History of West Africa
since 1800

Elizabeth Isichei, M.A. D. Phil.
Professor of History, University of Jos

Africana Publishing Company
New York

First published in the United States of America 1977
by Africana Publishing Company
a division of
Holmes & Meier Publishers, Inc.
101 Fifth Avenue
New York, New York   10003

Library of Congress Cataloging in Publication Data
Isichei, Elizabeth Allo.
   History of West Africa since 1800.

   Includes index.
   1.   Africa, West—History.   I.   Title.
DT476.2.I84   1977   966   77-4393
ISBN 0-8419-0311-5
ISBN 0-8419-0312-3 pbk.

Printed in Hong Kong by
Wing King Tong Co Ltd

Contents

12 Case Studies

List of Maps

Acknowledgements

I am delighted to have the opportunity to thank the following: Humphrey Fisher and Christopher Fyfe, who most generously commented on substantial portions of the text; Macmillan's anonymous reader, whose comments on a first version were instructive, and on a second immensely encouraging; my friend Jane Turner, who typed several versions of this book – and whose help with typing, in general, has been beyond all thanks; the librarians in Enugu and Nsukka, who have shown such consistent interest in my work and helpfulness in forwarding it; Professor W. T. W. Morgan for help with the maps.

To write a book of this kind to meet a publisher's dead-line, while still doing justice to my varied duties as a university teacher, meant a period of great overwork and strain – so much so, in fact, that I often found myself reflecting uneasily on the words of Bacon, 'To spend too much Time in Studies is Sloth'. Accordingly, I owe an indescribable debt of gratitude to my husband, Uche, and our children, Uche, Emeka, Nkem and Chinye, who bore with me while I wrote it, and whose affection makes them collaborators in all my undertakings, as I am in theirs.

The author and publishers wish to thank the following who have kindly given permission for the use of copyright material: Cambridge University Press for the extract from 'Rural Hausa' (1972) by Dr. Polly Hill; Oxford University Press for the extract from 'Education and Changing West African Culture' (1966) by John Wilson.

The author and publishers wish to acknowledge the following photograph sources.

Camera Press p. 301   Church Missionary Society pp. 74 top, 130 bottom, 157
Basil Davidson p. 297   E. C. P. Armees p. 260   Foreign and Commonwealth
Library p. 130 top   Illustrated London News pp. 65, 227   Info Senegal pp.
55, 249   Keystone Press Agency p. 261   National Archives, Ibadan p. 77
Nigerian Magazine p. 120   Popperfoto pp. 140 top, 114, 147   Public Record
Office p. 154   Radio Times Hulton Picture Library p. 160   Staatleche Museum
Berlin (West) p. 90   University of Liverpool p. 254   Wallace Collection p. 66

The photograph on p. 86 is taken from *Les Bas Reliefs Des Batiments Royaux D'Abomey* (*1926*) by E. G. Waterlot and is reproduced by permission of the Institut D'Ethnologie, Paris.

They also wish to thank Hakluyt Society; Librairie Hachette; and University Library, Ibadan for permission to reproduce photographs and John Freeman & Co. for taking several photographs.

Every effort has been made to trace copyright holder., but in the event that anyone has been omitted this will be put right at the earliest opportunity.

Publishers' Note
Many of the photographs included in this book are very old. They were chosen because they illustrate aspects of West African history in a unique way, which no modern copies could hope to reproduce. It does mean, however, that the quality of reproduction may not be as good as we would normally require.

Preface

History books are basically very abstract, and the wider the geographical area they cover, the more abstract they become. Although history deals essentially with the life of men, the sweeping generalisations of a general book may seem to become almost entirely divorced from the life of any specific men. To take an example at random – the peasant farmer on the cold Jos plateau, in his village ringed with cactus hedges, amid a splendid panorama of rocky hills, appears nowhere in this book, any more than the wild flowers which grow with such variety on those same hills, their butterflies, their glistening fragments of white quartz, will appear in a book on Nigerian geography. Yet the past of his village is as authentically part of West African history as that of Freetown, which appears in every account of the West African past.

All history books, whatever their scope, are highly selective. Large books have been written on small towns, but even then the writer is mainly conscious of what has been left out. Historians have to select some themes, and by the very act of selecting, leave out others. In this book, for instance, I might well have discussed the Mossi kingdom, instead of concentrating exclusively on Islamic states in the western Sudan. I could have discussed the kingdom of Igala instead of the kingdom of Benin, or taken Tivland instead of Igboland as my example of a small-scale society.

How are such decisions taken? Sometimes it is simply because the writer knows more about one subject than another. Sometimes it is because one has tried to cover the various geographical areas of West Africa as systematically as possible. But even in the societies studied, there is much omitted. We discuss Benin in the nineteenth century, not in the twentieth. Ivory Coast appears twice – in the discussion of resistance to European conquest, and in the study of nationalism and independence. All these places have, of course, a continuous history, and no period of that history is necessarily more interesting or worth studying than another.

Perhaps the most important factor is that historians are, like other people, very much influenced by convention. In African history – or European history – they have informally agreed to stress certain themes; this, by definition, means that others are excluded. Occasionally an inquiring spirit will appear and write the history of bubonic plague, or the potato, instead (to take the examples from European history), but for the most part, research, and especially textbooks, follow well defined tracks. This is essentially a conventional history. It is so because it is written partly for WAEC students, who follow a conventional syllabus and sit conventional examinations, and partly because I lacked the leisure to think out the subject in a wholly new way. In any case, the possible approaches are limited by the available materials; one cannot do original research on more than a small part of West Africa, and for the rest, one follows closely the paths cut by others. But one should at least be aware that there are serious imbalances in our 'conventional history', which accords more space to Blaise Diagne than the influenza epidemic, although the latter undoubtedly influenced men's lives much more.

In writing a book such as this, one is so conscious of what is left out, that one is tempted to make it longer and longer. Of those who read and criticised this book for me, one said I should make it much shorter and simpler, and another said I should make it much longer and even add another volume! In the end, the maximum length was decided by the publisher.

This is the first book I have written which has no footnotes, and this leaves me with the problem of how to acknowledge my indebtedness to others. Some of the sources of this book are listed in the Reading Guide, but this is essentially a list of books which will be profitable for teachers and learners. The sources which have influenced my own mind, or underlie specific judgements, are often not the same thing. Parts of this book are based on my own research, but for the most part it is distilled from the work of other historians. Of these, some are my personal friends. Others I have met briefly, in contexts such as conferences. The majority are known to me only through their writings, though sometimes one feels that, through their writings, one comes to know them very well indeed. And so I can hardly do better than follow the example of a distinguished predecessor in West African studies and borrow the words of Abdullahi dan Fodio, a brilliant Nigerian writer and intellectual, who died in 1828.

> Many a scholar or student other than these
> Has profited me with sciences, from the East and the West.
> May God give all of them, and the one who loves them
> To drink of the showers of abundant flowing rain of His approval.

Christmas, 1975.

To God the Holy Spirit

Veni Pater pauperum

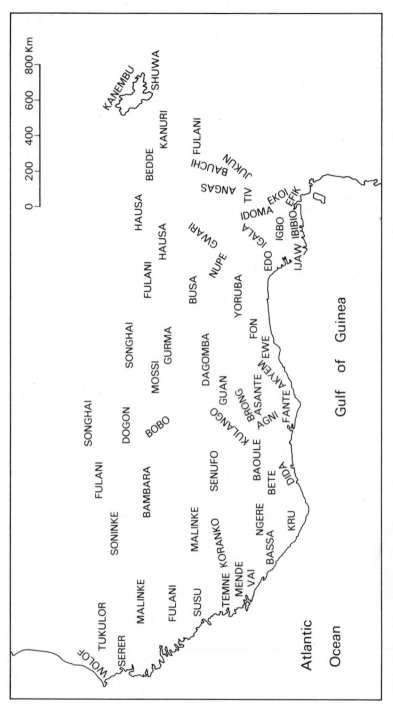

Ethnic groups of West Africa

I

West Africa and a Wider World in 1800

The natural setting

The history of all peoples has been greatly influenced by the natural environment in which they live. Most, though not all, of the peoples of West Africa live in one of two contrasting environments. There is, of course, no sudden dividing line between them, and they merge invisibly into each other, as the vegetation changes gradually, over hundreds of kilometres. One is the rain forest belt, just north of the sea. It runs from east to west, but is not of even width, or continuous. At its broadest it is about three hundred kilometres wide. It is broken in the middle, at Dahomey (Benin), where, apparently because of decreasing rainfall, the savanna comes down to the sea. Largely because of tse-tse fly, the people of the forest zone could not keep herds and flocks on a large scale, though they did have sheep, goats, and a special variety of dwarf cattle which was resistant to tse-tse fly. Their economy was based on agriculture. Many centuries of human habitation and farming have removed the original forest cover in many places, and have had the effect of making the savanna encroach on the forest zone. The forest zone – which is often called Guinea – has a great variety of economically useful trees, some indigenous, like the kola tree and the oil palm, and others introduced from elsewhere.

As one moves north, the trees thin out gradually. Desert varieties like the thorny acacia begin to appear. The dry season lengthens; in the dry season, the peasants put even the straw in the fields and the leaves on the trees to economic uses, and the hedged fields lie, orderly, but bare. Roughly north of a line between Jenne and Kano, the tse-tse fly ceases to be a menace (though there are fly-free areas much further south). Because of this, and because the land was relatively clear of forest, cattle herding became of great economic importance. This area is called the western Sudan.

Further north still, we come to the Sahara, an ocean of sand lying between north and west Africa. It has not always been so. Long before the period covered by this book – perhaps four thousand years ago – it was green and fertile. But gradually the climate changed, and many, though not all, of its people, retreated to moister areas north or south. Over the last thousand years or so, the Sahara has continued to expand,

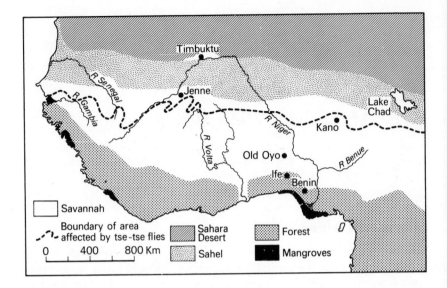

The natural setting

with many consequences for West African history. It is still doing so, creating tragic difficulties for the states of the Sahel.

Most, though not all West Africans, lived in one of these environments. There were, however, other contexts for human life, such as the Niger Delta, which is an area of water and mangrove swamps. Here the people adapted to their environment with great success, becoming first fishermen and salt manufacturers, and later brokers and long distance merchants.

Economic life and external trade

By 1800, West Africa was involved in international trade on two frontiers. But to see this involvement in perspective, it is important to remember that its economy remained basically self-sufficient and that trade between different West African groups was still more important than trade with outsiders. For many centuries, the peoples of West Africa had engaged in a great variety of arts and crafts; each area would build up a surplus in one or more products and exchange it for other goods which it could not produce so well or easily. In many different parts of West Africa, for example, iron smelters extracted iron from local iron ore. Blacksmiths made the iron into weapons and agricultural tools. Coastal peoples extracted salt from the sea. Inland, there were a number of salt lakes and salt mines. Some areas produced natron, which was valued as a medicine and as a meat tenderiser. Some produced gold, and their goldsmiths worked it into ornaments with exquisite skill. Coppersmiths made bronzes which are among the art wonders of the world, using copper from the Sahara mines or from further afield. Spinners and weavers made thread and cloth, not only from cotton, but from a variety of other substances, including bark. Dyers produced a great range of vegetable dyes – blue, green, yellow and red, among them. Weavers wove the thread into elaborate patterns. The leather-workers of Hausaland and elsewhere produced beautifully prepared leather goods which were exported through North Africa, and so became known, misleadingly, as 'Morocco leather'. Potters produced a great variety of decorated and useful pottery. Fishermen and farmers who reared animals or grew crops, also produced a surplus of one commodity and exchanged it with their neighbours for another.

West Africa was divided into a number of agricultural zones. The northern, drier areas produced sorghums and millets. A belt extending along the coast from southern Nigeria to Ivory Coast depended on root crops, especially yams. To the west of this, rice was the staple crop. All these crops were indigenous (though imported varieties of yam and rice were cultivated as well).

There were also a number of important crops which had been brought to West Africa from other parts of the world. Plantains came originally from Asia and spread across the African continent. A staple in East Africa, they only became of comparable importance in eastern Ivory Coast. Elsewhere in West Africa they are valued for the variety they add to the diet.

During the era of the slave trade, two very important crops – maize and cassava – were introduced from the New World. The cultivation of cassava took a long time to spread because of the elaborate preparation it requires before it can be eaten. But it had and has many advantages: it grows readily in poor soils, and the farmer only has to plant the stem, not an edible seed like maize or seed yams.

Over the centuries, West Africa built up a complicated network of markets and trade routes. States which were strategically situated on these trade routes became wealthy and powerful, maintaining splendid courts and relatively large armies.

The pictures on pages 4 and 5 show a few of these many forms of economic life, depicted in nineteenth-century photographs and eye-witness drawings.

West Africa had gone far beyond the barter stage. There were a large number of currencies, some locally invented and some introduced, some used over large areas, some used only locally. They included cowrie shells from the Indian Ocean, horseshoe shaped copper manillas, iron bars, and copper wires. Some areas used imported 'Maria Theresa dollars' which were specially manufactured for the African market. West Africans made much use of 'units of account' – abstract measurements of value – especially in their trade with Europeans.

Trans-Saharan trade

There were two types of international trade in which West Africa was involved. The first led across the desert, a trade pattern which probably goes back to the days when the Sahara was well watered. The trans-Saharan trade routes, which depended entirely on the use of camels, were extremely dangerous. Sometimes whole caravans died, if they lost their way, or if a vital well dried up. But all the hardships and dangers did

Forms of economic life

A Lake Chad fisherman

Pastoral life near Zinder

Iron smelting in Gurma

4

A Bambara weaver

Dyeing wells near Bonduku

Dyers and blacksmiths in Iddah

not deter brave merchants in search of a livelihood, or devout Muslims bent on the incredibly long and perilous pilgrimage to Mecca. But because of the dangers of the trans-Saharan trade and the time the journey took (two to three months) the quantity of goods that could be carried in this way was limited. Trade commodities included slaves and horses, both of which were self-transporting but often died on the way, and weapons. Salt from the mines of the Sahara was exchanged for gold from the mines of the south. For the rest, the trade was in luxuries whose value was high in proportion to their bulk. Some scholars think that the trans-Saharan trade reached its peak in the sixteenth century and had declined a good deal by the nineteenth. However that may be, it was certainly still important, in 1800, to the peoples of the western Sudan.

The Atlantic slave trade

From the late fifteenth century, a second line of communication with the wider world became available, as gallant little Portuguese ships ventured ever further down the desert coastline of Mauritania. By 1445 they had reached the mouth of the Senegal river. By 1475 they had reached Fernando Po.

The Portuguese came first, but other European sea-faring nations soon joined them, and for the peoples of the West African coast-line it meant an economic revolution. Previously the coast had been thinly populated by fishermen and salt makers, who looked out onto a pounding perilous surf, and an empty sea. Now it became a key area of international trade. (Not all areas, of course, were equally affected, and the impact was differently distributed at different times.) The first European visitors sought a wide variety of local products including gold, ivory, pepper and local textiles. These last they bought in one part of West Africa, and sold in another, so that they were actually acting as carriers in internal African trade. They also carried slaves from one part of West Africa to another, and exported a few to Europe, but the number taken to Portugal were low, for the Portuguese economy could not absorb large numbers of slaves.

It was perhaps the central tragedy of West African history that this external trade came to be dominated more and more by the trade in slaves. In this, ships financed and crewed by Europeans came to the shores of Africa, and in exchange for an assortment of goods purchased her men, women and children, who a little while before had been, for the most part, free citizens in their own land. They were carried across the Atlantic ocean, in conditions so terrible that many of them died on the way. In the New World, they worked as Europeans' slaves until they died. Their children, if they had any, were slaves after them.

It was a trade so terrible and barbaric, that it is sometimes hard to believe it really existed. It developed solely for the economic benefit of Europeans. Briefly, at the end of the fifteenth century, they had discovered the Americas. Here there was abundant farming land and mineral wealth. They experimented with different forms of labour, including Indian labour and white indentured servants, and finally concluded that the labour of enslaved Africans was the most economically profitable.

6

Effects

Historians disagree about the way in which the slave trade affected West Africa, and the numbers enslaved. The most acceptable modern figure is that between six and seven million were carried away from West Africa; this is much lower than older estimates, and some people think it too low. Certainly, it excludes the countless individuals who died, in Africa, as the result of slaving wars, or of the long journey to the coast. Some think that the numbers exported were too low to make much difference to the total size of West Africa's population. Some have even suggested that the slave trade led to an increase in population, because the Europeans brought new crops, such as maize and cassava, which provided more food for more people. Others think that because of the slave trade, the population of Africa remained static, at a time when that of Europe and Asia was expanding, and that, as a result, Africa lost the economic stimulus which an expanding population sometimes provides (for instance, by creating a demand for more goods).

The way in which the slave trade affected society depended very largely on how the slaves were obtained. Some were criminals, paying the penalties for their misdeeds, but these were a minority. Many were kidnapped; this was particularly common among small-scale states, such as the village democracies of Igboland. Larger, more powerful states, such as Asante, obtained most of their captives in war. Historians disagree about whether these wars were fought only in order to gain captives for sale. But where the sale of captives provides an important source of state income and individual enrichment, there is a very strong incentive to wage war. The slave trade, then, sowed a dreadful harvest of insecurity, bloodshed and misery, and discouraged the conditions which help the productive arts of peace.

Some historians think that although the slave trade caused much suffering to individuals, the net results were beneficial, because the Europeans brought valuable imports in return for the slaves they carried away. They say that the locally produced cloth, iron and salt were insufficient for the demand, and hence the trade brought advantages to the African consumer. There is some truth in this. In some areas salt had been so scarce that the people had to manage with inferior vegetable ash substitutes. Imported iron would have improved the supply of agricultural tools.

Nevertheless, there is a lot to be said on the other side. The unsatisfied local demand could have led local craftsmen to new technological advances. Instead, local crafts were undermined by foreign imports. Local textiles were sometimes swamped by imported ones (though often they resisted the challenge); the craft of the West African iron smelter ultimately died out altogether. Moreover, as the European slave traders freely admitted, the quality of the imports tended to be poor. The cheap guns sometimes exploded in the purchaser's face, and the cloth was falsely measured. And not all the imports benefited the consumer. Firearms and spirits were destructive, rather than constructive, in their impact.

Most fundamentally, West Africa was forced to export a labour force, which created new wealth for Europeans, and valuable raw materials, such as ivory, gold and dyewoods. (Not all of these contributed equally to Europe's development – ivory was used for billiard balls and piano keys!) In return, she obtained consumer goods which were either uselessly hoarded, or quickly used up or worn out.

Opposition to the slave trade

African rulers tended to co-operate with the slave trade, for several reasons. Often it was their only way of gaining foreign exchange, and especially firearms. And when the slave trade had been going on for generations, people grew up with it, and tended to take it for granted. Nevertheless, some far-sighted Africans recognised the evils and fought against them, often at great cost to themselves. The first and most remarkable came from Central Africa. He was Dom Affonso, who ruled the kingdom of Congo for some forty years, from 1506. He was a convert to Catholicism, and perhaps one of the most deeply Christian rulers in the world at that time. He struggled in vain to end the slave trade, and to obtain various forms of western technical aid, such as medical care, for his people.

Later, a European who had lived for ten years in West Africa, wrote, 'The discerning natives account it their greatest unhappiness, that they were ever visited by the Europeans. They say, that we Christians introduced the traffic in slaves, and that before our coming they lived in peace'. In the early eighteenth century, an obscure local leader in Guinea called Tomba waged his own war against the slave trade. He failed, and was himself enslaved, but showed the same splendid courage in enduring the cruel punishments inflicted on him, and in leading a slave revolt on the slave ship itself. Agaja, who died in 1740, was perhaps the greatest of all Dahomey kings. The scholar who has studied his career most closely* believes that his campaigns of the 1720s, which overthrew the coastal kingdoms of Whydah and Allada, were intended to end the slave trade.

By the end of the eighteenth century, many men in England had come to share Tomba's views on the evils of the slave trade. The lead was taken by a group of Evangelicals, who were Protestants of deep religious conviction, and who opposed it on humanitarian grounds. Throughout the eighteenth century, when the slave trade was at its height, England had controlled the lion's share of the trade. When she gave it up, as she did in 1807, it was partly as a result of the efforts of these reformers, and partly because economic circumstances had changed, and the trade was becoming less profitable.

Two points must be made, however. The first is, that in a very real sense, the damage had been done. The slave trade had developed Europe (and the Americas) and underdeveloped West Africa. When the Europeans first came to West Africa, Africa and Europe were at a comparable level of development. The first European visitors to Benin described it in the terms they would have applied to any great European city. But the Europeans had several advantages, and they used them to obtain many more. One was firearms, though this only became really important much later. Another was their command of ocean-going shipping. By harnessing the wind

* Professor I. A. Akinjogbin.

they travelled the world and set up a vast network of international trade, which was designed for Europe's advantage. By 1800 the technological gap between Europe and Africa was immense. England had gone through the first phase of an Industrial Revolution, which changed the history of the world. Historians disagree about where the capital necessary for this revolution came from; the profits gained from the slave trade undoubtedly helped.

The second point is that the slave trade did not come to an end in 1807, though in the past historians have sometimes written as though it did. In fact, it died a long lingering death. There was a sugar boom in Cuba, and a coffee boom in Brazil. Both needed slave labour and the last recorded slave ship from West Africa sailed in 1864.

Rich and poor, slave and free

It is difficult to make generalisations which are true of the many different societies of West Africa, of its great kingdoms covering vast areas, and its tiny village democracies. But it is clear that by 1800 there was a considerable and probably increasing gap between rich and poor, and slave and free. This had always been so in the empires of the western Sudan. In the early fourteenth century, a ruler of Mali went on pilgrimage to Mecca. He spent so much money on the journey that he devalued the currency of Cairo. His journey literally put Mali on European maps, and was a magnificent demonstration of his country's power and prosperity. Nevertheless, the wealth which was poured out abroad was created by the labours of many forgotten workers, the gold miners, the salt miners, and so on.

The armies of the western Sudan depended heavily on horses. The ownership of a horse represented a large financial investment. A soldier on horseback could be protected by heavy armour, which again, cost money. So just as in medieval Europe,

Cavalryman and foot-soldier from Borno

where a caste of armoured knights on horseback developed, the western Sudan too developed its own armoured mounted nobility. The picture on the previous page, from Borno, shows the difference between the horseman and the foot soldier.

There is a similar contrast between the wealth of the divine kings of Guinea, and their subjects, even where the forests and tse-tse fly made the use of cavalry more difficult. In all kingdoms, the gap tended to be lessened by generosity – by the African system which expects a ruler to show his wealth by his readiness to distribute it. We have a moving example of this in a description of early eighteenth-century Benin.

> The King, the Great Lords, and every Governor, who is but indifferently rich, subsist several Poor at their Place of Residence on their Charity, employing those who are fit for any work, in order to help them to a Maintenance; and the rest they keep for God's sake . . .

The gap between rich and poor was less in the village democracies of the so-called 'stateless societies'. This was basically because the total resources of such tiny states were much less, and the surplus which could be acquired by an elite accordingly limited. In the words of an eighteenth-century Igbo, 'Everyone contributes something to the common stock, and as we are unacquainted with idleness, we have no beggars'.

One of the ways in which the slave trade affected societies was that it greatly increased the social gap between rich and poor, and rulers and subjects. Kings became much richer, because they exacted customs, harbour dues and so on from the foreign visitors. They usually also engaged in private trade, on especially favourable terms. They tended to collect wealth, which could not be put to any productive use. One coastal ruler imported a fully furnished house from Europe, but did not live in it. Another buried huge quantities of iron and copper bars under his house.

Subjects, on the other hand, became less free. A historian who himself comes from the Niger Delta describes the process in the Delta in these words: 'The fisherman who went where he wished in his fishing canoe became the "pullaboy" in a large trade canoe'. The slave trade led to a great expansion in domestic slavery. In some parts of West Africa, domestic slavery had existed previously; in others, it had not. In one area where it had not, 'Upper Guinea'★ the picture had changed very dramatically by the eighteenth century. Those peoples most involved in the external slave trade – the Fulani, Mandingo and Susu – now owned whole villages of slaves. It is easy to see how the accumulation of slaves for export encouraged the accumulation of slaves for work at home. If the price of slaves fell, or an individual slave was unsaleable, it was the obvious way out. In the nineteenth century, an American slaver visited the capital of Futa Jallon, and went to the slave villages nearby. The slaves fled in terror, expecting to be sold.

The longer a slave was owned, the less likely he was to be sold. In recent years, historians have stressed the differences between slavery in Africa and slavery in

★ The area between the Gambia River and the Liberia/Sierra Leone border.

America, claiming that in Africa slavery describes the way in which an individual entered a society, rather than his later prospects in it. In most African slave-owning societies, one can find examples of individual slaves who rose to the top rungs of society, becoming rich merchants (and slave owners!), top civil servants, army generals, and even kings. Such were the exception, however, and the way most slaves felt about their status is reflected in the large numbers who voted against slavery with their feet and ran away. Sometimes the slaves banded together in revolt. There was a slave revolt in eighteenth-century Futa Jallon and afterwards it was compulsory for the free to carry weapons, lest it happen again. There were revolts in the great kingdom of Asante, and in the little village democracies of the Igbo.

In 1838 there was the most remarkable slave revolt of all. It took place in Sierra Leone, and was led by a man called Bilalé, the son of a Susu chief and a slave mother. He was twenty-seven years old. Bilalé founded a fortified town, where he was joined by many fugitive slaves, and they successfully fought off the repeated attacks of the slave owners. In 1872 Bilalé was still successfully defending the cause of freedom 'and rousing a large portion of the servile population, not only to a devotion to the idea of liberty at any price, but a strong attachment to himself and a hatred of all who hold slaves . . .' He was one of the most remarkable nineteenth-century West Africans.

In non-Islamic states there was a worse form of social oppression, which was closely linked with both the slave trade and domestic slavery. This was the sacrifice of human beings, who were often slaves, sometimes prisoners of war and criminals, as religious offerings. Sometimes it was to placate a god, or to make amends for the sins of a community; sometimes the king offered sacrifices to his ancestors; more often, slaves were killed at the death of an important man, to be his attendants in the world to come. In places as far apart as the Efik city of Calabar, and the Asante capital of Kumasi, terrified slaves fled into the bush when they heard the news of a great man's death. The slave trade seems to have expanded and distorted a practice which probably existed earlier. It cheapened the value of human life, and made a pool of potential victims readily available. It disposed of slaves who were of little economic value. The records often speak grimly of the sacrifice of the aged and infirm.

Just as the slaves often resisted slavery, so, on at least one notable occasion, in Calabar, they acted together to put an end to human sacrifice. This is how a missionary who was living in Calabar described the movement.

> In the end of 1850, and beginning of 1851, they began to bind themselves together by a covenant of blood for mutual protection, and thence were known by the name of 'blood men', their objects being to resist the encroachments of oppressions of the Duke Town gentry, and to preserve themselves from being killed on all occasions according to old customs.

This peaceful combination for a limited end was entirely successful (see page 117).

The general effect of the slave trade, then, was to make elites richer and more powerful, and to expand domestic slavery. The pictures on page 12 reflect a few of these contrasts.

Social contrasts

The king of Dahomey displays his wealth in an annual ceremony

A slave coffle

A human sacrifice

The wide gap between rich and poor was not, of course, peculiar to West Africa. We have spoken of the Industrial Revolution which enriched England. At first it enriched only a minority, and the factory workers suffered terrible hardships until, after a long time, the benefits of mass production were more equally shared.

In 1851 a European visited Kano market. He said that although superficial appearances were so different, basically, the social pattern in Europe and in West Africa was the same. He described:

> the manifold scenes of public and private life, of comfort and happiness, of luxury and misery, of activity and laziness, of industry and indolence, which were exhibited in the streets, the market-places, and in the interior of the court-yards. It was the most animated picture of a little world in itself, so different in external form from all that is seen in European towns, yet so similar in its internal principles.
>
> Here a row of shops filled with articles of native and foreign produce, with buyers and sellers in every variety of figure, complexion, and dress, yet all intent upon their little gain, endeavouring to cheat each other; there a large shed, like a hurdle, full of half-naked, half-starved slaves torn from their native homes, from their wives or husbands, from their children or parents, arranged in rows like cattle, and staring desperately upon the buyers, anxiously watching into whose hands it should be their destiny to fall. In another part were to be seen all the necessaries of life, the wealthy buying the most palatable things for his table, the poor stopping and looking greedily upon a handful of grain; here a rich governor dressed in silk and gaudy clothes, mounted upon a spirited and richly caparisoned horse, and followed by a host of idle, insolent slaves; there a poor blind man groping his way through the multitude, and fearing at every step to be trodden down . . .

The spread of the world religions

One of the most interesting aspects of West African history up to 1800 concerns the expansion (or, in some cases, the failure to expand) of Christianity and Islam. Both Christianity and Islam are 'religions of the book'. The followers of each believe that they hold true beliefs about God, which are of great importance for the individual's eternal welfare and which are embodied in the teachings of the Bible or the Quran. Both Muslims and Christians have, in theory, a strong obligation to seek the conversion of others. By 1800, Islam, which had come to West Africa across the trans-Saharan trade routes, was widely, and in some cases deeply, rooted in the western Sudan. Christianity, which came by the sea, had made scarcely any impression at all.

Traditional religion

When one describes the spread of Christianity and Islam, one should not neglect to mention the value of traditional religion. The followers of traditional religion, generally speaking, did not seek converts. They tended to believe that the full truth about God

13

cannot be known, and that each people has that version of religion which is most suited to its own culture and circumstances. West African religions tended to hold that the Supreme God is benevolent, but that He stays remote from the affairs of men. It is therefore believed that worshippers should give most of their devotion to many lesser spirits, who interfere constantly in daily life. So thoroughly is traditional religion integrated into the life of society that there is often no word for 'religion'. The concept was defined only in response to the questions of Muslims and Christians.

West African religion has produced countless men of deep religious feeling and insight. Because they did not write, their wisdom has usually died with them. For several exceptional cases where it has been recorded (among the Dogon, and among the Igbo), the reader is referred to the Reading Guide.

Islam

Islam reached the western Sudan by the ninth century, or even earlier. It was brought by Muslims from North Africa (probably merchants) and their Berber converts from the Sahara. By the eleventh century, it was well established. There was a thriving Muslim township at that time at the capital of ancient Ghana. A beautifully carved marble tombstone at Gao shows that a king who died there in 1100 was a Muslim. In Kanem-Borno the first Muslim king was Ume, who died in 1097. Islam reached Hausaland later, in the late fourteenth century. Oddly enough, it was brought from the west, by missionaries from Mali, rather than by its immediate Muslim neighbour to the east, Kanem-Borno.

Islamic learning and scholarship seem to have attained a golden age in the cities of the Niger bend, when the Songhai empire was at the height of its greatness. Timbuktu produced brilliant scholars, whose works are still used today, and the trade in hand written manuscripts was the most important item of commerce in the city. In 1591 Songhai was invaded by soldiers from Morocco, using firearms, and the mighty empire collapsed. The centres of learning at Timbuktu and Jenne were badly affected, and scholars have tended to suggest that in the two centuries that followed there was, in the western Sudan, a general decline in Islamic fervour and scholarship. In the words of one leading scholar, 'In those areas where Islam had once been strong there was an increasing tendency to seek accommodation with local custom – even when directly opposed to the law of Islam'.

It is not easy to say how extensive Islamic beliefs were in 1800, or how fervently they were practised. In Futa Toro and Futa Jallon, Islamic revolutions had taken place in the eighteenth century. States, in which government was based on Islamic principles, had been established. These anticipated the jihadist states of the nineteenth century. In Hausaland and Borno, the rulers were nominally Muslims, but their critics accused them of compromising with paganism. It is likely that Islam was found mainly at court and in the towns, especially among the trader community. But throughout the western Sudan, there were communities of scholars and clerics, for whom Islam was the major commitment of their lives. It was these communities which were to produce the jihadist leaders.

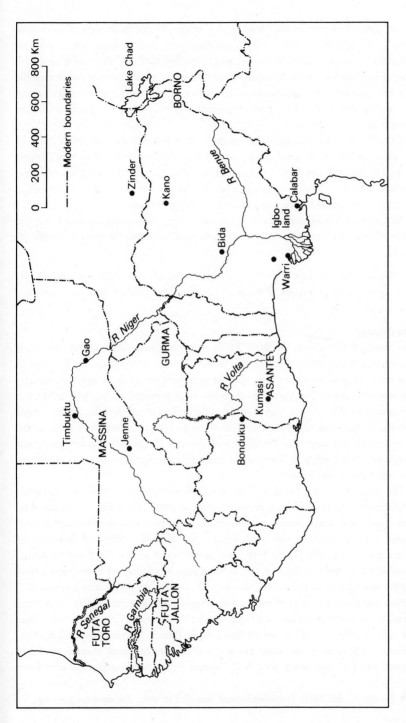

Places mentioned in Chapter One

The general picture scholars tend to give of the condition of Islam in the seventeenth and eighteenth centuries is, as we have seen, one of stagnation or decline. Nevertheless, several points should be noted. First, much of our information about the state of Islam in the eighteenth century comes from the jihad leaders of the nineteenth, and revolutionaries are not necessarily a good source of information about the society they seek to overthrow. They tend to exaggerate its evils in order to justify their own campaigns.

Secondly, here are two individual stories, which illustrate the strength of the hold which, even before the jihad, Islam had upon its children. Salih Bilali was a Fulani from Massina. He was born in 1770, and was sold into slavery when he was only twelve. After forty years as a slave in a non-Islamic environment (in the West Indies, and North America) he was still a devout practising Muslim.

Abu Bakr al Siddiq was born in Timbuktu in 1790, and brought up in Jenne. He was enslaved in 1805. After thirty years in Jamaica, he wrote the story of his life, in Arabic.

> I tasted the bitterness of slavery . . . and its oppressiveness. But praise be to God, under whose power are all things . . . Nothing can befall us unless it be written for us.

Christianity

The story of Christianity in West Africa to 1800 is essentially one of promising beginnings, which totally failed to bear fruit.★ There are two reasons for this. One is that missionary activity only took place at infrequent intervals. It was not until the nineteenth century that European churches were prepared to make a substantial investment in West Africa, and to send large numbers of missionaries, in the certain knowledge that many of them would die there. In 1597 a Catholic bishop explained why he could not keep Warri supplied with priests: 'This kingdom is very poor, and clergy would be unable to live there in reasonable comfort; moreover . . . the great unhealthiness of the climate'.

The second reason was that there was a fundamental contradiction between Christianity, which aimed to convert Africans, and the slave trade, which aimed to buy them. There is an amusing example of this in the recollections of an English slave trader, who, in the early eighteenth century, encouraged a citizen of Dahomey to follow the Golden Rule (i.e. to treat others as one would wish to be treated by them), 'And that our God had enjoined this to us on pain of very severe Punishment'. And yet the Englishman had come to Dahomey for no other purpose but to buy slaves.

Here and there, Christianity made a little progress. The Europeans who manned the forts on the Gold Coast maintained chaplains for their own services. These sometimes had a little influence on the surrounding people. Philip Quaque, who died in 1816, became a Christian in this way. He was a Ghanaian Anglican chaplain at Cape Coast Castle for some fifty years. J. E. J. Capitein, 1717–1747, was a former slave from

---

★ Except for the Sierra Leone settlement, founded in 1787, discussed on page 125.

the Ivory Coast, who studied at the University of Leyden, and who was ordained a minister of the Dutch Reformed Church and made chaplain at Elmina. A. W. Amo, of Axim, in the early eighteenth century became a doctor of the University of Wittenberg.

Catholicism, first introduced at Warri in the late sixteenth century, survived until the eighteenth, although for years at a time the Itsekiri saw no priest. We have a moving account of an aged ruler of Warri, in the early seventeenth century, making up for the lack of priests by his own exertions, instructing his people in Christian doctrine, and leading them in processions. Even at the end of the eighteenth century a visitor to the Olu's palace still found 'several emblems of the catholic religion'.

An eighteenth-century visitor to what is now Guinea described a pioneer African Christian – also a Catholic – who was the leader of a little Christian community. His name was Joseph and 'he has built a little Oratory for his People's devotions; erected a Cross; taught several of his Kindred Letters, dispersing among them little Romish Prayer-Books . . .'

Such men are inspiring forerunners to modern West African Christians. But all the same, by 1800 the impact of Christianity on West Africa was negligible.

2

Building New Societies: The Islamic Model

Of all the many aspects of nineteenth-century West African history, perhaps none has a greater relevance for our own time than the whole series of new Islamic states which were established as a consequence of jihad, or Holy War. Inevitably, in each jihad, there were political and secular motives as well as religious. Inevitably, after the jihad was over, the ideals which had originally inspired it were often neglected in practice. Nevertheless, the jihadist states of the nineteenth century were the result of a deliberate attempt to create new nations on a foundation of religion and social justice. According to Muslims, the rulers of the new states could only expect obedience if they followed the principles of Islam faithfully.

The jihads of the nineteenth century were partly the result of a tradition which was extremely ancient in the western Sudan, and which had born fruit most recently in the Islamic states founded in Futa Toro and Futa Jallon in the eighteenth century.

To a large extent, however, they were part of an international crisis in eighteenth- and nineteenth-century international Islam. This had many aspects. It was in part a reaction against the self-confidence and expanding aggression of Christian Europe, which overthrew the Moghul government in India, one of the world's great Islamic empires. It was linked with the evident weakness and decline of the once powerful Muslim Turkish empire. These threats to international Islam aroused two main reactions.

The first was the Wahhabi movement in Saudi Arabia, which was in many respects comparable with the Protestant Reformation in sixteenth-century Europe. The Wahhabi wanted a return to the original purity of Islam, which they thought had become corrupted.

One of the developments which the Wahhabi criticised was Sufism, which encouraged reverence for holy men, and the making of pilgrimages to their shrines. Sufism is the Islamic tradition of mysticism. Mysticism is something which can be found in all the great world religions. In it, an individual strives, by lengthy periods of prayer and self-sacrifice, to come to a living first hand knowledge of God. It is a long journey, which only a few individuals have the resolution to make. Their journey is of great significance to other believers, however, for it seems to them a confirmation of the reality of the unseen world, which most have to believe in without direct experience.

In Islam, the mystical tradition was closely linked with *tariqas*, or brotherhoods. These brotherhoods were founded by mystics, and were intended to lead their members to a living experience of God by their secrets – in practice, prayer, fasting and retreat. As we shall see, they were to be of the greatest importance in the nineteenth-century jihadist movements. Although the Wahhabi criticised Sufism, the main way in which West African Islam reacted to the crisis of the nineteenth century was in the creation of new brotherhoods, and the revival of old ones. Thus the West African response was very different from that of the Wahhabi.

Even those scholars like Usuman dan Fodio, who never went on pilgrimage, felt themselves to be a part of the international Islamic community, and had a reasonably good grasp of what was going on abroad. This knowledge came from returning pilgrims, and from long distance merchants, like the Moroccan, who, later on, warned the court at Sokoto about British imperialism. 'By God, they eat the whole country – they are no friends: these are the words of truth'.

The jihad in Gobir

Gobir

The first of the great jihads of the nineteenth century, which was the inspiration of the subsequent ones, began in Gobir, the most northern of the Hausa states, extending into the Sahara. The history of the Hausa states is very largely the story of how first one, and then another, went through a period of expansion, followed by decline. In the middle of the eighteenth century, it was the turn of Gobir to go through such a phase. For a time, her heavy cavalry, with their lances and plumed helmets, enabled her to conquer many of her neighbours. But like other states which have expanded and defeated weaker states, she soon found that her successes created new problems, particularly the enmity of other states, and the internal social strains caused by the expenses of war. By the late eighteenth century, Gobir was surrounded by enemies, and the weight of heavy taxation created much resentment among her own people.

The Muslims of Gobir were drawn from three ethnic groups; Hausa, Fulani and the Tuareg of the desert. Some Muslim scholars settled at the king's court, and made a good living as scribes, astrologers, writers of charms, and so on. Some, especially the Tuareg, continued to follow the nomadic life of their people, with all its hardships. We read of Tuareg scholars who owned superb libraries of hand-copied manuscripts, but lived in tents. Many of the Fulani scholars adopted a compromise between the two ways of life, and settled in communities of scholars in the country but kept close ties with their relatives, the pastoral Fulani, who travelled each year with their herds in a great migration, in search of water and pasture.

These scholars, whatever their origin, had at least one language in common – classical Arabic, the language of Islamic international learning, in the same way as Latin was for Christendom in the Middle Ages.

At court Islam was the official religion, but those who wanted reform complained

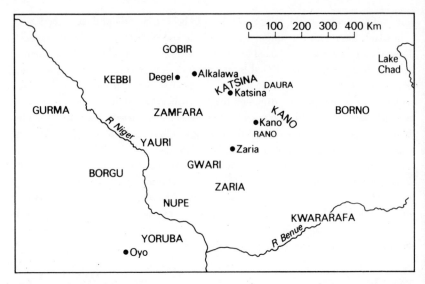

Hausaland before the jihad

that it was intermingled with pagan practices. Perhaps this was inevitable, because the king had tended to play a key role in traditional religion, and if he gave up traditional religion altogether, he was giving up one of his key duties, and sources of authority, in the eyes of the people. Nevertheless, the kings of Gobir were probably better Muslims than the jihadists gave them credit for. After a crushing defeat at the hands of the Muslims, Yunfa, the Gobir king, fleeing in terror, said all the five daily prayers expected of Muslims at once. The fact that he stayed faithful to prayer in these circumstances at all, surely shows him to have been a sincere Muslim.

Usuman dan Fodio

Usuman dan Fodio,* or Usuman, Son of a Learned Man, was born in 1754. He was a member of a learned Fulani clan which had settled in Hausaland since the fifteenth century. (The original homeland of the Fulani was in Senegal: from here they had spread to the east, until by the nineteenth century they had got as far as Cameroun, and Chad.) He grew up in a clerical community at Degel, near modern Sokoto. He studied at the feet of a number of reputed scholars, including Jibril, a Tuareg from the Sahara city of Agades, a fiery idealist who tried in vain to start a jihad among his own people. Usuman longed to go on pilgrimage, but his father forbade him. He wrote beautiful poetry in Arabic which expresses the intensity of his longing.

> Is there a way for me to Tayba,† swiftly,
> To visit the tomb of the Hashimite, Muhammad,

* This is the Hausa version of his name. The Arabic form is Uthman ibn Fodiye.
† That is Medina, one of the two holy cities of Islam.

When his sweet perfume diffuses in its sheltered places,
And the star of Muhammad urges on the pilgrims? . . .
Were I to visit Tayba, I would achieve the height of my ambition
Sprinkling myself with the dust of Muhammad's sandal.

The life of Usuman dan Fodio had three main dimensions; his endeavour to progress personally in religious devotion, his endeavour to convert others, by preaching
and writing, and, later, his endeavour to establish a righteous society through the
means of Holy War.

The first of these endeavours, which continued throughout his life, occurred within
one of the Sufi brotherhoods, the Qadiriyya, founded by a twelfth-century Persian
mystic and saint. From 1789 on, his Sufi devotion bore fruit in a series of visions. These
were of great importance, both to him personally, and to his followers, as an assurance
that he was specially chosen by God for some great work. One of these visions, in
1794, commanded him to take up the Sword of Truth, which he later saw as instructing him to take up a Holy War. He lived in great simplicity, owning one turban, and
one gown.

From the age of twenty, he devoted himself to various forms of missionary work.
He went on preaching tours, in which he tried to convert pagans to Islam, and nominal
Muslims to a more fervent practice of their religion. He wrote poetry and religious
works in Hausa, classical Arabic, and his mother tongue, Fulfulde. Altogether, over a
hundred separate works are attributed to him, which is an amazing output for one
man (though some, admittedly, were very brief). His son has described his public
lectures. Before he spoke, he always prayed in silence

> making a promise to God of sincerity in what he was going to do . . . He was
> never wearied by the people and never refused them. If perhaps he were asked a
> question in the middle of his speech, he would stop and answer it. His religion
> gave him strength, and he feared no criticism.

Like many Muslims of the time, he believed that the end of the world was near, and
this gave his message a compelling urgency. So did his vivid pictures of the horrors of
hell, and joys of paradise. He believed strongly in the education of women, and some
of the women of his own family were scholars and mystics in their own right. On the
next page is a picture of the room where one of them, his daughter Asma, lived. Asma
was a poet and a mystic.

The Shehu blamed his fellow teachers because:

> They treat their wives and daughters like household implements which are used
> until they are broken and thrown into the rubbish heap. Alas. How can they
> abandon their wives and daughters in the perpetual darkness of ignorance while
> they daily impart their knowledge to their students?

As time went on, Usuman became a famous and influential figure in Gobir, and
many disciples came to join him at Degel.

Asma's room

Conflict between Muslims and Gobir

An influential figure like Usuman dan Fodio created many problems for the kings of Gobir, who had already, as we have seen, serious internal and external difficulties. On the one hand, his great reputation made him a valuable ally – well worth keeping by concessions. On the other, much of his message looked like a direct criticism of the court, with his attacks on nominal Muslims, unjust taxation, corruption among officials and so on. King Bawa, who died in 1790, shortly after the death of his son in battle, decided on the first policy, of conciliation.

> Shaikh Uthman stood up before him and said to him: 'Indeed, I and my community have no need of your wealth, but I ask you this and this,' and he enumerated to him all matters concerning the establishment of religion. The Sultan replied to him, 'I give you what you ask, and I consent to all that you wish to do in this country'.

Bawa, who was already old, died soon afterwards. His successor was killed in battle four years later. The next king, Nafata, who ruled Gobir from 1794 to 1802, became afraid of dan Fodio's power and influence, since large numbers of disciples were flocking to his rural retreat. He feared dan Fodio as a potential rival, and adopted the second possible policy, that of restriction and limitation of the Muslim community. A whole set of new laws were passed, limiting the missionary work of dan Fodio and his followers. Only the Shehu (as he is always called in Hausaland) could preach, no new converts were to be made, and existing converts were to return to their original religion. Muslims were to give up their distinctive dress (veils for women, turbans for men). This was a serious attack, because these outward symbols strengthened the Muslims' sense of solidarity. Besides, many converts were won by example and especially, perhaps, by the Muslims' fidelity to prayer.

The final split occurred in the reign of Nafata's son, Yunfa (1802–1808). At first he showed deference to the Shehu, but soon he came to think that he was a rival focus of political authority. The breaking point came when Yunfa sent a punitive expedition against a Muslim community led by a Hausa scholar. Abd al-Salam. They were taken prisoner, and led past the Shehu's settlement at Degel. The Muslims of Degel rescued them. To avoid reprisals, the Shehu led his followers in hijra* to Gudu, a distant spot on the Gobir frontier: 'I will not forsake my community, but I will leave your country, for God's earth is wide'. This did not pacify Yunfa, who feared that many of his subjects would follow him. He sent troops in pursuit. Outnumbered and poorly armed, the Muslims fought with desperate courage. Their bowmen brought the horsemen of Gobir crashing to the ground, and they won the first battle of the war. The Muslims buried their dead with their bloody wounds unwashed, for their wounds were proof of martyrdom, and their passport to Paradise. Such were the small and unpromising beginnings of the jihad which was to overthrow the kings of Hausaland, and create the largest state of the time in sub-Saharan Africa. One of the dispossessed Habe† rulers compared it with a spark in the dry season, which turns into a terrible racing blaze.

The jihadists did not enjoy a chain of uninterrupted successes. On several occasions they were defeated with terrible losses. In one battle two thousand Muslims were killed, of whom two hundred knew the Quran by heart. The Shehu had been chosen as the leader of the new Islamic community. His personality gave it its inspiration, and assurance of God's favour. The actual military strategy and command was entrusted to the Shehu's brother, Abdullahi, and his son, Muhammad Bello. Gradually they carved a new state out of territory that had formerly belonged to Gobir, and the neighbour states of Kebbi and Zamfara. In 1808 they took Alkalawa, the capital of Gobir, and the survival of the new state seemed assured. Yunfa died fighting in his own palace.

After the victory of the jihad, the Shehu chose religious retirement. He divided his new dominions between his brother and his son. After his death in 1817, his son, Muhammad Bello, became Caliph of Sokoto, a position he held until his death in 1837. Sokoto was a new city, which Bello began to build in 1809. The Shehu lies buried there, his tomb a place of pilgrimage.

* Hijra, or flight from an oppressor, is sanctified in Muslim eyes by Muhammad's flight to Medina.
† i.e. Hausa.

Reasons for Muslim victory

One of the most interesting questions we can ask about the jihad in Gobir is this: why were the Muslims successful? How was a relatively small group of scholars able to overthrow a powerful military state? More surprising still – how was it that the jihad could expand so rapidly into neighbouring states (a process we shall study in the next section)?

A key inspiration of the jihad, and explanation for its success, lies of course in Islam. Islam provided the basic concept of Holy War, and the ideal of the just society which it might achieve. It gave Muslims dauntless courage in battle, for they believed that if they died they would receive a martyr's reward. Nevertheless, the jihad could not have been successful through the support of scholars alone. Jibril's experiences among the Tuareg show this clearly. There were many learned and devout men among the Tuareg, but, despite this, his jihad was a failure. To be successful, such a movement had to appeal to a number of sections in society, and offer a solution to a wide range of grievances.

One of the most important sources of support undoubtedly came from the Fulani. Hausa, Tuareg and Fulani fought in the Shehu's armies, but the majority, like the Shehu himself, were Fulani. Some Fulani were devout Muslims, some were not Muslims at all, some practised Islam imperfectly (because, for instance, the duty of caring for their herds made the long Islamic prayers difficult). They were drawn to the Shehu largely by ethnic solidarity. The Fulani clan leaders probably hoped for a larger share of political power, in a land where their forefathers had lived for centuries. Fulani herdsmen detested the cattle tax, *jangali*, which the Habe rulers imposed. Of the flag bearers who carried the jihad beyond Gobir, all but one were Fulani (the exception was Yaqub of Bauchi). The role played by non-Muslim Fulani probably helped reduce the original religious idealism, as we shall see later on. But there was a very important difference between the Sokoto jihad and wars which have been fought in the interests of a national or ethnic group. In principle, the jihad was above ethnic divisions. It was international, for the only true dividing line was between the Muslim and the unbeliever. For this reason, ethnic identities are seldom mentioned in lists of the Shehu's followers.

Some historians have interpreted the jihad primarily as a social revolution, in which Muslim intellectuals provided the leadership for the poor and oppressed. Certainly, the Shehu attacked many abuses which weighed heavily on the poor, such as the ostentatious luxury of the Gobir court, and the heavy taxes which made both this, and Gobir's wars of expansion, possible. He condemned the corruption of the officials, such as those who administered the markets, and the bad conduct of the law courts, which were concerned mainly with levying fines to swell the state's finances. Although the Shehu was a social critic, however, to him the world, and everything in it, was short-lived and corruptible, 'a mirage whose abundance is raging thirst'. His primary concern was with eternity.

When the jihad broke out, the Hausa peasants seem in the main to have supported the Muslims. But to maintain itself, the jihadist army was forced to live off the land.

Some of its soldiers went beyond this, collecting booty. This had the not surprising effect of turning many of the ordinary Hausa peasants against the movement.

The jihad spreads beyond Gobir

If Usuman dan Fodio's jihad had been confined within the borders of Gobir, it would not have been so important in West African history, or occupy so much space in this book. But Gobir itself is only a relatively small area on what later became the northern frontier of the Sokoto Caliphate. The jihad spread, until the Caliphate became the largest unified state in sub-Saharan Africa, at the time. Unlike most empires, it spread, not through military expeditions from the centre (Sokoto), but through a chain of local jihads, which were led by Muslims who freely gave their allegiance to the Caliphate.

The king of Gobir appealed to the other Habe rulers to unite with him against the jihad. There was no response. The Shehu was more successful when he appealed to communities of Muslim scholars scattered through Hausaland. Their leaders met together, and listened to a message from the Shehu. He said he was afraid to pray for their victory, lest they become like the Habe rulers. They must first take an oath that they would not be corrupted by power, or love of money, or strife and enmity, which 'makes a man a Muslim in the morning and a pagan by evening'. The leaders swore allegiance to the Shehu, and each was given a green flag, as a symbol of his support. The Shehu also appealed to the Habe kings to support him, but only one responded, the ruler of Zaria.

The jihad in Hausaland

Between 1805 and 1809, the jihad spread to Kano, Katsina and Daura. The Habe rulers of these ancient states united in opposition, but in vain, for they were defeated, after a bitter struggle in which five successive Katsina kings were killed in battle. The defeated Habe dynasties set up smaller states further north. The most important of these was Maradi.

In Zaria, the jihad followed a rather different pattern. When it began, the ruler of Zaria was Jattau* whom tradition remembers as a man of learning, wisdom and piety. Alone of the Habe rulers, he welcomed the jihad, and supported it till his death in 1806. After his death, Zaria rejected the Shehu's authority. Mallam Musa, one of the Shehu's students, was sent to attack the state, and established himself there with little difficulty. The defeated Habe dynasty fled south, and a little later built a new capital at Abuja, famous today for its beautiful pottery. Unlike the other Hausa emirates, Zaria included, to the south, many pagan peoples who did not acknowledge her authority.

* This is a nickname meaning fair-complexioned.

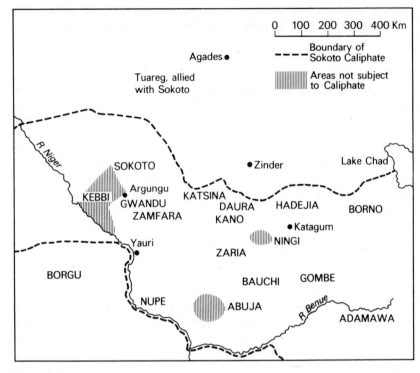

Hausaland after the jihad

The jihad in the south and east

In Hausaland, the jihadists inherited long-established states, with ancient traditions of centralised government. Further to the south, in the kingdom of Nupe, a follower of Usuman dan Fodio succeeded in gaining control of another established kingdom, this time by following a policy of divide and rule.

The kingdom of Nupe was founded in the late fifteenth century, and its rulers had become Muslims by the late eighteenth. By the early nineteenth century, the royal family was divided, and two cousins, Majiya and Jimada, were struggling for the throne. Mallam Dendo was a Fulani scholar who came to Sokoto in about 1810. He played off the rivals so cleverly against each other that he himself became the effective ruler of Nupe. After his death in 1833, however, his children, who had learnt nothing from the example of their predecessors, engaged in bloody civil wars among themselves, and against the heirs of the original Nupe dynasty. Finally, after many reversals of fortune, Masaba emerged supreme. He was Mallam Dendo's youngest son, by a Nupe mother. He took the ancient title of Etsu Nupe, and built a fine new capital at Bida.

The other emirates to the south and east were entirely new political creations. The Caliphate made an unsuccessful effort to conquer the ancient Muslim state of Borno (we shall look at Borno history on page 34). The jihadists were, however, able to carve two new emirates out of its western borderlands – Hadejia (1808) and Katagum (1810). The emirates of Gombe, Bauchi and Adamawa were all established by small Fulani minorities, amid numerous pagan peoples, in areas which had previously lacked political unity.

Perhaps the most interesting of these was Adamawa, which was named after its Fulani founder, Mallam Adama, and which covered a large area in what is now northern Cameroun, and north-eastern Nigeria. This beautiful mountainous region was inhabited by large numbers of pagan tribes. After a long struggle, the Fulani succeeded in imposing their authority, though they were frequently divided among themselves. Adama had to give no less than twenty-four jihad flags to his subordinates. He set up a new capital at Yola in 1841, and died in 1848.

One more important emirate should be mentioned. This is Ilorin, founded in the 1820s. We shall return to its history in Chapter Three.

By the time of the death of Usuman dan Fodio, the Caliphate had reached its geographical limits, except in Adamawa. To the west, an unsuccessful attempt had been made to conquer the warlike peoples of Borgu. To the east, Borno, reduced in size, had successfully resisted conquest. To the north was a ring of hostile Habe states, such as Maradi, and what was left of Gobir. The desert, in any case, made further conquests less attractive. To the south were a number of warlike peoples, like the Tiv, whom the British, in their turn, were to find very difficult to conquer.

The results of the jihad
The most obvious result of the jihad was the creation of the Sokoto Caliphate, with its component emirates. The emirs ruled their own states, though on occasion the Caliph intervened in their affairs, for example, if there was a succession dispute. The authority of the Caliph was essentially moral, as he embodied Islamic law and government, and the obedience of the emirs was essentially voluntary. They were expected to visit Sokoto each year, and send regular tribute. The Caliphate was ringed about with walled fortress towns, called *ribats*.

It would be wrong, however, to think that the Caliphate enjoyed perfect unity and security. To the north and south, lay the bitterly hostile Habe kingdoms. In the heart of the Caliphate, south-east of Kano, lay the Sultanate of Ningi, an independent Muslim state which rejected the authority of Sokoto. Bukhari, emir of Hadejia, successfully rebelled against the Caliphate in the mid-nineteenth century. A number of emirates, such as Gombe, Bauchi and Adamawa, had many pagan ethnic groups which never accepted the Caliph's authority, and against them, jihad became a permanent situation, a matter of annual wars and slave raids.

We have seen that the jihad was fought largely to achieve a more just society, governed according to Islamic ideals. One of the most important points to consider is the extent to which these ideals were maintained in practice. Did the Fulani of the Caliphate become just another privileged class, seeking their own interests, like the Habe kings? There is certainly considerable evidence that this happened. Hausa scholars became increasingly anxious and critical, and Abd al Salam even led a Hausa revolt after the Shehu's death. Even before the fighting was over, the Shehu's brother wrote a poem of bitter lamentation, that the lead had been taken by men

> Whose purpose is the ruling of the countries and their people,
> In order to obtain delight and acquire rank,
> According to the custom of the unbelievers . . .

Later in the century, Hausa poets wrote lines of stinging social criticism –

> Know that tyranny will be darkness on the Day of Resurrection . . .

The hated taxes of the Habe survived. Only their names were changed.

But to say that later Fulani rulers fell away from the high ideals of Usuman dan Fodio, is only to say that later rulers were not saints. No human society has ever put its ideals fully into practice. But part of the legacy of the Shehu remained. The authority of the Caliphate was primarily moral, not military. Its standing depended on its reputation for righteousness and justice. The judgements of its law courts depended on how closely they followed the Sharia (the law of Islam). The tradition of piety was never wholly lost. Abu Bakr, a Caliph of the 1870s, insisted on earning his own living by rope-making. And there is evidence of a continuing concern for the welfare of the common man. One small example dates from the lifetime of the Shehu, who tried to prevent boundary disputes by encouraging farmers to mark footpaths with a distinctive shrub.

It is clear that the jihad resulted in a great expansion of Islam among the Hausa peasantry, an expansion which continued in the days of colonial rule. One estimate suggests that half the Hausa-speaking population were Muslim at the beginning of the colonial period. Some pagan practices such as the *Bori* cult persisted, however. The geographical spread of the jihad brought people who had little experience of Islam, in places such as Adamawa, into contact with it for the first time.

The spread of Islam went hand in hand with a greater expansion of education and literacy. This included the elementary education of the Quranic schools, the higher education of the students who sat at the feet of famous scholars, and the brilliant literary achievements of the Shehu and his associates.

It is possible also that the Caliphate fostered economic growth, by breaking down political boundaries, and establishing greater peace and stability over a wide area. It is true that some states like Katsina suffered greatly in the jihad wars. Others, especially Kano, achieved great prosperity, but the foundations of that prosperity had been laid long before (by the collapse of the Songhai empire, and the resulting shift of trade routes further east).

The culture and brilliance of the Caliphate, like the culture and brilliance of Ancient Greece, rested on a foundation of slavery. One of the Caliphate's main sources of income came from slave raiding. Emirates with frontiers bordering on pagan peoples made annual wars on them, which were dignified by the name of jihad, and sent slaves as tribute to Sokoto. The first European visitor to Adamawa, in the 1850s, wrote, 'Slavery exists on an immense scale in this country, and there are many private individuals who have more than a thousand slaves'. In Zaria it has been estimated that the numbers of slave and free were equal. Some slaves, as we have seen, rose to positions of great wealth and power. Most worked on the land, and lived in the agricultural settlements dotted around the big cities. These slave farms were called *rinji*. It is difficult to know how their inhabitants felt about their situation. Certainly, there were no slave revolts in nineteenth-century Hausaland. The Shehu's slaves refused their freedom, preferring to stay with him. But there were many cases of slaves running away, sometimes on a large scale. The absence of revolts does not necessarily mean they were contented – they might have been unhappy, but feared the risk of rebellion. But the destruction and suffering caused by slave raiding was immense. This is a record of a conversation on the subject, in the 1850s, in Borno, which raided slaves in the same way.

> I took an opportunity to enter into a conversation with our friend the vizier, with regard to the policy which they pursued with these people, and the way in which they desolated these regions; and I asked him whether they would not act more prudently in allowing their natives to cultivate their fertile country with tranquillity, only levying a considerable tribute among them. But the vizier answered me, that it was only by the most violent means that they were able to crush these pagans, who cherished their independence and liberty above everything, and that this was the reason why he burnt all the granaries, in order to subdue them by famine.

The jihad in Massina

The jihad in Massina was very closely linked to that which established the Sokoto Caliphate. In its early stages its leader, Ahmadu (or Hamad) Lobbo★ wrote to Usuman dan Fodio, asking him if his own jihad was justifiable, although he was forced to take action before the reply, blessing his undertaking, came back. When he was successful, however, he refused to accept Sokoto's authority, or send tribute, and established his own independent Caliphate, with its capital at Hamdallahi.

The Hamdallahi Caliphate maintained a separate existence only from 1818 to 1862. It covered a much smaller geographical area than the Sokoto Caliphate, and most of the other Islamic empires studied in this chapter. But it has a special interest of its own, for of all the nineteenth-century jihads in the western Sudan it was probably the most purely religious in inspiration, and it was undoubtedly the one where the original ideals were adhered to most closely in later practice.

This jihad took place in the region of the Niger bend, where the great river breaks up into many lakes and narrower waterways, a region often called the inland delta of

★ His name appears differently in many history books. His surname is given variously as Lobbo, Cissé, or Bari.

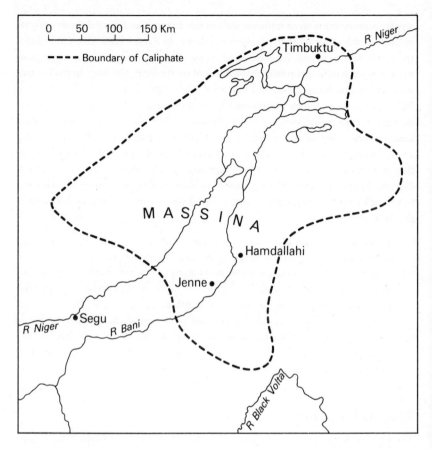

The Massina Caliphate

the Niger. It contains the great university cities of Timbuktu and Jenne, and attained the pinnacle of its wealth and learning in the sixteenth century, before the collapse of the Songhai empire. It is often regarded as the heart of the western Sudan, and of its Islamic culture, and historians have sometimes wondered why the early jihads were found, not in this heartland area, but on the periphery, in the Futa kingdoms, and in Hausaland.

Were it not for the inland Delta, Massina would have lain deep in the Sahelian zone. But the waters of the Niger made flourishing agriculture possible, as well as fishing industries and good water transport. Timbuktu and Jenne were strategically situated from a commercial point of view. They were at the southern ends of the trans-Saharan trade routes, where caravans of camels unloaded Saharan salt, and imports from north Africa, and where long-distance traders, such as the Dyula, brought gold, kola and other goods from the south. Historians have sometimes compared them with seaports, lying on the edges of a vast ocean of sand.

There is undoubtedly a close link between the prosperity of the area, and its fine tradition of scholarship. Books cost money, especially in societies where most of them were copied by hand, and it is hard for learning to flourish in a subsistence economy where men struggle for bare survival. Similarly, the learning of Usuman dan Fodio and his followers was ultimately made possible by the wealth of Hausaland, its commercial cities and flourishing agriculture.

Political background

The political situation in the area was extremely complicated. In 1591, the great Songhai empire had collapsed as a result of its conquest by an army from Morocco. The Moroccan soldiers and their descendants intermarried with local women, and founded a new ruling caste, the Arma, who ruled over a number of small fragmented states, for they were not able to recreate the unity of Songhai. Part of the political vacuum was filled by the growth of the new states of Segu and Kaarta, which were ruled by the Bambara, a pagan branch of the great Mande-speaking family.

Although these cities included a substantial Muslim community, their rulers clung to their traditional religion. In 1796 the great Scottish explorer Mungo Park came to Segu, a hungry and destitute traveller. He received the utmost kindness both from the king and from the women of the city, which he described as 'a prospect of civilisation and magnificence which I little expected to find in the bosom of Africa'.

By the early nineteenth century, the Bambara kingdoms had weakened themselves by their rivalries and internal jealousies. Further to the north and east, Berber tribes from the desert, for whom the waters of the Niger were always an attraction, had established their dominance in the area round Timbuktu. One Berber tribe, however, the Kunta, specialised not in conquest, but in religious study and teaching. They produced a famous Timbuktu scholar, Al Mukhtar, who died in 1811, and did much to increase the influence of the Qadiriyya.

The Massina area was one where many different ethnic groups lived side by side. Some were nomads, and some were settled agriculturalists. We have already noted the role of the Arma, the Bambara, and the Berber tribes. There were other Mande-speaking groups in the area, such as the Dyula (Muslim long-distance traders), the Marka (Muslim traders and scholars) and the Bozo (fishermen, long settled in the area). But the leadership of the Massina jihad was to come from none of these groups, but from the pastoral Fulani, who had lived in the area since the fifteenth century. The different Fulani clans were ruled by their own chiefs, called ardos. The ardo in the Massina area was a member of the Diallo clan.

Ahmadu Lobbo

Ahmadu Lobbo was born in 1775, a member of the Bari clan. He spent his youth and early manhood studying Islamic branches of learning, and tending cattle. Like Usuman, he was an ardent follower of the Qadiriyya. He was much less of an academic; he wrote little himself, and later used Usuman's books as a guide in the government he established. He was austere, and critical of his environment. He thought the famous scholars of Jenne spent too much time discussing futile questions, whereas the real way to save souls was through prayer. He fell out with them, and was forbidden to enter the Jenne mosque. He settled in a small town near Jenne, much as Usuman had settled at Degel, and devoted himself to religious teaching, attracting an increasing number of disciples around him.

In about 1807, he had a vision telling him that he was destined to establish a new state in the area of the Niger bend. As his followers increased, they came to pose a problem for the local ardo, as Usuman's followers had for the king of Gobir. Finally, the underlying tension broke into open conflict, and one of Ahmadu's disciples killed the ardo's son. Ahmadu performed his own hijra to Noukouma. The ardo appealed to his overlord, the ruler of Segu, for help, and Ahmadu's followers, who numbered only a thousand, faced an overwhelmingly superior army. He was invited to surrender, but his reply showed his complete confidence that his cause was that of God. 'We know the importance of the pagan armies, but the army of God is uncountable: it fills heaven and earth'.

Despite the odds against them, his followers won. Like the jihadists in Gobir, they were certain of God's support, and did not fear death, since a martyr's death would bring them straight to Paradise. As in Gobir, this initial victory was very significant. It showed that the new movement had a real chance of success, and won over many doubters.

Ahmadu's first supporters came from his own disciples, from the Marka scholars, and from many of his fellow Fulani, especially from his own clan. The ardos, abandoned by their people, in many cases adopted Islam, and supported the jihad. Others opposed it, and, ultimately defeated, had to move elsewhere.

Government of Massina
As Muhammad Bello founded a new capital at Sokoto, Ahmadu founded his own new capital, which he called Hamdallahi, which means 'Praise God'. Whereas Usuman dan Fodio sought to preserve his own spiritual life by living in retirement, and giving the role of political leadership to others, Ahmadu kept the reins of government in his own hands, but took the greatest pains to ensure that all its actions were in accord with his religious ideals. He invited a hundred leading scholars to write memoranda on how the state should be run. When they presented their work, Ahmadu studied it and chose the authors of the forty best efforts to form his governing council. All important issues were taken in conjunction with it. Since a body of this size could not be in constant session, he chose two especially outstanding scholars to be always at his side, to advise him. To make sure that his high ideals were consistently put into day to day practice, he appointed agents, *sa'i*, who kept a watch on the behaviour of public servants. The *sa'i* were specially chosen for their indifference to wealth and incorruptibility – the 'poor just ones'.

The new city took three years to build. Its mosque was plain and unadorned. Ahmadu showed a great concern for education. There were over six hundred Quranic schools in the capital alone, with their masters paid by the state, and no-one could open one unless his competence was first tested. An area near the governing council's meeting hall 'was reserved for lodgings for travellers, orphans, and old people, for all those without means of support who were fed and lodged at the expense of the state'.

The standard of hygiene was much higher than that of early nineteenth-century European cities, where the water often ran brown with sewage. It was forbidden to urinate in the streets or let the blood of a slaughtered animal flow there. Dogs were not allowed to roam at will. Milk-sellers were forced to keep their utensils spotless, and the quality of meat on sale was rigidly controlled. Ahmadu's concern extended to horses and donkeys, and cruelty to animals was forbidden.

The policing of the city was controlled by seven clerics. They were concerned not only with what we should now regard as crimes, but with areas of life which modern people would regard as within the sphere of private morality. Married people who were found in the streets late at night had to explain their presence there before a tribunal. Horsemen were forbidden to look over garden walls into private homes. Husbands returning home after a long absence were expected to give prior warning of their arrival, because to arrive suddenly might indicate a harmful lack of trust.

There were limits to Ahmadu's idealism, however, and when some scholars urged him to abolish all distinctions of caste (which divided the local people into higher castes, lower castes, and slaves), he refused – perhaps because he thought the undertaking would arouse too much opposition.

Ahmadu himself always lived with great simplicity, showing a concern for the opinions and feelings of others which was remarkable in the founder and ruler of a great state. When Hamdallahi was founded, he ordered the Niger boatmen to transport goods to its neighbourhood, as necessary. Another scholar told him that he was being just as arbitrary as the pagan kings he had criticised. He agreed, and took the order back. On another occasion, when he was hungry and no food had been prepared, he ate the rough provisions intended for the horses, despite the protests of his wife. Many years later, when Ahmadu was dead and his empire overthrown, his wife, a prisoner, was expected to eat equally coarse food. Remembering the example of her husband, she accepted it with a tranquil heart.

Perhaps inevitably, Ahmadu's austere government brought him into conflict with the twin commercial cities of Jenne and Timbuktu. On page 34 is a mid-nineteenth-century picture of Timbuktu.

Their wealth tended to lead to a luxurious way of life which could not be approved by Ahmadu, as well as practices contrary to Islam, such as taking alcoholic drinks. Jenne inevitably lost much of her importance when he built his own new capital in the same area. The wars between Segu and Massina undermined the cities' economic prosperity, by cutting them off from their gold supplies. To make matters worse, Ahmadu destroyed Jenne's mosque – in theory because it was too ornate, but perhaps because he remembered his own exclusion from it, long ago. In Timbuktu the Kunta, who had produced so many great religious leaders themselves, resented him as an upstart, and led a number of risings against him. In the 1840s, shortly before Ahmadu's death, the governing council of Hamdallahi blockaded Timbuktu, and starved it into

Timbuktu

submission. Typically, Ahmadu tried to make provision for the poor of the area, to prevent excessive suffering, but he died before his plans were fully implemented.

Although much of his government was concerned with the regulation of cities, he did not forget his own pastoral Fulani, and he arranged to give them military protection as they travelled on their long annual migration with their herds.

Ahmadu died in 1845, and was succeeded by his son, and then his grandson. He had been remarkably successful in creating a new unified state in an area with several different religions, and many different ethnic groups. Although he appealed to his own Fulani, it was not a Fulani rising in the sense that the war in Gobir tended to be. The first phase of the jihad was a conflict with a pagan Fulani ruler, supported by the pagan dynasty of Segu. Ahmadu's Islamic fervour united Muslims of many different tribes in his support, but he was still opposed by some Muslim groups, such as the scholars of Jenne and Timbuktu. Some of the inhabitants of Massina probably saw the movement in nationalist terms, as a return to self-government, after throwing off the yoke of Segu. The readiness with which many Fulani rejected the ardo and Segu, suggests that their rule may have been unjust and oppressive, but of this there is too little evidence to be certain.

Massina lost her autonomy within twenty years of Ahmadu's death. She fell, not through internal opposition, but to another Islamic ruler. This was Al Hajj Umar, whose career will form the subject of a later chapter.

Renewal without jihad: Borno

The original heartland of this ancient state lay to the north and east of Lake Chad in Kanem. In the fourteenth century its people were forced to migrate to the south-west of Lake Chad, to Borno. The move was due in the first instance to political conflicts, but these in their turn were probably caused by the progressive encroachment of the desert which meant that people were competing for fewer economic resources. The Kanuri nation developed from the intermarriage of these Kanembu migrants and the original pagan inhabitants of Borno, whom the invaders called 'So'. Like all empires, Borno went through phases of expansion and decline. It reached the height of its expansion in the sixteenth century when most of the states of Hausaland paid it tribute and it controlled a vast Saharan empire stretching north to the Fezzan, which meant that it controlled the valuable trans-Saharan trade routes and the salt mines of Bilma.

It is generally agreed that by the end of the eighteenth century Borno was one of the most thoroughly Islamicised states in West Africa. One account describes Birni Gazargamu as a city where there 'were many God-fearing Mallams and many blameless nobles and many unworldly people and learned saints'. The scholars of Borno used to export copies of the Quran to North Africa where they were greatly prized. It seems that Islam was not confined to the scholar class but was also spreading steadily among the peasantry, although, as in Hausaland, with a fair admixture of pagan practices.

Borno in 1800

Borno in 1800 was an ancient and internationally famous kingdom, but its power was more apparent than real, and it contained a number of weaknesses and internal contradictions which made it especially vulnerable to jihad. It had lost most of its imperial possessions and was in its turn the subject of external attack, being raided by the Tuareg to the north, the peoples of the mountain kingdom of Mandara to the south, and Baghirmi and Wadai to the east. It had lost control of the desert trade routes and their valuable salt mines and to make matters worse there appears to have been an agricultural crisis in the late eighteenth century and early nineteenth, a period of famines, pestilence and locust plagues.

Although Borno was an ancient Islamic state, its political institutions were shaped by pre-Islamic ideas of divine kingship. These are brought out very well by this picture of the Borno king, or Mai.

The court of the Mai of Borno

The ritual seclusion of the Mai is symbolised by the bars which divide him from his audience and the veil covering his face. His courtiers out of respect turn their backs to him. Both he and his courtiers wore many layers of clothing to give them the appearance of superhuman stature. This seclusion tended to make it difficult for him to supply vigorous leadership in a crisis. Earlier Mais had done this, but the tradition had weakened. More fundamentally, there was a contradiction between this idea of divine kingship and Islam.

There were a large number of immigrant groups in Borno society. These included Kanembu, recently arrived from Kanem, Shuwa Arabs and Fulani, who were concentrated mainly in the western provinces of the kingdom. For these last, the jihad of Usuman dan Fodio was to prove a golden opportunity to challenge the situation of Borno and seize political power.

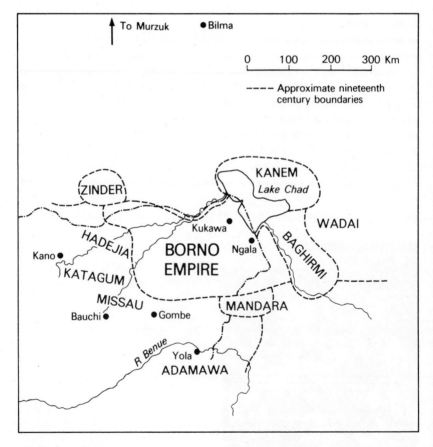

The Empire of Borno

The rise of Al-Kanemi

As soon as Usuman dan Fodio declared his jihad in Gobir, Fulani leaders in western Borno sent an emissary to him to obtain his flag. The leading role was played by Umar ibn Abdur, Ardo Lerlima and Ibrahim Zaki. The southern Fulani were led by Goni Mukhtar. The Mai protested to the Sokoto leadership that he and his people were Muslims, but to no avail. The Fulani leadership rapidly overran vast areas of Borno territory, and in 1808 sacked the capital of Birni Gazargamu itself. The Mai, Ahmad, who was old and blind, abdicated in favour of his son, Dunama. Dunama, with his capital lost and much of his kingdom in enemy hands, turned in desperation to a well-known religious teacher, who had had some success in resisting the Fulani at a local level. This was Al-Hajj Muhammad al-Amin, generally known as al-Kanemi.

Al-Kanemi was the son of a Kanembu mallam who had settled in Murzuk, in the Fezzan, in what is now Libya. His mother was the daughter of an Arab trader. He grew up and studied in the Fezzan, and then went with his father on pilgrimage, spending about ten years studying in the east. He returned to Africa, and ultimately settled at Ngala, south of Lake Chad, where his learning and piety attracted a number of scholars.

Al-Kanemi provided both practical military leadership and a theoretical justification for opposing the jihad. The jihadists claimed that Borno was a land of disbelief because people took bribes there and the law courts were often unjust. Al-Kanemi replied that these were sins but did not of themselves render the sinner a non-believer. Moreover they could be found in all Islamic countries.

> If praying and the giving of alms, knowledge of God, fasting in Ramadan and the building of mosques is paganism, what is Islam? . . . We love the Shaikh [i.e. Usuman dan Fodio] and the truth when they agree. But if they disagree it is the truth which comes first.

If the people of Borno were in error, Muslims should teach them rather than fight them.

With the help of Al-Kanemi, Dunama briefly succeeded in regaining his capital, only to abandon it soon afterwards as being too close to Fulani strongholds. The Mai then wandered from place to place, mockingly known as 'the Mai of the calabashes' (in which his people carried their possessions). He was deposed by courtiers dissatisfied with his leadership and from 1809 to 1813 his uncle reigned in his stead. In 1813, Al-Kanemi restored Dunama to his throne. This was the decisive step by which Al-Kanemi became the most powerful man in Borno, for the Mai owed him his throne and Al-Kanemi had demanded as his price the right to tax and administer half Borno's territory. (Borno had shrunk considerably by this time, for the Fulani succeeded in keeping control of the western provinces.)

It seems that for many years Al-Kanemi was torn between his original religious idealism and the political career into which circumstances had thrust him. As late as 1820 he wrote that if obligations did not keep him there he would have liked to leave Borno. Earlier he wrote to the people of his father's homeland:

I am concerned about your dependence on worldly things and the pleasure you derive from them. You should not look to them at all. God is concerned about your soul, so pray for his mercy upon it.

Although his example and preaching led many Muslims to practice their religion more fervently, his views, as we have seen, were basically tolerant and he does not appear to have made many efforts to spread Islam or reform religious practices. He was a man of towering personality, sometimes ruthless, sometimes overwhelming his opponents with his generosity. Something of his dynamism is revealed in this contemporary portrait of him.

Al-Kanemi

From 1813 on, one can isolate various milestones in his political career. He took the title of Shaikh (Shehu), as Usuman dan Fodio had done, with its implication of religious leadership. He built his own capital at Kukawa in 1814. This is a picture of his palace, with a broad promenade in front of it.

Al-Kanemi's palace

In 1820 he struck his own seal. In that same year Dunama, tired of his role as a shadow king, made a last bid to regain his lost power, conspiring with his country's enemy, Baghirmi. But the plot misfired and it was Dunama himself who was killed in battle, meeting his death with great courage and dignity.

From now on, Al-Kanemi was king in all but name. Wisely, he did not take the title of Mai which might have aroused the hostility of many sections of Borno society. Instead he installed Dunama's younger brother, Ibrahim, as a shadow king. The real power in the kingdom, however, was in the Shehu's much simpler and more informal court at Kukawa. His six most trusted companions became his advisory council. As we have seen, Al-Kanemi was born abroad and was of partly foreign origin. His political organisation depended heavily on the support of foreigners, his Kanembu and Fezzani kinsmen and the Shuwa Arabs. He also placed much reliance on slaves and posted slave generals called *kachella* on the crucial western frontier. His dependence on immigrants and slaves may have reflected his imperfect acceptance by the traditional Kanuri nobility who were almost bound to see him as an outsider and an upstart.

He was a decisive and successful military leader. He fought a series of wars with Baghirmi, which was finally defeated in 1824, and a number of wars against Sokoto. On one occasion he pursued a fleeing enemy as far as the gates of Kano. In his military as in his political organisation, he made extensive use of foreigners, often employing North African mercenaries.

Even under Al-Kanemi's able leadership, Borno had certain weaknesses. These had begun before his time and were to become of decisive importance in the lifetime of his son. One of these was the decline of the kingdom's external trade. Borno's economy had depended heavily on trade with North Africa. In the nineteenth century this trade was declining. The export of slaves to North Africa declined as a result of European intervention and anti-slave trade agreements there. For a time, the slave trade was replaced by a trade in luxuries, especially ivory and ostrich feathers, but the market for these was uncertain and when Europe went through a phase of economic recession, the demand was severely affected. These economic difficulties had important political consequences. The political prestige of a ruler depended largely on his ability to reward his followers. Al-Kanemi's descendants, lacking the necessary means, lost political prestige accordingly.

Another aspect of Borno's weakness can be seen in the basically unjust structure of her society, with its opulent and privileged court, and an oppressed peasantry. This is reflected in the song of a Borno nobleman:

> The peasant is grass, fodder for the horses.
> To your hoeing, peasant, so that we can eat.

It reached its culmination in the reign of Al-Kanemi's grandson, Bukar, who in 1883 tried to find a solution to his economic problems by confiscating half the possessions of the peasantry.

Borno after Al-Kanemi

Al-Kanemi died in 1837. The crucial question now became whether his authority was purely personal or whether he had founded a new dynasty. Mai Ibrahim tried to assert his independence but Al-Kanemi's son, Umar, successfully established his own authority. In 1846 Ibrahim conspired with the Sultan of Wadai, a central Sudanese state then going through a phase of expansion. The Sultan invaded Borno and even sacked part of Kukawa but was ultimately forced to retreat. Ibrahim and many of his followers were killed. The survivors fled or gave their allegiance to Umar. It was the end of the ancient Seifawa dynasty which had ruled for perhaps a thousand years, one of the longest surviving dynasties the world has known.

Umar reigned until his death in 1881, a reign marked by economic decline and the loss of power and territory to Wadai which gained control of Baghirmi and Kanem. Borno was left a relatively small state, sandwiched between the Sokoto Caliphate and the Sultanate of Wadai. Umar's last years were marked by intense rivalry between his sons who were never sent on a campaign together lest one should take the opportunity to seek his brother's death. In fact, the three of them ruled successively, each having a fairly short reign.

An outside observer would have thought that Borno, weakened and divided, would fall an easy prey to European imperialism. In fact Al-Kanemi's dynasty was overthrown by an African, Rabih Zubair, a general from the eastern Sudan who succeeded in carving out for himself a substantial, if short-lived, empire. He conquered Borno in 1893. We shall consider his career in Chapter Six.

The jihad in the Bambara kingdoms

Al Hajj Umar

The leader of the last great jihad of the western Sudan was born in Futa Toro in 1794, a Tukulor of the clerical caste, *Torodbe*. His name was Umar b. Said Tall but he is generally known as Al Hajj Umar. As a young man, he joined the Tijaniyya, a new Sufi order which had been recently established in Algeria (though its real home was Morocco). He decided to go on a pilgrimage to Mecca and with typical initiative, he went to St Louis, then under French rule, to collect donations for the purpose. He set out on his pilgrimage in 1825. In Arabia he succeeded in winning the confidence of the Tijani representative, overcoming the initial racial prejudice he met with his sophistication and wit. He was entrusted with the innermost secrets of the order and was appointed its Khalifa (representative) for the western Sudan.

Some historians have seen the Tijaniyya as an essentially democratic order with a strong appeal to the common man, while the older orders, such as the Qadiriyya, were more learned and aristocratic. But in fact the main dividing line between the Tijaniyya and the other Sufi brotherhoods lay in its higher pretensions, which have always seemed to non-Tijani to be ill founded and arrogant. Its founder claimed to have had a direct revelation from Muhammad and to be the culmination of all Sufis, as Muhammad was the culmination of all prophets. He claimed that the Tijaniyya enjoyed much greater spiritual privileges than the other brotherhoods. He forbade its members to join any other brotherhood and said that if they left it, they would jeopardise their salvation. These teachings had a special relevance to Muslims in the early nineteenth century when, as we have seen, many believed that the end of the world was at hand. Tijani differed from other Sufis, too, in his attitude to wealth and material possessions. Whereas most other Sufis had practised and advocated asceticism, Tijani said that his followers should enjoy the blessings given by God and be grateful for them. This gave his teachings an obvious attraction for the prosperous. The practices enjoined on the Tijaniyya were basically the same as those of the Qadiriyya, the daily recitation of litanies, the prayers of which were counted by the thousand.

Between 1829 and 1840, Al Hajj Umar returned slowly from his pilgrimage. He spent long periods in Borno and Sokoto, where he married daughters of the ruling families and gained many disciples by his teachings. It is even possible that he hoped to succeed Muhammad Bello as Caliph, but if this was his hope, he was disappointed. He then visited Massina and Segu, where he was imprisoned, presumably for attacking the paganism of its ruler. Wherever he went, his status as a Hajj and his learning and talents attracted disciples, attention and gifts, but he was basically unacceptable to other Muslim rulers for he advocated a new brotherhood which challenged the authority of the Qadiriyya order to which they themselves belonged, and, by implication challenged their religious leadership.

He settled down, not in his native Futa Toro, but on the boundary of Futa Jallon. He shifted his headquarters several times, but the centre especially associated with his name is Dinguiray. When he returned from pilgrimage, he was already an influential and wealthy man, surrounded by disciples and slaves. Now, using their services, he set out deliberately to build up his economic resources, engaging in long distance trade in commodities which included gold, and in agriculture. With the profits, he bought firearms from French and British merchants in Senegal, the Gambia and Sierra Leone. He was the first jihadist leader to recognise the importance of firearms and make a systematic attempt to acquire them. The Sokoto jihad, it may be remembered, was won primarily by Fulani bowmen. His policy reflects his strategic capacity and insight and also his recognition that the trans-Saharan trade had been overtaken in importance by the trade of the Atlantic coast. He continued to attract disciples, mainly from the Futa kingdoms, and went on extensive preaching tours.

The wealth he had accumulated was only a means to an end, and his main ambition was to carve out a new Islamic state. Historians differ as to what extent he was inspired by Tijani missionary zeal, and to what extent by the ambition of an empire builder. Since both motives led him in the same direction, it is fruitless to try and estimate their relative importance, but for Al Hajj Umar, as for dan Fodio and Ahmadu Lobbo, the primary reality was religious and the primary good to be sought salvation.

Conquest of Segu and Kaarta

In 1852 he had a vision in which he was inspired to establish an Islamic state in the pagan Bambara kingdoms of Segu and Kaarta in the east. As the map on the opposite page shows, it was the obvious way to expand, for to the west lay the theocratic states of Futa Jallon and Futa Toro and the danger of conflict with the French in Senegal.

By 1854 he had conquered Kaarta and nothing seemed to prevent his further expansion eastward, but as he began to build up his empire – a process some historians describe as the 'African partition of Africa' – he was forced to develop a policy towards French imperialism based in the coastal settlements in Senegal. In the very year in which he conquered Kaarta, a new expansion-minded French Governor was posted to St Louis. This Governor, Faidherbe, built a fort high on the Senegal river at Medina to contain Umar's expansion. Umar was in a quandary. He did not wish to conquer the Islamic kingdom of Futa Toro, but neither he nor his Futa followers were willing to see Christians conquer their Islamic homeland while they themselves fought jihads elsewhere. This extract from a letter he wrote to a French governor of Senegal shows the way he viewed Europeans, and the role he saw for them in Africa:

> The whites are only traders; let them bring merchandise in their ships, let them pay me a good tribute when I'm Master of the Negroes, and I will live in peace with them. But I don't wish them to expect permanent establishments or send war-ships into the river.

In 1857 he made desperate attempts to take Medina but failed narrowly, despite the reckless courage of his followers. In the words of Faidherbe, 'they march against our fire as if to martyrdom. It is clear that they wish to die'. This was the first military encounter between European and Islamic imperialism in the western Sudan. His failure at Medina and the casualties he suffered encouraged Umar to make peace with the French. In 1860 he made a truce with them in which their mutual boundary was established and in which both sides promised to safeguard each others trading interests. Interestingly enough, a number of Muslim skilled craftsmen from St Louis abandoned their homes to follow Umar, and people from Futa Toro crossed the boundary under fire from the French guns to do likewise. On the facing page there is a picture of Koundian, a fortress town on the western frontier, built by Umar against French aggression.

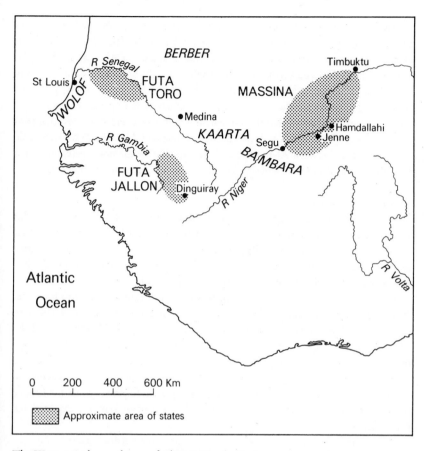

The Western Sudan on the eve of Al Hajj Umar's jihad

Al Hajj Umar's border fort of Koundian

Having settled the French question, at least for a time, Umar marched on the other pagan Bambara state, Segu, which he conquered in 1861. His advance, however, alarmed Massina, now ruled by Ahmadu III, the grandson of Ahmadu Lobbo, who was unwilling to see a powerful Tijaniyya neighbour at the boundaries of his relatively small state. He negotiated an agreement with the ruler of Segu, in which he promised military aid in return for the adoption of Islam. Umar, finding pagan shrines in Segu after its conquest, claimed that the agreement was insincere and hence his own conquest justified. The theoretical debate between Umar and Ahmadu III is comparable with the debate between Al-Kanemi and Muhammad Bello. Both were concerned with their own justification and neither debate had any real impact on events.

Conquest of Massina

Having conquered Segu, Umar turned on Massina and after a fierce struggle his soldiers, through their use of firearms, overwhelmed the Massina cavalry in 1862. Umar had probably not originally intended this tragedy, whereby one jihadist state destroyed another. Had Massina not intervened in Segu, he would perhaps have bypassed it and invaded the pagan states further to the south.

Ironically enough, it was his war with Massina which brought Umar to his death. After conquering Massina, his armies marched on the ancient Islamic university city of Timbuktu but led by a local religious teacher, the people of Timbuktu and the Tuareg of the desert rose against him. The rebellion spread to Massina where Umar himself was beseiged in Hamdallahi. Segu joined in the rising, cutting off provisions from his armies. In 1864 Umar was killed, burnt to death in a fire lit by his enemies to prevent his escape. He was seventy years old. Many of his followers could not believe that he had really died and, to the end of the nineteenth century, expected his reappearance.

This picture reminds us of the price that the wars of the jihadists exacted.

A war victim

After the death of Al-Hajj Umar

Some historians think that the state created by Umar's conquest had much in common with a modern nation. They point to the way in which it included many different ethnic groups and was receptive to modern technology, especially armaments, which were obtained through external trade. They point, too, to the way in which he utilised the abilities of Africans trained in western skills. But in fact his empire had many serious weaknesses, which became very apparent in the reign of his successor. There is no way of knowing how successfully Umar would have tackled them himself.

The first was the problem of unity. Umar had faced widespread revolts among conquered peoples but had no difficulty in maintaining the unity and enthusiasm of his followers, who were inspired both by religious zeal, and the hope of plunder. After his death, his sons fell out among themselves. His chosen heir was his eldest son, Ahmadu bin Shaikh (Ahmadu Seku). Since he was the son of a Hausa woman of slave descent, many of his brothers found his leadership unacceptable. One brother, Aguibu, established an independent state in Dinguiray. A cousin, Tijani, put down the rising

Ahmadu

45

in Massina, and established his own state there. Other brothers revolted in the 1870s, though Ahmadu was finally able to suppress the rising. Ahmadu's own authority was concentrated in the kingdom of Segu. Here he had to cope with constant risings among the Bambara population. These two pictures show two contrasting faces of empire, his palace, and the execution of a Bambara prisoner of war.

Ahmadu's palace at Segu

The execution of a Bambara prisoner of war

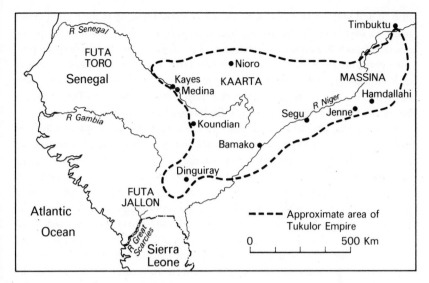

The Western Sudan at the death of Al Hajj Umar

The disunity of Umar's sons was matched by the dissatisfaction of his followers, the *talibes*, or disciples, who had followed him originally from Futa Toro. Many did not think a hereditary monarchy should be set up at all. None found Ahmadu an inspiring religious leader like his father, although he tried to fill that role. The ending of conquest meant the end of plunder. To pacify them, Ahmadu gave them excessive rights and privileges, and they plundered and exploited the subject populations. This, together with Umar's policy of forcible conversion to Islam, explains the perpetual dissatisfaction of the Bambara, which the French were able very cleverly to exploit.

Relations with France

The empire's disunity weakened its resistance to the danger from without of French expansion from Senegal. Well aware of this, Ahmadu made every effort to avoid a direct confrontation with the French, relying instead on diplomacy. In 1880 he made an agreement with the French which has been described as a brilliant diplomatic triumph for the Tukulor. The French, in return for trading privileges, recognised his empire and even any future conquests he might make. But the French Governor in Senegal refused to ratify it and so later on did Ahmadu when he learnt that the French were interpreting it in a sense quite different from the way in which he understood it.

In 1883 the French reached Bamako, a key point on the railway which they were building from the coast. They then linked it with Kayes, their military outpost in Senegal, so that there was a chain of forts cutting across the empire. Ahmadu made no effort to prevent the capture of Bamako or even to hinder the passage of the French gunboat on the Niger as it passed his capital at Segu. Soon afterwards he shifted from Segu to Nioro, the capital of Kaarta, but this was apparently less to avoid the French than to deal with internal rebellions. He still continued to cling to the path of diplomacy. In 1887 he made a further agreement with the French by which he accepted a nominal French Protectorate in return for a French pledge not to invade his empire. Two years later the French attacked his border fortress of Koundian (there is a picture of it on page 43). It fell after a desperate resistance. In 1890 the French took Segu, installing a Bambara as the new ruler. They hoped that he would be a French puppet but in fact he was shot soon afterwards for his anti-French activities.

For years Ahmadu had tried to resist the French by diplomacy. Now he was faced with a choice. He could give in to the French and gain what personal advantages he could from the deal (as his brother Aguibou did), or he could fight a war which he saw clearly to be doomed. His troops with their ill-assorted weapons were no match for the well-trained and well-armed French Senegalese forces and the stone walls of his fortresses could not withstand artillery fire. Nevertheless, he decided to fight. The French marched on Nioro, meeting bitter resistance all the way. They reached Nioro only to find that Ahmadu had moved on to Massina. There, too late, he tried to form an alliance with other Muslim rulers (previously he had refused an alliance with Samori and had actually helped the French suppress Mahmadu Lamine). In 1893 the French, with the help of his own brother, defeated him at Massina. His brother, Aguibou, was given the rule of Massina as his reward. Undaunted, Ahmadu moved further east and set up another little kingdom. When once more the tide of European expansion reached him, he set off for Sokoto but died on the way. His companion in exile observed 'that the respect that was due to him continued to be shown to him by all the princes and chiefs among whom he sojourned'.

Although the French overthrew the Tukulor empire with relative ease, it should be noted that on one occasion they suffered a serious defeat – at the hands of the Tuareg at Timbuktu in 1894.

The Senegambia

The Senegambia is the general name given to the area drained by the Senegal and Gambia rivers. Relatively large numbers of different peoples live there. North of the Senegal, in the deserts of Mauritania, live Arabised Berbers or 'Moors'. Inland, in the early nineteenth century, lay the Islamic Tukulor states of Futa Toro and Futa Bondu. Between the Senegal and the Gambia were a number of Wolof states. The main ones were Cayor and Jolof. Further south were the Serer states of Sin and Salum whose people spoke a language closely related to Wolof. Along the Gambia river was a chain of small Mandingo states.

How deeply Islamicised were these states? In the mid-fifteenth century, an Italian visitor, Ca' da Mosto, said of the Wolof and Mandingo: 'The faith of these first blacks is Muhammadanism; they are not, however, as are the white moors [Berbers of Mauritania] very resolute in this faith, especially the common people'. Later accounts of the area describe a situation where there were some very devout Muslims,

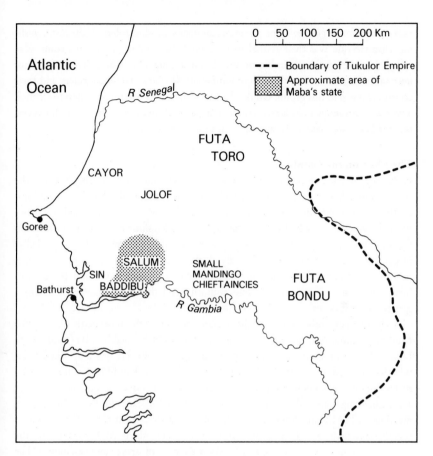

The Senegambia in the mid-nineteenth century

some nominal Muslims and some pagans. In 1818 a French visitor gave an interesting description of the Wolof state of Cayor.

> Mahometanism will soon become the universal religion of the country of Cayor. The court indeed remains attached to paganism, probably as more indulgent to the passions . . . The Mahometan negroes are devout votaries to the external forms of their religion. They will rise frequently in the night to chant chapters of the Koran, and one part of the day is allotted to repeating prayers on a long chaplet suspended from their girdle . . . To procure admission into the class of Marabouts, an irreproachable character and some knowledge of the Arabic language are requisite.

In the Senegambia generally there were two opposed groups. The first were called Marabouts. This word originally means a Muslim cleric and teacher but it came to be applied to fervent Muslims generally. Some of these earned their living as scribes or makers of amulets (*gris-gris*) for pagan or nominally Muslim rulers. Their distinguishing characteristic was their refusal to take alcoholic drinks. The other group were called Soninke★ in the Gambia or the Tiedo among the Wolof. They were not necessarily pagans – often they were indifferent Muslims. The local rulers and their courts belonged to this group. Unlike the Marabouts, they had no objection to alcohol. These two groupings cut across ethnic and political divisions. The Serer, however, resisted Islam and have only welcomed it in quite recent times.

The jihad on the Gambia

In the early nineteenth century there was an increasing number of clashes between the two groups. They came to a head in Baddibu, one of the small Mandingo kingdoms on the Gambia. An open conflict broke out here in 1861. Its background has many parallels with the pre-jihad situation in Gobir. The Muslims resented their exclusion from political power, and the taxes they were forced to pay which they regarded as illegal and which fell particularly heavily on them, as many of them were prosperous traders. They accused the king of plundering their wives, slaves and possessions. Increasingly, the king tended to lose authority and the situation worsened into a general state of chaos.

As in so many other states of the western Sudan in the nineteenth century the Muslim community threw up an outstanding leader, Maba Diakhou Ba (1809–1867). Like Al Hajj Umar, he was originally of Torodbe descent. He was a devout scholar who had studied in Cayor and Jolof before returning to Baddibu, accompanied by many disciples. A contemporary eye-witness account describes him as very tall, with a commanding personality and a severely pockmarked face. In 1850 Maba had a meeting with Al Hajj Umar. Tradition relates that they spent three days in prayer together and then agreed on the areas of their respective jihads. Maba was to have the Gambia. The next ten years, however, Maba devoted to prayer and teaching – 'The jihad of the hand and voice' – in a small town, Kir Maba, 'Maba's Town', amidst his disciples.

Like the ruler of Gobir, the King of Baddibu inevitably saw this clustering of Muslim disciples round a revered leader as a challenge to his authority. The tension came to a head when the British, stationed at Bathurst, intervened in Baddibu to protect the interests of their traders. Baddibu was a valuable source of groundnut exports. Maba helped arrange peace terms and the King of Baddibu blamed him for the British intervention. He sent a party to kill him but they were driven out and the King's son was killed. The Marabouts rallied to Maba's support and easily drove the Soninke from the area. At this point Maba wanted to return to his farm and his school, but circumstances made this impossible. In a speech of 1863 he said, 'Let all remember that a holy war is not waged for private ambition but it is a sacrificial act in which the

★ Soninke properly speaking refers to a group of northern Mande. On the Gambia it became equivalent with Pagan, as Bambara often is. Tiedo refers to the Jolof warrior class who were the last to be converted and therefore became equated with paganism.

love of God is placed above personal desire'. As in other jihads, his followers did not always adhere to his ideals in practice. He never fought in person but would pray on the battlefield surrounded by a group of blind priests. Having established his power in Baddibu, he moved into the Serer kingdom of Salum, replacing its king with a Muslim and establishing his disciples as judges throughout the conquered areas.

Lat-Dior of Cayor and Alboury N'Diaye

Interestingly enough, he converted two Jolof kings to the fervent practice of Islam. One was Lat-Dior, the ruler or Damel of Cayor (1842–86). He had been Damel from 1862–3 but was driven from his throne by a rival who was supported by the French. In a search for allies to help him regain his throne, he allied with Maba and the Marabout party and announced his conversion to Islam. This may have been originally a political conversion but he remained true to Islam until his death. In 1869 the French approved his return to Cayor and in 1871 he was recognised as Damel.

The eleven years which followed were full of significance for Wolof history. He ardently supported the extension of Islam and historians see this as a most important turning point in the history of Islam among the Wolof. He realised that the French were mainly interested in trade. He allied with the farmers rather than with the Tiedo warrior class and exported vast quantities of groundnuts to the French ports. He is an outstanding example of a modernising nineteenth-century African ruler – modernisation in this case being closely linked with Islam. Cayor may be seen as the meeting point of two cultures and two worlds, the world of Islam in the western Sudan and the world of European commerce on the Atlantic coast. But his understanding with the French was a fragile one and it broke down in 1882 when the French began work on a railway to the interior. Both Lat-Dior and the French realised the importance of this railway with perfect clarity. It was bound to mean an extension of French colonial rule and the undermining of the sovereignty of the African rulers in the area. Lat-Dior was deposed as Damel and replaced by a French nominee but he continued to struggle against the French in guerilla warfare until his death in 1886. On the day of his death he foretold that he would say his evening prayers with Maba, dead long before.

Maba also converted another Jolof ruler, the Burba Jolof, who had in the past been the ruler of all the Wolof states and who still retained considerable standing. Alboury N'Diaye, Lat-Dior's nephew and Maba's brother-in-law, who became Burba in 1875, was his convert and became a devout Tijani. He was the moving spirit of a series of anti-French alliances but he successfully avoided open conflict with the French until war was finally forced on him in 1890.

Maba and the French

The French were alarmed by Maba's growing power and especially, perhaps, by his alliance with the Wolof kings. In 1862 his forces were defeated by the French but this was only a temporary setback as large numbers of Muslims flocked to his banners. A British visitor said that he had never seen, 'even in India, so imposing an array of warriors'. His army was estimated at 11,000 fighting men. Visitors were astonished to see the whole army prostrate in prayer. Dying Marabouts were congratulated by their friends on their nearness to heaven, and prisoners were given the choice between death or conversion.

In 1864 the French recognised Maba as the Almami of Baddibu and Salum. This was the high point of his career, but the agreement was an unstable one. It was difficult for Maba to restrain his followers from further expansion. Lat-Dior may well have been a decisive influence in this direction. The French for their part were bound to fear the growing power of an African ruler, especially as Maba extended his alliances not only to the Wolof kings but also to the Moors of Mauritania and the ruling class of Futa Toro. No one has ever come closer to making the Senegambia a single political unit.

In 1865 and again in 1867 the French sent forces against him. They caused much destruction but the French themselves suffered heavy casualties and new recruits flocked to Maba's side. But divisions were growing among Maba's followers. Many of his judges had been appointed from among his Wolof disciples. On the Gambia these seemed to be foreigners from the north. The continuing jihad exacted a heavy financial burden and some of the Muslims on the Gambia revolted against his authority.

In 1867 Maba was killed in battle with the pagans of Sin. Lat-Dior and his forces had fought on his side but fled when they saw the day was going against them. Maba's head was sent to the French on the coast to prove that he was really dead. His body was buried at a spot on the frontiers with Salum which is still a place of pilgrimage.

Maba is a less celebrated figure in West African history than Usuman dan Fodio or Al Hajj Umar. The area of his operations was relatively small and his regime lasted only six years. After his death no leader of comparable stature emerged and divisions grew among his followers. As with other jihads, a heavy price had to be paid for his wars, in the deaths of all those who fell in battle, and in the raiding of slaves to be exchanged for horses and guns. His significance, perhaps, was two-fold. On the one hand, like Umar, he established a new state overriding ethnic divisions. Of greater lasting importance, his jihad made a great contribution to the spread of Islam in the Senegambia.

Mahmadu Lamine

Maba was not the only Islamic warrior the Senegambia produced. High on the Senegal, another Islamic scholar and sage repeated much of his career some twenty years later. Al Hajj Mahmadu Lamine (Muhammad al Amin) was a Soninke,* born not far from Medina in about 1835. Like Al Hajj Umar he went on a lengthy pilgrimage to Mecca and, like Umar, was imprisoned for a time at Segu on his way back. The crucial difference, of course, was that Lamine was imprisoned by the Muslim Tijani ruler Ahmadu, whereas Umar had been imprisoned by the pagan Bambara. It is not quite clear why Lamine fell out with Ahmadu, though various suggestions have been

* Many books use the alternative name Sarakole which can be spelt in a wide variety of ways. Soninke is the name by which the people describe themselves. They are, as we have seen, a northern Mande group.

made. It may have been basically the same factor which had produced tension between Umar and his successive Muslim hosts. His learning, his holiness, his status as a pilgrim, made him seem a rival Islamic authority. He may have acted or spoken as a supporter of Soninke as opposed to Tukulor nationalism. He may even have been a member of yet another order, the Sanusiyya, but there is little real evidence of this, and it is more likely he was a Tijani.

He returned home in 1885, determined to announce a jihad and carve out a new state in the borderland between the French and Tukulor empires. His reputation for learning and holiness attracted many disciples and his message had an immediate appeal to his fellow Soninke. Circumstances were favourable. The Tukulor, as we have seen, were deeply divided among themselves and the energies of the French were diverted into fighting Samori, whose career we shall study in Chapter Six. An opportunity for decisive action came in Bondu, where the Almami died and was replaced by an unpopular French puppet ruler. Lamine intervened and in 1885–6 he built up the core of a new state in Bondu, the gold-producing area of Bambuk and surrounding areas. He had an army of volunteers which, as with Umar, included Muslims with European skills from St Louis. The French could not stand by and watch the establishment of a new state in an area which was for them of decisive strategic importance, since it was astride their route to the western Sudan. A bitter struggle followed, in which Lamine's cavalry proved an unequal match for a well-armed, modern, professional army. This picture of one of their battles clearly shows the differences between the two armies.

Mahmadu Lamine's forces in battle

A fierce struggle ended with Lamine's death in battle in December 1887. His son, Soybou, had been captured by the French some months earlier and executed by them after a mock trial. He died with heroic dignity before a firing squad, thanking his

The death of Soybou

executioners for sparing him an ignominious death which might have made him unworthy of paradise. He was, incredibly, just eighteen years old.

Men of peace
There were a number of other formidable Islamic warriors in nineteenth-century Senegambia but if jihads gave the initial impetus to the spread of Islam in the area, the hold of Islam was greatly deepened and strengthened by men of peace. For all their piety, warrior Muslims had been largely responsible for a long process of war and destruction. The French had conquered all, fervent Muslims, indifferent Muslims and pagans alike. A new generation of Muslim leaders arose who refused to interest themselves in politics, leaving unto Caesar the things which were Caesar's, and concentrating on scholarship and religious life – what their most famous member called the 'Holy War of the Soul'.

Malik Sy, 1855–1922, was a famous Islamic teacher, a Tijani, who took no part in politics. Ahmadu Bamba, 1850–1927, was celebrated for founding a new religious brotherhood, the Mourides (Muridiyya), which had 700,000 members in Senegal in 1970. Bamba was a Muslim saint who lived very simply, spending much time in solitude. His reputation for holiness attracted many donations, but he gave them all away. When others spoke to him of jihads, he said that the true jihad is in the soul. This is the only surviving picture of him.

Ahmadu Bamba

His teachings seem to have had a special appeal in a time of foreign conquest and revolutionary change. A number of Christian prophets flourished in the same circumstances. The Mourides established an alternative social order based on agriculture, which readily absorbed the unemployed and the landless (see also page 248). Where Lat-Dior had fought against the railway, the Mourides made good use of it to open up new farming areas. A modern Mouride has said of Ahmadu Bamba, 'He was the first marabout not to carry a gun, only the Quran'.

To some extent, his teaching was a reaction against the violence of the jihadist era, and especially the unsuccessful violence which tried in vain to prevent the imposition of colonial rule. But one would misrepresent the spirit of earlier West African Islam if one failed to point out that one finds here and there in earlier times a similar pacifist and quietist spirit. This was extremely characteristic of the Diakhanké (pronounced 'jaxanké'), a Malinke-speaking group who showed no interest in political power, devoted themselves to Islamic teaching, and were strongly pacifist in outlook. They still preserve these values into our own time. A scholar has recently written, perhaps with nostalgia, of the life of a 'holy village' of Diakhanké, living in voluntary poverty, 'out of the world and out of time'.

Innovation and Reform in the States of Guinea

In the last chapter, we studied the extraordinary chain reaction which took place in nineteenth-century western Sudan, when so many new states were founded in an endeavour, which was not always realised in practice, to organise human affairs on a basis of religion and social justice.

The history of the nineteenth-century states of Guinea has no such single overriding theme. As far as Islam is concerned, in Dahomey, Asante and in Yoruba states such as Ibadan, there were important Muslim communities, and in 1801 his conversion to Islam cost an Asantehene his throne. A later, greater, Asantehene did not formally become a Muslim, but always emphasised his love for Muslims, and their holy Book. A revolt of enslaved Muslims in Ilorin was one of the key events which overthrew the mighty Oyo empire.

Christianity made real progress in Guinea, for the first time, in the nineteenth century, largely through the work of black missionaries from Sierra Leone. Sierra Leone and Liberia were the scene of a fascinating social experiment. This was an attempt to form 'a nation of free black Christians', with a thorough command of western skills. Because settler communities were at the heart of this experiment, we shall discuss them in a separate chapter. But not all Christians were formed through Creole influence. In 1797 a king of Dahomey was deposed for his preference for Catholicism.

In a number of instances, a number of West African peoples made a deliberate attempt to introduce western political forms. Examples are the Egba United Board of Management in Yorubaland, the Fante Confederation in the Gold Coast, and the Grebo Reunited Kingdom in Liberia.

As the fall of a Muslim Asantehene, and a Dahomey king inclined to Christianity, showed, the two religions of the Book remained marginal to most of the Guinea kingdoms,* where traditional religion, and reverence for ancestors, were held to be inseparably linked with the power and prosperity of the state. In Dahomey, most major political decisions were taken during a great traditional religious festival. But it is essential to realise, and this has tended to be overlooked by historians, that there

---

* Bonny, in the second half of the nineteenth century, was an exception.

was, in the nineteenth century, a powerful impulse to social reform among those who held traditional beliefs. We shall see a number of examples in the pages which follow. Gezo of Dahomey limited human sacrifice, restricted the death penalty, campaigned against drunkenness, and planned more reforms to follow. As Gezo pointed out, an innovating ruler had to move slowly: 'He considered it dangerous among a people so long accustomed to these usages to revolutionise the whole at once'. The last Oba of independent Benin loathed human sacrifice, but felt himself powerless to change it. In Igboland, the men of Nri had long ago embarked on one of the most revolutionary political experiments in human history. This was the establishment of a purely pacifist 'empire' based on influence, not force, which resolutely condemned the shedding of blood. An early nineteenth-century Eze Nri proclaimed to all who would listen, the sanctity of human life.

This is the impulse to social reform from above. The history of Guinea is full of examples of reform from below. Some are well known, such as the revolt of the Calabar Blood men, or the long slave rebellion led by Bilalé in Sierra Leone (see page 11). Some are almost unknown, such as the slave exodus from the Niger Igbo state of Ossomari.

Innovation, of course, could take many different forms. Some rulers, while retaining traditional religious, social and political structures, were extremely interested in technical innovation. This was very true of such great eighteenth-century figures as Opuku Ware of Asante, and Agaja of Dahomey. The hunger for what we would now call technical aid was equally strong in the nineteenth century. In 1842 an Efik ruler requested technical aid for Calabar.

> We . . . want something for make work and trade. And if we have some seed for cotton and coffee, we could make trade, plenty sugar cane live here; and if some man would come teach way for do it, we get plenty sugar too; and then some man must come teach book proper.

King George Pepple of Bonny requested machinery for cracking palm kernels. Cracking them by hand was unbelievably tedious and time-consuming. 'It is . . . incumbent upon all intelligent educated Africans to use every cogent means in their power to develop or devise some means of developing the resources of their country'.

King Ja Ja of Opobo was deeply attached to the religion of his fathers. Opobo, although a new state, retained traditional political and social institutions, including slavery. But in many ways he was a man of startling modernity. This can be seen particularly in his attempt to break expatriate control of the import-export trade, and especially, perhaps, in his support for secular education. Opuku Ware, Gezo of Dahomey and Ja Ja, all employed at least one expatriate in their service. These examples, therefore, demonstrate that some Africans were choosing elements from other cultures which they felt they could profitably assimilate, and leaving out the others. This can be contrasted with the violent break in continuity which colonialism meant, when Africans lost much, though not all, control over the pace and direction of change.

It is essential to realise that there are other important strands in the history of the nineteenth-century Guinea states. Three loom large in this book. One might be called the problem of political balance. All the Guinea states analysed here had very sophisticated political institutions, designed to combine effective central direction with safeguards against tyranny. In some kingdoms these continued to work well. In others, there were breakdowns, sometimes linked with external aggression and economic problems. We have the collapse of the great Oyo empire, and the successor states' long struggle to inherit its power. We have frequent succession disputes in Benin together with some provincial revolts, and a good many provincial revolts in Asante.

The second theme, which also overshadows, in the end, the western Sudan, is that of the rising tide of European encroachment. Looking at the nineteenth century from the present day, it appears like a tragedy on the stage. Whatever the capacities of the actors, their concern for reform and innovation, their struggles for state unity and prosperity, whatever their diplomatic cunning, military preparedness and personal courage, all fell, in the end, to a foreign conqueror.

The third theme concerns their responses to the crisis caused by the decline of the Atlantic slave trade, which had been, in varying degrees, a major source of state revenue. The states of the Niger Delta and Dahomey turned energetically to palm-oil exports. Asante strengthened her economic links with the north. Benin underwent an economic recession. This economic context is, of course, of the greatest relevance to their political history.

Asante*

The beginnings of empire

At the beginning of the nineteenth century there was a tremendous contrast between Asante and Fante. The Fante lived in small states on the coast, and were badly disunited among themselves. Asante, with its capital at Kumasi, was an extremely powerful kingdom which covered most of modern Ghana and large areas which are now in Togo and the Ivory Coast, with a population of perhaps three to four million.

This contrast had not always existed. Until the late seventeenth century, Kumasi was a small clan among other similar small Akan clans, comparable in size and power with the Fante coastal kingdoms. In the late seventeenth century, its great ruler Osei Tutu laid the foundations of its empire, instituting the Golden Stool as a symbol of political unity. Interestingly enough, one has the same basic pattern in Dahomey of a powerful inland kingdom and small, weak, disunited coastal states. It is possible that in each case the coastal kingdoms remained small and weak as a result of the European presence among them.

In the eighteenth century, the power and wealth of Asante were extended by another great ruler, Opuku Ware, who died in 1750. Asante was wealthy, selling

---

* The older spelling of 'Ashanti' is still widely used as well.

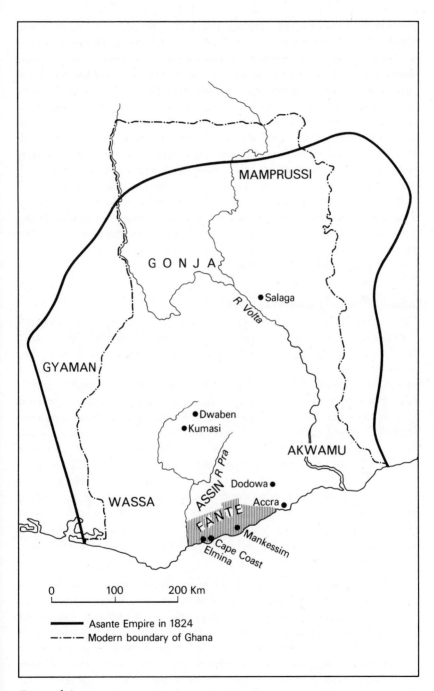

Fante and Asante

slaves to the Europeans and exporting gold both to the south and to the north. Opuku Ware himself was much more than a successful general. He showed a great interest in economic development, introducing the use of imported thread in the Asante textile industry. He tried to set up a distillery with the aid of Dutch technical experts, an early attempt at import substitution, which means producing goods locally which would otherwise have to be imported. In the late eighteenth century, new developments took place in Asante government. Officials were employed who were not hereditary but appointed, and who could be sacked for inefficiency. They dealt with the various spheres of government – taxation, provincial administration, foreign affairs and so on. They were responsible only to the king, and therefore his power increased. It was a career open to merit, where many non-Asante played an important role.

It seems surprising that the Asante kingdom, which succeeded in conquering the relatively large and powerful states to the north, never conquered the small divided Fante kingdoms to the south. This was probably because its economy was basically orientated towards the north. It is likely, too, that successive Asante rulers wanted to avoid a confrontation with the Europeans.

Asante in the early nineteenth century

The abolition of the slave trade was very unwelcome to Asante, for it removed one of her main sources of foreign exchange and deprived her of a safe way of disposing of her war captives. Her rulers feared that if these accumulated in large numbers, they might threaten the security of the state. But since Asante had a number of alternative sources of income, the end of the slave trade did not plunge her into an economic crisis. The northern trade in gold and kola nuts was still important, and some gold was still sold to the Europeans on the coast. But the Asante, like nearly all nations, hated reducing their gold reserves, and in the nineteenth century, the northern trade, which involved commodities besides gold, became increasingly important. Salaga, a market city, well-situated on the important trade route between Asante and Hausaland, became larger than Kumasi itself. The Asante heartland was an area of flourishing agriculture, and one where a wide variety of crafts were practised, especially spinning, dyeing and weaving, and above all the goldsmith's art. Every year the Asantehene's gold ornaments were melted down and re-made. The first European visitors to the Asantehene's court at Kumasi, in 1817 and 1820, gave a picture of almost unbelievable splendour and magnificence.

> The king, his tributaries, and captains, were resplendent in the distance, surrounded by attendants of every description, fronted by a mass of warriors which seemed to make our approach impervious. The sun was reflected, with a glare scarcely more supportable than the heat, from the massy gold ornaments, which glistened in every direction. More than a hundred bands burst at once on our arrival, with the peculiar airs of their several chiefs; the horns flourished their defiances, with the beating of innumerable drums and metal instruments, and then yielded for a while to the soft breathings of their long flutes, which were

truly harmonious; and a pleasing instrument, like a bagpipe without the drone, was happily blended. At least a hundred large umbrellas or canopies, which could shelter thirty persons, were sprung up and down by the bearers with brilliant effect, being made of scarlet, yellow, and the most showy cloths and silks, and crowned on the top with crescents, pelicans, elephants, barrels, and arms and swords of gold . . .

This is a picture of an Asante war captain, dressed in scarlet with gold and silver ornaments and embroidery, and wearing thigh-length boots of red leather. A European spoke of their 'aristocratic air and courtly polish'.

An Asante war captain

The palace of the king's nephew

This is a picture of the palace of the king's nephew in Kumasi in 1820.

These pictures and descriptions date from the reign of Osei Bonsu who ruled from 1801 to 1824.

State organisation under Osei Bonsu

Osei Bonsu continued the process begun by his predecessors of replacing hereditary chiefs as much as possible by appointed officials. This was more efficient since they were appointed for their abilities and could be dismissed if their work was unsatisfactory. Since they were responsible to the king, this had the effect of increasing the royal power. Osei Bonsu appointed some expatriates amongst his staff, among them a Frenchman and a Dane.

The court at Kumasi was the centre of a highly developed bureaucratic system. The Minister of Finance (Gyaasewahene) held a daily court of exchequer. The state was financed by tribute from conquered areas, a poll tax levied in Kumasi, death duties and tolls. A large sector of the economy was controlled by the state, including the royal mines, worked by slave miners, ivory hunting and much of the area's trade.

One of the most interesting aspects of state organisation under Osei Bonsu was his recognition of the value of written records in administration. He employed Muslims who kept records in Arabic, and set up an Arabic school in Kumasi.

Like Dahomey, Asante acquired in European eyes the image of a warlike and blood-thirsty regime, but if one examines Asante policies carefully one finds that the opposite is the case and that they often went to great lengths to avoid war. A European visitor to Osei Bonsu's court said that it was 'a maxim associated with the religion he professed, never to appeal to the sword while a path lay open for negotiation'. The higher levels of the Asante diplomatic service were staffed by *akyeame*, whom Europeans called 'linguists'. One of the most eminent of the linguists was a non-Asante. He was an Akwamu who started life as a salt carrier, until a series of accidents brought his hidden talents to the king's notice. All administrators and diplomats were entirely subject to the king: 'No man must dare to do good out of his own head'. The king's absolute authority was reinforced by an elaborate system of espionage (this was also the case with some absolute European rulers).

The Asante empire was in two sections. There was the Asante heartland extending for sixty or eighty kilometres around Kumasi. Here each area had its own local ruler, called the *omanhene* (plural *amanhene*), who enjoyed much local autonomy, levying taxes and holding his own court. The other part of the Asante empire, Greater Asante, consisted of peoples who had been conquered by the Asante and here they practised a kind of indirect rule.

> It was no part of Ashantee policy to alter the government of the conquered country. The chiefs of the different tribes remained in possession of what power the conqueror thought fit to leave them, with the style and rank of a captain of the king; and in that capacity they acted as so many lieutenants . . .

An Asante representative was placed in each of these areas as well.

The Asante army was made up of contingents sent by the various local rulers. The most recently conquered peoples were placed in the vanguard. The army was under the control of military officers commanding divisions – it was these who overthrew Osei Kwame in 1801. They had no cavalry and their soldiers were armed partly with muskets and partly with bows and arrows. Thus relations with the south, the source of arms and munitions, were of great strategic importance. To guard against the danger of a further military coup, Osei Bonsu established a household regiment of foreigners. One of his successors took this process much further, building up a Hausa regiment and recruiting deserters from the British army.

The general pattern of Asante government in the early nineteenth century was that the king's power was becoming greater, and that positions in his service were increasingly open to talent, irrespective of social origins. This was to be seen in the king's council where instead of members attending through hereditary right, individuals were summoned to attend meetings for specific purposes. The king had a deliberate policy of limiting the growth of the merchant class, since this might ultimately challenge his authority. He restricted the accumulation of capital by imposing high rates of interest and exacting heavy death duties. On the other hand he favoured foreign merchants who posed no political threat.

One aspect of the growth of royal absolutism was the attempt to undermine the rights of the *amanhene*. This led to conflict with Dwaben, the most powerful of these states and for a time its king and people fled into exile.

As in other kingdoms of Guinea, such as Dahomey, the glory and authority of the state were further maintained by elaborate state festivals and the preservation of state history by professional groups such as the state drummers.

By the early nineteenth century, Asante was a highly centralised, bureaucratic state with a high degree of economic planning.

The growth of Islam

The gradual spread of Islam was one of the most interesting aspects of the history of many of the states of Guinea in the eighteenth and nineteenth centuries. There were Muslims at the court of Oyo in the sixteenth century and we have many references to Muslims in eighteenth-century Dahomey. If colonial rule had not been imposed in West Africa, it is likely that this steady spread of Islam would have continued. Osei Kwame, 1777–1801, was an Asantehene who apparently lost his throne as a result of his personal conversion to Islam. His chiefs feared that Islamic ideals of human equality would undermine the hierarchic structure of the state, and they resented his abolition of a number of festivals involving human sacrifice. Osei Bonsu, warned by the fate of his predecessor, never formally adopted Islam but he surrounded himself with Muslims, many of whom were widely travelled men of great learning. Among them was a Hajj from Katsina and a cleric from Mamprussi with a beautiful collection of illuminated Arabic manuscripts. Osei Bonsu made no secret of his love for Islam. 'The book [Quran] is strong and I like it because it is the book of the great God . . . I love all the people that read it.'

The southern factor

The most striking aspects of Osei Bonsu's reign were his campaigns against Fante and his attempts to reach the sea. These were reflected in the name he took – Bonsu, the whale. Asante had attacked Fante on at least three occasions in the eighteenth century. They had had good reasons for doing so. The Fante excluded them from direct trade with the Europeans and made the most of their role as middlemen, interfering with the quality of both European imports and Asante gold. But in the early nineteenth century Asante policy to Fante showed surprising moderation. In 1807 two rebel chiefs from Assin, a southern state of Greater Asante, sought refuge in Fante. The Asante invaded Fante only after repeated attempts at a peaceful settlement. After a successful campaign, smallpox broke out in the Asante army and they returned to Kumasi early in 1808.

The Fante were not forced into submission by this defeat. In 1809 and 1810 they allied with their neighbours to attack Asante's allies, Elmina and Accra. After a series of defeats by Asante, the Fante finally submitted and Asante sent resident commissioners among them. In 1823 the British joined an anti-Asante alliance with the southern states. In 1824 Governor MacCarthy and his small army were defeated at Asante hands.

In these and later campaigns one can see the same pattern occurring again and again. Britain and the small states of Fante tended to ally against Asante. This, for the British, was a policy going back to the eighteenth century. They preferred to practice a strategy of divide and rule amongst small states, rather than be at the mercy of a large and powerful one. The Dutch on the other hand tended to ally with Asante. The second element of the pattern is that conquest tended to be impermanent. Asante conquered the south but did not establish lasting control there. The same was true of the British conquest of Kumasi in 1873.

Subject peoples
The persistent revolts of the southern states suggests another dimension of Asante history. If one looks at Asante, as it were, from the viewpoint of the centre, one sees its effective administration and the splendour of its cosmopolitan court, thronged by merchants and scholars from far afield. But the vassal kingdoms saw it differently, and the accession of every new Asantehene tended to be a signal for widespread revolts. This was the pattern in the eighteenth century and it continued in the nineteenth, with revolts not only in the south but in northern states such as Gyaman and Gonja. Their persistent revolts show that they saw Asante rule as oppressive. They objected, for instance, to the annual tribute in slaves which was demanded. If we condemn European imperialism as imposed on unwillingly subjected peoples, should we not also condemn African imperialism? We have already noted the revolts against the Tukulor, and the same was true of Samori.

Asante in decline, 1824–96
Asante reached the peak of its power in the reign of Osei Bonsu. He died at the same time as MacCarthy, perhaps on the same day. For the rest of the century, Asante was to grow steadily weaker, the power of the British in the Gold Coast steadily stronger. Later, in 1824, the Asante were defeated in the south and retreated. In 1826 they

attempted a further invasion but suffered a crushing defeat at the battle of Dodowa. The British now refused to pay rent for their forts.

In a treaty of 1831 the Asante renounced their southern territories. From 1834 to 1867, Asante was ruled by Kwaku Dua I. He ruled peacefully over his reduced kingdom until near the end of his reign, when, apparently, he gave in to the pressure of a pro-war party. In 1863 the Asante again invaded the south and later they sent two expeditions to the north. Again, they won victories but no lasting extension of their empire. Kofi Karikari, 1867–74, attempted to regain the lost states of the south. In 1868–70 the Asante invaded the south but with no lasting results. In 1873 they sent another successful army to the south but it was plagued with disease and had to withdraw to Kumasi, its numbers reduced by half. This led in its turn to a large-scale British expedition which invaded Asante in 1874. Here is a picture of the British forces (most of the soldiers are Africans!) crossing the Pra with their heavy artillery.

British forces crossing the Pra in 1874

The Asante resisted the expedition's progress fiercely, but their muzzle loaders were no match for rifles and artillery. When the British finally reached Kumasi they found it empty. They burnt it, exacted an enormous indemnity in gold, and returned to the coast without bringing Asante permanently under their authority. Here is a picture of

An Asante death mask

an Asante head, a fine example of African craftsmanship, which is now in a London museum, part of the plunder taken on this occasion.

The Asantehene himself was dethroned soon afterwards for stealing the treasures from his ancestors' graves (this was, of course, a consequence of the poverty resulting from the plunder of Kumasi and the indemnity). This was Asante's lowest point. They renounced all claim to their southern provinces and the northern states took advantage of their weakness to revolt. The empire shrank to the heartland round Kumasi and even here there were revolts.

The reign of Prempeh, 1888–96

In 1888, Prempeh was chosen as Asantehene elect, after a civil war. He was aged about sixteen. Despite his youth, he showed great diplomatic ability, and tried to restore the vanished glories of his empire and to defend its independence against the rising tide of British imperialism. In 1895 all the Asante paid a tax to finance the sending of eight ambassadors to London. They stayed in England six months, and were entirely ignored. When Prempeh was asked to accept a British protectorate over his state, he rejected it with calm dignity.

. . . My kingdom of Asante will never commit itself to any such policy. Asante must remain independent as of old, at the same time to remain friendly with all white men. I do not write this in a boastful spirit, but in the clear sense of its meaning . . . the cause of Asante is progressing and there is no reason for any Asante man to feel alarm at the prospects . . .

The British sent an expedition, which was not resisted. Prempeh submitted completely, but he could not raise the huge indemnity of 60,000 ounces of gold which was demanded from him, and he was deported with a group of his relations and chiefs.

The Asante bitterly resented the deportation of their king. The final straw came when the British demanded the Golden Stool, the sacred symbol of the Asante nation. In 1900 they rose in a final bitter struggle against the British, but were again defeated. It was not until 1924 that Prempeh was allowed to return from exile. He died in 1931.

Fante

We have already seen the basic political situation in Fante, how the struggle against the Asante forced them into an alliance with the British. As in Sierra Leone, a mission-educated elite developed in the coastal states, producing a number of prosperous merchants and professional men. They included James Bannerman, a wealthy English-educated mulatto who acted as Lieutenant-Governor and was nearly made Governor. George Ekem Ferguson studied surveying in England and his explorations and the treaties he signed did much to determine the northern boundaries of modern Ghana. J. Mensah Sarbah, who qualified in 1887, was the first Gold Coast lawyer of entirely Gold Coast ancestry.

In the mid-nineteenth century, this elite played an active role in local government. At least half the Justices of the Peace appointed in 1851 were Africans. Later, as in Sierra Leone, they were crowded out by white officials, and suffered greatly from white racism. It was an official of the Colonial Office who wrote, 'The "educated native" such as Messrs Bannerman, Brew, etc., is the curse of the West Coast'.

One of the most interesting aspects of nineteenth-century Gold Coast history concerns experiments in western forms of government. The first of these experiments took place under the control of the British, and involved chiefs, who had not, in fact, had a western education. In 1851 the chiefs were formed into a Legislative Assembly and the people were asked to pay a poll tax. Because this was intended to provide money for schools, hospitals and roads, the people paid it readily, but when the poll tax seemed to be yielding no clear benefits, being swallowed up in officials' salaries and tax collectors' corruption, opposition grew and the British gave it up.

The real pioneer of modern political nationalism in West Africa was John Aggery, who became king of Cape Coast in 1865. He steadfastly defended his own political authority in the face of British encroachment which had, in his own words, 'in a very peculiar, imperceptible, and unheard-of manner, wrested from the hands of our Kings, Chiefs, and head men, their power to govern their own subjects'.

This was in the year when a Select Committee of the House of Commons recommended withdrawal, when possible, from all British settlements in West Africa, except Sierra Leone. But for King Aggery, his attitude led rapidly to his arrest in 1866 and deportation. In 1869 he was allowed to return as a private citizen, but died the same year. Here is a drawing made in 1841 of the home of his father, King Joseph Aggery.

The home of King Joseph Aggery

Knowledge of Parliament's resolution of 1865 rapidly reached the educated elite in the Gold Coast. They were delighted with the news, for it corresponded exactly with their own wishes. Africanus Horton, a Sierra Leonean army doctor working on the Gold Coast, played a key role in defining and directing these wishes. In 1868 he wrote *West African Countries and Peoples*, a plan for self-government which included a Kingdom of Fante and a Republic of Accra.

The Fante Confederation

The Fante Confederation was a conscious attempt to put his ideas into practice. Because they thought that the British planned to withdraw, the Fante assumed that the British would approve of their initiative towards self-government. The recent Asante invasions also gave them a compelling reason to unite in self defence. It is interesting to note that nearly all the leading roles were filled by zealous Methodist laymen. The Confederation was active between 1868 and 1871, then it declined, coming to an end in 1873.

One of their first aims was to oppose the proposed exchange of Dutch and British forts in 1868. They disliked the Dutch for their traditional pro-Asante policy, and were indignant that their own political fortunes should be settled without consultation. This grievance was removed when the British bought the Dutch forts in 1871.

In 1868 the Confederation declared itself independent of Britain. In the years that followed they drew up three successive constitutions. Their critics say that they spent most of their energies in drawing them up, and had few practical achievements to show. The 1871 Constitution was drawn up at Mankessim, the traditional centre of Fante. There was to be a King President, elected by the Confederation's constituent kings and a Representative Assembly, where each state was to send one chief and one educated man. They committed themselves to the construction of roads and schools and to agricultural and industrial development, to be financed by a poll tax and by import and export duties. They had a National Seal struck, showing an elephant and a palm tree. They recruited an army of 15,000 men, and set up a Fante National Supreme Court. A similar, though smaller and weaker movement existed briefly in Accra in 1869.

After 1871 the movement collapsed. It had been inspired partly by fear of Dutch rule, but now the Dutch had sold their forts to the British. It had been inspired, again, by fears of Asante, which were allayed when the British sacked Kumasi in 1874. The movement had been weakened by the rivalries of the chiefs concerned, but the essential reason for its collapse was the hostility of the local British officials who, for a time, imprisoned its leaders. The Fante had assumed that the British would encourage and support it, and were not able to sustain it in the face of British hostility. This was especially the case for educated men, who tended to look to the state for employment.

In 1874 southern Ghana became a British colony, and the self-government to which the Fante had aspired did not become a reality until 1957.

The Yoruba

In the period of West African history we are considering, scarcely any episode is as exciting and dramatic and as hotly debated among historians as the collapse of the Oyo empire, the subsequent creation of new states, and the struggles of these new states for supremacy.

At the beginning of the nineteenth century, there was no such area as 'Yorubaland'. The very word Yoruba first referred to people from Oyo and only later came to include Yoruba-speaking people generally. But many links bound the Yoruba-speaking communities together, especially their reverence for Ife, where, according to tradition, Yorubaland was first settled, or the world created. Here the great kings of Yorubaland obtained their beaded crowns, whose fringes hid their faces, a symbol of their sacred status.

The Oyo empire
By far the largest political unit was the Oyo empire, with its capital to the north, near Nupe and Borgu. Its political power was partly a reflection of its wealth, both as a producer of excellent textiles and as a merchant state strategically situated between

north and south. Kola nuts, cloth, salt and possibly slaves were sent from the south to the north, in return for leather, knives, natron, and especially horses. Oyo's cavalry, which depended on the constant import of horses, became the key to her military might, striking terror amongst surrounding peoples.

The Oyo empire embraced a number of subject states. In practice these were largely self-governing, but they paid Oyo annual tribute and their rulers came annually with grass to mend the Alafin's roof, as a symbol of their allegiance. The empire included non-Yoruba states, such as the warlike kingdom of Dahomey. It did not include some Yoruba areas such as Ekiti and Ilesa. It reached the peak of its power in the first half of the eighteenth century.

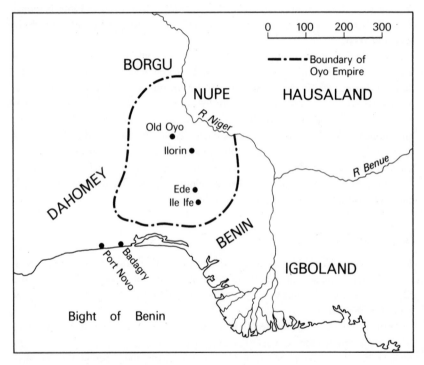

The Oyo Empire and its neighbours

Oyo government

The Oyo empire was basically a limited monarchy. At its centre was the sacred king, the Alafin. His life was mainly confined to his palace where he lived in splendid ceremonial among his wives, slaves, palace eunuchs, court officials, drummers and praise singers. He was sacred, and deeply revered by his subjects, but he was not absolute.

The Alafin ruled in conjunction with the Oyo Mesi, a council of seven nobles. By far the most powerful of these was the Basorun. The Alafin had little say in their appointment, but they played a key role in the selection of the Alafin. For much of Oyo's history the eldest son did not succeed to the throne and indeed the crown prince died with his father. They controlled promotion in the army, and if a difference of opinion with an Alafin became acute, they could demand his suicide by a symbolic gift of parrots' eggs.

A counter-balancing council saved the Alafin from being the puppet of the Oyo Mesi. This was the council of the Ogboni society. Its chairman, nominated by the Alafin, was the interpreter of the Ifa oracle.

The final important element in the Oyo state was the army, commanded by the Kakanfo, at the head of seventy war captains. He was appointed by the Alafin and swore allegiance to him. Several factors prevented the Kakanfo from developing political ambitions of his own. He was of slave origin and was forbidden to enter the capital. The system of checks and balances operated in the army, as everywhere else in the Oyo state, for promotion of the war captains was in the hands of the Oyo Mesi.

At its height the Oyo empire seems to have provided considerable peace, prosperity and stability for its citizens. In 1826 when its collapse was far advanced, a European visitor wrote:

> I cannot omit bearing testimony to the singular and perhaps unprecedented fact, that we have already travelled sixty miles in eight days, with numerous and heavy baggage, and about ten different relays of carriers, without losing so much as the value of a shilling public or private; a circumstance evincing not only somewhat more than common honesty in the inhabitants, but a degree of sub-ordination and regular government which could not have been supposed to exist among a people hitherto considered barbarians.

Crisis in Oyo

In the late eighteenth century, Oyo was plunged into an external and an internal crisis. She was defeated by both her powerful neighbours, Nupe and Borgu, although this was in the area where her cavalry operated best. The difficulties in the north may have made it difficult for her to obtain new supplies of horses. More serious still was the successful revolt of the Egba under Lisabi, the Liberator, in 1797. This endangered her trade routes to the sea and showed other subject peoples that Oyo could be defied successfully.

Oyo's defeats were linked with her internal troubles, which centred basically round a political crisis, a conflict between the Alafin and his officials. In the eighteenth century not a single Alafin died a natural death. This conflict reached its height in the 'Age of Gaha', 1754–74. Gaha was a Basorun who made himself supreme in Oyo, putting four successive Alafins to death until he in his turn, old and partially paralysed, fell victim to the violence by which he had lived. The Alafin who overthrew him, Abiodun (who died in 1789), was a strong ruler whose reign is remembered as an Indian summer of peace and prosperity before the gathering storm.

What caused the collapse of the Oyo empire? It is likely that there were a variety of factors. One cause was probably the power and ambition of the Oyo nobility (there is a close connection between cavalry and a strong ambitious nobility, since the purchase of horses demands considerable wealth and horsemen require extended training). The slave trade can also be blamed for the collapse of the Oyo empire, since in general it encouraged violence and unrest and discouraged peaceful productivity, and more specifically, it shifted the focus of wealth and power further south. A suggestion in the opposite direction is that it was possibly the abolition of the slave trade which weakened Oyo by removing one of the main forms of her external trade. All these arguments, however, exaggerate the importance of the slave trade to Oyo, which was basically a northern empire where northern trade and internal commerce and productivity were much more important. It was Oyo's internal weaknesses which were therefore probably more important.

One other factor which contributed to the final collapse was the role of religious and ethnic minorities. There were many Hausa slaves in Oyo whose skill in handling horses made them of crucial importance to the cavalry. In the final downfall, a key role was played by Muslim revolt.

Afonja's rebellion

After the death of Abiodun in 1789 the empire's collapse proceeded very rapidly. His successor fell victim to an army mutiny as a result of which he had to commit suicide in 1797. Before doing so,

> he stepped out into the palace quadrangle with face stern and resolute, carrying in his hands an earthenware dish and three arrows. He shot one to the North, one to the South, and one to the West uttering those ever-memorable imprecations, 'My curse be on you for your disloyalty and disobedience, so let your children disobey you . . . To all the points I shot my arrows will ye be carried as slaves' . . .

Many local rulers seized the opportunity to declare independence – this was the period of the Egba breakaway. The decline in prosperity was reflected in a popular song:

> In Abiodun's day we weighed our money in calabashes,
> In Awole's reign we packed up and fled.

Among the rebels was the Kakanfo, Afonja, who was stationed at Ilorin. Related to the royal family on his mother's side, he was a man of blazing ambition and reckless courage. Although not a Muslim himself, he formed an alliance with a group of Yoruba Muslims, called on the support of the Hausa Muslim slaves, and invited to Ilorin a Fulani religious leader known as Alimi. For the slaves it was a golden opportunity to win their freedom. They flocked to Afonja's banner, forming themselves into brotherhoods (Jamaa). They lived off the country, revenging themselves on unkind masters.

Afonja's arrogance soon cut him off from the rest of Yoruba nobility. He came to depend increasingly on the Jamaa but these, as Muslims, could not give their full loyalty to a pagan master. In 1824 they overthrew him.

> Seeing the day was lost, some of his followers became disheartened and deserted him, but the rest chose to die with him. He fell indeed like a hero. So covered was he with darts that his body was supported in an erect position upon the shafts of spears and arrows showered upon him.

Alimi, the Fulani teacher, now became the ruler of Ilorin and his son, Abdussalami, was later recognised by Sokoto as its Emir.

The Brothers' Wars

The history of the relationship between states in nineteenth-century Yorubaland is largely a history of war. The wars were many and complex and this is a brief analysis of the main ones. Their military details are less important than their long term effects on Yoruba society.

The Owu War (c. 1813–23)

This was fought between southern Yoruba groups. The Owu attacked Ife as an act of loyalty to Oyo, for Ife had been kidnapping Oyo citizens. But a dispute between Owu and Ijebu traders made the war escalate. Ijebu entered the conflict on Ife's side and won a crushing victory, largely through the use of firearms (Ijebu as a southern kingdom was in a particularly good position to purchase these). After a desperate siege, Owu was sacked and wiped out of existence.

Wars with Dahomey

In the eighteenth century the warrior kingdom of Dahomey paid tribute to Oyo. In the 1820s, it not only stopped paying tribute but began invading Yorubaland, largely in order to obtain slaves. The defence of Yorubaland fell on the Egba state of Abeokuta. In 1851 and again in 1864, Dahomey besieged Abeokuta unsuccessfully. In 1886 Dahomey was able to take Ketu, a westerly Yoruba state, which had struggled long and unsuccessfully to maintain her neutrality.

Wars between Oyo and the Fulani

After the fall of Afonja, the Alafin and his people made a number of attempts to stem the Fulani advance. The conflict which resulted is called the Locust Fruit War, because when the soldiers ravaged the farms the contestants could find no other food. Later, the Alafin called on allies from Borgu but finally, in 1835, the ancient capital of Oyo was abandoned. A new Alafin was appointed, Atiba, and he built a new capital, far to the south, in the city we know today as Oyo. On page 74 is a picture of his court and palace there.

In 1840, at the battle of Oshogbo, the new state of Ibadan won a great and decisive victory over the Fulani and halted their southern advance.

Atiba's court

The wars of the successor states

After the fall of Oyo, many of her people moved south. They founded a number of new states of which the most important were Ijaye and Ibadan. The Egba founded the state of Abeokuta. This is a picture of Ogundipe, 'the uncrowned King of the Egba'.

Ogundipe of Abeokuta

These states became plunged in a series of conflicts which we have called here the Brothers' Wars. The states concerned made strenuous attempts to maintain peace. In 1855 Ibadan called a conference of Oyo towns. They agreed to settle disputes without war, to pay voluntary tribute to the Alafin, and to live in peace and friendship with the Egba and Ijebu. But within five years, they were locked in war and a few years later a still more extensive and long lasting war broke out. What were the factors which produced the Brothers' Wars?

The most important cause seems to have been the balance of power. The old balance of power was destroyed by the fall of Oyo. Now three new powerful states grew up in close proximity to each other. Each desired to avoid domination by the others. As Ibadan appeared to grow ever more powerful, her neighbours ended up by allying with each other to prevent domination by Ibadan.

A second important factor concerned the control of trade routes. The victory of Ijebu in the Owu war showed the vital importance of access to firearms and ammunition. These were obtained in exchange first for slaves and later for palm oil. Ijebu and the Egba had their own access to the sea. For the inland state of Ibadan, free movements on the trade routes was vital to her survival and if necessary she would fight to maintain it.

A third reason which tended to encourage war was the need to obtain slaves, first for export and later for use in palm oil collection, agriculture and the army. Some minor skirmishes were undoubtedly fought solely in order to obtain slaves which were a major source of income both for the state and for the war captains within it.

The Brothers' Wars can be divided into three main stages.

Ibadan expansion in Ekiti
Ekiti is the hilly eastern border country of Yorubaland. Like Fante it consisted of many small states. Tradition speaks of the sixteen kings of Ekiti. By 1854 the whole of Ekiti was ruled by Ibadan.

The Ijaye war, 1860–5
According to Oyo tradition, a crown prince died with his father. When Atiba died the tradition was broken and in accordance with Atiba's wishes the crown prince became the next Alafin. Kurunmi, the military ruler of Ijaye, refused him allegiance and attacked Ibadan. Other powers, Abeokuta and Ijebu, jealous of Ibadan's might, joined Ijaye. The war ended with Ibadan's victory and the destruction of Ijaye.

The last stage of this war was marked by British intervention. The allies attacked the Ijebu of Remo who had used the war to seek their own independence and had smuggled arms to Ibadan. The British, who had sold the arms, attacked the army of the invading Egba although Abeokuta had been one of the most promising centres of Christian missions. The Egba promptly responded by expelling both the missions and their supporters. The Ijebu for their part stoutly resisted both missions and European penetration until they were compelled by military conquest in 1892 to admit them.

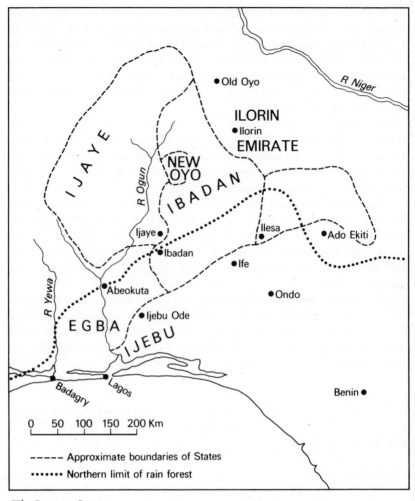

The Successor States

Kurunmi himself, who lost his eldest son in the war, was shattered by his defeat. He went round asking himself pathetically, 'Was I then in the wrong?', and died soon afterwards, of a broken heart.

The conflict had a sequel in a war with Ilesa, which had attacked a town favourable to Ibadan in its closing stages. In 1870 Ibadan took Ilesa, after a painful siege.

The Sixteen Years' War, 1877–93
The Ijaye war was followed by a stalemate but not a peace. The basic issues remained unsettled. Still to be resolved were the question of access to trade routes and the grow-

ing might of Ibadan, surrounded by a ring of defeated but still restless powers to whom Ibadan's rule seemed oppressive and unfair.

In 1877 conflict broke out again when the Egba closed the trade routes in response to an Ibadan expedition to the coast to buy gunpowder. Like earlier conflicts, the war escalated rapidly. The Ekiti towns attacked the local Ibadan representatives and formed, with Ilesa, a new military organisation called the Ekitiparapo. Here is a picture of its general, Ogedengbe, with his war councillors.

Ogedengbe and his war councillors

Educated Ijesa supporters in Lagos supplied them with modern weapons and instructors in their use. Ijebu, Ilorin and even Ife entered the alliance against Ibadan but their combined force was unable to defeat her. Weary of the war, the educated elements began to seek a peace initiative from the British. In 1886 the governor of Lagos sent two Yoruba clergy to negotiate a cease-fire, in which the independence of the Ekitiparapo was recognised, but the war between Ibadan and Ilorin continued until the imposition of British rule.

Why did Ibadan fail in her attempt to establish a new empire to replace that of Oyo? Her failure is often attributed to the fact that she lacked the tradition of authority, but all growing empires must lack this in their early years. The real difference between them was that Oyo's rule did not weigh heavily on the peoples concerned. Ibadan, a new military state struggling for survival, inevitably made much heavier demands on her subject peoples. Her exactions were the most resented as they went in large part to maintain the luxury of a new leisured privileged class, the Ibadan military aristocracy. It was the war weariness and exhaustion resulting from these extended conflicts which paved the way for the extension of British rule over Yorubaland.

Social changes

The refugees

The fall of the Oyo empire caused a basic re-distribution of population. The area immediately south of old Oyo had been extremely densely populated. Now it became one of the most sparsely populated regions of Yorubaland. The bulk of the population moved south into the forest zone. Many ancient cities entirely ceased to exist. Old Oyo itself, far from villages and roads, is visited only by archaeologists. The ancient capital, where visitors once admired the carving and sculpture, is marked only by pottery fragments and grinding holes. Ijanna, where all possible surfaces were ornate with carving and where the people made fine cloth and pottery, is another vanished city, as is Bishop Crowther's home of Osogun. The twentieth century has seen many examples of the sufferings of refugees all over the world. It is difficult, however, to imagine the suffering and hardships undergone by these innumerable Yoruba refugees in the past. This dispersal of Oyo refugees had the effect of spreading a number of aspects of Oyo culture, such as the Sango cult.

New towns for old

'Out of this nettle, danger, we pluck this flower, safety'. These famous words of Shakespeare can be taken as a summary of the response of the Yoruba to their difficulties. From warfare, flight and disaster, they constructed a series of great new states, each with its own distinctive institutions. Atiba built new Oyo, and Modakeke was founded by refugees in Ife, but the most powerful and important of the new states were Ijaye, Ibadan and Abeokuta. Each embodied experiments in political and social organisation. Each was a triumphant adaptation to the perils and difficulties of the age.

Ijaye was settled in 1830 by Oyo warriors who captured it from the Egba and expelled their people. It was fundamentally a military dictatorship under the general Kurunmi, who took the ancient title of Kakanfo.

Abeokuta was founded in the same year by a group of Egba, who had first settled in Ibadan. Their great leader was Sodeke. Abeokuta did not develop new centralised political institutions. Its citizens, who were refugees from other towns, preserved their original groupings and offices and the city was essentially a federation of many small groups.

Ibadan was founded in 1829 on a strategically chosen site, a cluster of hills, by soldiers and refugees of different ethnic groups, among whom chiefs from Oyo became dominant. In theory they retained their allegiance to the sacred Alafin. In practice, Ibadan was a military republic, where both civil and military offices were open to talent and where the gifted and courageous could attain wealth and power, whatever their origins. War captains tended to form a new leisured aristocracy. The military power of the city attracted many refugees. It captured many slaves in war, some of whom worked on plantations around the city, while others were incorporated in the army. So secure did they feel themselves, that they did not feel the wall of protective bush which surrounded most Yoruba cities was necessary. Here is a drawing of Ibadan about twenty-five years after its foundation.

Ibadan in the mid-nineteenth century

The militarisation of life

War dominated the life of nineteenth-century Yorubaland to an extent for which there were no earlier parallels. Ibadan was a classic example of a state organised for war. The conflicts of the time were fought with the ruthlessness of total war. Owu, razed to the ground and with rebuilding prohibited, was a good example. In the terrible sieges, men ate maize stalks or weeds, and children bartered their freedom for a plate of beans.

A professional military class of generals and soldiers ('warboys') grew up, who lived by the profits of war. Firearms replaced horses and weapons became steadily more sophisticated until by the 1870s breach loaders and repeating rifles were common.

Nevertheless, it would be quite wrong to see nineteenth-century Yoruba history purely in terms of war. Oluyole, Ibadan's great general, took a passionate interest in agriculture and undertook experiments to improve agricultural productivity. Here is a description of another chief who was highly esteemed in the same warlike city.

> He did not aspire to the leadership of the people, preferring private life to the responsibilities of government. He was a man who loved peace; he would never carry arms nor allow any to be carried before him, even in those turbulent days, except in the battlefield. A bundle of whips was usually carried before him . . . and with this token of authority he was able several times to disband men in arms and put an end to civil fights. The combatants as soon as they saw the bundle of whips coming would cease firing, saying to one another, 'Baba mbo, baba mbo' (father is coming, father is coming).

But men such as Labosinde were exceptions in the context of the time.

The growth of enslavement

The slave trade was both a cause and a consequence of the Brothers' Wars. It boomed at the old slave ports such as Whydah and Porto Novo and the newer slave ports of Lagos and Badagry. Kidnapping became widespread and with it a chronic insecurity. A special gag was invented to silence its victims.

What this meant in the life of a single family can be seen from the life of Ajayi Crowther who was captured in 1821 with his mother and sisters. He was separated from them and ultimately liberated in Sierra Leone. Meanwhile another brother had ransomed his mother and sisters. Incredibly, years later, mother and daughter were again kidnapped on the way to market and again ransomed.

The spread of Islam

Islam spread rapidly through Yorubaland in the nineteenth century, partly as a result of the dispersal of Oyo Muslims. Numerically, Muslims were a minority, but they included traders, warriors and other influential citizens. In 1871 a Muslim became ruler of Ibadan. By 1878, there were twelve mosques in New Oyo. Ibadan became a centre of Islamic learning, under the leadership of a mallam from Kano, and another of Ibadan origin, who attracted pupils from elsewhere and organised a group of pilgrims for the long journey to Mecca.

Things to come

Another very important strand in nineteenth-century Yoruba history concerns the spread of Christian missions and the influence of educated repatriates from Sierra Leone. Christian mission work began in Yorubaland in 1842 and in the years that followed missions were established in Abeokuta, Ibadan, Oyo, Ijaye and Ogbomosho. Only the Ijebu rejected them. If you look carefully at the picture of Ibadan on page 79, you will see the mission buildings in the foreground. Christianity went hand in hand with western education and the spread of western skills. In 1859 Yorubaland's first newspaper was established in Abeokuta, *Iwe-Irohin*. In 1863 another newspaper, *The Anglo-African*, was started in Lagos. Some of the repatriates embarked on a study of Yoruba language, culture and history. Bishop Crowther made pioneering linguistic studies and Samuel Johnson was the first of a large body of outstandingly gifted Yoruba historians, who have, in our own times, immensely enriched our understanding of the African past.

The Fon kingdom of Dahomey

Dahomey was a kingdom with a very eventful and interesting history. The traditional centre of the Aja-speaking peoples was Allada. Dahomey was founded by a breakaway movement from Allada to the Abomey plateau in the interior, in about 1625. Throughout the rest of the century the kingdom gradually built up its strength, while the coastal kingdoms remained relatively small and divided. (It is interesting to compare this with the history of Asante and Fante.) Under their great king Agaja, who ruled

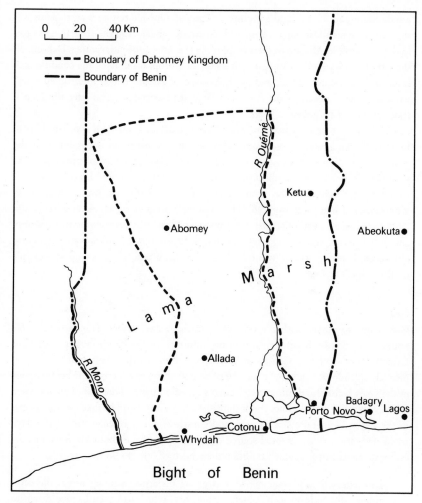

Dahomey in the nineteenth century

from 1708–40, the Dahomeans conquered Allada and the wealthy slave-trading port of Whydah. But it is one of the ironies of history that just as Dahomey was carving out an empire in the south, it in its turn was conquered by another, greater, empire to the east. Repeatedly, Dahomey was invaded by Oyo cavalry and these invasions caused much havoc and destruction. In 1730 Dahomey agreed to pay Oyo a heavy annual tribute. However, she kept her freedom of action in the south and west.

Professor Akinjogbin, the Nigerian historian who is the chief authority on eighteenth-century Dahomean history, believes that Agaja's invasion of the south was originally inspired by his desire to suppress the slave trade, but that this soon proved impracticable. Dahomey soon became deeply involved in the slave trade, which was a state monopoly under rigid government control. One interesting aspect of this was the way in which Dahomey compelled expatriates engaged in the slave trade to pay high wages to the Africans in their employ. In the late eighteenth century Dahomey's slave trade declined. This was partly because the Europeans disliked the conditions of trade and rigid state control, and partly because of factors which interrupted international trade in general – the American War of Independence and later the French Revolution and Napoleonic Wars.

The economic crisis which this caused went hand in hand with a political crisis. In 1797 the king was deposed and killed, because of his people's discontent at the economic situation, or because of the welcome he extended to Catholic missions. The king was the head of the traditional religion and his officials feared his conversion. It is interesting to compare this with the coup four years later against the Asantehene who favoured Islam (see page 56). His successor, Adandozan, made an unsuccessful attempt to lessen his nation's dependence on external trade by diversifying the economy and, in particular, sponsoring a revival of agriculture. But his efforts were apparently unsuccessful and in 1818 he was overthrown by his brother, Gezo, who was to rule until his death in 1858.

Gezo

Gezo came to power with the help of a Brazilian slave trader, Francisco Felix De Souza, who was to benefit greatly in the future from the king's favour. The king created the new office of Chacha of Whydah for him, and for many years he lived in princely splendour, although, as a result of accepting too much credit, he became poor in the years before his death in 1849. Gezo's accession marked the end of an era when the slave trade was in decline, and it flourished from now until its final collapse began in the 1840s. Gezo followed an open and conscious policy of encouraging the slave trade. He saw it as an essential source of revenue to finance both his wars and the elaborate annual rituals which tradition demanded of him. In his own words,

> The state which he maintained was great; his army was expensive; the ceremonies and customs to be observed annually, which had been handed down to him from his forefathers, entailed upon him a vast outlay of money. These could not be abolished. The form of his government could not be suddenly changed, without causing such a revolution as would deprive him of his throne, and precipitate his kingdom into a state of anarchy.

The palm-oil trade, on the other hand, was 'a slow method of making money, and brought only a very small amount of duties into his coffers'.

In striking contrast with the relative poverty of the late eighteenth century, Gezo maintained a splendid court, though, like his son after him, he chose to dress with great simplicity. Like his son, he detested drunkenness and energetically suppressed it amongst his subjects. Here is a picture of Gezo and his son the Crown Prince Badahun (the future king Glele) in 1856.

*Gezo and his son, the
future king Glele, in 1856*

Gezo took it for granted that his state was comparable in power and influence with
Britain. A British visitor to his court recorded a conversation with one of his great
officials:

> 'These', said the mayo, pointing to two tumblers on the table, 'are alike in size,
> in make, in shape; this is Dahomey, that England. See, I turn round, and looking
> again I cannot distinguish; they are coequal, the greatest white and the greatest
> black nations. Your queen can conquer all white nations, Gezo can take all
> blacks.'

Although he was committed, for economic and political reasons, to the continuance
of the slave trade, and to war, Gezo showed, in a number of respects, the attitudes of
a social reformer. We have already noted his campaign against drunkenness. He reduced the incidence of human sacrifice, by restricting its practice to the king alone, he
established a court of appeal, and he limited the infliction of the death penalty so that
it could only be imposed by the king. These were, according to one English visitor,
intended as a first instalment of reform.

> As many of the old, absurd customs, which still existed, were of a comparatively
> harmless nature, he had hitherto permitted them to remain, as he considered it
> dangerous amongst a people so long accustomed to these usages to revolu-
> tionise the whole at once; but he approved of commencing with the most
> unreasonable and injurious, and gradually progressing, as in fact he had done.

When he died, some of his people believed that his death was due to his neglect of the old ways. His officials were divided into two parties, one advocating the abolition of human sacrifice, and the other, which was successful, and to which the new king apparently belonged, supporting its continuance.

War against the Yoruba

One of Gezo's great achievements was to throw off his country's vassalage to Oyo which had lasted for so long. Not only did Dahomey cease paying tribute in the 1820s, but she began a series of energetic attacks on territories to the east. In this, of course, she was greatly assisted by the collapse of the Oyo empire, described in the last section. These wars were inspired partly by the desire for slaves for export, partly by the need for sacrificial victims for annual ritual ceremonies, partly no doubt by a desire to throw off the memory of a long period of political subjection. In the words of a Dahomey song,

> Yoruba and Dahomey!
> Can two rams drink from one calabash?

The task of defending Yorubaland against Dahomey fell primarily to Abeokuta. Their first clash, in 1844, was a major setback for Dahomey, in which Gezo himself was nearly captured. But the Dahomeans continued to raid in the area and made two further unsuccessful onslaughts in 1851 and 1864. Ultimately a section of Dahomean opinion came to see Abeokuta as an 'elephant' which it was impossible to conquer, and argued for concentration on easier targets. Much later, Dahomey did succeed in destroying the western Yoruba kingdom of Ketu, though its final overthrow in 1885 was made possible only by treachery.

The palm-oil trade

For most of the reign of Gezo, the profits of the slave trade supported a magnificent court, the wealthy Dahomean officials, and about 2,000 royal relations who did not work. It also enriched the prosperous Brazilian slave traders, who were often, though not always, of part African descent. It stimulated agriculture in the coastal areas as provisions were necessary for the slave ships and the slaving establishments on shore – the excellent agriculture of the area had been noted at the beginning of the eighteenth century. The soldiers of the Dahomean army, who were given a payment for each living captive or skull they brought back, prospered likewise.

From 1848 onwards, as the British naval blockade intensified, the slave trade began to decline seriously. The decline worsened after the British conquest of Lagos in 1851, and the trade finally collapsed in the 1850s. Dahomey responded to this economic crisis by switching over to palm-oil production, although the Brazilian slavers opposed the change, as they feared that in legitimate trade they could not compete on equal terms with the British and French. But the change seems to have been welcomed by a large section of Dahomean society, which was tired of war. A British visitor stated in 1863:

People have no time for peaceful pursuits: war, war, war is alone thought of, and the King gives them no rest. Many of the Chiefs complain of this, and seem heartily tired of it.

Palm-oil exports began in the 1840s, and expanded rapidly. But, as Gezo had prophesied, this brought in less wealth, and observers commented that Glele's court and ritual celebrations were much less magnificent than those of his father. It also meant that Dahomey lost in relative power and prestige, for her palm-oil exports were little more than those of her small tributary state, Porto Novo. This was probably one of the factors leading Porto Novo to reject her tributary status. This relative decline in income was not due to any lack of aptitude for agricultural pursuits. A visitor who had lived in Asia made favourable comparisons between Dahomean and Chinese agriculture, and was enthusiastic about the country's farms and plantations. The end of the external slave trade did not mean the end of social oppression, for the plantations were worked by slaves. Some of the palm oil was exported via the river Ouémé to the port of Cotonu and some was rolled overland in barrels, 140 kilometres to the sea. When the French invaded Dahomey in 1892, these slaves seized their opportunity and revolted. Most of them were Yoruba and, as they went home, they took revenge on their former masters. Observers remarked that they created more havoc than the French.

The government of Dahomey
The king of Dahomey was absolute, but he was not a tyrant. His power was greater than that of many other African monarchs. But as a British visitor noted,

> The Ministers, war captains, and fetishers may be, and often are, individually punished by the King: collectively they are too strong for him, and without their cordial co-operation he would soon cease to reign.

Each year the king's officials and soldiers gathered for great ritual celebrations. The king took the opportunity to hold a council which discussed important matters of state and frequently he refused to reach a decision on such matters before he had been advised by his council.

The power of the king, and the obligations of citizens towards him, were described in a Dahomean proverb: 'The state is like a calabash of water and the citizen has a duty to block holes in the calabash with his finger'. The kings lived in an enormous palace. Each successive king added to it, and it was surrounded by walls three and a half metres high. Guilds of craftsmen such as metal workers, jewellers and wood carvers, devoted their talents to the royal service. The palace was decorated with paintings and bas reliefs. On page 86 is an example of one of them.

Each year, the king held an elaborate ceremony which the Europeans called the 'Annual Customs', and the Fon called 'Xwetanù' (there were very similar ceremonies in Asante). This served a number of different purposes. It was primarily religious in nature. The Fon saw their kingdom as something sacred, embodying the dead, the living and the unborn. It was their religious duty to honour their ancestors by providing

A bas relief from the Abomey palace

human sacrifices for their service. But it also filled political purposes. It was, as we have seen, a time when the king met his officials, who came with their umbrellas of office, covered with heraldic devices. It was at this time that the king held his court of appeal. He received tribute from his people and he in his turn showed his wealth and generosity by throwing money and goods to his officials and soldiers and by putting to death criminals and war captives, who might otherwise have been sold or put to work. Reliable estimates of the numbers involved in the nineteenth century range between thirty-six and eighty. Europeans tended to exaggerate vastly the scale of this human sacrifice. In the mid-nineteenth century the celebrations included a huge model ship on wheels, a symbol of the importance of external trade to the Dahomean economy. On page 12 there is a picture of another aspect of these ceremonies, the procession of the king's wealth, when the king's treasures were shown to his people, as a visible demonstration of the wealth of the state. Note the umbrellas carried by officials and the royal tent in the centre. This was scarlet in colour, nine metres high, and covered with elaborate decorations.

Few states, past or present, have made as much use as Dahomey of the capacities of their women citizens. Each state official had a counterpart – a 'mother' – among women of the palace whose duty it was to watch over him and check any abuses. The system of checks was, in fact, very elaborate, since he had a male double to report on his activities as well. Dahomey had two armies, one of men and one of women, the

An Amazon in the Dahomey army

latter generally described by European writers as 'Amazons'. Here is a picture of an Amazon in her army uniform.

The Amazons were greatly feared. They were looked on as the king's wives and therefore held in much honour, but forbidden to marry. They also provided the king with the personnel for the highly dangerous activity of elephant hunting. Dahomey was a state very largely geared to war, which maintained a large standing army in terms of its size and resources. Its permanent standing army is thought to have numbered 4,000, half of whom were women, but it could field 12,000 after a call up.

There were a number of important royal officials. The Yovogan was in charge of Whydah and therefore exercised much control over external trade. The Chacha who was chosen from among the Brazilian community was concerned specifically with foreign trade. Possibly by appointing expatriates to this office, the king was trying to restrict the impact of foreign influence on his kingdom. He kept foreign traders within strict geographical limits, and left foreign trade under the control of a foreigner.

The chief state officials were the Migan, the Minister of Defence, Meu, the Minister of Commerce, and Gau, the Commander of the Army. Although there was a Muslim community in Dahomey, its people do not seem, like Asante, to have experimented with written Arabic records. Instead, great reliance was placed on memory. Each year at the Annual Customs, professional historians related the history of the state. A foreign visitor described them as 'a human archive'. It was said of a Meu who was very old in the 1860s that he 'could so class facts that he never forgot name or event: with the poor memonical aid of a few beans or seeds he managed the complicated affairs of Dahome'.

Similarities between Dahomey and Asante

There are many parallels between the history of Dahomey and Asante. Each built up a strong, centralised, militarised state inland from the coast and away from direct European influence, in striking contrast with the small fragmented states of Fante or the southern Aja. The external slave trade was, for each, an important source of foreign exchange. Asante reacted to the abolition of the slave trade largely by developing her northern trade further. Dahomey responded by producing palm oil for export with slave labour. In each, the king enjoyed great power. Each had an elaborate bureaucracy and a well organised army. Each held elaborate annual ceremonies which were basically religious in intent, but which also served to display the king's wealth and power. Each, despite its splendid court and effective administration, contained real elements of social oppression. One has the magnificence of the court on one hand, the slave labourers and human sacrifices on the other. Each experienced, though at different times and in different degrees, slave revolt.

Conquest by the French

For many years, the kings of Dahomey tried to avoid an open confrontation with the French, which they knew they were almost sure to lose. In the prophetic words of Glele, 'He who makes the powder must win the war'. But if Dahomey was determined to keep her independence, and France was, as time went on, determined to expand to the interior, conflict was bound to ensue, and it did in the reign of Behanzin, who came to the throne in 1889.

Predictably, the area where conflict between the French and the Dahomeans first broke out was Cotonu. This port, at the mouth of the Ouémé river, was of key importance to Dahomey, as one of the main outlets of her palm-oil exports. In 1890 Dahomey was forced to recognise the French occupation of the area. Two years later, French forces went up the Ouémé and advanced towards the capital, Abomey, led by a brilliant Senegalese, General Dodds. The Dahomey forces fought fiercely against the French advance, but in vain. When they finally reached the capital, the Dahomeans set it and the royal palace ablaze, to prevent it falling into the hands of the enemy. The king, Behanzin, fled further north with his followers. There on the northern fringes of his kingdom, he began to reorganise his army. The Dahomeans were willing to enter into peace negotiations, but not to accept the French demand that they depose him.

In 1893 the French mounted a further expedition. Again, the king escaped, but now with only a handful of followers. He fled, almost alone, from village to village, protected from the French by the villagers who fed and sheltered him. It is a very interesting demonstration of their attachment to the monarchy. Perhaps they felt that as long as the king was free, the kingdom of Dahomey survived, in some sense, in his person.

Finally, under pressure from the French, some Dahomean officials whom the French had captured agreed to choose a new king, and Behanzin gave himself up. But the monarchy as it now existed, under French control, was a hollow shell, and even this was abandoned in 1900.

Benin

The background

The first Europeans to visit Benin, from the late fifteenth century on, have left us an extremely attractive picture of it. They thought it comparable in every way with a European city. A sixteenth-century Englishman wrote, 'The people are very gentle and loving', and a little later a Dutchman described it in these words:

> The towne seemeth to be very great, when you enter into it, you goe into a great broad street, not paved, which seemeth to be seven or eight times broader than the Warmoes street in Amsterdam . . . The Houses in this Towne stand in good order, one close and even with the other, as the Houses in Holland stand.

One gets a similar impression from this seventeenth-century drawing of Benin (some people think that it is idealised, but there is evidence of its authenticity, for the design of the buildings is similar to that of a brass box found in the Oba's palace, which was a miniature model of it, and a modern visitor to Benin will see the same low hills).

Seventeenth-century Benin

Benin craftsmen produced works of art in bronze and ivory, which are among the art wonders of the world. Many of them were reliefs, where the relative size of the people depicted reflected their relative social importance. This one shows a Benin nobleman, sword in hand, with his attendants on either side, drawn to a smaller scale and in the two upper corners, smaller still, two Europeans drinking from flasks.

A Benin bas relief

Benin was a kingdom whose ruler, the Oba, was thought to be divine. The dynasty traced its origins to Ife, to a son fathered by an Ife prince, Oranmiyan, who is also thought to be the ancestor of Oyo. This legend refers to the origin of the dynasty and not of the state, which had existed long before. The Oba who was ruling in Benin at the time of its conquest by the British in 1897 was the 35th Oba of this dynasty.

The Oba had two functions, as ritual priest and warrior king. They were perfectly combined in Ewuare the Great, who ruled in the late fifteenth century, a great 'magician' whom tradition credits with the capture of two hundred and one towns, and who built an enormous ditch and wall around his capital, part of which still survives.

As time went by, the ritual aspect of the Oba came to dominate. One indication of this can be seen in the introduction of human sacrifice, through which the Oba can be seen as lord of human life, which is not mentioned at all in the first descriptions of Benin. The first account of it dates from 1535 – the Portuguese first visited Benin in

1486 – and strangely enough it was probably introduced by an Oba who had been baptised as a Christian. The sixteenth century was an age of great military expansion and was also the period when Benin bronze production reached its greatest heights.

In 1600 the Oba Ehengbuda was drowned on an expedition to the Lagos area. After that the Obas no longer led military expeditions in person. In the seventeenth century the Oba was relatively weak and dominated by his great chiefs. He lived secluded in his palace. The rule of primogeniture, whereby the eldest son inherits the throne, lapsed. This always weakens kingship because if the identity of the heir is not certain, chiefs and officials can exploit the situation to their own advantage. At the end of the seventeenth century the power of the Oba was reasserted after a major civil war. Akenzua I who died in about 1713 is remembered by tradition as 'one of the richest kings who ever sat on the throne of Benin'. He restored the rule of primogeniture, reinforced his power over his chiefs by creating many new titles and introduced the practice of trying criminals by administering a kind of poison called sasswood (again, the Oba seen as lord of life and death). He reintroduced the export of male slaves which was previously prohibited, possibly as a way of getting rid of those who had rebelled against him. His son, who reigned after him, was so rich that the floor and walls of his house were lined with cowrie shells, the money of the time.

Benin government

The Oba, as we have seen, was revered by his people, but he was not absolute. The basic structure of Benin government remained the same as that established by Ewedo in the thirteenth century. Benin city, which was surrounded by a high wall, was divided into two sections separated from each other by a wide avenue – the Palace and the Town. This geographical arrangement corresponded to two categories of chiefs. The Palace Chiefs were appointed by the Oba, and so remained readily subordinate to him. There were three grades of Palace Chiefs, covering various duties in the court. All freeborn Bini were theoretically the king's servants. They did not work in the palace in practice, but the system identified them with the government. The Palace Chiefs were responsible for the guilds of craftsmen, the bronze casters and so on. They advised the Oba and formed a Council of State together with the Town Chiefs.

The Town Chiefs were also appointed by the Oba, with one exception. There were thirteen of them by the 1890s. In some ways they filled the function of an opposition party, for they alone had the right to argue with or censure the Oba in public. This was especially the function of the *Iyasere* and when he died his jaw bone was sent to the Oba, to show that the jaw which had disputed with the Oba in life became the Oba's in death. Both the Palace and the Town Chiefs were wealthy and powerful, controlling large estates and numerous followers. The Oba, to gain his will, had to balance them against each other.

There was a third category of chiefs of less political importance. These were the *Uzama*, who represented the government of Benin before the foundation of the dynasty. Successive Obas undermined their powers as time went on, and added the crown prince, *Edaiken*, to their number.

The king's wall in Benin

The Benin empire

The heartland of the empire was the Edo-speaking area around Benin. As we have seen, the empire attained its maximum expansion in the sixteenth century. Lagos (Eko) was founded from Benin and Benin expeditions pushed even further to the west along the coast. The chiefs of Lagos sent the Oba tribute, and he confirmed them in office. Benin conquered the small states of Ekiti. The boundary with the Oyo empire was at Ottun. The same process of expansion extended south towards the Niger Delta and the sea. Tradition relates that in the late fifteenth century, a son of the Oba who could not succeed to his father's kingdom because of his unpopularity set off to establish his own kingdom in the south. He founded the Itsekiri kingdom of Warri.

It is not clear whether Benin was simply following a policy of expanding as far as possible in all directions, or if the movement towards the coast was stimulated by the advent of European traders and the commercial possibilities this opened up. Benin also maintained its authority over the small states of western Igboland. Many of these modelled their government on Benin, miniature kingdoms ruled by an Obi instead of an Oba. The title of *Iyase* was extremely common among them. Each year the Oba sent his troops to fetch water from the Niger. If they went there and returned undisturbed, it was a sign that his authority was unquestioned. But all these tributary states, whether in Ekiti, Lagos or Igboland, were practically self-governing in their day-to-day affairs.

In the nineteenth century the ancient kingdom faced an internal and external crisis.

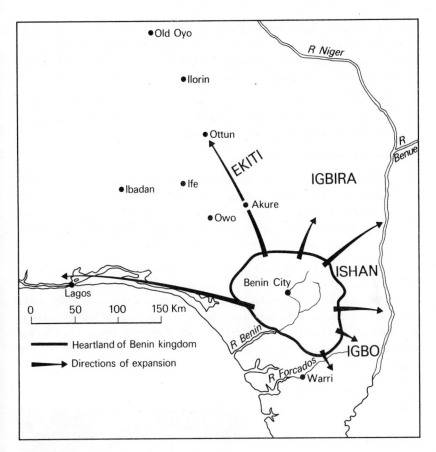

The Benin Empire

The internal crisis

In the eighteenth century it had become the normal pattern for the death of an Oba to be followed by a civil war. Although primogeniture was established in theory, it was not always clear in practice who the Oba's eldest son was. This was because the Oba had many wives and children, and there was no satisfactory way of recording the date of each child's birth. The confusion was compounded by the practice of sending the Oba's wives away from Benin to have their children.

This pattern of civil war continued into the nineteenth century. In 1804 Obanosa succeeded to the throne, after a conflict in which tradition states over a thousand people died. When Obanosa died in 1816 his two elder sons fought for his heritage. The loser took refuge in Ishan, where he raised an army and ultimately succeeded in overthrowing his brother. His brother burnt his palace, destroyed its treasures and then committed suicide. The victor ruled as Osemwede from 1816 to 1850. When he died, he was succeeded in 1851 by his son, who took the name of Adolo, and who was to reign until 1888. Again, he won his throne after a civil war with his brother, who was, in fact, older than he was. As in the previous reign, the loser fled to Ishan, where he raised a series of revolts until his death in 1880. When he died, a courtier told the Oba that his enemy was dead. The Oba replied:

> Do not say that Ogbewekon was my enemy. He was no enemy to me at all, but was my real brother. We were born on the same day. If he is dead it is an indication that my own death is also approaching.

Oral tradition remembers Adolo as

> a kind-hearted and prudent Oba, beloved and respected by his subjects for his just and wise rule. He was rich and industrious. He purchased many slaves and founded many towns and villages for them to dwell in. He encouraged commerce and established various markets such as Ekiadolo, which bears his name. He was very generous and provided for the upkeep of the aged and helpless.

In 1888 Ovonramwen, the last king of independent Benin, succeeded to the throne. He avoided a civil war by taking action before his enemies could and putting many of his opponents to death, but this left a heritage of bitterness and division which was to weaken the kingdom in the face of an external enemy. Ishan, as before, remained rebellious and in 1896 the western Igbo kingdom of Agbor revolted. The Oba was raising an army to put down this rebellion at the time of Britain's conquest of Benin in 1897.

Ovonramwen

As we have seen, Benin's internal crisis can be seen in the conflict within the governing class. But it seems likely that there was another source of tension as well, to be found in a conflict of interests between the governing class and the people they ruled. We have seen that one way in which eighteenth- and nineteenth-century Obas overcame political opposition was by creating new titles. All these chiefs enriched themselves in many ways by levying tribute, by exacting fees and by making use of the people's labour. This wealthy governing class was expanding at the very time, as we shall see, when external trade, and therefore the income of the state, was declining. It is likely then that it imposed a heavy burden on the resources of the state.

The external crisis

By the nineteenth century the Benin empire had shrunk considerably. One result of the increased economic importance of the sea coast was the growing importance and economic independence of Lagos and the Itsekiri kingdom. Benin's control over Lagos, which had been slight in preceding years, came to an abrupt end in 1851, when the British conquered it. The subjection of the Itsekiri to Benin was little more than nominal in the nineteenth century. They were, indeed, a serious economic threat, for they monopolised the growing trade in palm oil, from which Benin might otherwise have profited. Ishan, as we have seen, was the seat of constant rebellions throughout the nineteenth century.

Even more serious than this loss of control over her tributary states, was the growth of an external threat from not one, but a number of militant expanding powers. This was, of course, the century of the jihads, and the Emir of Nupe was raiding the Ishan area from the mid-nineteenth century onwards. To the west, when the new military power of Ibadan conquered the little states of Ekiti, Benin was powerless to intervene, and the defence of the area was left to the people concerned, in the Ekitiparapo. Some Bini fought in the wars as individuals and for a brief period Benin made an economic profit by selling arms to the combatants, but essentially her role in the conflict was minimal.

More dangerous than either Ibadan or Nupe was the expanding power of Britain. When the Yoruba wars came to an end, the right bank of the Benin river was established as the eastern boundary of the colony of Lagos. The Royal Niger Company (see page 170) had its headquarters at Asaba and made its presence felt in at least part of the western Igbo interior. In the Niger delta yet another colonial jurisdiction was established, the Oil Rivers Protectorate, and it was from this base that Benin was finally to be conquered.

Although in the nineteenth century the Benin empire was on the defensive and there was a tendency for it to shrink towards the Edo heartland, one should not forget that successive Obas made energetic attempts to defend their heritage. Obanosa won a war in Owo, Osemwede enjoyed military successes in Akure and Ekiti, and Ovonramwem was raising an army of 10,000 men against Agbor on the eve of his fall.

But it was not difficult to see the direction in which events were tending, and in 1890 the Ife oracle predicted that a great calamity was about to fall on Benin.

The role of external trade

Over the last ten years or so, many of our previously accepted ideas about Benin history have changed completely. According to the old view, Benin was a society which was very seriously affected by the slave trade. This view maintained that it was the corrupting effects of the slave trade which explained the contrast between the harmonious society of the first European descriptions and the much less favourable accounts by Europeans in the nineteenth century (these last laid much emphasis on human sacrifice and called Benin 'a City of Blood'). This view, too, held that the expansion of Benin in the sixteenth century was made possible by firearms bought from the Europeans, and that the decline in the quality of Benin social life was parallelled by a decline in the quality of its art.

In recent years, research has shown that almost every element in this analysis is wrong. Far from being deeply involved in the slave trade and corrupted by it, Benin followed a conscious policy of restricting it. The slave trade was marginal in Benin life and went hand in hand with the export of other products. Pepper, ivory and high-quality cloth were the most important exports but some gum and camwood were sold as well. As early as 1516 the Oba began to restrict the sale of slaves. This soon developed into a total prohibition on the sale of male slaves, which lasted until the last decade of the seventeenth century. It ended then, probably because of the desire to deport those who had opposed Akenzua. The slave trade was still restricted, and was under the control of the Crown. In the eighteenth century Benin sold slaves, but on a very small scale. In 1798, for instance, English ships bought 19,450 slaves from the eastern delta, and only a thousand from the Benin river, and even of these last, most were bought from the Itsekiri.

It is clear that external trade in general, and the slave trade in particular, were of marginal importance in Benin life. In one way, however, the political importance of external trade was greater than its bulk would suggest. Most of the important exports were controlled by the Oba and his chiefs and thus external trade in practice provided a subsidy for the ruling class. When external trade declined in importance, the ruling class lost the subsidy.

The old view of the link between Benin military expansion and the purchase of firearms from Europeans has been shown to be false. The Portuguese made the supply of firearms conditional on Benin's adoption of Christianity. Since this condition was not fulfilled, firearms were not supplied, and Benin's sixteenth-century wars of expansion were fought with traditional weapons. Firearms were not imported on a large scale until the end of the seventeenth century. The question of the decline of Benin art is a separate and complicated question. Most people do, in fact, prefer the earlier to the later art works, but this is simply a matter of personal preference. The earlier works are more realistic, the later more abstract. But even if the earlier works are 'better' than the later works, there is no necessary connection between the standard of the art a society produces and the other aspect of its social, cultural and political life.

Since the slave trade was not very important in Benin, and since she had traded over a long period of time in a number of other commodities, one would have expected

Benin to have been exceptionally successful in making the transition from the slave trade to legitimate trade. This did not, in fact, happen. The trade in, for instance, cloth and ivory was not on a sufficiently large scale to attract European firms in a big way. The most important export commodity for the area was to be palm oil, but this was dominated by the Itsekiri, who had the all-important advantage of controlling the rivers where the trading factories were situated. Therefore, in the nineteenth century, the external trade of Benin declined and this in its turn had an adverse effect on the power, wealth and prestige of the Oba and his chiefs.

The changing image of Benin

We are still left with the problem, how did the city of 'very gentle and loving people' of the sixteenth century turn into the 'city of skulls', or 'city of blood' of the nineteenth? Nearly all European visitors to nineteenth-century Benin laid great emphasis on the prevalence of human sacrifice, just as they did in Asante, Dahomey or Igboland. There are several possible explanations for this.

It is possible, and indeed likely, that human sacrifice really was increasing in nineteenth-century Benin, and that the divine king turned increasingly to divine protection and the exercise of his religious powers, as he felt himself increasingly under external attack. Muslims were invading his kingdom from the north, and Christians from the south. The divine kingship of Oyo had collapsed and so had kingship in Warri. It seems that the Oba and his officials responded by practising traditional religion with a more intense and desperate devotion. When the British finally captured Benin they found many corpses there. These were individuals who had been put to death in a last desperate attempt to preserve the kingdom by placating the gods. It is important to realise, however, that the change was only partly in Benin itself and partly in the eyes of the foreign observers. Not all the corpses the British saw in Benin were human sacrifices – and this was true also of the other peoples of Guinea. Many of them were simply unburied as a result of different burial customs. People did not wish to defile the sacred earth by burying, for instance, criminals in it, and therefore these were simply thrown away in areas specially designated for the purpose.

On the European side, it was undoubtedly a century of increasing racial prejudice. By the 1890s when the conquest of southern Nigeria was well under way, it was impossible that the autonomy of the ancient kingdom should be permanently respected. The British magnified the abuses of Benin society in order to justify its conquest. Their anxiety to conquer Benin was intensified by their exaggerated idea of its natural resources and, in particular, by a desire to tap the rubber of its mighty forests. The pneumatic tyre was patented in 1888, the year of Ovonramwem's accession, and the great demand for rubber which this generated was undoubtedly one of the reasons which led to his overthrow.

Finally, as in Dahomey, we have indications of changing attitudes within the state itself. Ovonramwem told a visitor before his kingdom's conquest, with reference to human sacrifice, that 'he was sick of it all but that he could not discontinue the customs of his ancestors'.

British conquest

We have already noted the factors which pointed towards a British conquest of Benin – the economic factor and the steady expansion of colonial boundaries. In 1892 the British signed a treaty with Benin. The British official who signed it ranked Benin as of the same order of importance as Dahomey. In it the Oba announced his political independence in both internal and external matters. He threw the trade of his kingdom open to all comers and he opened the door to Christian missions. Its terms were so wholly at variance with Benin policy, both before and afterwards, that it seems impossible that it was interpreted to him accurately.

In the years that followed, tension between Benin and the British mounted. The officials of the Oil River Protectorate were making plans for its military conquest from 1894 on. In that year, they overthrew the Itsekiri ruler, Nana, an event which caused much alarm and consternation in Benin. In 1897 the Consul went on leave. A young official, anxious to make his mark while he had the opportunity, was appointed to act for him. He asked for permission to embark on a military expedition, but the Foreign Office ordered delay. He therefore set out with a large party on a diplomatic mission. The Oba, who was engaged in important religious ceremonies, refused to see it, sending messengers repeatedly to ask the party to turn back. The party continued to advance. Against the Oba's wishes, his warlike chiefs chose to interpret this as an invasion of their sovereign state, and practically the whole party was put to death on the Gwato–Benin road.

A sketch of Benin made before it caught fire

With amazing rapidity the British launched a major three-pronged attack on the city. The Oba stayed in his capital until shells were falling within his palace walls, and then agreed to flee. Two days after its defeat, the entire city was accidentally destroyed by fire. Fortunately, the superb art works were saved, but instead of being left in the city they were taken as plunder to Europe. Later, the Oba came in and surrendered. The war chief, Ologboshere, continued to wage guerilla warfare until mid-1899 when he was finally defeated and executed. The English had originally intended that the Oba should stay in office, but as the result of a trivial misunderstanding he was deported, and spent the last sixteen years of his life in exile. In 1914 his son returned as Oba to Benin, taking the name of one of his greatest predecessors, Eweka.

Small-scale states

All the sections of this book, so far, have dealt with unified states, which were in most cases headed by a king, or a figure comparable with a king. But many of the peoples of West Africa, perhaps as many as thirty-five million, lived in what many historians call stateless societies, but which I prefer to call small-scale states. The actual peoples included depends on how one defines stateless, or small-scale states. But there is certainly a large concentration of such societies in eastern Nigeria and west Cameroun, roughly in a square between the Jos plateau, the Forcados estuary, the Cameroon mountain and the Mambila plateau. They include the Igbo, whose history we shall study in this section, the Ibibio, the Tiv, the Idoma, Birom, Angas, Yako, Mbembe and Ekoi. Some would include the Efik state of Calabar, and Ijo states such as Bonny and Okrika. There is another region with many small-scale societies between the Volta headwaters and the Niger bend. These include amongst others the Dogon, Konkomba, Birifor, and Bobo. There is a further concentration of small-scale societies in Ivory Coast, Guinea and Liberia. These include the Kru, Grebo, Bete, Basa and Koranko. One should also include the clans of pastoral Fulani, scattered right across the western Sudan.

These small-scale societies have been, in many cases, little studied by historians. It is much easier to write the history of a united state such as Benin or Asante than that of numerous small-scale societies such as the small states of Igboland or Tivland. There are several reasons for this. Centralised states tend to have attracted early European visitors, so there are more written records. Often, but not always, they have preserved more elaborate oral histories. The larger the state the more likely it is to be able to afford such luxuries as professional historians of various types (drummers, praise-singers and so on). Another important reason is that the rule of kings and the varying impact of their personalities in centralised states provides a ready made focus for historical study.

The account which follows isolates some of the key themes of the history of the Igbo, who are probably numerically the most important of the various peoples who come into this category, apart from the pastoral Fulani, in West Africa.

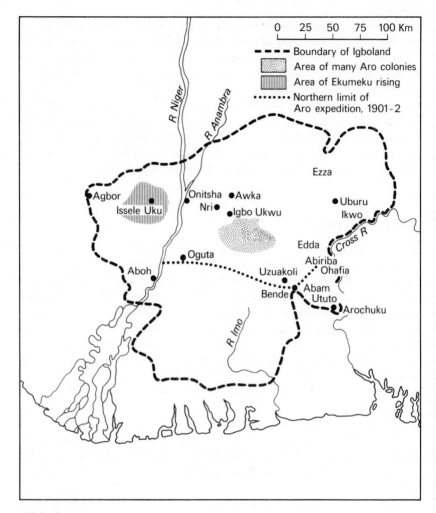

Igboland

The Igbo

The role of Nri

One of the key themes in Igbo history undoubtedly concerns Nri, which an early missionary described as 'a kind of Holy City, the Rome or Mecca of the Igbos'. Nri traditions describe the invention of agriculture and iron working, and the introduction of the four-day week. They tell of an original focus of settlement in the Anambra valley, and a common historical heritage with Igboland's northern neighbour, the kingdom of Igala. The antiquity of Nri civilisation was strikingly attested by archaeological excavations at Igbo-Ukwu. Igbo-Ukwu is very close to Nri, and one of the

A bronze from Igbo-Ukwu

sites excavated is thought to be the burial site of a ninth-century king of Nri. The objects discovered include beautiful and elaborate bronze ornamental and ritual objects, a roped vase, an altar stand, a human portrait, bronze shells, bowls, and so on. They reflect the wealth of the society a thousand years ago, and the superb quality of its craftsmanship.

The dominion of the king of Nri (Eze Nri) could be described as a unique political experiment, remarkable by its pacificism. The Eze Nri was essentially a 'spiritual potentate'. He and his people had the right to confer certain titles, especially the important *ozo* title. He had ritual control over various crops, especially yam, the staple crop, over epidemics, and over insects such as locusts. In the era of the slave trade, when kidnapping was common, men of Nri travelled unharmed, distinctive because of their deep facial scars, and their staffs of peace. They conferred titles, and cleansed the sacred earth from abominations.

Many communities to the west and east of the Niger have sectors which were founded by Nri men. During the era of the slave trade, when human sacrifice became common, the Nri continued to avoid it, bearing steadfast testimony to the sacredness of human life. Ewenetem was an Eze Nri who died in about 1820, and who is remembered for his clear teaching 'that a slave was a human being and to kill one was abomination'. The Nri did not participate openly in the slave trade, though individuals sometimes dealt in slaves secretly. They turned the weapons of aggression into the ritual implements of purification and peace. The spear became the staff of peace, *otonsi*, or the staff of political authority, *alo*. The club became the *ofo*, symbol of truth and justice. The cutlass was used in the yam cult. The Nri authorities arranged for travelling Nri ritual specialists to visit different areas, to avoid the possibility of disputes. The authority of the Eze Nri was essentially religious. Thus, he could place an embargo on a community, which meant that the Nri ritual specialists would avoid it, and it would be left with its abominations uncleansed, and would be shunned by other towns. This religious authority was suggested by a saying recorded in the 1890s, 'The street of the Nri family is the street of the gods, through which all who die in other parts of Igboland pass to the land of Spirits'.

Long ago, perhaps in the tenth or eleventh centuries, part of Nri migrated to another town a little to the south, Oreri, which in due course built up its own, smaller, sphere of influence.

Some of the qualities attributed to Nri men were conferred by them on others, on whom they conferred the *ozo* title. To gain an *ozo* title, a man needed to be wealthy, for it involved heavy financial payments. He went through complicated rituals, by which he was purified and reborn to a new life. Thenceforth, he was sacred. His purity was safeguarded by numerous regulations which he must follow, and, like the men of Nri, he was safe from outside attack.

In the nineteenth century, and indeed before this, the area of Nri influence was shrinking. There seem to have been several reasons for this. Its religious pacifist nature meant that it was ill-equipped to withstand more aggressive military powers, such as Benin in western Igboland, or Igala to the north. In fact, it may have been the military threat of Igala that led to the original withdrawal from the Anambra in the first place. Within Igboland, the Nri were unable to act effectively against the Cross River Igbo warrior groups which terrorised the area in the nineteenth century. Secondly, the travelling men of Nri sometimes settled down in the towns they visited, or founded new ones. These Nri sons abroad tended to fill the same ritual role in the new local area, thus weakening their attachment to the Nri metropolis.

But although its authority was declining, widespread reverence for its spiritual and ritual role persisted. In a sense, Nri history appears as a unique political experiment, since it was a state based not on force, but on pacifism and religious values. In the words of an elder from Nri:

> We Nri brought peace within communities when we ruled. We are doing all we can to bring peace between communities, but the slave trade did not allow

us to, and the white men came and stopped us from ruling. White men have arms and we do not believe in fighting. Fighting spills blood on the earth and this is an abomination . . . We Nri never did so; we tried to persuade and convince people not to do so . . .

Aro diplomats

Arochukwu was another state which had an importance which extended far beyond its own boundaries, and, in fact, beyond the boundaries of Igboland. (The Ijo, to the south, consulted the Aro oracle, and the Aro were well known for their trading role among the Igala and Idoma to the north.) The Arochukwu state was probably founded at the beginning of the seventeenth century (though, of course, people had lived in the area long before). It was founded in the extreme south-east of Igboland, near the Ibibio border, and was the result of intermarriage between Igbo and Ibibio. Some of the Aro villages look back to an Igbo, and others to an Ibibio origin. They made use of these links in their trading operations, forming economic ties with the relevant areas. Aro tradition states that the Aro learnt the art of long-distance trading from another group involved in Arochukwu's foundation, the Akpa, and that they began to build up their long-distance trade network from the middle of the seventeenth century on.

The eighteenth and nineteenth centuries were when the Arochukwu trading network was at its greatest extent. The Aro established a large number of colonies – an Aro historian lists ninety-eight – especially in the area south of Awka. They traded primarily in slaves, and in imported goods. The oral traditions of Igbo communities show that their impact on the rest of Igboland was twofold. On the one hand, the growth of enslavement led to a great growth in insecurity, for in Igboland practically all slaves were obtained by kidnapping. On the other, they introduced a large number of new commodities, and, in some cases, new crops. In the words of oral tradition:

> We were told that external trade brought many good things into the clan but that its evils were perhaps greater. Before the external trade, we were told that the clan was comparatively quiet and that everything moved orderly. We were told that everything turned topsy turvy with that trade. Traders from Awka, Arochukwu and Uzuakoli brought new articles . . . Later they brought gin . . . and tobacco . . . It was these traders that first brought guns into the clan . . . At that time it was very unsafe for any child to go out alone from its father's compound even in the day time . . . So that the trade with these foreign traders brought many new things into the clan but it also brought wars and chaos.

One of the most striking characteristics of the Aro was their wonderful talent for diplomacy. They built up excellent relations, both with the 'hosts' of the Aro colonies, and with other Igbo communities whose interests were linked with their own. Since they concentrated mainly on trade, they bought their provisions from nearby communities, such as Ututo, which concentrated on farming. All Aro, whether living at home, in Arochukwu, or abroad, in one of the Aro colonies, always remained very united among themselves. For transporting their goods from place to place, they made agreements with Igbo groups which specialised in contract porterage.

The heart of the Aro economic system lay in the great monthly trade fairs. These were not held in Arochukwu itself. One was at Bende, the name of which was familiar to Europeans long before they were able to visit it. The Aro 'owned' the fair; and they established very friendly relations with the Bende hosts. In the words of Bende tradition, when the founder of Bende was first approached by the Aro:

> He agreed to give up trading to concentrate on farming. It was understood though that he would do this on condition that the Aro made Bende town their market centre and so gave the Bende people an opportunity to profit as hotel keepers and money lenders to the visiting traders. Hence Bende and Aro always worked together on the friendliest terms.

In 1896 the Aro had a dispute with Bende, and transferred the fair to the nearby town of Uzuakoli.

The other great fair was further to the north, at Uburu, which was famous for its salt production. Here, too, there was a rival fair at Okposi.

We have seen that the commercial life of the Aro centred round the slave trade. But in 1807, the British, who had dominated the Delta slave trade, gave up their role in it. The real period of decline in the external slave trade was not until the 1830s, and even then the slave trade in Igboland seems to have been little affected. The palm-oil trade which developed in the Delta required a large labour force, to purchase and transport the oil. As late as the 1890s, up to six bands of one hundred to two hundred each left the Aro colony of Ndizuogu for the fair at Bende, every twenty-four days. Many Igbo slaves were assimilated into the Ijo states of the Delta, and some of them rose to be important chiefs. The Efik state of Calabar purchased many slaves, who were employed on agricultural plantations. The states of Igboland itself, similarly, made much use of slave labour. Since the society continued to enslave individuals, but they could no longer be exported overseas, slaves became cheaper and more abundant. One bad effect of this was an increase in the practice of human sacrifice. But as we have seen, Nri had always condemned it, and as the nineteenth century progressed, we have evidence of a more general rejection of the practice, especially in the Niger towns, which were subject to mission influence. We have seen a similar pattern in Benin and Dahomey.

Igboland had many oracles, but the most famous of them was at Arochukwu. It developed out of a small Ibibio shrine, and rose to prominence in the generation after the state's foundation. It attracted people involved in disputes from much of Igboland, and indeed from beyond its borders. In a way, it was a classic case of how religious credulity could be used for gain; the Aro asked for heavy fees from those who sought the oracle's verdict, and those whom the oracle condemned were later sold as slaves. But, like Igboland's other oracles, it filled useful functions in society. Its continuing reputation depended on the justice of its judgements, and travelling Aro merchants, who guided individuals to the oracle, made every effort to find out the truth of a case. The oracle undoubtedly did much to prevent internal disputes and conflicts, by providing an external arbitrator, speaking with all the authority of God, which could give a decision acceptable to all concerned. The fame of Arochukwu had reached Europeans long before they went there. A missionary who visited the Niger in 1841 learnt that:

> There is a town in the Ibo country – where I could not sufficiently ascertain – which is called Tshukunga, or God's town; there God dwells and gives his oracle from the ground. Any matter of importance is left to his decision; and people are travelling to the place from all parts of the country. The people of Aboh say they can reach it in three months . . . Tshuku* cannot be seen by any human eye; he speaks every language on earth, discerns thieves; and if there is any falsehood in the mind of the inquirer, he is sure to find it out.

Cross river warriors

We have already mentioned the wonderful skill which the Aro showed in reaching agreement with other communities whose interests were linked with their own, such as the agriculturalists of Ututo, the contract porterage specialists of Ibeku, or the fair 'hosts' at Bende and Uburu. But the most remarkable relationship of this kind concerned the warlike Igbo groups of the Cross river area, such as the Edda, Ohafia and Abam. These peoples developed a warlike culture, in which the greatest esteem was paid to the man of courage, the hero, and a coward was looked down on and despised. But how was one to judge who were heroes, and who cowards? The societies concerned developed a concrete test; to prove his courage, a man had to produce the head of an enemy killed in battle. (The head, still whole, was first inspected, to make sure it was really that of an enemy.) Because a man needed to produce a head to be an honoured member of society, the Abam, Ohafia and so on were always very eager to find a legitimate war to take part in.

The Aro fully exploited the warlike dispositions of their northern neighbours. For all their diplomatic talents, they sometimes found themselves in a situation where they needed to exercise force, for example, when customers would not pay their debts. They did not wish to fight themselves, and so they used the services of the Cross river warriors. (Some accounts call them mercenaries, but in modern times the peoples concerned insist that they fought, not for gain, but purely for glory.) Not only did they use Cross river warriors in their own conflicts, but the Aro acted as brokers, or go-betweens, hiring out Cross river warriors to other communities. Sometimes corn cobs were sent, to indicate the number needed. Those hiring them had to take care that the warriors did not get involved in any other conflict on the way, for if they did, they considered their obligations fulfilled, and went home again.

Okoli Ijeoma was a famous general from the Aro colony of Ndikelionwu, who

---

* Tshuku (modern spelling, Chukwu) is Igbo for supreme God.

waged war in the Awka area on a very large scale, largely, it seems, in order to obtain slaves. The Cross river warriors instilled terror in the hearts of Igbo communities over a very large area east of the Niger. A missionary visiting Awka was asked not to whistle, for 'our way now lay through the dreaded Abam country', though the Abam area was in fact many kilometres away.

The Cross river warriors were not always, of course, successful, and in the late nineteenth century the communities who suffered from their attacks developed a number of ways of defending themselves. One was by forming defensive alliances. (The people of Nri joined such an alliance, but it was unsuccessful, and in the end they had to negotiate an agreement with Okoli Ijeoma.) Other defensive measures were adopted, including the building of defensive fortifications, elevated platforms, and so on. Here is a picture of a nineteenth-century tower in Awka.

A clay tower in Awka

Awka

In Igboland, as in many other parts of Africa, the blacksmith was a highly-honoured member of society, because of the skills he possessed, and because of his special usefulness to his fellow men, in producing, for instance, agricultural tools, and weapons of war. Almost every area in Igboland had a local blacksmith community, but certain

Igbo towns developed metal working to such a degree of excellence that they were able to travel far and wide, practising their skills. These famous centres of metal working included Abiriba, Awka and Nkwerre. The most famous of all was Awka.

Awka was an exceptionally large town, by Igbo standards, comprising no less than thirty-three villages. Not all the inhabitants were blacksmiths; some villages concentrated on agriculture, while others developed various professional specialities, such as wood carving and traditional medicine. Originally, blacksmithing was confined to a group of seven villages, called Agulu. The blacksmiths travelled to Agbaja, some kilometres away, where there were rich deposits of iron ore at a hill called Akputakpu. Because of this, the blacksmiths' shrine was also called Akputakpu.

The Awka blacksmiths were highly organised, so that disputes could be avoided, in the same way as the Nri ritual specialists were. Half the blacksmiths would travel abroad, while the other half stayed home, to protect their families. The following year, the section that had stayed home would have its turn to travel. Each year, all the Awka people at home and abroad met for a great festival called *Otite*. This enabled them to check up if anyone was missing. If anyone stayed away without an excuse, he had to pay a heavy fine.

The Awka blacksmiths divided 'the known world' among themselves. Each village had its own journey route, leading, in many cases, well beyond the Igbo area. As well as making objects from iron, they worked in copper, and were gunsmiths. Like other African peoples, they could make all the parts of a gun except the barrel and here they were prevented by the fact that the metal available to them was not of good enough quality. This is a picture of the traditional tools of an Awka smith.

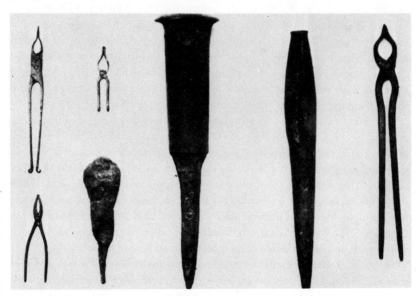

The traditional tools of an Awka smith

As time went on, the knowledge of blacksmithing spread beyond Agulu. A woman from Agulu who married a man from another village would beg her relations to teach the skill to her children. A man from a non-smithing village might seek the same favour from a friend. Amikwo was a section of Awka which had originally specialised in traditional medicine, but by the nineteenth century many of her members had mastered blacksmithing as well. Economic competition between Amikwo and Agulu, over journey routes, finally erupted in civil war between the two in 1903. The war was fought with a bitterness and destruction which were unusual in wars within Igbo communities; many lives were lost and much property destroyed. Finally, Agulu, which was fighting to defend its traditional control of routes, seemed to be losing. They sent a deputation asking the British to intervene, behaving like many African peoples who thought they could use the colonial powers to gain their own ends. The British did, indeed, intervene and stopped the civil war but the result was that Awka lost her independence to the British, who, in their turn, threw open the blacksmiths' trade to every section of Awka.

Like the travelling Aro merchants, the smiths of Awka often combined their travels with slave trading. They also made use of their journeys to bring clients to their own oracle, Agbala. This was organised with the same elaborate stagecraft as the oracle of Arochukwu, filling all who visited it with awe at the divine presence. But although it was famous and widely revered, it never had the same reputation as the oracle of Arochukwu.

The north-east Igbo

We have seen that in the nineteenth century, the Abam, Edda and Ohafia were engaged in almost constant warfare, often at great distances from their homes. But they fought purely because they sought glory in warfare as individuals, not in order to expand their own territories. In the north-east of Igboland there were three large clans, who believed that they were ultimately related to each other, and who fought a constant series of boundary wars with each other and their neighbours to gain more farming land for themselves. These clans were the Izzi, the Ikwo and the Ezza.

Their hunger for land has been explained in terms of their geographical environment. In Igboland, yam is the king of crops, and on it the livelihood and well-being of the whole community depends. In most parts of Igboland, the number of yams an individual can plant is limited by the fact that if yams are left for long in the land they rot there. This means that the planting and harvesting seasons are fairly short. But in the north-east, the climate is much drier. Yams can be left in the ground much longer; hence it is possible to start planting much earlier, and an individual can plant a much larger area. The Ezza and their neighbours were extremely energetic and dedicated yam farmers, in constant search of more and yet more land to farm.

This explains why the north-eastern Igbo were anxious to expand at the expense of their neighbours, but it does not explain why they were able to. The three big clans of the north-east were numerically much stronger than their relatively small Igbo and non-Igbo neighbours, and hence they were able to displace them with relatively little difficulty. When the British imposed their rule on the area, in the early twentieth century, these wars were still going on. Although the British put the whole weight of colonial government into suppressing internal African conflicts, the Ezza still continued to fight wars of territorial expansion in the colonial era. They continued to press to the west in particular, until the British marked the boundary with concrete pillars in 1923.

If colonial rule had not intervened, one cannot tell how far these wars of expansion would have carried these clans. They were practising, in fact, imperialism on a small scale, and it is not impossible that in time their territories would have expanded until they formed a substantial state like Dahomey. Historians have sometimes written as though expansion of this sort is a form of progress, but this is very doubtful, and the small-scale democracies of Igboland were probably a preferable form of government.

Like the Abam and Ohafia, the Ezza paid a price for their conquests. Daily life became militarised and brutalised; duelling was common, and sometimes the young men rioted in the market, plundering the stalls. An early party of missionary visitors wrote, 'The Ezzas . . . lived as uneasy conquerors in constant fear of attack'.

Traditional Igbo government

The typical form of government in pre-colonial Igboland was village democracy, and it is impossible to say exactly how many of these separate states, each covering a small geographical area, there were. The typical Igbo village group had a number of different political institutions. These gave most influence to the community's elders, but they also gave scope to the other sections of society as well. A typical village group might have an assembly of elders, and also an assembly of all male citizens which would meet when a matter of great moment, such as a declaration of war, was at stake. Each family, and extended family, had a particular elder at its head.

Each village group contained a number of component villages. There was always a danger that the component villages might go their own way and have difficulty in acting together. To guard against this, a number of political devices were developed. One was the age grade, linking together all the community's men of a particular age. Each age grade had its own duties. Some areas had secret societies. In some towns they were dominated by young men, who thus gained a say in the affairs of the town, which was otherwise denied them. In others they were dominated by rich influential men, and were much like the title system. We have already mentioned the title system. A man qualified for a title both by his success in life and his personal character. Some Igbo towns had a special woman official who controlled the affairs of the market, which was of key importance in the town's economic life.

Traditional Igbo society gave its members a great deal of say in the matters which affected their lives – more say than a modern democratic state gives its citizens. People were free, to a very great extent, to achieve a position and status in society by their own efforts. It was a society in which many different kinds of talents were recognised and welcomed; the outstandingly successful farmer took the title of Yam King. Orators, outstanding soldiers, craftsmen such as blacksmiths, priests of traditional deities, specialists in herbal medicine and divination, long-distance traders, all had their own kind of success and place in society.

There was a fault in Igbo democracy. The same fault had existed in the famous democracies of ancient Greece. This was the existence of slavery. Some individuals were even worse off than ordinary slaves. These were those who were sacrificed in religious rituals, and those dedicated to divinities, who were not put to death, but were shunned by the community as 'cult slaves', or *osu*.

The Niger monarchies

Village democracy was so typical of Igboland that it became a proverb, 'The Igbo have no kings'. But there were in fact some Igbo kingdoms, in the Niger area and in the west. These seem to have modelled their institutions to a considerable extent on those of their great neighbour, Benin. These kingdoms included Onitsha, Issele-Uku and Agbor. In each case, the king was seen as sacred; he lived in seclusion in his palace, emerging occasionally to dance before his people at great festivals. He played a key role in religious, as well as political matters. But the king was not an absolute despot. He shared his power with a large number of chiefs, and with representatives of other groups in the town as well. Every morning, the royal drummer warned the king of Aboh, 'Watch your step, watch your step!' An essentially democratic spirit was present therefore in Igbo monarchies as well.

One of the most powerful and successful of these states at the beginning of the nineteenth century was Aboh, which was strategically situated at the apex of the Niger Delta, where it joins the River Niger proper. It was therefore ideally situated for acting as a middleman between the merchant states of the Delta, which traded with the Europeans, and states further north. It retained the advantage which its location gave it, by maintaining a fleet of three hundred heavily armed war canoes. When the first Europeans visited Aboh in 1830, the wealth of the state was reflected in the magnificence of her king, Obi Ossai, who was dressed in scarlet and gold lace, and an abundance of coral ornaments.

A later European expedition, in 1841, negotiated with Obi Ossai on the abolition of the slave trade. They promised to bring 'legitimate' trade to the lower Niger instead, but the promise was not kept. The various descriptions of Obi Ossai emphasise his diplomatic skill and intelligence. His actions towards the 1841 expedition showed his kindness and courtesy as well:

> If I had been pleased with Obi's character before, I was much more so now. I had been completely in his power: the vessel's decks were crowded with his people; they were aware that out of the five white men I had living, three were confined to their hammocks; and yet I was received with more kindness, and had more respect paid to me, than when I visited the place before, with all my crew living, and in full health and strength.

To prevent conflicts, the states trading on the Niger agreed on a series of trading conventions. The two main states trading on the lower Niger were Aboh, and the

Obi Ossai of Aboh

Igala kingdom, with its capital at Iddah. Their representatives met at a boundary market near Asaba. In the Delta, Aboh's main trading partner was the Ijo state of Brass.

When the Europeans finally began to trade on the Niger in person, from the late 1850s on, the effect on Aboh was disastrous, for its role as middleman was completely undermined. To make matters worse, it was not chosen as a centre of mission work (which meant schools and probably trade as well) and when trading posts were established there, they were soon given up. The result was a catastrophic decline in the wealth and power of the Aboh kingdom. As her people complained to a missionary, in 1879:

> A long time ago the Abohs were regarded as the most powerful amongst their neighbours, both for riches and strength, and as such were feared by all; but now . . . places . . . once their slave grounds are lifting up their heads against them . . . they could not describe their feelings to me whenever they saw ships laden with merchandise passing away from them to villages further up . . .

Aboh's old trading partner, Brass, suffered even more acutely from these changes. Surrounded by creeks and mangrove swamps, her people depended on trade for their livelihood. When the Royal Niger Company obtained its charter in 1885, it used its power to exclude them from their old trading grounds on the Niger altogether. Finally, in desperation, the people of Brass launched a military assault on the company in 1895.

Canoes in Aboh Creek

Systems of writing

It is widely believed that the peoples of sub-Saharan Africa did not invent systems of handwriting, so that they were forced to rely on other ways of keeping records, such as the elaboration of aids to memory. We shall see one exception to this generalisation, in the Vai of Liberia who, in the early nineteenth century, invented their own alphabet and established schools to teach it (see page 137). Another, less well known, system of writing was in use among the south-eastern Igbo and their neighbours. This system, called *nsibidi* is particularly interesting because it owes nothing to European models, and works on an entirely different principle.

In *nsibidi*, as in Chinese, a symbol, or combination of symbols, represents, not a letter, but a concept. This means that it could be used as a means of communication between speakers of different dialects, or even different languages. This is, in fact, what happened. It was apparently invented by a small group living in the Cross river area. It spread to Ibibioland and to south-eastern Igboland. We have records of at least one school where it was taught. In many societies, the knowledge of reading and writing is the carefully guarded privilege of an elite, and this was the case with *nsibidi*. The knowledge was confined to members of a secret society. But there were indications that the knowledge was becoming more widely spread. Had colonial rule not intervened, it is likely that the knowledge of *nsibidi* would have become more general, and that it would have acquired more and more symbols, as Chinese did, becoming a suitable vehicle for recording any kind of literature, science or philosophy.

Now, *nsibidi* has died out entirely, and many Igbo are unaware that it ever existed. Opposite is an example of it. It is the account of a court case, recorded at the beginning of this century, Other African peoples, in Cameroun, Sierra Leone and Liberia, also invented scripts – often, in the twentieth century, as a form of cultural patriotism

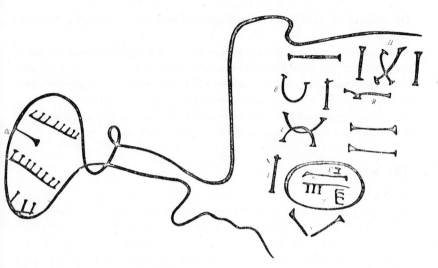

The account of a court case in nsibidi

The Igbo resistance to colonial rule

It is surprising, but true, that the invading colonial powers often found it easier to conquer large unified states than peoples whose organisation consisted of many small independent units. In the case of a unified state, once the capital was taken, and the army defeated, the war was lost. But thoroughly defeating the many small independent democracies which made up Igboland was a task which often seemed to the British a hopeless and almost endless one. The real conflict between the two developed in the 1890s, though there had been isolated clashes earlier. The largest single British expedition was the famous Aro expedition of 1901–02 which attacked not only Arochukwu, but many other states of southern Igboland. But much of Igboland was still unvisited and undefeated, and even those states which had been supposedly conquered by the expedition renewed their defiance once it had passed by. Thus a British official reported from the Bende area:

> I heard from Bende and from all sides that the two tribes had given it out as their intention to remain hidden in the ravines and farms until we left the country, that they would never come in and we could destroy their towns if we wanted to.

Every dry season, year after year, the British persisted in sending military forces against the various states of Igboland. The large ones were called 'expeditions', the smaller ones 'patrols'. In 1909 a British colonel told a London audience that Igboland 'is really quite a small portion of Nigeria . . . but it has been the most troublesome section of any'.

During the first World War of 1914–18, some Igbo states, like many other West African peoples, seized their apparent opportunity and broke once more into revolt.

The defeat of the little democracies of Igboland took the British well over twenty years to achieve.

The individual states of Igboland were defeated relatively easily in war, because of their small size. But it was difficult to maintain lasting control over them. In one area, the people concerned realised this, and formed a union of previously disunited states, to fight the invader, not once, but in a series of campaigns extending over a period of twelve years. This was the Ekumeku movement in western Igboland, which attacked the British in a number of campaigns between 1898 and 1910.

The Niger Delta

The background

The Niger Delta is an area of over twenty-eight thousand square kilometres of mangrove swamps and meandering waterways. Most discussions of the Delta include not only the rivers which actually flow from the Niger, but states such as Opobo, situated at the mouth of the Imo river, and even Calabar, situated much further east at the juncture of the Cross and Old Calabar rivers. Much of the area consists of salt-water swamp which can grow nothing but mangroves, though the fresh-water swamps further inland have limited agricultural possibilities, on their small areas of higher and drier land.

Despite the difficulties of their environment, the peoples of the Delta had a well-organised political and economic life before the Europeans came. The Niger Delta city states, which are thought to date back to about 1400, had developed a relationship with the hinterland which was beneficial to both sides. The Delta peoples exported

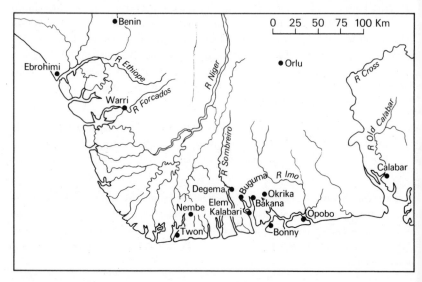

The Niger Delta

salt and fish to the hinterland, and obtained agricultural produce in return. Different parts of the Delta also traded with each other in various commodities, especially the all-important canoes, for in the words of a Nembe drum song:

> Tall as the mangrove grows
> It makes no canoes.
> The Nembe make no canoes.

The first European visitors came in the late fifteenth century. As time progressed, the Niger Delta became a major exporter of slaves. By the eighteenth century, it was West Africa's largest slave exporting area, with the island kingdom of Bonny enjoying the greatest share. In a sense, the Delta states became wealthy and powerful by exploiting their neighbours, especially those from the densely populated Igbo hinterland. But since the Europeans did not need to come to West Africa to buy salt and fish, it was, during the era of the slave trade, the only kind of foreign trade open to them.

The era of the slave trade brought about a number of political changes in the Delta states. The king, *amanyanabo*, became richer and more powerful, his revenues increased by the customs duties paid by Europeans. Not all slaves were sold abroad, however; some were kept to build up the population of the city state. This influx of new members meant that the original pattern of the organisation of society gave way to a new institution – the canoe house.

The canoe house was 'a compact and well-organized trading and fighting corporation capable of manning and maintaining a war canoe'. One could be born a member, or one could join it voluntarily, but the most common means of recruitment was through enslavement. But a slave who joined a canoe house, even though against his will, became a member in a very real sense. He joined the 'kitchen' of a woman member, who acted almost as his mother. He took the surname of the house's founder. If he proved himself an energetic and capable businessman, he could even rise to be a house's head. (A house head was elected at a general meeting of members.) The heads of the canoe houses met together to form the governing council of the state.

The canoe house was largely, though not solely, a business organisation. It was expected to be successful, prosperous and dynamic. A flourishing canoe house would produce other, junior, canoe houses, which would keep connections with the mother house. A declining, impoverished house might attach itself to another, more successful one, or even cease to exist altogether.

The large influx of Igbo slaves meant that there was a very real danger that the culture of the state might be submerged in the process. The city states took steps to avoid this. This was most successful in Elem Kalabari. In Bonny, however, the indigenous tongue, Ubani, was replaced, in every day use, by Igbo.

In both Bonny and Elem Kalabari, adjustment to the existing culture was encouraged by the masquerade society, Ekine. Whatever his origins, a man could join this very important society if he thoroughly mastered the local culture To join it, however, he had to pass a difficult test, performing dances to the commands of the drum.

Among the Kalabari, another secret society challenged those found out at night. If they answered with a foreign accent, they were sold abroad or put to death.

The Efik state of Calabar developed rather differently. The different lineage groups, or wards, which numbered six by the early nineteenth century, did indeed incorporate large numbers of slaves, but they kept to traditional lineage government through elders. This contrasts with the extremely fluid society which developed in Bonny or Kalabari, where successful slaves rose to the headship of a house, and where canoe houses rose, fell, divided and reunited.

To meet the conditions of international trade, the Efik developed a new type of secret society, called *Ekpe* (Europeans called it Egbo), which seems to have come into existence in the mid-eighteenth century. It became the chief law enforcement agency in Calabar (a masked figure, representing the forest spirit *Ekpe*, went round Calabar with a whip). As such, it enforced the repayment of debts, which was obviously vital in a community geared to international trade, where the whole economic system rested heavily on the extension of credit, or 'trust'. So useful was it, in this respect, that some Europeans joined it. It consisted of nine grades; slaves could only join the five bottom grades, and were thus excluded from the decision-making levels.

Warri, accessible by the Forcados river, was an Itsekiri state, which drew its slaves largely from Urhoboland, and, to a lesser extent, from the Kwale Igbo. Nembe (Brass), deep in the Delta, was relatively inaccessible. It had a port at Twon, and traded up the River Niger. Bonny and Elem Kalabari were trading rivals, situated close to each other, and tending to compete for the same markets. Bonny's main trading empire was on the navigable reaches of the Imo river. Okrika, Bonny's ally, traded with Europeans through Bonny until the late nineteenth century. The Kalabari controlled the markets on the Sombreiro river. They, and Bonny, tended to contest markets like Ndelle, which lay in between. Opobo, at the mouth of the Imo river, was founded by a breakaway movement from Bonny, in 1870, and took over its oil markets. It later developed markets on the Kwa Ibo river as well. Calabar had the Cross river for its hinterland.

Each city state consisted of three sections. There was the capital, which gave its name to the state, where land for settlement was usually extremely limited. There was a cluster of related towns and villages, which included the port, which provided pilots (Twon in the case of Brass, Finnema for Bonny, Ifoko for Kalabari). Thirdly, each state had its own trading empire, extending, as we have seen, along navigable rivers. The Delta state did not rule such an area, but enjoyed a monopoly of its external trade.

The palm-oil trade
For the first third of the nineteenth century, the slave trade and the palm-oil trade existed side by side, and it was in the 1830s that the slave trade began seriously to decline. Some historians have written as though the development of the palm-oil trade ushered in revolutionary changes in the life of the Delta states and, in particular, led the slaves to fight for their rights, both as individuals and in corporate slave risings.

In fact, although there were two slave revolts in the Delta, and although all the leading city states, except Brass and Okrika, experienced a severe internal crisis, the observer is more impressed by the continuity of their institutions. One has cases of new men, rising from slavery to become wealthy chiefs, but there had been such men in the era of the slave trade. Many of the characteristic aspects of traditional organisation continued; the canoe house, the absorption of slave recruits into it, the great importance of credit in commercial transactions.

It is important, too, that the social mobility enjoyed by individuals should not be thought of as making a democratic society. In this respect, Niger Delta society was very much like the first phase of industrial capitalism in England or America. In theory, it was possible for a poor man to rise to wealth and power, though in practice it was very much easier for the son of a rich man to do so. But the poor man who joined the ranks of the wealthy, whether as a Delta chief or a European factory owner, was extremely exceptional, and his rise did nothing to improve the lot of his fellows, the factory workers or slave pullaboys, who did not have the luck and talent to rise in this way. Individuals might cease to be exploited and become exploiters in their turn – the familiar sight of a slave turned slave owner – but the bulk of Delta slaves in the nineteenth century were a submerged proletariat, with little hope of a change in their fortunes. At the worst, in the first half of the century, they might be sacrificed in the name of religion. Alternatively, they spent their lives as pullaboys, in the case of Bonny, or labourers on plantations, in Calabar, cut off from the profits of trade.

What difference did the palm-oil trade really make to social organisation? It seems to have increased the already existing tendency to incorporate slaves into the Delta states. This was partly because of the large amount of labour needed to purchase and transport oil, and partly because the supply of slaves from the hinterland was still available, even when the external outlet had ceased to exist.

From the viewpoint of the Delta merchant, the palm-oil trade posed a number of new challenges. It required a substantial investment in transport and storage facilities, and hence large supplies of capital. Credit, important before, soared to new heights. The relative impoverishment and decline of the Bonny monarchy, in the nineteenth century, may have been because none of her kings could rise to these challenges.

Political crises in the Delta states

Slave revolt in Calabar

We have already looked briefly at the revolt of the Blood Men in Calabar in 1850–1 (see page 11). Essentially, what happened is that the slaves working on plantations outside the town banded together to put an end to human sacrifice, and to oppression by the ruling sections of *Ekpe*. They had no desire to take over the government of the state, or abolish *Ekpe*, though their numbers would have made this possible, but simply to obtain a specific improvement in their condition by non-violent means, behaving very much like a modern trade union movement. They won the support of many of the poorer freemen; in fact, one scholar has described it as a revolt of the poor rural masses against the rich urban privileged classes.

The movement was a remarkably successful exercise in peaceful agitation. When the Efik rulers seized some of the rebels, their comrades on the plantations retaliated by seizing the rulers' property until they were released. It is tempting to speculate on the relationship between the movement and Christian teaching. But since Christian missions had only come to Calabar in 1846, it is unlikely that they had penetrated the plantations in four years. In any case, in the words of an outstanding Delta historian, 'the issues to which the Blood Men addressed themselves were ones of whose justice they scarcely needed an outside agent to persuade them'.*

Revolt in Warri

Mid-nineteenth-century Warri experienced an extremely severe political crisis which, unlike the disturbances in the other city states, seems to have really been caused by the transition from the slave trade to the palm-oil trade. The slave trade died away in the 1820s, because slavers felt that they were liable to be captured by the British squadron while sailing over the Forcados bar. As the palm-oil trade developed, it was based not in Warri (Ode Itsekiri), the capital, but on the Benin river, about eighty kilometres away.

The effect on the Warri king (called the Olu) was disastrous, because he lost almost his entire source of revenue, both from customs and from his own activities as a slave trader. To make matters worse, his subjects began to move away to the flourishing commerce on the Benin river. New towns grew up there, and Ode Itsekiri was almost deserted. The Olu who died in 1848 is remembered as being harsh and overbearing. This tradition may well have developed to explain the basic conflict of interests which had grown up between him and his people.

After the Olu's death, the two princes who were his likely heirs died in rapid succession. Benin tradition says this was the result of a curse imposed by the Oba. Since no likely candidate had the necessary qualifications of wealth and royal birth, an interregnum followed, which lasted until 1936.

The slave revolt mentioned in the heading occurred at the crisis caused by the Olu's death. It seems that the slaves of the two dead princes decided that since their masters could not succeed to the throne, nobody else would do so. In the words of tradition, 'they were so formidable in wealth and men, that no power or force could withstand them in those days'.

Like the Blood Men, the slaves of Warri do not seem to have tried to take over the government of the state; in fact, several candidates for Olu were disqualified because they had slave mothers. But they seem to have played an important part in ending the rule of the royal dynasty and after their success, a number of them established themselves in independence on the Benin river.

* Recently a scholar has put forward another explanation which was that human sacrifice had already been abolished, and that the Blood Men were intervening in sectional politics in Calabar. But the truth seems to be that they feared the new regulations could not be enforced.

In the second half of the nineteenth century, there were civil wars in both Bonny and Kalabari, which had momentous consequences for those concerned, for many of the inhabitants of Bonny left to found the new state of Opobo, and the ancient settlement of Elem Kalabari was given up altogether, when its inhabitants moved to three separate sites further inland. (It is interesting to note that there was a comparable division in the eighteenth century in Nembe, which led to the foundation of a separate (but subordinate) kingship across the river, at Bassambiri.)

The conflicts in Bonny and Kalabari were clearly not slave risings. Rather, they were struggles between competing clusters of canoe houses. In Bonny, the last rich and powerful king was Opubu, who died in 1830. After his death, no ruler of his stature emerged, and the Bonny political scene was dominated by the rivalry between the house he had founded, Annie Pepple, and the house founded by his brother, Manilla Pepple. Both were branches of the ruling Pepple (Perekule) dynasty. Their affairs were dominated by able ex-slaves of Igbo origin. Annie Pepple house was ruled first by Madu, a protégé of King Opubu, and then by his son Alali. Alali was succeeded by his brother, but when the brother died, the dynastic chain was broken and Ja Ja, whose career we shall study in more detail below, was chosen as the new house head.

Manilla Pepple, likewise, was dominated by able ex-slaves of Igbo origin. By the time of Ja Ja's accession to power, it was dominated by Oko Jumbo.

The rivalry between the two houses affected every aspect of Bonny life. They struggled to put their members on the throne. After a mission was established in Bonny in 1864, religion became a dividing point as well, since the Manilla Pepples supported Christianity while the Annie Pepples remained hostile, a hostility which was to be characteristic of Ja Ja until his death.

King William Dappa Pepple (of the Manilla Pepple branch), became king in 1835, was exiled in 1854, recalled in 1861, and died in 1866. In exile he became a Christian, and acquired a good command of English. When he returned from exile, anxious to spread the knowledge of western skills, he brought with him 'a chaplain, schoolmaster, carpenter, gardener, school mistress, doctor and nurse'. His efforts were unavailing, partly because of his poor health, but mainly because he lacked the wealth which alone could command respect in the commercial centre of Bonny.

His son, King George Pepple, had been educated in England, and was an ardent Christian. He had the same zeal for modernisation as his father: in his own words, 'It is incumbent upon all intelligent educated Africans to use every cogent means in their power to develop or devise some means of developing the resources of their country'. A Bonny resident said that he could have become 'a model king in West Africa'. But the same poverty which had hampered his father made him an ineffective ruler. He was deposed in 1883, and restored by the British in 1886.

The tension between Annie Pepples and Manilla Pepples shifted from economic rivalry to war. The rift became irreparable when, in 1855, many of the Annie Pepples were massacred. In 1869 civil war broke out between the two factions. Ja Ja, who was losing, led the Annie Pepples to a new site at the mouth of the Imo river, thus at a stroke cutting Bonny off from her inland markets, and turning defeat into victory.

In Kalabari, similarly, the ruling dynasty of Amakiri had split into two rival factions, the Amakiri and the Barboy. In 1879 Will Braid, a leader of the Barboy group, decided to follow the example of Ja Ja, seceding from Elem Kalabari and settling at Ewofa, which controlled the entrance to the New Calabar river. Ja Ja advised him against the step, for his financial resources were inadequate, and he was heavily in debt to other Kalabari leaders. He failed, essentially because, unlike Ja Ja, he was unable to attract the European traders to his new settlement.

He was forced to leave Ewofa, and settled instead at Bakana. The other Kalabari, probably fearing they would be cut off from their markets, also shifted to the northern edge of the Delta. The Amakiri settled at Degema, and then Buguma. A section of the Barboy group, which had refused to follow Will Braid, settled at Abonnema. The area where the Kalabari state had been situated for so long was left almost deserted.

Two merchant princes
Ja Ja
Ja Ja, the founder of Opobo, was a man of commanding abilities. He was an Igbo, born in the Orlu area, in the heart of Igboland, in 1821. Different sources give different accounts of how he became a slave – perhaps kidnapping is the most likely. He ended up in Bonny, belonging to the lowest section of Bonny society, that of slaves born

Ja Ja

outside. He became a member of the Annie Pepple house, and by sheer ability worked his way up until he was a well known and dynamic trader. Like the contemporary kings of Dahomey, he disliked the effects of imported alcoholic drinks, which he avoided altogether. He scraped together a little capital for himself, largely from dashes from European traders, and bought first a cask of oil, and then a small canoe. His resources expanded rapidly.

In 1863 the head of his house died, leaving an enormous burden of debt (over £10,000). The senior chiefs were reluctant to assume this burden. The position was offered to Ja Ja, then in his early forties, who accepted it and paid off the accumulated debts in two years. He, in his turn, encouraged young men in commercial activities, and was prepared to guarantee them. The prosperity of Annie Pepple house encouraged others to join it, but provoked the jealousy of its traditional rivals. In 1869, as we have seen, he led his followers away from Bonny, and civil war, and established the new state of Opobo, commanding Bonny's traditional markets, leaving Bonny 'a ruined and impoverished country'. In 1873 a treaty with the British recognised his sovereignty, and his exclusive rights to his commercial hinterland. To show his good will, he even lent the British troops for the Asante expedition. With characteristic foresight he first obtained written confirmation that 'his was not to be taken as a precedent!

Ja Ja's career, for the eighteen years he reigned as king of Opobo, is a fascinating example of selective modernisation. In government, he retained traditional forms, such as the canoe house, the secret society which effectively policed the state, the association of warriors who had slain a foe in battle. In religion, he excluded missionaries and showed a deep attachment to traditional forms. This may have been linked with the original religious conflict in Bonny, and confirmed by his experience of the disruption which Christianity brought to Bonny life. It may have been linked with that reverence for the past which made him call his new state after the great King Opubu. On one occasion he defined traditional religion as 'the celebration of our forefathers' lives and deaths'.

He rejected Christianity, but welcomed western secular education. In 1873 he set up a school in Opobo, run first by a Sierra Leonian, and later by an Afro-American woman called Emma White. He sent two of his sons to school in Scotland, but insisted that they should not be turned into Christians.

He showed his great shrewdness in his development of his commercial empire, in the way in which he preserved good relations with his Annang, Ibibio and Igbo oil suppliers, and in the attempt he made to beat the white traders at their own game, and export his oil to England himself. In 1884 when a British consul was signing treaties in the Delta, he asked for and obtained a written guarantee that 'the Queen does not want to take your country or your markets'.

Ja Ja was ultimately overthrown because his political and commercial power and independence were incompatible with British interests. The white traders were upset by his attempt to rival them in the export trade, and thought, wrongly, that they would make greater profits if they dispensed with the African middleman and traded

direct with the original producers. And the very existence of an independent unconquered sovereign African state at their doorstep seemed a challenge to the officials of
the newly-established British protectorate in the Delta. In 1887 Ja Ja sent a deputation
to London, in an attempt to have the texts of his treaties honoured. But it was in vain,
for Ja Ja, who had overcome so many dangers and difficulties, at last fell victim to
treachery. The acting British consul invited him to a friendly meeting on a British
gunboat to discuss their differences. Ja Ja, shrewd as ever, asked for a white hostage,
but in the end was satisfied with a written pledge of safe conduct. Once on board, he
was given the choice between the bombardment of his town and his own deportation.
To save his people, he chose the latter. He never returned to Opobo alive. He died in
exile in 1891, a death he clearly foresaw: 'Last night I close mine eyes to die and I
could see no man but God'.

His people showed their love for him by paying the cost of having his body
repatriated, and by giving him a royal funeral.

Nana

We have seen how many of the people of Warri migrated to the Benin river, and how
the long interregnum created a vacuum in Warri political life. The vacuum was filled
by an official chosen from among the traders on the Benin river, called Governor of
the River and recognised as such by the European trading community. Originally, he
had been the Olu's customs collector and trading agent. The Governor was chosen in
turn from the royal family, and from the second most important family, Ologbotsere.

Olomu, who was Governor of the River from 1879 until his death in 1883, was an
extremely wealthy and powerful merchant, with a great palm-oil trading empire
among the Urhobo clans on the Warri and Ethiope rivers. He had over a thousand
people working for him, partly slaves, and partly poor freemen. When he died, he left
his whole wealth to one son, Nana, instead of following the usual practice of dividing
it among his sons. Nana thus succeeded to his father's full wealth and power, and, in
recognition of the fact, was elected Governor of the River. This broke the system of
alternation between the two leading families. This, and his near monopoly of the trade
of the Ethiope and Warri rivers, made him many bitter enemies among his fellow
Itsekiri traders.

His capital, Ebrohimi, was founded by his father on an almost impregnable site,
created by dumping sand in the middle of a swamp. This is a picture of his state canoe.

Nana's state canoe

Like Ja Ja, Nana was slowly but relentlessly overwhelmed by the rising tide of imperialism. In 1884 he signed a treaty with the British. Like Ja Ja, he had the wisdom to restrict the rights he surrendered; in particular, he and his fellow Itsekiri refused to grant general access to their trading empire, or to admit missionaries. As time went on, his relations with the British worsened. British officials mistrusted his great authority and influence; British traders hoped to do away with his middleman role. He appealed to the Governor of Lagos to mediate, but without success, and he was deposed from his position as Governor of the River. Finally, he was summoned to a meeting on government premises. He refused to attend, remembering Ja Ja's fate, and his refusal was taken as defiance.

In 1894 Ebrohimi was assaulted and taken by a massive combination of British armed forces, the crews of three gunboats, and Nana's local rivals. As in other similar wars, the British won through their superior armaments, among them machine guns and rockets.

From 1894 to 1906, Nana lived in exile. This is a picture taken of him then.

Nana in exile

When he returned, he began to build a new town and the welcome he received from his former trading associates reflects his popularity. So does the fact that some of his former slaves, now freed, worked for him voluntarily. He died ten years after his return.

The extremely interesting comment (in 1915) of a European who knew him well suggests that Nana, too, belongs to the number of frustrated African modernisers:

> . . . it is with pain and sorrow that he now views the country (which he so wisely governed) in the occupation of those who do little or nothing to develop it.

Both Ja Ja and Nana have attracted very sympathetic attention from historians, and it is easy to see why this is so. Their great abilities and their resistance to European encroachment, made them attractive to later nationalists, as did, in the case of Ja Ja, his rise from humble origins. But as was recently pointed out,* it would be wrong to idealise these merchant princes unduly: 'Their world view did not extend much beyond their local commercial interests, their visions of social justice did not include the emancipation of their own slaves'.

---

* By A. G. Hopkins.

4

Building New Societies: Western Models

The Creoles of Sierra Leone

The background

The relatively small area of modern Sierra Leone contains a large number of ethnic groups. The largest of these are the Mende, who are about 750,000 strong, in a population of about three million. As their name suggests, they form part of the great Mande family, and they may be at least partly descended from the mysterious 'Mane' who invaded the area in the sixteenth century, and whose identity has given rise to much speculation. They were divided into a large number of independent chiefdoms, but the different states were linked by several powerful secret societies; the Poro, or Wunde, for men, and the Sande for women. Early Portuguese accounts of the area give us a strikingly clear picture of these societies, as they functioned in the sixteenth century.

The second largest group were the Temne, who now number 600,000. They were divided into twelve kingdoms. Unlike the Mende rulers, whose power was mostly secular, the Temne had a form of divine kingship. The Temne king was thought never to die. He came from Futa Jallon, and returned there when on the point of death; his successor was seen as the same king, returning.

There were many other smaller groups, including the Bullom, who live along the coast, and the Limba, both of whom speak languages related to Temne. The Loko are historically linked with the Mende. Further north were the Susu and Fulani (called Fula in Sierra Leone).

When the Portuguese first visited the area, they were extremely impressed by the superb craftsmanship of the coastal peoples, presumably the Bullom.

One interesting example of this can be found in the so-called Afro-Portuguese ivories, which were made by African craftsmen for European customers. On the next page is a very famous example. (The Edo did similar work for the Portuguese.)

One of the unsolved mysteries of Sierra Leone history is: why did this tradition of craftsmanship die out completely? Was it due to the impact of internal upheavals, such as the Mane invasions? Was it the result of the external slave trade, which, in the

An example of the
Afro–Portuguese ivories

coastal areas, undermined the peace and stability which favour the creative arts? There are parallels elsewhere in West Africa (the short-lived bronze casting schools of Igbo-Ukwu, in Igboland, and of Ife in Yorubaland), and nobody really knows why.

One could well write the history of nineteenth-century Sierra Leone in terms of the history of its indigenous peoples, who formed, and still form, most of the population. One could describe the long series of wars fought between the Temne and Loko, the expansion of the Mende, whose warrior leaders often took part in others' wars, the trade wars of the 1880s, and so on. Instead, this chapter concentrates on the Creoles of Freetown, who have always been a tiny minority, and who were not, originally, for the most part, indigenous to the area at all. This concentration follows the emphasis in the historical literature on Sierra Leone. The Creoles have had a special fascination for historians, for they seem to have anticipated, in so many ways, the achievements of educated West Africans in our own time.

The Province of Freedom★

The word Creole means different things in different countries. In Sierra Leone it refers to the descendants of a number of groups who settled in Freetown in the late eighteenth century and the first half of the nineteenth.

The first band of settlers came in 1787. They settled on the rocky peninsula which the Portuguese had called 'Serra Lyoa', or lion mountain. This was the beginning of Freetown.

These first settlers were free blacks who had been living in England. Some had been taken there as attendants to American or West Indian slave owners; some had become free by fighting for the British during the American War of Independence. But they soon discovered that freedom means little without the means of livelihood. The settlement was encouraged by those who hoped that it would be an island of Christian influence, and that by its example, and prosperity, it would discourage the slave trade. One of the organisers in England was Olaudah Equiano, born in Igboland, who was enslaved, won his freedom, and settled in England, where he married an English wife and became a well-known writer and public speaker. Another was the outstanding British humanitarian, Granville Sharp. Others were anxious to get rid of the social problem which the free, but poor, blacks represented. Thus in 1787 a party of 411 settlers sailed from England.

The little settlement started with high hopes. It was called the Province of Freedom and had a constitution much more democratic than England did at the time. On the next page is a famous and beautiful picture of the area.

But in practice it was dogged with disaster. The settlers had little knowledge of tropical agriculture. They suffered terrible hardships and many died. Finally the Temne, the original owners of the area, scattered them. The survivors, ironically, turned to slave trading!

★ Strictly speaking, this name applies to the period 1787 to 1791, but it is often taken as appropriate for the whole Creole experience.

The Province of Freedom

At this point, the settlement was saved by two new groups of arrivals. In 1792, a body of a thousand 'Nova Scotians' arrived. They were former slaves who had fought for the British in the American War of Independence. They had been settled in Nova Scotia, but it was bitterly cold and in many cases the land they were promised was not forthcoming. They gladly agreed to settle in Sierra Leone and in 1792, about a thousand of them reached it. Ardent Christians, they went ashore singing hymns. Like the original settlers, they suffered from economic hardships and high mortality rates.

In 1800, another, smaller, group arrived, consisting of 550 Jamaican Maroons. They had escaped from slavery and set up their own state in Jamaica – no easy task on a fairly small island. When they were finally conquered by the British, many were deported, despite the promise that they would not have to leave the island. They, too, were sent, first to Nova Scotia and then to the Province of Freedom.

By the beginning of the nineteenth century, then, there were several small groups of free black settlers on the peninsula, less than 2,000 of them in all. Each had, in different ways, a history of fighting for freedom. They were ardently Christian, and had been exposed to European culture. But they faced serious economic problems, and were few in number. The company which had been formed in 1791 to rule the area made such losses that it could not continue, and in 1808 it became a British Colony. As the map shows, the Colony was very small – just the area round modern Freetown.

The liberated Africans

In 1807 the British parliament passed an act prohibiting British nationals from taking part in the slave trade. (There is a lively controversy as to whether this was because of humanitarian considerations, or because changing economic circumstances had made it less profitable, but that dispute lies beyond the scope of this book.) The British

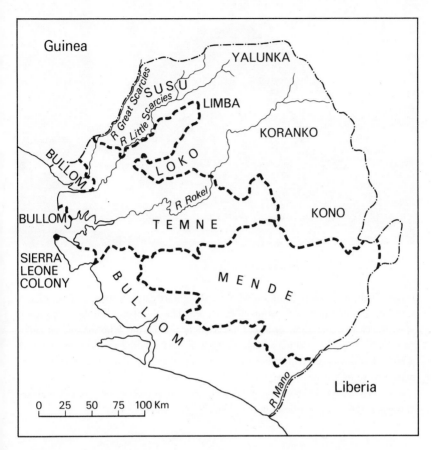

Sierra Leone

were naturally unwilling to see others continue to take part in it, and wherever possible they signed anti-slave trade agreements with other nations. A naval squadron was established on the West African coast, to capture illegal slave-ships. As we shall see, many ships still slipped through, and the slave trade continued to flourish until the 1850s. But many slave ships were captured, and their living cargoes released at Freetown. (It was impracticable to restore them to their widely-scattered homelands.) Each year, ship-loads of Liberated Africans, or Recaptives, as they were called, were landed and released. In time, they transformed the size of the Creole community. By 1834, when twenty odd years of Recaptive settlement still lay ahead, the number of Creoles was estimated at 32,000. On the next page is a picture, taken in 1870, of the yard where they were released.

The Liberated Africans faced tremendous problems of adjustment. They had been snatched away from their homes and families. Some of them have left accounts of their lives, which nearly always include touching details of wives and children left

The yard where Liberated Africans were released

behind. They had passed through a whole series of terrifying experiences. People from some areas would find compatriots in Freetown. The Yoruba, called Aku, and Igbo, were the two largest ethnic groups. Others might find no one who spoke their language at all. It was a situation which might well have reduced them to collapse and despair. But the success with which they adapted to the demands of their new environment was to be a major triumph of the human spirit.

Since Freetown could not absorb them all, they set up a whole series of new villages in the area. Here is a picture of one of them, Regent, in about 1820.

Regent village

Christian missionaries, especially members of the C.M.S. and Wesleyan Methodists, made an important contribution to the rehabilitation of the Liberated Africans. For the most part, these responded to Christianity eagerly; they were far away from their traditional shrines and deities which had, in any case, proved unable to protect them from the misfortune of enslavement. The Nova Scotians were an example, close at hand, of a community of fervent black Christians.

However, not all the Liberated Africans became Christians. There was a flourishing Muslim community in Freetown, and a few kept to their traditional religion. Sometimes the first generation kept a foot in both camps, while their children became more committed Christians. We have the example of one family where the parents decided to retain the traditional Yoruba cult for twins. When one of the children, the future 'Holy' Johnson, grew up and attended mission schools, he put an end to the cult.

Charles MacCarthy, the British governor of the colony from 1814 until his death in 1824, made important contributions to its development. He encouraged the work of the missionaries, and spent much government money on building.

Livelihood of the settlement

The small rocky Freetown peninsula did not offer the expanding Creole community an adequate means of earning its living. The original plan had been for an agricultural community, but generations of Creoles learnt by hard experience that farming seldom led to prosperity. Even rich Creoles who went in for farming as a sideline, usually lost by it.

Usually, the Creoles decided instead to earn their living by trade. The penniless Recaptives coming off the slave ships engaged in petty trade in the streets. They clubbed together to buy the cargoes of captured slave ships. Some travelled far into the interior to buy the palm oil which became the colony's main export. Others earnt their living by exporting timber (destroying, in the process, an irreplaceable natural resource).

The colony's most successful businessman was Charles Heddle, the son of a Scottish doctor and a Senegalese mother. He was the first to see the possibilities of groundnut and palm-kernel exports. He made an enormous fortune and retired to a chateau near Paris! Others, who lacked his initial advantages, also built up substantial fortunes. Emmanuel Cline, a Hausa Recaptive, embarked on land subdivision and when he died, endowed a church for the area concerned. John Ezzidio, a Nupe, imported goods worth £3,000 annually, and rose from slavery to membership of the Legislative Council.

The uses the Creoles made of their wealth was strikingly like that of the modern West African elite. They built houses in Freetown, and rented them out. But above all, they educated their children. There was a large network of elementary schools, grammar schools for boys and girls were established in the 1840s, and from 1876 Fourah Bay College, founded in 1827, was empowered to award degrees of the university of Durham. Some Creoles studied abroad, and in the 1870s, Creoles graduated from the universities of Oxford and Cambridge.

As the result of this investment in education, a distinguished body of Creole professional men developed. There were a number of doctors and lawyers, and many clergymen. Africanus Horton was the son of poor Igbo parents in the Colony. A black West Indian Chief Justice, who financed the education of a number of poor boys, sent him to secondary school. From there he won a scholarship to study medicine at King's College, London. He qualified in 1859 and won a number of distinctions and prizes. He went on to a distinguished career as an army doctor, finally becoming head of the army medical services in the Gold Coast. He was a man of extraordinary energy, who wrote books on tropical medicine and related sciences, and on politics, and drafted blueprints for the government of the West African colonies when they became independent – a day he thought to be close at hand. Originally called James, he chose the name Africanus to show his pride in his African identity.

J. F. Easmon was another distinguished Creole doctor, who became head of the government medical department on the Gold Coast. He was the first to isolate black-water fever – one of many brilliant West African doctors who have made original contributions to medical science.

Sir Samuel Lewis, who qualified in 1872, was the most famous Creole lawyer. He refused to work for the government, preferring private practice, where he devoted himself to his clients' interests with ferocious and single-minded industry. He became the first Mayor of Freetown, and the first West African knight. It is said that he refused to hold a party, as Mayor, on the grounds that the poor would not be invited, although it was the poor street hawkers whose payments for licences would have financed it.

The Creole community was generous and public spirited. Some Creoles contributed money to a number of Christian churches as well as their own. Muslims subscribed to the building of a church, and Christians to the building of a mosque. They were equally generous to less immediate needs, and gave money to appeals in aid of the Syrian Christians, or the widows left by the Crimean War (a European and Asian conflict which had nothing to do with Africa). Like Usuman dan Fodio or Shaikh Ahmadu, they offered a striking example of how religious ideals could be translated into practice, and we can learn much from them.

The search for an identity
The Creoles in the nineteenth century faced a problem which has also confronted educated West Africans in our own time. This problem was how to reconcile African and Western culture in their lives and attitudes. Because they had been physically uprooted from their own cultures, they tended, especially at first, to identify strongly with Britain. They took pride in the name black Englishman, called England 'Home' and called Queen Victoria 'our mother' (in Krio, 'we mammy'). They tended to look down on the indigenous peoples of Sierra Leone, calling them 'natives', as Europeans called Creoles!

But elements of African culture were always strongly embedded in their lives, for example, in the lavish expenditure on funerals, the tradition of helping the extended family, and in African methods of food preparation. Traditional African masquerades and secret societies still flourished, and the Creoles developed their own distinctive language, Krio, a fusion of English and African elements. Here is an example. (The first paragraph was written by recent converts to Methodism in 1860; the second, in modern Krio, was written in 1960.)

> Then we na fraed again, we say country fashion him na true God. Then we give our heart to true God. O Scroo Masser, we heart good now, we heart sweet now, we heart laugh now . . .

> Den we say contry fashin nar from God he camm. Den we gee we heart to do true God. O school master, we heart don good now, we heart sweet now, we heart gladie now . . .

Many Creoles were very ambiguous in their attitude to things African. They often felt a sense of loss in their own separation from their cultural heritage. A few took African names, and a shortlived society for African dress was founded. (It soon disappeared, because its members felt ridiculous.)

The Creoles in eclipse

In the third quarter of the nineteenth century, the Creoles of Freetown were a prosperous and successful community. It seemed clear that there was no position which they could not fill satisfactorily. There was a fundamental harmony, in those years, between British policies and Creole aspirations. In 1865 a British committee recommended Britain's withdrawal from all her West African colonies except Sierra Leone. It was difficult to recruit European professional men to work in Africa, so the British gladly made full use of the training and talents of men like Africanus Horton. A whole series of Englishmen – Granville Sharp, Governor MacCarthy, and Henry Venn (for many years secretary of the Church Missionary Society) – had done their best, according to their lights and opportunities, to further the growth and development of Creole society.

In the 1880s, things began to change. The British became far more intolerant towards the subjects of their colonies. Strangely, they often seemed to reject precisely those cultures which were modelled most closely on their own. In India, they preferred the hill tribes to the educated 'Babu'. In Africa, they felt more sympathy with traditional rulers, or peasants, than the black Englishmen of Freetown. Not surprisingly, the Creoles themselves suffered from a bitter feeling of rejection. As one of them put it in 1916:

> The upset of the Sierra Leonian began with the upset of the thought of his white rulers concerning him . . . Those who had been fathers now rose to arms, and in many and strange ways proclaimed that Arcady was gone, and the idyllic must be superseded by a reality which must go hand in hand with sternness. Segregation was the first blast of the trumpet; then other things and other things . . .

This sense of rejection often undermined their collective self-confidence, turning the Creoles, as one of them put it, into 'self-detractors, self-depreciators, distrustful of our own possibilities'.

European racism was not confined to attitudes; it had many practical effects. As health conditions improved, an increasing number of Englishmen wanted to make a career in West Africa. Deliberately, the British kept the Creoles down. A regulation passed in 1902 laid down that no African doctor, no matter how senior or highly qualified, could hold a post senior to any European doctor, no matter how junior. At a time when only two white officials in Sierra Leone, apart from the doctors, had university degrees, a Creole Oxford graduate found himself jobless and had to go back to England to study law. The pleasant multi-racial society of nineteenth-century Freetown withered and died. White officials moved out of Freetown to the Hill Station, and a special railway was built for their benefit.

The eclipse of the Creoles in the professions went hand in hand with their eclipse in business. Big foreign firms moved ever further into the hinterland, where Creole traders had operated, and the Creoles lacked the capital to compete with them. Although they prospered as individuals, their wealth was often spent in discharging family obligations, or in educating their children. Some Creole fortunes vanished in lengthy legal disputes; Africanus Horton had planned to endow a college of science in Freetown, but his intentions were made impossible by long years of legal battles after his death.

Even in petty trade, there were new competitors; those very Syrians whom the Creole philanthropists had once helped. These immigrants, called 'corals' from one of the items they traded in, prospered by using the techniques which had worked so well for the Liberated Africans. They clubbed together to make joint purchases, and built up capital by strict economy.

The Creoles abroad

The energies and capacities of the Creole community could not be absorbed in the small area that was then the Colony of Sierra Leone. Some, as we have seen, traded in the Colony's hinterland. A few, such as P. P. Hazeley, the apostle of the Limba, worked for the conversion of its peoples to Christianity. But most Creoles were more interested in the settlements along the coast than in the hinterland. Creole traders were to be found from the Gambia to Calabar. One enterprising Creole set up plantations in Fernando Po. Most of these left Freetown in search of economic opportunity. A classic example of a successful Creole merchant abroad was Richard Blaize of Lagos, who died in 1904, and who was so rich that he used to drive round Lagos in a carriage, complete with coachman and footman!

Many Creoles, especially the Yoruba, never lost their attachment to their original homeland. In 1839 three Creoles of Yoruba descent clubbed together to buy a condemned slave ship, which they used to transport passengers to their homeland. This idea caught on, and soon there were substantial Creole communities in many Yoruba cities, including Abeokuta, Lagos, Ibadan and Badagry. Just as the Nova Scotians in

Sierra Leone had influenced the Liberated Africans, by giving them an example of a community of black Christians with western skills, similarly the Creoles who left Freetown influenced those around them by their example. In Abeokuta, they encouraged an important experiment in western-type government (see page 149). The writings of Africanus Horton, then working on the Gold Coast, inspired another such experiment in the form of the Fante Confederation, which in its turn inspired a similar experiment among the Grebo.

Many Creoles left Freetown as Christian missionaries, to spread the Gospel in their homeland or elsewhere. We shall look at the most famous example of this, the Niger Mission, later in this book (see page 157). Some who left Freetown to work in this way were famous and eminent, like Bishop Samuel Ajayi Crowther, or Bishop James Johnson. But some were obscure men of little education, whose steadfast Christian witness has been, for that reason, almost forgotten. One was Simon Jonas, Igbo-born, who acted as interpreter for three Niger expeditions, and who (in 1841) was the first man to preach the Christian message in Igboland. Another was Thomas Samuel, who worked for years as a humble devoted catechist on the Niger and who was said to have no education but the Bible.

The Creole community tended to be more interested in the land they originally came from, especially in the case of Yorubaland, rather than in its Temne, Mende or Limba neighbours. They were to pay a heavy penalty for this gulf dividing them from their neighbours, in the Mende war of 1898, which we shall discuss in a later section of this book.

An assessment of the Creoles

As we have seen, the Creole community was uncertain in its assessment of itself. Sometimes the Creole prided himself on being a black Englishman, sometimes he tried to identify more with his African heritage. In the face of white racism, the community's collective self-confidence was often undermined. Sometimes they sought to compensate for this by emphasising the glories of the African past; not the black African past, about which they, like everyone else, knew little, but the glories of ancient Egypt, or the North African church.

The same wide range of attitudes has persisted into modern times. Most books, including this one, emphasise the achievements of the Creoles, their successful struggle with adversity, their impact on West Africa. They were, in the words of the historian who has contributed most to our knowledge of their history,* 'the intellectual leaders, the vanguard of political and social advance in West Africa'. A recent Nigerian interpretation† is more critical. In this they are called 'Deluded Hybrids', scorned by Nigerian communities for their slave origins.

Most of the criticisms which are made of present-day West African elites can be made with equal justice of the Creoles – that they created a little island of prosperity

---

* C. Fyfe.
† By Professor E. A. Ayandele.

for themselves, without real concern for the condition of the rural masses around them.

However, much of the Creole achievement – the work of their writers, scientists, doctors – is a glowing example of West African accomplishment, before the onset of the long darkness of colonialism. Then, the memory of Creole culture was a constant proof that there is no sphere of human endeavour in which Africans cannot excel. In the nineteenth century, Creoledom had produced its bishops, its doctors, its experimental scientists, even the first historian of Creole achievements (the schoolmaster and amateur artist, A. B. C. Sibthorpe). And for West African Christians, there can scarcely be anything more inspiring than the memory of the Creole missionaries, such as the great and holy Bishop Crowther, of whom an Englishman, who was singularly well placed to judge, wrote, 'that in all my large experience I never met with more missionary wisdom, nor . . . more of the Spirit of Christ . . .'

Liberia

Liberia, Sierra Leone's south-eastern neighbour, has a history which is parallel in many fascinating ways, though the differences are as important as the similarities. Both are of comparable size; the population of Liberia is smaller – under a million – and divided into many ethnic groups. Many, such as the Vai, Mende and Kpelle, belong to the great Mande-speaking family, and have the men's and women's secret societies so characteristic of Sierra Leone. The Vai belong to the small number of sub-Saharan African peoples who invented handwriting.* In the nineteenth century, Islam was

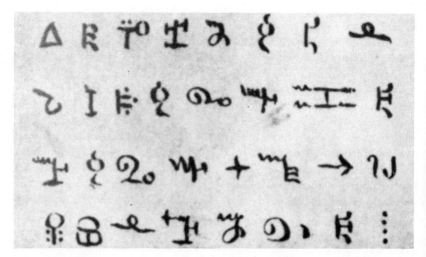

An example of Vai script

* See the account of *nsibidi* at page 112 above. There are other examples, as well.

spreading among the Vai, especially the chiefs, and it was probably in response to the stimulus of this or of European influences that one of their number invented an alphabet, which was systematically taught by the Vai in their own schools. Later, it was partially superseded by the Roman one.

In southern Liberia, a group of peoples including the Grebo, Kru, Bassa and Dey, spoke related languages, belonging to the West Akan family. The Kru played an outstanding role in the economic life of coastal West Africa. Outstandingly brave and skilled sailors, they prided themselves on the fact that they had never been enslaved, and they manoeuvred boats through the dangerous and sometimes shark-infested surf with a confidence which won the admiration of all who saw it. European captains made a practice of stopping at Cape Palmas to take on Kru sailors. Some stayed away from home for many years – there was a Kru settlement in Freetown – and the various 'British' expeditions to the Niger were so heavily dependent on their aid that they could equally well be called 'Kru' expeditions.

One of the Englishmen who relied so heavily on their services wrote this of them:

> They never desert their employers in danger or distress; they are constitutionally brave, and are easily kept in order: they are the life and soul of the trade on the coast; without them the cargoes could not be stowed, nor could boats be manned . . . They are generally tall and well-proportioned, their limbs are muscular, their gait erect and firm. I was informed that they are never taken as slaves, in consequence of the unyielding spirit they have always displayed; and indeed there is a certain air about them which proves that they were born free and will still remain so.

They worked on ships in teams, under their own leader. He was the one they obeyed, and the only one who could flog them.

The Grebo, like the Kru, were passionately eager for western education. Such was their enthusiasm for it, and Christianity, that missionaries originally wanted Liberia College sited among them. In the nineteenth century, they had a long history of disputes with the Settlers, whom they felt excluded them from opportunity, and who they claimed, had cheated them of their land. In 1873 they formed the Grebo Reunited Kingdom which was a strongly Christian body, consciously modelled on the Fante Confederation.

The Settlers
Like Sierra Leone, Liberia was the site for a nineteenth-century settlement of black immigrants. In Liberia, the settlers were blacks* from America. The numbers involved

---

* In the past, the black population of America have usually been called Negroes. This is now unacceptable to those concerned, who prefer 'black'. Afro-American is perhaps the most acceptable word, but it is too cumbersome for constant use. In America, both 'Negro' and 'black' include those of mixed European and African descent. In West Africa, these last are called mulatto, or, in French, métis.

were fairly small, since less than 17,000 ever migrated to Liberia. There was a small body of Recaptives (liberated by the American navy) but these numbered less than 6,000. There was thus the opposite situation to Sierra Leone, where Recaptives outnumbered Settlers.

As in Sierra Leone, the settlement sprang from a number of considerations – the desire of black men for freedom, and the encouragement of humanitarians, who despaired of obtaining justice in America for the black man. But one of the strongest pressure groups behind the American Colonisation Society, which was founded in 1816, to settle American blacks in Africa, consisted of white slave owners. These were unhappy about the substantial free black population in early nineteenth-century America which numbered about 200,000. Its existence made it easier for slaves to escape. More important, the sight of black men earning their own living and regulating their own lives openly contradicted the slave owners' theory that blacks needed coercion to work, and a long period of 'preparation' for liberty. (In fact, of course, the only experience which equips men to live at liberty is to live at liberty, and the tenth generation of blacks in America were no more or less ready for this than the first.)

All slave-owning societies have lived in the shadow of slave revolt. In 1822 a free black American planned a massive slave rising, which was betrayed before it came to fruition. In 1831 a Virginian slave called Nat Turner led a hopeless heroic revolt; only seventy men were involved, but it cast a lasting shadow of terror over the south.

The injustices from which free blacks suffered in America were, moreover, a denial of the principles of the Declaration of Independence, which claimed that it was 'self evident' that 'All men are created equal, that they are endowed by their Creator with certain inalienable rights, that among these are life, liberty, and the pursuit of happiness'. The author of the Declaration of Independence, himself a slave owner, was one of the first to propose that the problem be solved, not by giving blacks equality in America, but by resettling them in an unspecified 'far away place'.

Faced with a choice between fighting for justice in America and emigrating, Afro-Americans have nearly always chosen the first alternative. As we have seen, less than 17,000 out of 200,000 emigrated to Liberia, and many of those were forced to do so, since they were emancipated on that condition. America was the land of their birth, they spoke no African language, and Africa was as remote and unfamiliar as Europe to white Americans. Since they had long since lost their immunity to West African diseases, they had a well-grounded fear of its sickness and mortality rates. Black Americans, like white, wrote about 'the savage wilds of Africa'.

Both the Settlers and their American supporters hoped that Liberia would be a centre for the spread of Christianity and western culture. This was the same hope which lay behind the Sierra Leone experiment. Like the Freetown Settlers, they were ardent Christians, mainly Methodists or Episcopalians. Whites assumed that because the immigrants and the people of the area had the same complexion, they would easily identify with each other. But the Liberians saw themselves, not as returning Africans, but as exiled Americans. Fleeing from oppression, they still identified with the culture of the oppressors. This is clearly and poignantly reflected in the words of the free blacks of Baltimore, in 1826:

> Though, under the shield of your laws we are partially protected, not totally oppressed, nevertheless our situation will and must inevitably have the effect of crushing, not developing, the capacities God has given us . . .
>
> We shall carry your language, your customs, your opinions, and Christianity to that now desolate shore, and thence they will gradually spread, with our growth, far into the continent.

The establishment of the settlement

After an unsuccessful attempt to settle in the Sherbro, the representatives of the American Colonisation Society bought land at Cape Mesurado, forcing the local ruler to sell at gunpoint. The settlers formally took possession of the area in 1822. The new state was called Liberia, and the capital, which it was originally intended to call Christopolis, was finally named Monrovia after the American President of the day (Monroe). Paul Cuffee, who might well have led the new settlement, died shortly before it was founded. He was an American Quaker merchant and shipowner, one of the outstanding humanitarians of his time, who had previously settled some people in Sierra Leone at his own expense. His father was black and his mother an Indian. As it turned out, the leading role in the 1820s was taken by Jehudi Ashmun, a white American pastor, who paid for his devotion to Liberia with his own life and that of his wife.

The first site was paid for with 300 dollars worth of trade goods, and defended soon afterwards by force from the sellers. From Monrovia, the colonists extended further inland, signing treaties which were often not fully understood by the local people. The price, to be paid in miscellaneous trade goods, was often not paid in full. Perhaps the black settlers of Monrovia were not very different from white settler communities elsewhere in Africa.

In the 1830s, after Nat Turner's revolt, American slave owners became enthusiastic about black emigration. Often slaves were freed specifically for this purpose. A whole chain of settlements developed along the coast. With unconscious irony, they echoed the names of the societies whose oppression they had fled – Maryland, New Georgia . . . In 1837 all but one amalgamated to form the Commonwealth of Liberia. The remaining state, Maryland, joined Liberia in 1856.

The new state moved rapidly towards political independence. Initially it was ruled by the American Colonisation Society, a private body which welcomed the prospect of independence since this would release them from a heavy responsibility. Liberia was not an American colony, nor could it well become one, since it was less than a hundred years since the Americans had fought their own war against colonial status. Until she became an internationally recognised state, it was difficult for Liberia to finance her own government. Where there was little cash available for direct taxation, customs duties were the obvious source of revenue, but European merchants were reluctant to pay these, and used Liberia's irregular legal status as an excuse.

Celebrations in Liberia of ninety years of independence

In 1841 Joseph Jenkins Roberts became the first Afro-American governor of Liberia. In 1847 Liberia became an independent republic, with the motto, 'The Love of Liberty brought us here'. It should be noted, however, that although the motto reflects the settlers' enduring love of freedom, it explicitly excludes the indigenous people of the area. Liberia's government was closely modelled on that of America, with a Declaration of Independence and a written constitution.

Britain recognised the new state in 1848; the United States delayed recognition until 1862, apparently out of reluctance to receive a black ambassador in Washington.

Liberia's Crest

In its early years, especially, Liberia attracted some individuals of outstanding talents. Lott Cary, a Baptist preacher, played a leading role in the settlement until his accidental death in 1829. Unlike many of his fellow immigrants, he felt a deep concern for the welfare of the local people. He set up a school over a hundred kilometres in the interior, paying its teacher, for a time, from his own pocket.

John B. Russwurm had been one of the first black American college graduates, and co-founder of the first black American newspaper. From 1836 until his death in 1851, he was an outstandingly successful Governor of Maryland. He was the first black Governor of an African colony.

One of the most famous Liberians, Edward Wilmot Blyden (1832–1912), was born in St Thomas, in the West Indies, and migrated to Liberia in 1851, having been refused admission to three American colleges. He was a self-taught intellectual of great learning, who mastered many languages, including Hebrew and Arabic. He stressed the greatness both of the African past and of the black man's contribution to the development of the New World: 'the commercial and agricultural history of nearly the whole of the Americas is the history of the negro.' He held a number of important positions. He was Professor, and then President, of Liberia College, he was Minister of the Interior and Secretary of State, and represented his country as ambassador.

But he achieved much less than his great gifts would have led one to expect. On several occasions he was forced to flee from his adopted country. Tragically, his experience of racial discrimination turned him into a racist, and much of his energy was wasted on a pointless hatred of mulattoes, whom he tried to keep out of Liberia. He infected the Colonisation Society with his views, so that prospective immigrants were asked if they were dark or light coloured, and the Society was duly puzzled when they answered 'Ginger'! Like many brilliant men, he lacked the tenacity and robust sense of reality which have often enabled those less gifted to achieve greater things.

Benjamin Anderson was an outstanding black explorer who made important journeys to the Liberian interior in 1868 and 1874. His books describing them are among the classics of West African exploration.

Political history

Most historians interpret the mid-nineteenth century history of Liberia in racial terms, concentrating on the conflict between mulattoes and black settlers. The mulattoes tended to form a wealthy self-sufficient elite. Their feeling of unity was strengthened by the fact that they tended to be Freemasons, and either Methodists or Episcopalians. Each political party came to be dominated by one of the two racial groups. The Republican party, which ruled Liberia, with one brief interlude, from 1847–78, was dominated by the mulattoes. Roberts himself was so fair-complexioned that he looked much like a European.

If this is a true analysis of Liberian politics it is indeed a tragedy that a society which had been established explicitly as a protest against racial discrimination began at once to build it up again within its own boundaries. But it is possible that the element of racial antagonism has been exaggerated, and that later historians have seen events too much through Blyden's eyes. Roberts was succeeded by a black President – Stephen Benson – and there is no trace of black-mulatto antagonism in present-day Liberia.

In 1869 the Republican monopoly of office was broken, and their opponents, the True Whigs, won the election, under the leadership of Edward James Roye.

Roye was a black man of outstanding abilities. He was an American college graduate, and a wealthy trader and shipowner. He realised that the development of his country was being stifled by lack of capital, and planned to raise money abroad, to invest in education, financial reconstruction, and a railway. But the only loan he was able to negotiate, which was with Britain, was on disastrously unfavourable terms. Of the £100,000 loaned, £30,000 was kept by the lenders, as discount and advance interest! Nothing constructive was done with the money that remained, and the loan, instead of making rapid development possible, tied a millstone of debt round the country's neck. These financial disasters played into the hand of Roye's political enemies. In 1871 he was violently deposed in the only successful coup in Liberian history, and he was drowned while trying to swim to safety. He was accused of embezzlement, and of aiming at dictatorship. It is difficult to know the truth of the matter. The whole episode – a loan on unfavourable terms, charges of corruption, a coup – anticipates with astonishing precision much West African political history in the 1960s.

The Republicans returned briefly to office, but in 1878 the True Whigs came to power and have kept it ever since.

This long period of one party rule, has, of course, exposed Liberia to a great deal of foreign criticism. A number of points can be made in her defence. There is no mention of parties in the Liberian, or American, constitutions, and the founding fathers of American democracy, like George Washington, had a poor view of them. Some commentators compare Liberian 'stability' favourably with nineteenth century Latin America's constant series of coups and wars. Nearer home, one is now less likely to criticise the Liberian experience in a West Africa where effective two party government has almost entirely vanished.

A more fundamental criticism of Liberian government, last century and this, is that the Americo-Liberians formed a prosperous closed corporation, dividing the spoils of office among themselves. Much of the state income went on salaries (this has been equally true of many independent West African states in recent years). The Americo-Liberians had a very long history of tension with the indigenous peoples, who felt that they were excluded from adequate educational opportunities, and that even if they were educated, they were excluded from employment. In the nineteenth century, the Americo-Liberians had a series of disputes with local peoples, which sometimes reached the point of war. In 1875 the Grebo Reunited Kingdom fought a successful war in which Liberia was saved only by American intervention. In 1915 the Kru declared war on Liberia, preferring British rule, and asking, in vain, for British assistance: 'We can stand them if we have ammunition'. A few local people were granted citizenship but the conditions for this status were very difficult to fulfil. It was not until after the Second World War that the franchise became general, and it was not until 1952 that it was exercised. The long Presidency of William Tubman (1944–71) saw a deliberate effort to tackle the grievances of the local people, and there is now an increasing tendency for the two groups to work together and intermarry. In 1950, however, the attempt of the Kru, Didwo Tweh, to become President was a failure. Most observers still see Americo-Liberian society as an island of privilege, far removed from the sea of rural poverty around it. In the words of one commentator in the 1960s:*

> Tubman's claims to guide democracy in Liberia are mocked by the still profound backwardness of the indigenous peoples, the great gulf between them and the dominant Americo-Liberian class in Monrovia, and the monopoly of politics by his True Whig Party. His famous yacht . . . cannot dazzle the labourers in the rubber plantations who earn the equivalent, in cash and subsidised rice, of two or three shillings a day . . .

Economic history

As in other countries, the various aspects of Liberian history are very closely linked with the changing fortunes of her economy. Political independence, territorial integrity, educational and development projects, or the lack of them, all rest on an economic base. Until perhaps 1870, the Americo-Liberians prospered; later generations looked back wistfully to the mid-nineteenth century as to a golden age, comparable, in many respects, with the great days of Creoledom in Sierra Leone, though the Liberians tended to concentrate on business, rather than the professions. Liberians such as Roberts and Roye were wealthy merchants. Liberia exported the finest coffee in the world, as well as palm products, camwood, ivory and piassava (raphia palm fibre). A number of Liberian shipowners exported the country's products in their own vessels.

The golden age soon ended. Liberian shipowners found they could not compete effectively with European lines. This meant that the whole economy became heavily dependent on foreign shipping. British steamers stopped calling at Monrovia in 1858, and trans-Atlantic shipping was irregular. Camwood exports were ruined when the Germans invented synthetic dyes. Liberian sugar could not compete successfully with European sugar beet and American sugar cane. Worst of all, Liberia lost her leading position as a coffee producer. In 1876 the Liberians sent coffee specimens to a Trade Fair held in America to celebrate the anniversary of the Declaration of Independence. Brazil acquired these varieties, and became the world's leading coffee producer.

Liberia still had some saleable exports, such as palm products, but in the late nineteenth century England and France preferred to buy these from their own colonies where they had secured political control and could secure favourable terms of trade. America might well have traded with Liberia, but South America was a much larger and closer source of tropical products. This left Germany, whose tropical possessions

* Ronald Segal.

were too few to supply her industries with the products they required. In the years before the First World War, the Liberian economy was dominated by trade with Germany, but her income was still grossly inadequate for her needs.

This lack of income had a damaging effect on many areas of Liberian life. It was impossible to finance an adequate system of education and this of course increased the dissatisfaction of the local people. Liberia College, founded in 1862, the second institution of higher learning in West Africa, aroused high hopes which it never fulfilled. It was closed for long periods of time, the staff appointments were politically determined, and between 1877 and 1900 it produced no graduates at all. Motor roads and harbour construction waited till the 1940s. The railway of which Roye had dreamed was not built until the 1950s. Poverty thus proved a vicious circle, for capital is required to build roads and railways, and without means of transport, the economy cannot develop, since products cannot be sold outside the area in which they are grown.

Because Liberia was poor, she could not maintain adequate embassies abroad. Most of her diplomatic representatives were wealthy whites who did the work for nothing, because they enjoyed diplomatic life. More seriously, her lack of resources made it impossible for her to establish effective government in her own hinterland but by the 1880s 'effective occupation' was necessary to justify all territorial claims. Liberia was unable to prevent her neighbours taking large slices of her territory. Sierra Leone took eighty kilometres of coastline with its economically valuable hinterland. France adjusted the northern frontier in her own interests so that large areas of the Nimba mountains, one of the world's best sources of iron ore, became part of Guinea. France similarly took much territory on her eastern frontier, so that much of the former Maryland became part of Ivory Coast. Again, there was a vicious circle. Liberia's

Liberia College

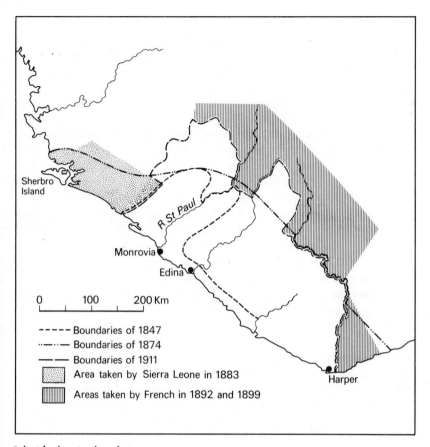

Liberia's changing boundaries

weakness and poverty made her unable to maintain her territorial integrity. The shrinking of her boundaries robbed her of part of her economic resources and made her weaker and poorer.

As the state of the Liberian economy worsened, the settler community came to rely increasingly on government employment, and a disproportionately large part of Liberia's small income went on salaries. To some extent, this was inevitable. The smaller a state's income, the larger the proportion which is consumed by administration, just as the smaller the individual's income, the larger the proportion which is spent on food. But more fundamentally, the elite, just as in many modern African states, was consuming too large a slice of the national cake. This left little surplus for development, which alone might make the cake larger. In the 1920s, Liberia's income was twenty-one per cent of that of her comparably sized neighbour, Sierra Leone. Ninety per cent of it went on salaries.

Like many modern developing nations, Liberia tried to supplement her inadequate income with foreign loans. The results were often disastrous, since the money was lent on terms which took advantage of Liberia's weak economic position, and on conditions which undermined her sovereignty. The Roye loan was only the first of its kind. In 1906 a famous Englishman arranged another loan for Liberia, of $500,000. Part went to repay the Roye loan, but much of it went into a company he established, supposedly for the development of Liberia's resources. No accounts were presented, and there was no development to show for it, but in the process the company acquired control of Liberia's customs revenue. In 1912 a loan from the U.S.A. was negotiated to repay the British loan – again, in return for the control of her customs revenue.

In 1914 war broke out in Europe, and all colonised Africa was brought into a conflict which was not its own (see pages 258–9). Liberia's President realised with great clarity that his country's real war was with poverty, and tried at first to stay neutral. But real neutrality proved impracticable; Liberia's French and British ruled neighbours cut her off from the German shipping on which her economy depended. In 1917 Liberia entered the war. This meant a German bombardment, but it earned Liberia one great benefit, since she was able to send a representative to the Peace Conference, and thus averted the danger of probable partition. But nevertheless, deeply in debt and with her sovereignty gravely endangered, Liberia seemed almost to have reached the end of the road.

Firestone in Liberia

In 1926 came a major turning point when the American tyre-producing company, Firestone, moved into Liberia on a very large scale because of the increasingly high cost of Asian rubber. The Liberians gave Firestone a ninety-nine year lease on over 400,000 hectares of land for rubber plantations. By 1950 rubber formed 90 per cent of Liberian exports, though more recently her exports have diversified and iron has become increasingly important as well.

Opinions vary about the significance of Firestone's arrival in Liberia. On the one hand it is ironical that what was then the only independent state in West Africa was the only one to make an agreement which alienated much of her land and brought in a plantation economy. Many observers have described Liberia's situation since then as neo-colonial, meaning that the formal political control of a foreign nation has been replaced by the vast informal economic power of a private corporation. On the other hand, Liberia was rescued from bankruptcy and preserved her political sovereignty. Belatedly, the money was now available for the building of roads and railways. The economy was helped greatly when in 1945–8 the U.S.A. built a modern harbour at Monrovia for strategic purposes.

The whole history of Liberia is equally controversial. Most observers emphasise the gap between the settler elite and the indigenous masses, though this has been shrinking in recent years. They have said that the Americo-Liberians are very much like a white settler community, and have condemned them for diverting so much of Liberia's national income into the pockets of wealthy settler clans. The history of Liberia is

Rubber being processed in modern Liberia

particularly poignant, because for so long Liberia and Haiti were the only free black Republics in the world. African nationalists looked to their experience with the greatest anxiety and the Nigerian political leader, Azikiwe, wrote a substantial study of Liberia.

Liberia undoubtedly had her weaknesses but like the problems of Haiti they were rooted not in any black political incapacity, but in particular circumstances. The chief of these was poverty. Liberia had to search for a long time for a viable export commodity and this made it difficult for her to maintain true independence in a colonial world. Nevertheless, in an age when black Americans were oppressed and nearly all Africans ruled by foreign masters, the Liberians created a state where a black man could live free from foreign domination. The Liberians have never lost their passion for freedom which is incorporated in their national motto. A man born in America put it simply, when he said, 'I have never been happy until I made Liberia my home'.

The Egba United Board of Management

One of the most interesting strands in nineteenth-century West African history concerns the various attempts made to establish or modify states on western political lines. We have already noted two instances of this – the Fante Confederation and the Grebo Reunited Kingdom (see pages 68 and 137).

Another fascinating experiment in westernisation was the Egba United Board of Management, which was established in Abeokuta in 1865, partly in order to deal with the newly-established colony of Lagos on its own terms. The Bashorun became the President-General and the Seriki the High Sheriff. Interestingly enough, the man behind the experiment was somebody who himself had fairly little western education. He was the Sierra-Leone born G. W. Johnson, a tailor by trade. The Abeokuta experiment was partly a reaction against white racism and a fear of colonial encroachment. A Sierra Leonian said at Abeokuta in 1865, 'For we come to find, that the more a Black man is enlightened in Africa, the better his opposition, and hatred by a White man'.

The Board of Management was particularly interesting for the very modern way in which it made a distinction between western technical achievements and Christianity, considering, in the words of a missionary, 'civilisation . . . a thing by itself, and able to stand without Christ'. They set up a postal service to Lagos and a school and tried to improve hygienic conditions in the town, and to establish a court to settle trade disputes. A white missionary said,

> These Sierra Leone men are . . . forcing on civilisation and English custom, teaching the people the use of writing and printing and bringing about the adoption of written laws. They are doing what we cannot . . .

Interestingly enough, Bishop Crowther condemned them for their rejection of European missionary influence.

In the years that followed, Johnson's influence in Abeokuta diminished, even though he renounced his British citizenship and adopted an Egba name. He spent long periods of time away from the city and his involvement in its internal political disputes made him unacceptable to many. In 1895 he was expelled from Abeokuta at the request of the Governor of Lagos, dying in Lagos four years afterwards.

5

Patterns of External Change

The decline of the slave trade

In 1807 Britain abolished her own slave trade. Denmark had abolished her slave trade earlier and the United States did likewise in 1808, as did Sweden and the Netherlands soon afterwards. But Britain's abolition was by far the most important, for she had dominated the eighteenth century slave trade and now took an active part in suppressing the slave trade of other nations. This took several forms. She exercised diplomatic pressure on slave-trading powers to sign anti-slave trading conventions and stationed a squadron off the coast of West Africa to intercept slavers. At first, ships could only be seized when they actually had slaves on board. Later, evidence that they intended to transport slaves was sufficient to convict them.

Since a number of states signed anti-slaving agreements unwillingly, they often did not enforce them and many slave ships managed to elude the squadron's vigilance. Therefore it would be quite wrong to think that the slave trade came to an end in 1807, and in fact the first half of the nineteenth century was a period when the slave trade continued to flourish. According to the most recent estimate, 1,898,400 slaves were imported into the Americas between 1811 and 1870. Perhaps a fifth again of this number died during the hardships of the Middle Passage. It is likely then that during this period 2,278,000 slaves left Africa, which, in round figures, is over $2\frac{1}{4}$ million. Sixty per cent of these went to Brazil and most of the rest to Cuba.

To the historian of Africa, however, it is less important to know their destinations than their areas of origin. There are various ways of determining this – one of the best is by analysing the origins of the Recaptives in Freetown.* The map shows the picture which results.

The vast majority of the slaves came from the area between southern Dahomey and the Niger Delta. A very large number were Yoruba. Scarcely any Yoruba had been enslaved before 1800 but now the victims of the Yoruba Civil Wars of the nineteenth

* The main disadvantage is that Africans enslaved in southern and central Africa are under-represented.

century made them the largest single ethnic group in Freetown. The second largest were the Igbo. The large number of Hausa and Nupe reflects the wars and slave raids of the Sokoto Caliphate.

The slave trade came to an end at different times in different places. In the Niger Delta the time of real decline was the 1830s, though the last recorded slaver left in 1854. Lagos had a relatively brief career as a slave trade port, beginning in the late eighteenth century, increasing in importance after 1810 and coming to an abrupt end in 1851 when a British Consul was posted there. When the British were established at Lagos, they were able to maintain a closer blockade of Porto Novo, Badagry and Whydah, where the slave trade shrank to a trickle in the 1850s. Paradoxically, the slave trade lingered longer on the margins of the Province of Freedom, on the borders of Sierra Leone and Liberia and in those rivers such as the Rio Nunez and Rio Pongas which the French called the Rivers of the South and the British the Northern Rivers, and which are now part of Guinea Conakry. Here in these areas of tangled waterways and swamp, slavers were able to conceal themselves and carry out their business, despite the nearness of the naval squadron at Freetown. In the 1840s the British navy attacked the slaving establishments on shore in the southern area, Gallinas.

In 1850 Gallinas signed an anti-slave trade treaty. In the Northern Rivers the slave trade lingered on into the 1860s and the very last slave ship to be captured, in 1864, was taken in the Northern Rivers. In the end the main factor which brought the slave trade to an end was the loss of the overseas market as both Brazil and Cuba, largely as a result of foreign pressure, put an end to importing slaves.

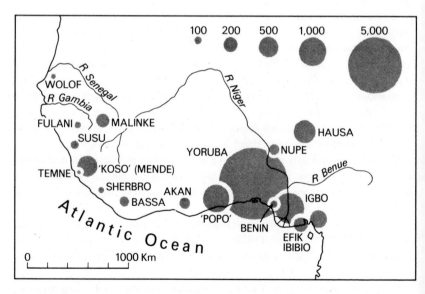

Origins of West Africans enslaved in nineteenth century (After Curtin)

The British navy attacks slaving establishments in the Gallinas

The growth of legitimate trade

Historians usually refer to the various forms of trade which gradually took the place of the slave trade as 'legitimate' trade. It is important to realise that for the first half of the nineteenth century, the two often co-existed. Calabar began exporting palm oil in the late eighteenth century and in the first three decades of the nineteenth century, the Niger Delta exported slaves and palm oil simultaneously.

The most important export commodity in the nineteenth century was vegetable oils. By far the most important of these was palm oil, which was produced along most of the West African coast but supplied most abundantly by the ports of the Niger Delta. Palm oil was used in Europe primarily for making soap. Before the commercial exploitation of petroleum began in 1850, palm oil was used as lubricant (especially on the railways). It was also used in the manufacture of candles, which were later replaced by kerosene lamps.

West Africans had been processing palm oil for centuries, for local use. Since there was no shortage of palm trees, since extraction required no elaborate equipment and since the oil could be sold in small or large quantities, some historians have thought that it was easier for ordinary individuals to take part in than the slave trade. They say that palm oil could be produced by large numbers of peasant families, whereas the profits of the slave trade tended to go mainly to the ruling class. The rulers' military resources were an advantage in rounding up slaves, but no one could round up palm trees! They point out, too, that by the nineteenth century European exports to West Africa had become much cheaper as a result of the Industrial Revolution and were thus more readily available to the average man.

But this theory that the palm-oil trade was essentially democratic is only partly true. Palm-oil production was very laborious and sometimes dangerous, but brought very small returns to the individual involved. The real profits were made by those responsible for bulking and transport, and this lay in the hands of a class of wealthy merchant princes employing slave labour. The importance of the Niger Delta was due only partly to the abundance of palm trees in its hinterland. It was due mainly to the many navigable waterways such as the Niger, the lower Imo river, the lower Kwa Ibo river and the Niger's many tributaries, which enabled the oil to be readily transported. The actual work of buying the oil and paddling the canoes was done by slaves called pullaboys, and a German doctor who visited Bonny in 1840 has left a vivid picture of their pathetic attempts to build up a little capital by selling bits of fruit. Dahomey had only one navigable waterway, and in some cases her slaves rolled the oil in barrels 140 kilometres to the sea.

In the nineteenth century slaves were increasingly used in agriculture as well as in the palm-oil trade. States such as Calabar or Ibadan were surrounded by slave plantations, just like the cities of the western Sudan. After the Atlantic slave trade came to an end, slaves were still purchased in Sierra Leone and sold in Guinea, where they worked on groundnut farms. Too often, an economy in which the slave was exported, was replaced by an economy in which the slave was employed in farming, or in collecting and transporting agricultural products.

But if the palm-oil trade was not democratic, it still represented a triumph of African organising power and ingenuity in the face of a major technical challenge. Previously only small quantities of palm oil had been processed, for food and locally-made soap. Now, suddenly, the amount expanded enormously. In 1810 a thousand tonnes of palm oil were exported to England. By 1855 this had risen to forty thousand tonnes. To respond so quickly and efficiently to this challenge, with all that it implied in credit and finance arrangements, and in the provision of transport, was a major achievement. At first the palm kernels were discarded because the Europeans had no use for them. They were first exported from Sierra Leone in 1841, their export pioneered, as we have seen, by the mulatto, Heddle. The trade became really important in the 1870s. The Germans discovered how to process the fine oil that they contained for making margarine, and the residue was used for cattle food.

Another important source of vegetable oils, which developed later than the palm-oil trade, was the growing groundnut industry in the Senegambia. Here again the people were familiar with the crop, since an indigenous variety of groundnut existed, but to produce them in commercial quantities for export, as they did from the 1840s on, meant a major adaptation. By the late 1880s, the Senegambia was exporting an average of 29,000 tonnes a year.

The export of these bulky products was greatly facilitated by a revolution in ocean transport which occurred in the second half of the nineteenth century. This was the changeover from sailing ships to steamships.

Historians have sometimes written as if the trade in vegetable oils was conveniently supplied by Providence to replace the slave trade and give African communities an alternative source of foreign exchange. But in fact, of course, not all areas which were involved in the slave trade were able to make the transition to legitimate trade. Slaves were self-transporting, and could be obtained anywhere where men lived. Participation in legitimate trade depended upon the existence of a suitable local export crop and above all on nearness to the sea or navigable rivers. Some parts of West Africa were plunged into a desperate search for a suitable export commodity. We have already seen the difficulties which Liberia experienced in this regard. On the Gold Coast the supply of gold remained static and it was not until the introduction of cocoa and its widespread cultivation, beginning in the 1880s, that an adequate export crop was available. In Senegal the gum trade declined in the late nineteenth century, as a result of rival supplies of gum from Egypt and, more important, because of the development of chemical substitutes. Timber was an export commodity which tended to be quickly exhausted, as happened with the forests of Sierra Leone. In the late nineteenth century there was a brief boom in wild rubber, but it could not compete with Asian plantation rubber and inexpert tapping tended to destroy the trees. Cotton was a commodity for which there was a great demand but only a limited supply for export, in the nineteenth century. The map below shows the areas of export crops.

It is easy to exaggerate the importance of the Atlantic export trade, however, both to Europe and West Africa. Only a very small sector of the African economy was involved in it, and some important branches of long-distance trade, such as the trade in kola nuts, were purely internal. West Africa provided less than one per cent of Europe's foreign trade, since it was only one of many sources of oils. This proved to her disadvantage, as it meant that she had little control over prices. For example, palm-

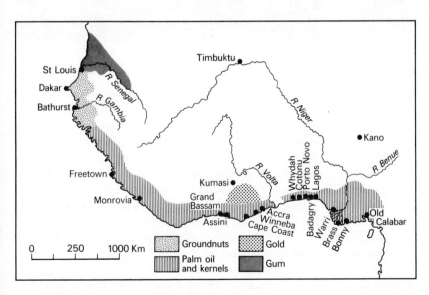

The Atlantic export economy in the nineteenth century

A gin label, showing the commodities of West African trade

oil prices sank in the late nineteenth century as a result of competition from mineral oils and oil extracted from Indian groundnuts and Australian tallow.

To understand the importance of external trade to those communities involved in it, we must ask ourselves, of course, not only what was exported but what was imported. Textiles were the most important import, followed by spirits, guns and gunpowder. With the exception of spirits, tobacco and firearms, these imports were of real value to West African consumers but they were, nevertheless, goods which were soon used up or worn out and added nothing to the productive power of the economy. A number of West African rulers realised this and asked instead for western education, industrial plant and various forms of industrial training, but such requests often, though not always, went unanswered.

For much of the nineteenth century, the trans-Saharan trade continued to flourish. It could not compete, however, in the export of commodities such as palm oil or groundnuts, which were very bulky. In 1875 its value was one-fifth of that of the seaborne trade. After that year a serious decline set in and it had almost ceased to exist by 1900.

The Christian missionary presence

It is one of the puzzles of history that the command 'Go ye and teach all nations' has been seen at some times, by some Christian groups, as a most urgent and compelling duty, whereas at others it has been neglected. As we have seen, Christianity made practically no headway in West Africa between the fifteenth and eighteenth centuries. But in the nineteenth century the nature of the Christian presence in West Africa was totally changed, essentially as a result of changing attitudes in Europe.

In the late eighteenth century, there was a great movement among English Protestants called the Evangelical revival. Evangelicals had an overriding sense of the importance of eternity, which tended to make them active in good works. As we have seen they led the crusade against the slave trade. Evangelicals stressed that man is saved by faith which made the work of converting non-Christians seem extremely urgent, though it tended to produce a low and condescending view of non-Christian cultures. In the words of an Evangelical hymn:

> The heathen are foolish and brutish and blind,
> They are mortals in body but demons in mind,
> Yet their souls we must seek though their sins be abhorred
> For our labour shall not be in vain in the Lord.

The concern for foreign missions led to the establishment of a number of missionary organisations. Two important ones in West Africa were the Church Missionary Society (founded and run by Evangelical Anglicans), established in 1799, and the Wesleyan Missionary Society. Both of these were soon at work among the Settlers and Recaptives of Freetown, and Creole Christians, sometimes professional missionaries, sometimes not, soon carried their teachings the length of the West African coastline.

The Catholic missionary revival began perhaps half a century later. It led to the formation of a large number of fairly small missionary congregations, often with only several hundred members each. Whereas the Protestant societies included both clergy and laymen, and a large number of lay supporters at home, the Catholic congregations consisted only of priests, nuns, or brothers. Funds were collected by a number of separate organisations, which pooled small amounts from large numbers of humble contributors. The most important of these was the society called the Work of the Propagation of the Faith.

The Catholic congregations which had the greatest impact on West Africa were the Society of African Missions, and the Congregation of the Holy Spirit. The latter grew out of a congregation founded in France in 1844 by a converted Jew, Father Libermann. In 1848 it joined an older body, taking the name the Congregation of the Holy Spirit. The Society of African Missions was founded in 1858 by Bishop Melchior de Marion Bresillac, a French aristocrat who had previously worked in India.

The Catholics had much the same view of non-Christians as the Evangelicals. In fact, they had a great deal in common, though they did not recognise this, and each looked on the other as gravely misguided. The founder of the Holy Ghost Fathers' mission to the Lower Niger wrote to his nephew: 'All those who go to Africa as missionaries must be thoroughly penetrated with the thought that the Dark Continent is a cursed land, almost entirely in the power of the devil'.

However absurd this attitude, it was, in a sense, what made the sacrifices of the missionary life possible. Nineteenth-century missionaries to West Africa looked forward to the likelihood of sickness and death. In one missionary congregation the average length of life in West Africa, for a time, was two years ten months. Of a party of ten first sent out by Father Libermann, six died and two were invalided home. Fifteen years later the first party of four missionaries of the Society of African Missions, including the founder, died almost as soon as they reached West Africa. In West Africa there are many quiet mission graveyards, both Protestant and Catholic, the last resting place of men and women who died in their late twenties or early thirties. Strangely, too, the nineteenth-century missionary, for all his views about the heathen, often mastered African languages and customs better, and shared village life more fully, than his modern counterpart.

Sometimes the individual foreign missionary was unable to translate the high ideals which brought him to Africa into day-to-day practice. Many were high-handed and authoritarian with their converts, and exacted work from them, much in the fashion of forced labour for colonial governments. For some, the strains of an unfamiliar environment, and culture shock, were too great. Thus of the first little band of Catholic missionaries at Lokoja, in the 1880s, it was said of one, 'He likes neither Africans, nor what pertains to them', and of another, 'for him, it is necessary that the Africans speak French'. Finally, the leader of the mission, in discouragement, went back to Europe, and the post was given up.

Some, on the other hand, gave years of devoted service to Africa. Father Coquard worked in Abeokuta from 1890 until his death in 1931; although he had not studied medicine formally, he specialised in the care of the sick. Father Piotin, who worked among the Afenmai of mid-west Nigeria in the early years of this century, gave all his small income to his parishoners and lived on pieces of yam. Father Burr worked in another part of mid-west Nigeria from 1907 until his death in 1951. In all that time, he only went on leave once. He grew his own food, including coffee beans, and went by cycle round his far-flung parish, even when motor cars were in general use. At the age of seventy, cycling from a funeral in another town some kilometres away, he was run over by a car, and died.

So far we have looked at a few of the European missionaries. But perhaps the most important fact about mission work in nineteenth-century West Africa was the extent to which it was spread by Africans. One of the most famous chapters in the spread of Christianity in Africa was the Niger Mission, established in 1857 by the Church Missionary Society. This was staffed entirely by black Sierra Leonians, under a black Bishop, the saintly Samuel Ajayi Crowther. For years they worked patiently on the

A chapel built by Delta slaves

banks of the Niger and in the Delta. Their greatest success was in the Delta, especially among the slaves of Bonny. Like the early Christians, they carried the Christian message as they went about their daily work, and as they went to the palm-oil markets in the interior. There they built little churches; above is a sketch of one of them.

One Bonny Christian, Joshua Hart, met a martyr's death in 1875. The Niger Mission was alight with promise, and was the pride and joy of the parent missionary society. But in the late 1870s the sky darkened. The Niger Mission was subjected to a rising torrent of white criticism, and ultimately a white take-over, which was completed in 1891 when Bishop Crowther died, and was replaced by a European. Some of the criticisms were justified, since no mission is perfect, but those who had destroyed it realised too late that it is harder to build than to destroy. The training institute for local youths was sold at a bargain price to the Royal Niger Company, for use as an army barracks! The European critics soon died or left the mission, and by 1896, their sole survivor recognised, too late, the errors of the past.

> I greatly long to see an African Diocese formed . . . May God forgive us the bitter slanderous and lying thoughts we had . . . in those dark days of 1890 . . . We condemned others, and we ourselves have done less than they did.

African agency was equally important outside the ranks of the C.M.S. A Ghanaian historian* has written the history of the African role in the spread of Methodism among the Fante. The mulatto, Thomas Birch Freeman, was one of the fathers of Gold Coast Methodism, and the pioneer of the modern phase of missionary work in Nigeria as well. The Presbyterian mission established at Calabar in 1846 was partly staffed with black West Indians. The Catholics had far fewer black clergy than the

---

* F. L. Bartels.

Protestants, though there were a few striking examples, such as Father P. D. Boilat, a Wolof who wrote a multi-volume study of Senegal, and the black clergy of San Thomé, who worked in some parts of West Africa, such as Whydah. A British observer cited these last as examples of 'the extraordinary capacity of the African mind' – 'these sable fathers assist materially towards the great object, the civilisation of Africa'. Perhaps the most remarkable African Catholic missionary, however, was a layman, Antonio. Antonio had been enslaved, and had ended up working for Carmelites in Brazil, becoming a devout Christian. When freed, he had no desire to return to Africa. But when he learnt that there was a flock of Catholic 'Brazilians' in Lagos, without a pastor, he went there and led the little congregation until Catholic priests came, when he became a 'humble auxiliary' until his death, at eighty.

Impact of the missions

But the impact of Christian missions was still very limited in the nineteenth century. They were most successful in the Colony of Sierra Leone, where the Recaptives, abruptly torn from their traditional cultures, were most responsive to their teachings. Elsewhere, even in states such as Bonny, where the missions were most successful, many remained attached to their traditional religion. In the words of one disillusioned missionary, in an old mission area, 'In a small district we perhaps touch one per cent of the people . . .' And the majority of West African communities remained quite untouched by mission influence.

We have a number of interesting descriptions of the encounter between missionaries and traditionalists. When warned of the dangers of hell fire (very real to both nineteenth-century Catholics and Evangelicals), the people of Whydah and of eastern Nigeria, in different centuries, made much the same reply: 'We are not better than our ancestors, and shall comfort ourselves with them'. Traditionalists often claimed that each people had its own form of religion, suited to its own circumstances. In the words of Glele of Dahomey, 'White people have their customs and black have theirs'. It was said of another traditional ruler elsewhere, 'He regarded all religions as equally true'.

A handful of West Africans who visited Europe realised with a shock that the religious earnestness of the missionaries was not typical of Europe as a whole, and that many Europeans were indifferent or even hostile to religion. (This was also true of many white traders and officials in Africa.) A Bonnyman, returning from England, held Sunday meeting at the same time as the missionaries, telling the young men that 'In England they do not believe that there is God!' Muslims who engaged in debate with Christians often found that the technological knowledge of the latter was counter-balanced by their theological ignorance. An English explorer recorded an encounter with Muhammad Bello of Sokoto:

> He continued to ask several other theological questions until I was obliged to confess myself not sufficiently versed in religious subtleties to resolve these knotty points, having always left that task to others more learned than myself.

European exploration

In the late eighteenth century Europeans had been trading on the West African coast for centuries but they were almost unbelievably ignorant about the interior, although they had visited a few points such as Benin which were not too far from the coast. The first half of the nineteenth century was to see a number of major journeys of exploration which entirely transformed Europeans' knowledge of West Africa.

Many historians nowadays object to the words 'exploration' and 'discovery'. They point out that West Africa had been explored long before, by West Africans, and that it is absurd to talk about the discovery, for instance, of the sources of the Gambia which Africans knew perfectly well already. Nevertheless, the expansion of European knowledge of Africa was an important strand in its history and was in particular an indispensable prelude to its conquest. Most of the exploring journeys made in West Africa, however, before the 1850s were inspired not by imperialist aims but by a disinterested spirit of scientific curiosity. They were supported moreover by missionary bodies, humanitarians and opponents of the slave trade, who hoped that exploration would open up new mission fields and reveal new forms of trade to undermine the export of slaves.

In 1788 the African Association was founded by a group of leading British scientists. They resolved to concentrate on the problem of the course of the Niger, since the map of inland Africa was 'but a wide extended blank, on which the Geographer . . . has traced, with a hesitating hand, a few names of unexplored rivers and of uncertain nations'. Nothing reflects Europeans' ignorance of Africa better than the fact that they did not know that the Niger Delta, where they had traded for centuries, was the termination of the great river. Some people thought the Niger was linked with the Gambia, some with the Congo, and some with the Nile. Others thought that it flowed into the Great Sink of Africa (which did not of course exist).

The first three explorers the African Association sent to tackle the problem were unsuccessful. One was forced to turn back, and two died on the way. In 1795 a Scottish doctor called Mungo Park – one of an astonishingly large number of Scotsmen and medical men who have contributed to the exploration of Africa – set out from the Gambia. He travelled through Medina and Kaarta and finally, after suffering innumerable hardships and difficulties, reached the Niger at Segu. Now, at least, it was known that the Niger flowed from west to east and not, as many had previously thought, from east to west. Still, no one knew where the Niger ended. A German explorer was next sent, via North Africa, but died in the desert before even reaching his destination. In 1805 Park was sent on a much larger expedition with forty-five Europeans. Many of his companions died of sickness but the survivors embarked on the Niger at Sansanding, and managed to travel over 1,200 kilometres to Bussa in modern Nigeria, only to lose their lives there.

In 1822 Oudney, Denham and Clapperton travelled from Tripoli to Lake Chad. Oudney died, but Denham explored the Bornu area and Clapperton travelled to Sokoto where he learned that the Niger flowed south. Immediately after his return home, Clapperton set out for the Niger again and travelled to Sokoto from Badagry. He died there in 1827 and his young servant, Richard Lander, tried to follow the course of the Niger alone. Difficulties arose and he returned to Badagry and England. He then persuaded the British Government to sponsor him and his brother on one more journey of Niger exploration. They travelled from Badagry to Bussa, where they embarked in canoes and floated down the river. They were kidnapped on the lower Niger but after various difficulties found their way to the Niger Delta. Thus these two young men of little education succeeded where so many others had failed and established that the so-called Oil Rivers were in fact the gateway to the Niger.

In 1818 a Frenchman called Mollien had solved the last remaining major geographical problem, in establishing the sources of the Gambia and Senegal rivers.

Another topic which has always fascinated Europeans was the ancient university city of Timbuktu. In 1828 a young Frenchman called Caillé succeeded in visiting it, travelling from the Rio Nunez, and returning to Europe via the Sahara. This is the drawing he made of it.

Caillé's drawing of Timbuktu

The man who is generally regarded, however, as one of the greatest explorers of West Africa is famous, less for discovering new areas, than for his splendid observation and description of areas previously visited by Europeans. He was the German, Heinrich Barth, who set out from Tunis in 1849 as a member of a British expedition to explore the possibility of developing the Saharan trade on a large enough scale to destroy the slave trade. In the course of time, his companions died, but Barth bravely travelled alone through Bornu, Adamawa, the Sokoto Caliphate and Timbuktu, keeping a superbly detailed and accurate record of all he saw. The five large volumes which he published after his return to Europe in 1855 are one of our most valuable sources of information on West African history.

This map shows the routes followed by these various explorers.

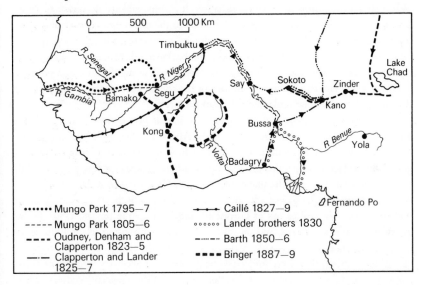

Explorers in West Africa

Now that the Landers had revealed the course of the Lower Niger, both traders and missionaries were eager to make use of the information. In the 1830s several expeditions were sent to the Niger. In a sense, they were disastrously unsuccessful, as so many of their members lost their lives, among them Richard Lander himself, but they did prove that the Niger was navigable by steamer. In 1841 an ambitious expedition was sponsored by the British Government which aimed to establish an agricultural colony of freed slaves at Lokoja. This, it was hoped, would become a centre of Christianity and legitimate trade comparable with Freetown. But this expedition, too, was ravaged by sickness and one-third of the Europeans involved lost their lives. For some years this disillusioned the British with the possibilities of Niger trade, but in 1854 another Scottish doctor, William Balfour Baikie, led another expedition up the Niger, and preserved the health of its members with regular doses of quinine. This opened the door to an era of intensive trade and missionary work on the great river.

The journeys of exploration described were not, as we have seen, inspired by colonialist aims. But mention should be made of an important later journey of exploration. Between 1887 and 1889, a French officer, named Binger, travelled from Bamako to Kong, Salaga and Mossi, ending his journey at Grand Bassam, in Ivory Coast. This directly paved the way to French conquests in the Ivory Coast hinterland, where Europeans had previously thought expansion was blocked by the (non-existent) Mountains of Kong!

European political encroachment

When studying a complex historical situation, it is impossible to do justice to all its aspects at once. Older books on African history in the nineteenth century tended to concentrate on the exploits of European explorers, conquerors, administrators or missionaries, to which Africa becomes simply the background. Modern books, usually but not always, concentrate on the history of Africa itself, seeing the European presence as one of many factors affecting the history of the continent from the outside. This is the viewpoint which has underlain this book so far.

In this section, we adopt, for a moment, a different perspective, focusing on the total picture of the European presence in West Africa, the 'Scramble', the reasons for it, and what went before. In the next chapter we look at the process of imperialist conquest, and the factors which made that conquest, impermanent as it was, possible at all.

We have seen that until the nineteenth century, European–West African relations were dominated by the slave trade, and that it was not until the 1850s that the slave trade died out. The real period of European conquest began in the late 1880s. In the intervening years a different, and, in some ways, more promising relationship developed. In the era of the slave trade Africans were regarded as objects to be bought. In the colonial period, they were subjects to be governed, if necessary by force of arms. But in between these two periods, in the third quarter of the nineteenth century, when there was a black Anglican bishop on the Niger, and a flourishing black commercial and professional class in Liberia and Sierra Leone, at least part of Europeans' interest in Africa was inspired by genuine concern for African welfare and sympathy for African aspirations. This was partly the reflection of religious movements such as the Evangelical revival, partly the result of a sense of guilt about the slave trade. It fitted in well with the search for new export commodities. The combination of different interests was reflected in the motto, 'Christianity, Commerce and Civilisation'. It was hoped that there would arise on the Niger 'a kingdom which shall render incalculable benefits to Africa and hold a position among the states of Europe'.

The humanitarian phase, however, had its limitations. It tended to identify civilisation with European culture. And it had a more sinister implication. Europeans forgot with convenient rapidity the infinite harm that they had done to Africa in the long centuries of the slave trade. Now, they could see themselves as bringers of Christianity, crusaders against the slave trade, agents of 'civilisation'. In a sense, it fostered a low view of Africans, who were seen mainly as the recipients of European good deeds. It directly paved the way to colonialism, which could be defended only in terms of the supposed benefits it would bring, and which could only exist at all when Europeans had a lively belief in their own cultural superiority.

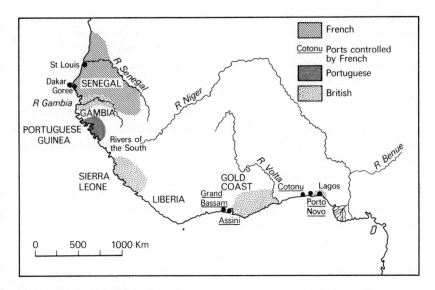

Areas under European rule in 1879

The pattern of events

If you look at this map of West Africa in 1879, you will see how little of it was ruled by any colonial power. What colonies there were were small and strung out along the coast, and European statesmen had had many hesitations about the value even of these.

French conquests

In the 1870s the largest block of colonial territory was French Senegal, its economy resting on the expanding trade in groundnuts and the declining trade in gum. St Louis was the capital; there were also French posts at Gorée Island and, after 1857, on the mainland opposite, at Dakar. These settlements were islands of French cultural influence, comparable in many ways with Liberia and Sierra Leone. There was a small body of Creoles, who identified strongly with French culture,★ but most of the inhabitants, despite their command of the French language and French culture, were Muslim Wolof. French rule in Senegal was consolidated and expanded by General Louis Faidherbe, who ruled the colony from 1854–61 and from 1863–5, which was an unusually long spell of office for nineteenth-century West Africa. He built up the Senegalese army which later conquered the western Sudan for France. It was Faidherbe who came into conflict with Al Hajj Umar, and deposed Lat-Dior for the first time (see page 51).

★ Note that the word 'Creole' means different things in different places. In Sierra Leone it refers to the descendants of African Settlers and Recaptives but in Senegal it refers to people of mixed European and African descent (métis).

The French had a few other posts on the West African coast as well in 1879, established in response to pressure from French palm-oil traders. From 1843, these included Grand Bassam and Assini, in the future Ivory Coast. They were concerned to maintain a presence in southern Dahomey, especially after the British conquest of Lagos in 1851. The situation was rather similar to that in the Gold Coast. Just as the British allied with the small Fante states against the powerful inland kingdom of Asante, so the French allied with a petty coastal ruler – Tofa of Porto Novo – against his overlord, the King of Dahomey. By 1883 the French had established a protectorate both in Porto Novo and in the crucially important port of Cotonu, which was the main outlet for Dahomey's palm oil.

We have seen how long the slave trade lingered in the southern rivers of the future Guinea. Creole traders from Sierra Leone and French traders from Gorée competed there for groundnuts, from the late 1840s on. Faidherbe strongly advocated the extension of French rule to the area. In the late 1860s French forts were established there, and in 1882 it became a colony.

In 1879 the French began the military conquest of the western Sudan. This was the first step in a chain of events which was to re-write the political geography of West Africa in the short space of twenty years. It was to create a vast bloc of continuous territory, to be known as 'French West Africa'. It should be remembered, however, that much of it was deep in the Sahelian zone where, in the words of one Frenchman, 'Nothing can be grown except the decorations that flourish on the uniforms of officers impatient for promotion'.

The first step was a railway project, launched in 1878–9, to link Dakar and St Louis, and continue to the Niger at Bamako. It was this railway which Lat-Dior correctly realised was a threat to his sovereignty, and which he opposed until his death in 1886. In 1882 the French came into contact with Samori for the first time. The epic story of their long conflict belongs to the next chapter. In 1885–7 they fought, as we have seen, a bitter war with Mahmadu Lamine, which finally ended with his defeat and death. Had the various Muslim rulers been willing to combine in joint action against the invader, the course of events might have been very different. A series of defeats might well have persuaded the French that the cost of conquest was too high. But as on other occasions, before and later, foreigners profited from African disunity.

Continuing French expansion brought them, as we have seen, into conflict with the Tukulor empire, whose ruler tried unsuccessfully to protect himself with treaties. (It was a famous seventeenth-century English political philosopher who said, 'Covenants without the sword are but words, and of no strength to secure a man at all'.) In 1880 the French made Upper Senegal-Niger into a separate military command. In 1888 this was put under Colonel Louis Archinand, a soldier of ruthless ambition. Unauthorised, he began the invasion of the Tukulor empire. It is interesting to note that some of those who had opposed the French unsuccessfully in Senegal, among them the Burba Jolof and a contingent from Futa Toro, fought for the Tukulors, just as some Tukulors after their defeat fought for Samori. As we have seen, Ahmadu was forced ever further to the east, dying at last in Sokoto.

In 1887 the French signed a treaty establishing their frontier with Samori. It was an agreement they had no intention of keeping. They at once supplied arms to Samori's enemy, the ruler of Sikasso. When he realised their treachery, Samori sought an alliance with Britain instead, sending representatives to Sierra Leone. The Creoles rejoiced at the prospect, but the British government declined it, for if they began to disregard French treaties, France would doubtless begin to disregard theirs. So great was the sense of wasted opportunity that a British businessman sent his own diplomatic mission to Samori, but the British government refused to ratify the agreement reached. In 1892 Samori sent his own mission to London, but in vain.

From 1891–8 the French fought an epic war with Samori. He conducted a gradual retreat to the east, building a new empire as he went, until finally he reached the frontiers of British power in the Gold Coast – and there was nowhere left to retreat to. The possibilities narrowed . . . capture and exile, and death.

The next great state which the French encountered in their drive to the east was the Mossi kingdom, with its capital at Wagadugu. This has a special interest, as a western Sudan state which resisted Islam until well on into the present century.

In 1895 when a French representative sought a treaty, the Mossi ruler would not hear of it.

> I know that the whites wish to kill me in order to take my country, and yet you claim that they will help me to organise my country. But I find my country good just as it is. I have no need of them. I know what is necessary for me and what I want: I have my own merchants: also, consider yourself fortunate that I do not order your head to be cut off. Go away now, and, above all, never come back.

The kingdom was conquered by force, and many of its people were destined to become conscripts in the French army, or forced to labour on the Ivory Coast, thus fulfilling the fears of their ruler. In 1892–3, as we have seen, the kingdom of Dahomey fell to a French force led by General Dodd, who was a Senegalese métis, like Paul Holle, who led the defence of Medina against Al Hajj Umar.

The French had thus established their rule over a vast bloc of territory, joining their possessions in Guinea (where they signed treaties with the rulers of Futa Jallon), Ivory Coast, and Dahomey. In many areas their rule, however, was still precarious. In the next chapter we shall see how the small communities of Ivory Coast struggled against French dominion for well over a decade. Their drive to the east brought them into potential conflict with the British, then establishing their rule in northern Nigeria. This came to a head in the Borgu area, which was of great strategic importance, since that is where the Niger becomes navigable to the sea. The English and French 'race' for the area brought them within striking distance of war. Much further north, the French pressed on to Chad. A French column led by Voulet and Chanoine was supposed to move from Zinder to Lake Chad, where it was to join up with columns from North and Equatorial Africa. This column was responsible for some of the grimmest episodes in the bloody story of Europe's conquest of West Africa. Crazed with blood, they slaughtered and plundered their way through what is now Niger, until they were finally overthrown by a mutiny of their own men. Under a new leader, the column moved on to its destination, and the war with Rabih, which we shall examine in more detail in the following chapter.

This completed the French advance in West Africa. They had established their rule over a vast expanse of territory, and limited the expansion of Liberia and the British colonies. The British colonies, however, were economically more valuable. In the colonial period, the whole of French West Africa together produced only twenty-five per cent of West Africa's exports.

British expansion
The Gambia and Sierra Leone

The scramble for West Africa was to end with the British in control of two small colonies, the Gambia and Sierra Leone, and two large ones, the Gold Coast and Nigeria. The British presence on the Gambia dates from 1816. France and Britain had just fought a long war, in the course of which the British had taken Senegal from the French. At the end of the war, Senegal was restored to the French, so British merchants moved to Bathurst (now Banjul). Britain controlled a narrow strip of territory along both banks of part of the Gambia; French expansion soon cut it off entirely from its natural hinterland. On several occasions in the nineteenth century, an exchange of the Gambia for French territory elsewhere was suggested, but it never came to anything, mainly because of opposition from British merchants on the Gambia. In this instance, colonialism meant the creation of a small country, where economic development would be difficult, and which was cut off by political and linguistic factors from its neighbours.

We have already looked at the beginnings of the colony of Sierra Leone, which began as a small area around Freetown. The Colony was established in 1808, partly as a sequel to the various settlements made there, and partly because of the strategic value of Freetown harbour. During the nineteenth-century, the Creoles, who traded far and wide in the interior, repeatedly asked for an extension of British authority. But by the time the Protectorate was finally established in 1896, the French had already taken much territory which might well have formed part of Sierra Leone, and which instead became part of the Republic of Guinea.

The Gold Coast

On the Gold Coast, a number of European nations had competed for centuries for gold, and for slaves. They had built a number of stone or brick forts, but they continued to acknowledge African sovereignty, since African rulers held the Notes which showed that they owned the land, and that the Europeans must pay them rent. By the beginning of the nineteenth century, three European nations remained on the Gold Coast; the Dutch, the Danes, and the British. All faced economic difficulties after the abolition of the slave trade. Palm oil and gold found their way to the coast, but in insufficient quantities. The Dutch and Danes finally withdrew from the area, and the British came close to doing so on several occasions.

In the early nineteenth century the British forts were administered by the Company of African Merchants. This had been heavily involved in the slave trade, and in 1821 it was abolished. The British forts on the Gold Coast were then placed under the Governor of Sierra Leone, who happened to be Sir Charles MacCarthy, whose contribution to Freetown development was noted in an earlier chapter.

In 1824 he was killed in a battle with the Asante and the British came close to withdrawing from the area entirely. The merchants trading in the area protested, and in 1828 the forts were handed over to a committee of merchants. In the years that followed, the head of the governing council they appointed, Captain George Maclean, did much to strengthen and consolidate the British presence in what is now southern Ghana. Maclean had a number of European enemies, but he won and kept the confidence of the African peoples with whom he had dealings. Like MacCarthy, he was one of the most outstanding Europeans in government service in nineteenth-century West Africa. One example of his dealings may suffice. He made an agreement with the Asante. As a guarantee that they would keep their side of the bargain, the Asante supplied hostages, and a large sum in gold. The hostages were sent to England for education (the Royal Niger Company officials used young hostages as domestic servants) and the gold was later returned in the original bags!

Largely as a result of criticisms made by his enemies, the crown resumed control in 1843, though Maclean remained in the area, in a judicial capacity, until his death in 1847. In 1844 the Fante states signed agreements with this new government, called Bonds, giving the British limited rights in the judicial sphere. The British sometimes called these states a 'Protectorate'. They formed about a quarter of modern Ghana (see map on page 59).

The British presence in southern Ghana was gradually becoming more like that of a colonial government. But there was one great obstacle to the formation of a colonial government. The existence of three European powers side by side meant that none of them could levy customs duties. If the British had attempted to do so, traders would simply have gone to the Dutch area, and so on. In 1850 the British acquired the Danish forts, but the Dutch were still there.

In 1863 the Asante mounted a very successful invasion of the 'Protectorate'. At this time, as we have seen, many people in Britain had doubts about the value of colonial possessions at all. They were, said one civil servant, 'expensive and troublesome'. A famous political leader called them 'millstones'. In 1865 a Select Committee of Parliament was appointed to report on the British West African settlements. It recommended that all should be given up except Sierra Leone. 'The object of our policy should be to encourage in the natives the exercise of those qualities which may render it possible for us more and more to transfer to them the administration of all the governments.'

This corresponded exactly with what the western-educated class among the Fante wanted. They embarked on the Fante Confederation, as we have seen (see page 68), confident of British support and sympathy. They were disappointed. The tide turned with amazing rapidity. In 1872 the Dutch withdrew which meant that a British colonial government, financed by customs revenue, became possible. In 1873 the British embarked on a successful expedition against Asante. In 1874 southern Gold Coast became a Crown Colony. Until 1886 it was under the same Governor as Lagos.

Despite their conquest of Asante, the British did nothing for many years to establish their own rule in the area. The way to the extension of British rule over what is now northern Ghana was paved by a Fante surveyor, George Ekem Ferguson, who signed treaties with, among other states, Dagomba, Mossi and Mamprussi, ultimately losing his life in the process. In 1896 under an imperially-minded British home government, and anxious to prevent French encroachment, the British conquered Kumasi. Treaties signed with rulers further north had, by 1898, taken the northern boundary of what is now Ghana to its present limits. As elsewhere, the boundaries were not determined by the preferences or cultures of the people concerned. Dagomba, and the Ewe people further south, were divided between the Gold Coast and Togo.

Nigeria

The British established their first bridgehead in Nigeria by the conquest of the small state of Lagos in 1851. It was at the time weakened by a succession dispute. It was justified as a blow against the slave trade, which was certainly weakened as a result. Modern historians tend to see the British conquest of Lagos as an act of economic imperialism: 'the economic desire to control the trade of Lagos from which they had hitherto been excluded and from where they hoped to exploit the resources of the vast country . . .' Ten years later, Lagos island and a small area of coastline became a colony.

In 1849 the British had appointed a consul for a wide coastal area stretching from Dahomey to the Cameroons. A clause which was crossed out in the letter of appointment stated that the government 'have no intention to seek to gain Possession, either by purchase or otherwise, of any portion of the African Continent in those parts . . .'

This consul's successors came to concentrate on the Niger Delta. They were not, of course, colonial rulers. They were diplomatic representatives to sovereign states. They did not even live there, but, until 1882, on the distant island of Fernando Po. But supported by the 'moral authority of a "man-of-war" ' they often intervened in Delta affairs, with decisive effect.

In the middle 1880s, the nature of the British presence in southern Nigeria changed dramatically. In 1884–5 an international conference was held at Berlin, where it was decided that 'effective occupation' was necessary before claims to colonial teritory in Africa could be recognised. (At first this applied only to the coast; later the interior was included as well.) Before the delegates had left Berlin, German representatives arrived in Togo and the Cameroons, and obtained treaties, which established their claims to these areas. The British presence in the Cameroons had been much like the British presence in the Delta. There had been many British traders there, but nothing like a colonial government. Hurriedly, to avoid being forestalled by another European nation, the British established a protectorate in the Delta.

On the lower Niger a number of British firms had been engaged in cut-throat competition for trade in the 1870s. The man whom history knows as Sir George Goldie, originally a shareholder in the smallest firm, succeeded in bringing about an amalgamation which brought great economic advantages to those concerned. But there was no way in which he could prevent new firms entering the lower Niger trade, and he could not continue the amalgamation process indefinitely. The British government, on the other hand, needed to establish 'effective occupation' to forestall other European nations. In 1886 Goldie's firm was given a charter to govern, becoming the Royal Niger Company. It kept these powers until the end of 1899. For the British government, this was a cheap and trouble-free way of creating the appearance of effective government, though the Company's real authority was limited to a narrow strip along the river banks. For Goldie, it provided in practice, though not in theory, the power to exclude trade rivals.

The Company was very unpopular with the lower Niger peoples, and caused great suffering to the men of Brass, whose whole livelihood had depended on trade with the area, from which they were now excluded. To economic injustice were added a number of instances of cruelty and brutality. Finally in despair the Brassmen revolted against the Company in 1895. The rising failed, and the Brassmen suffered much in consequence, but they had at least obtained a hearing for their grievances. This is how they described them:

> The ill-treatments of the Niger Company is very bad. They said that Brassmen should eat dust . . . we see truly that we eat the dusts. Our boys fired, killed, and plundered, and even the innocent provision sellers were captured and killed likewise . . . instead of we Brass people die through hunger we had rather go to them and die in their sords . . .

One British official compared the British presence in southern Nigeria with soap in a sponge – once there, it could never be entirely removed. In the late 1880s effective British control in Nigeria was limited to the Niger Delta, a narrow strip along the banks of the lower Niger, and Lagos, and a narrow strip of coastline nearby. From all these starting points, there was a steady process of conquest and expansion. In 1897 the Royal Niger Company conquered Ilorin and Nupe: on the next page is a picture from the Ilorin campaign. It is interesting to compare it with the picture on page 53 of a battle between the French and Mahmadu Lamine. It shows precisely the pattern which was to recur in the British conquest of northern Nigeria – a futile gallant cavalry charge, against artillery.

In 1887, as we have seen, Ja Ja was abducted and exiled; in 1894 Nana was overthrown, after fiercely defending his capital at Ebrohimi. In 1897 the British conquered the ancient kingdom of Benin, looting its incomparable art treasures. In 1901–2 they mounted the Aro expedition against southern Igboland, to be followed by countless more obscure wars in the years that followed.

The extension of British rule in Yorubaland followed a different pattern. For decades Yoruba communities had looked suspiciously at the island of British authority

A battle between the Royal Niger Company and Ilorin

at Lagos, and feared that it would lead to further encroachment. But Yorubaland's capacity and will to resist the invader were weakened by its divisions and wars. In 1881 the British Colonial Secretary declined a proposal to mediate in these wars: 'Such a course would not fail to involve the Colonial Government in dangerous complications . . .' In 1886, despite this, two Christian Yoruba went on a largely successful peace mission with the support of the Lagos government; they failed in one important respect, as Ilorin remained outside the agreement. In 1888 a Frenchman obtained a treaty at Abeokuta, and the possibility of the French moving in on the area, the one event which could infallibly move a British government to action, appeared. (In the event, the boundary was negotiated much further west, leaving most, but not all, Yoruba communities in Nigeria.) In 1892 the British invaded the southern Yoruba kingdom of Ijebu. They chose this particular area for a show of force, it appears, because of the Ijebu's refusal to admit Christian missions, and western influence. The overthrow of the warlike and well-armed Ijebu had a great psychological effect on the rest of Yorubaland, and the following year the Governor of Lagos was able to make treaties in the various Yoruba states, again with the exception of Ilorin.

The establishment of British authority in Yorubaland followed a quite different pattern from that in the other areas and states we have studied in this book, and is to be explained by the exhaustion created by incessant war. To some educated Yoruba, the establishment of British rule was a blessing: 'It was like the opening of a prison door'.

In 1900 the Royal Niger Company lost its charter, obtaining an absurdly heavy compensation in exchange. In that year, Lugard was placed in charge of the new Protectorate of Northern Nigeria. His base was at Lokoja, although he made several expensive changes of headquarters subsequently, and his authority extended little beyond it. It appears that he deliberately refused to use diplomatic means to establish

Different victors at the Victor's Gate, Kano

his regime, preferring that it rest on a basis of conquest. In 1903 the British took the great city of Kano; this picture shows British soldiers standing in front of the Victor's Gate, formerly used for triumphal processions.

Rather than live under the rule of unbelievers, the Caliph of Sokoto embarked on hijra. People from all walks of life followed him. The British pursued them, and defeated them at the battle of Burmi. Despite this, a large body continued on through the desert to the eastern Sudan, where their descendants still live. This photograph of the dead, after the battle, gives a moving testimony to the price exacted by colonial conquests.

The victims of Burmi

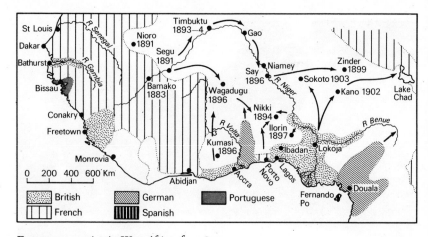

European expansion in West Africa after 1890

In 1906 the Protectorate of Southern Nigeria (based on the Delta) and the Colony and Protectorate of Lagos, united to form the Colony and Protectorate of Southern Nigeria. The administrative division between northern and southern Nigeria, which was to be perpetuated by later administrative arrangements, was largely the work of Lugard. It is generally regarded as the source of many evils in later Nigerian history.

By 1906 the external boundaries of Nigeria were established as far as other colonial powers were concerned, but there were still many areas within it which the British had never seen, much less conquered.

By the early twentieth century, most of West Africa was under French or British rule. Liberia preserved a precarious independence, Portugal retained the little enclave of Guinea-Bissau, Germany ruled the narrow strip of territory which was Togo and the much larger colony of Kamerun. Both Togo and Kamerun were to be divided between Britain and France after the First World War.

Some reasons for imperialism

In the next chapter we shall analyse the factors, technical and otherwise, which made it *possible* for European nations to conquer West African ones. A tremendous amount of attention has been devoted by scholars to a different question, which we must now briefly consider; why did they *wish* to do so? Why did the trading relationship which had existed for centuries, in various forms, give way to one of conquest and subjection? Why, in particular, was the attitude of the 1860s, which sought to limit imperial responsibilities, replaced so soon by a scramble for empire?

National prestige
One clear motivating force for imperialism was the concept of national prestige. Even when anti-imperial sentiment was strongest, statesmen tended to be reluctant to sur-

render colonies once acquired, because they were so easily identified with national standing. In the 'eighties and 'nineties, the possession of colonies came to be regarded as a symbol of a so-called 'First Class Power'. Some historians believe that the whole French invasion of the western Sudan was really motivated by the desire to win imperial glory, to compensate for France's disastrous and humiliating defeat in the Franco–Prussian war of 1870–1.

Much of the scramble for West Africa was inspired by the fear of being excluded by another European power. The extension of British authority in the Delta was described explicitly as 'the scheme . . . for keeping the French away . . .' In 1882, several Cameroonian rulers, in the Douala area, invited the British to establish a protectorate there. The relevant British minister declined because 'the climate of all parts of West Africa is very pestilential . . . the extension of British occupation would probably lead to wars with the interior tribes and heavy demands upon the British taxpayer'. Two years and a change of policy later, the British were just about to move in, when Germany forestalled them. British traders, long established in the area, soon withdrew. Thus the scramble for Africa was very largely self-generating. When other potential colonisers appeared indifferent to empire, it was easy to be indifferent too. When a European rival began to lay claim to large tracts of territory, other colonial powers were impelled to do likewise.

Individual initiative

To a surprisingly large extent, the policies of metropolitan governments were often determined by the man on the spot. The military command of Upper Senegal-Niger was almost a law unto itself. We have already noted, in an earlier period, how much Faidherbe contributed to French expansion in Senegal. A good example of initiative taken by the man on the spot was Johnston's abduction of Ja Ja. The Foreign Office thoroughly disapproved of his action, but did nothing to reverse it, and Ja Ja died in exile. Local government representatives tended to favour expansion, in the hope of furthering their careers by leaving their mark on events. Professional soldiers practically always favoured war, because only in war could decorations be won, and promotions accelerated.

One famous interpretation, which very few scholars accept, but to which all have given serious consideration, finds the key to the scramble, not in sub-Saharan Africa at all, but in Egypt! Egypt was of the utmost strategic importance to Britain. From 1876–82, France and Britain controlled Egypt jointly. In 1882 Britain occupied Egypt alone, thus terminating the earlier arrangement. French resentment, the theory runs, led her to carve out empires elsewhere. Germany profited by the situation, for she was one of the powers which controlled Egypt's revenue, which gave her a powerful bargaining counter when staking out claims elsewhere. But the present writer believes that in the scramble for West Africa this was, at most, of marginal importance. The real factors were local conditions, the mirage of national prestige, and especially economic factors.

Economic reasons

There was an undoubted link between imperialism and economic considerations. A British official wrote, 'Trade is our sole object in West Africa'. But it is not always easy to say exactly what the nature of the link was. West Africa played only a minor role in the whole complex of Europe's foreign trade – less than one per cent of the total. But there was a group of French and British merchants whose trade was mainly with West Africa. These put pressure on their governments when their immediate interests were affected. But although a colonial government was likely to protect their interests, the traders did not necessarily always seek the spread of colonial rule, since colonial governments levied import and export duties.

The middle 'eighties were a period of economic depression in Europe. This affected political events in West Africa in several ways. To continue to make a profit, European manufacturers had to obtain their raw materials more cheaply. European merchants in West Africa believed, often wrongly, that this could be achieved by bypassing African middlemen and trading direct with the producer. Since no middleman was going to agree without protest to the loss of his livelihood, this had to be done by force; hence the abduction of Ja Ja and the sack of Nana's stronghold. At least one of the factors which lured the British to the conquest of Benin was the rubber of its forests. Since colonial governments were financed by duties on imports and exports, their local personnel tended always to be sympathetic to advances which might 'extend trade'.

The establishment of a colonial government was not necessarily founded on a rational calculation of the economic benefits the area was currently yielding. Often, those concerned were moved by the thought that it might yield as yet undisclosed riches in the future, by what one historian has called 'uncosted hopes of future benefits', from which another colonising power might exclude them forever.

Changing attitudes

A final factor in the rising tide of imperialism has been linked with changing intellectual attitudes in Europe itself. Many factors, into which we cannot go here, encouraged Europeans to overvalue their own culture, and undervalue the cultures of African peoples, about which, in any case, they knew practically nothing. We observed the rising tide of white racism in miniature, in the history of the Niger Mission. This sense of cultural superiority led Europeans to think for a time, that they had a right to rule other peoples. The whole edifice of colonialism, in a sense, rested upon this collective self-confidence, this illusion of superiority. When the hard historical experience of twentieth-century Europe shattered the illusion, imperialism vanished, too. Conversely, one of the most essential elements in the experience of independent Africa has been the sustained attempt by both African and expatriate scholars to attain a truer understanding of the African past and the African cultural inheritance. 'People will not look forward to posterity who never look backward to their ancestors'.

The real reasons for the colonial presence in West Africa are a different thing from the many arguments which were brought forward, at various times, to justify and defend that presence. But a famous French colonial administrator summed up the whole matter honestly enough, in 1921:

> It is not altruism that leads us to Africa, at least not as a nation ... At times we wished to ensure outlets for our trade, and sources of raw material for our industry, at others we felt the need to protect the security of our nationals or the need not to be outdone by foreign rivals; sometimes we were moved by the obscure and unconscious desire to procure a little glory or grandeur for our country, at others we simply followed hazardous caprices or the tracks of an explorer, believing that we could do nothing different. In no case do I find as the motive force of our colonial expansion in Africa the real and reasoned wish to contribute to the welfare of our subjugated peoples.

6

Resistance to Alien Conquest

Why European conquest was possible

In the previous chapter, we looked at the scramble for Africa, and the years of changing policies and gradual encroachment which preceded it, from the point of view of
the colonising powers. In it, the present writer tried to present a bird's eye view of the
whole picture of European encroachment, and to answer the question: why, in fact,
did the Europeans compete for African territory? Why, after Africans and Europeans
had traded on equal terms for some four centuries, did the relationship suddenly give
way to aggression and conquest on the one hand, and resistance on the other?

This chapter seeks to look more closely at African resistance. It is one of the aspects
of African history which scholars have concentrated on most in recent years. It is not
difficult to see why this was so, for the memory of how their predecessors struggled to
resist alien rule in the first place was an inspiration to nationalists struggling to regain
their independence.

When one studies West African resistance to alien rule, one is immediately confronted with the question; why was it possible for European states to conquer African
states at all? It was, in fact, a surprising phenomenon which needs explanation, though
the question is not asked as often as it should be, for historians tend to take whatever
actually did happen as what was to have been expected.

Several factors, above all others, explain why it was possible for Europeans to
subjugate the states of West Africa.

The firearms revolution

Until the middle of the nineteenth century, the firearms available to Europeans were
relatively inaccurate and inefficient. Their heavy cannon, which were capable of causing great damage, were too difficult to transport along the narrow footways of West
Africa, so could in practice only be used against states near the sea or near a navigable
river. In the second half of the nineteenth century, a series of dramatic improvements
took place, both in hand arms and in artillery, which amounted to a firearms revolution, and which created an enormous armaments gap between Europe and the African

states which had, for the most part, old-fashioned types of firearms, or none at all. Rifling the barrel, which meant that the bullet spun, for greater accuracy and range, became general; it was a feature of the Enfield rifle, in general use in the British army from 1855 on. The older type of guns were muzzle-loaders. This meant that they were very slow and cumbersome to reload. From 1848 on they began to be replaced by breech-loaders. These last had a great advantage in that they could be reloaded lying down, thus giving their user much more protection from enemy fire. In 1867 an improved model combining breech-loading and rifling was introduced, and in the years that followed successive technical improvements developed rapidly.

A much more deadly weapon of war, however, was the rapid-firing machine gun. Early models were used in the 1860s – such as the Gatling gun, used in the American Civil War, which worked on the principle of rapidly revolving barrels. In 1889 Maxim invented the modern machine gun, which was at first called the maxim, after its inventor. It worked on a new principle. The recoil from one shot reloaded the gun for the next and it was able to pour out bullets at the rate of eleven per second. Unlike the cannon, it was relatively light and easy to transport.

European armies in Africa were supplied with the most up-to-date weapons. Some were even tried out for the first time in Africa. The impact was devastating. In the words of an English writer:

> The difference is that we have got
> The maxim gun, and they have not.

A maxim gun in action

177

As the armies of Europe were equipped with the new rifles, their out-of-date weapons were sold off cheaply. Arms dealers made a great profit, reselling them in West Africa, and in other parts of the world where there was a market for them. Some West African rulers such as Ja Ja, Nana and Samori, recognised the importance of rifles and managed to acquire them. The Dahomey army did so, at the eleventh hour, just before the French invasion. But in general, the most common gun in West Africa was the old-fashioned Dane gun, a flintlock musket, which could not possibly compete in accuracy, range, or rapidity of fire with a rifle, and was totally inadequate to cope with a machine gun. Some African peoples resisted the Europeans without firearms; the forces of the Sokoto Caliphate fought with their traditional weapons, the sword, the spear, and the bow. No African state ever succeeded in obtaining a machine gun for use against the invaders.

Some firms in Birmingham made a speciality of manufacturing cheap muskets of poor quality for Africa. An English gunmaker called them 'horribly dangerous', for they were liable to explode in the owner's face. Fortunately, the gunpowder sold to Africa was usually so cheap and inferior that it was too weak to burst the barrel in this way.

In 1890 a European convention agreed to ban the export of precision weapons to Africa. Even where these weapons were obtained, African states faced the problem of maintaining them, and of supplying ammunition. These problems were solved with varying degrees of success. Generally, the shortage of ammunition meant that their troops had inadequate target practice.

The gap in firearms went hand in hand with a gap in military organisation and training. West Africa produced some superb strategists, such as Samori, who adjusted with triumphant success to the new weapons and the new conditions of war. But sometimes African commanders clung to the tactics of the past, which had proved successful in different circumstances. Such tactics included the defence of walled towns, and the cavalry charge. Both of these were fatal in the face of modern artillery. (See the pictures on pages 53 and 170 above.)

The resources gap

Underlying the gap in firearms, and ultimately causing it, was a tremendous gap between the technology and material resources of the industrial nations of Europe and the states of West Africa. In the late eighteenth century, England had embarked on a process of industrialisation which is one of the great turning points in the history of the world. This spread, though unequally, to other nations within Europe, and America and Japan.

In the case of England, the capital for industrialisation had been built up largely through the profits of international trade, and a far-flung empire. By the late nineteenth century, the African state which tried to resist British or French encroachment was, in fact, resisting an international empire, with a highly industrialised metropolis.

On the following page is a picture of a French gunboat being constructed on the Niger.

A French gunboat being constructed on the Niger

Disunity in Africa

After the firearms gap, nothing helped the European conquests more than the divisions of Africans themselves. These can be viewed under two aspects:

The policies of African states

The typical African statesman of the late nineteenth century did not see the political and diplomatic situation in racial terms – black against white, or African against European. Rather, he saw his state as surrounded by many other powers, some hostile, or potentially hostile, some friendly, or potentially friendly. Often the Europeans appeared as an almost unknown quantity. It was difficult to appreciate what they wanted, or what their rule would mean. Meanwhile, the African statesman had to consider his African rivals and enemies. The superior firepower of the whites often made them seem an ideal ally, to be used against his traditional enemies.

And so, in most of their campaigns, if not in all of them, the Europeans worked in conjunction with African allies. Ja Ja of Opobo, who would soon himself fall victim to colonialism, supplied a contingent of men for the invasion of Asante in 1873. The Tukulor empire aided the French against Mahmadu Lamine. To overthrow the Tukulor, the French sought the support of the Bambara. Against Samori, they supported his enemy, the ruler of Sikasso. When the Muslim rulers of the western Sudan finally brought themselves to consider an alliance, it was too late.

The African conquest of Africa

It is one of the ironies of African history that the rank and file of the so-called British or French forces were actually Africans. The Aro expeditionary force, for instance,

*Senegalese soldiers in the
French forces*

comprised 74 European officers and 3,464 African soldiers and carriers. The Royal
Niger Company's forces consisted of 5 Europeans and 416 Africans from the Gold
Coast, Yorubaland and Hausaland. In the French forces, the officers too were sometimes
men of African descent. It was the Senegalese métis, Paul Holle, who led the defence
of Medina against Al Hajj Umar. Another Senegalese métis, General Dodds, planned
and led the campaign which conquered the kingdom of Dahomey. It has been said
that 'Empires make their victims their defenders', and this is very true.

Non-military confrontations

It is not always recognised that some of the confrontations between Africans and the
invaders took non-military forms. One of these might well be called violence by
example. When the colonial powers overthrew an African state, that state's African
neighbours learnt by the experience. Sometimes states which had intended to put up a
fight realised that if their powerful neighbour was defeated they themselves had little
chance of victory. The overthrow of Nana in the western Delta created great appre-
hensions in Benin. The overthrow of Benin, in its turn, had a great effect on the
smaller kingdoms on Benin's borders, for if Benin had failed, how could they hope to
succeed? Sometimes the British provided a practical demonstration of the power of
their artillery, to discourage resistance. In several small-scale states in southern Nigeria

they deliberately shattered some mighty forest trees by machine gun fire. The lesson was not lost – if the machine gun was so effective against trees, what would it do to men?

There was another type of non-military confrontation, however, which has been relatively neglected by historians. Some states sought to resist, not by military means, but by seeking religious or magical protection. We have already noted the large-scale sacrifices with which Benin tried to stave off invasion. Many of the small states of Igboland tried to repel the British by calling on the services of famous diviners and experts in ritual and magic, who summoned epidemics, snakes, insect pests and so on. The modern reader is not likely to be impressed by this kind of technique, but, strangely enough, both the written records left by the British and Igbo oral tradition suggest that it was often effective! It is possible, in fact, that these traditional diviners possessed real powers and skills in the sphere of what we would now call extra-sensory perception, and that the coming of colonial rule diverted Africa from the pursuit of a new, different, branch of knowledge, and impoverished humanity accordingly.

The collaborators
Not all African statesmen, of course, thought it their duty to lead their people in armed combat against the colonial powers. Some recognised that the conflict, ultimately, was a hopeless one, and that they had no real chance of expelling the invaders. They therefore thought it best to avoid bloodshed and accept the situation, using the techniques of diplomacy to win for themselves and their people the best deal they could.

Modern historians have assessed those who took this line, who are often described as 'collaborators', differently. Some historians have condemned armed resistance as a 'romantic, reactionary struggle against the facts'. Others claim that resistance was not entirely fruitless. There is no doubt that African societies, large or small, which fought heroically against alien domination, left an imperishable heritage to later nationalism, in the memory of their courage, their passion for freedom, in the fact that they cherished the inherited values of their society so strongly that they believed them worth dying for.

It would, of course, be quite wrong, to think of West African leaders as divided into two camps, of resisters on the one hand, and collaborators on the other. We have seen repeatedly in this study that many African peoples, such as Asante or the Tukulor, made every effort to avoid conflict, until circumstances turned them finally into resisters. Most African states were, in fact, resisters at some times, and collaborators at others.

Fighting empires: 1) Samori

In the whole history of West African resistance to European invasion, a history full of remarkable and heroic figures and episodes, none is more remarkable and heroic than that of the fighting empire of Samori Touré. This, in its origins, was a purely African empire, which developed in response to internal challenges, in isolation from direct contact with Europeans. Samori first came into direct contact with the French in 1881. He was finally captured in 1898. In the words of the French scholar who is the leading authority on his life, 'No other confrontation between colonised and coloniser had ever lasted so long without the former surrendering his liberty'.

The Dyula revolution

Samori was born in the Guinea Highlands in about 1830, in a village in the valley of the River Milo, one of a number of rivers which flow north until they empty into the Niger. The people of the area were Malinké, part of the great Mande-speaking family. Some kept to their traditional religion, and it was this group which provided the rulers and warriors of the region. Some, the Dyula, were Muslim in religion and traders by profession. For centuries they were contented to live the life of peaceful merchants, and leave the conducting of government and war to others. In the early nineteenth century their attitude changed, for two reasons. First, they were influenced by the jihads in other states, especially, perhaps, by the jihad in Massina. Secondly, since they controlled the trade of the region, and the supply of firearms, they were in a good position to seize power.

In the early nineteenth century, several Dyula clans set up small new states in the region of Samori's homeland. They were involved in numerous wars, with each other, and with surrounding traditionalists.

Samori was born to a Dyula family which had given up both trade and Islam. When he was young, his mother was captured by another Dyula clan, the Sisé, and he joined their forces in the hope of rescuing her. After some years in the Sisé army, he offered his services to traditionalists in the early 1860s. He rapidly began to build up an army of his own, centred round a solid nucleus of friends and relations. For some years he followed a brilliant strategy of divide and rule, among both Muslims and pagans, until by 1881 he was master of a large empire, which included the gold-bearing area of Bouré. His expansion had brought him into conflict with Kankan, a very wealthy Dyula city, which he conquered in 1880, because it had refused to support him in another struggle.

As early as 1850 Samori had become a Muslim. In the 1880s, with his power apparently secured, he began to identify more closely with Islam. He renounced the pagan title *Faama*, and instead called himself Almami, like the Muslim rulers of Futa Jallon. Different scholars assess the importance of Islam in his life differently, but it is generally agreed that he was first and foremost a military leader. Some have suggested that he adopted Islam in the hope that it would provide a unifying ideology for his vast empire, established, as it was, in an area previously divided among many small states. He seems to have been influenced both by Futa Jallon, his neighbour, with which he remained on friendly terms, and by the Tukulor empire to his immediate north. In 1886 he announced that all his subjects must become Muslims. This led to much discontent, and was one of the causes of the Great Revolt against him in 1888. After that, he relaxed his demands.

Although Samori is primarily regarded as a military figure, his attachment to Islam was sincere and deep rooted. As we have seen, he risked his empire in an attempt to compel the conversion of his subjects. A Frenchman who visited his empire in 1887 left the following account of his efforts concerning religion and education.

The almami-emir is commander of the faithful and interprets the Koran, whose teaching, however, does not appear to worry his subjects overmuch. He is assisted in this task by a very mild and tolerant young marabout, trained by the Trarza Moors, who he has made his spiritual guide . . . The building of a more or less rudimentary mosque in each village, and the maintenance of a marabout to serve it, are generally regarded as adequate public demonstrations of religious devotion.

The only duty which the alimami strictly enforces on his leading subjects is to send their children regularly to school. He ensures that this rule is carried out by unexpectedly summoning, and personally interrogating, some child of good family, even from the most distant parts of the empire. If the child's ignorance shows that he has not been following the marabout's course of instruction, a heavy fine is imposed on the parents.

Samori

Political and military organisation

The government of his empire centred, to a very large degree, on his own personality. His aim seems to have been to create a large unified state where Islam would flourish, and where peaceful conditions would promote trade. He often said that he wanted to create a situation where it would be possible for a woman to travel safely alone to Freetown. This emphasis on unrestricted and peaceful trade won him the devotion of the Dyula merchants.

Samori's empire was divided into two sections. The central section, comprising almost half the whole, remained under his personal government, and maintained a large reserve army of between 8,000 and 10,000. He was himself surrounded by a corps of crack troops, who wore uniform. The outlying parts of his empire were divided into five large provinces. Their government was entrusted to his relatives (first his brothers, later his sons), or his close friends. Only once did any of these provincial governors rebel against him.

The army was recruited from many sources. Conquered warriors were given their freedom in return for enlisting in his army. Conquered areas provided a tribute of soldiers. All, however, came from different Mande-speaking groups, which helped them to develop a sense of national unity. The soldiers were grouped in units, which had no relation to their place of origin. These units soon developed a strong sense of *esprit de corps*. Although they were called sofas, which means 'horse fathers', they consisted, in fact, primarily of infantry. By 1888 his army comprised between 30,000 and 35,000 men.

He had a very clear appreciation of the merits of modern rapid-firing rifles, which he began importing, from the late 1870s, from Sierra Leone. He studied various models, and selected the most satisfactory. He mobilised his craftsmen, as well as his soldiers, for war; bands of skilled blacksmiths studied the rifles and imitated them. Some of

Samori's blacksmiths

them even went to work in a French armaments factory in St Louis to learn their skills. 3,000 to 4,000 men worked in his own arms factory. But he never succeeded in arming more than a minority of his soldiers with rifles. By 1888 only a few hundred were equipped with them. By the 1890s he had about 6,000. After that, his retreat to the east cut him off from his sources of supply in Sierra Leone.

How did he finance his arms purchases, his army, and the administration of his empire? Until he lost the gold-fields of Bouré to the French, he paid for them partly with gold. He exported ivory, and sold slaves to the north. These slaves were rebels and prisoners of war; their numbers have been estimated at 2,800–3,000 a year. This picture of his forces pursuing captives reflects part of the social cost of his empire.

Samori's forces pursuing captives

At the capital, Bissandugu, an area of 200 square kilometres was laid out in splendid agricultural plantations. In addition, each village cultivated a field for his benefit. The size of the field depended on the size of the village. In times of war, this produce was carried to the army by 'immense convoys of women and children'.

The encounter with the French

If Samori had lived a hundred, or even fifty, years earlier, he could have devoted the rest of his life to developing the organisation and economy of the state he had founded, or to trying to extend its boundaries. In the event, as he expanded towards the north, he came into collision with the French, who were simultaneously advancing towards Bamako and the Niger bend. As with Al Hajj Umar and the French enclave in Senegal earlier, an expanding European imperialism and an expanding African imperialism met, and conflict was almost inevitable.

185

The first actual clash came in 1882, when a French officer led an unauthorised raid to Kenyera, deep in Samori's territory. The raid led to an inglorious retreat but it was, for Samori, the first contact with the Europeans' superior technological resources and for the French, it was their first indication of Samori's military might. They had not even heard of Samori before 1878, and Samori had not looked previously on the Europeans as a potential threat. Soon afterwards, the two imperialisms converged on the same goal – Bamako. Samori sent his brother to capture Bamako. Arriving there, he found the French in possession, and tried to dislodge them but failed, with great loss of life.

In 1885 the French tried to seize the valuable gold area of Bouré. They were repulsed, but again, at the cost of great losses among Samori's forces.

At this point it suited both the French and Samori to seek an agreement. Samori was anxious to end the threat from France; and anxious, too, to devote his full attention to a war with an African rival – the wealthy city of Sikasso. The French looked on the agreement as a temporary one; anxious to fight with one enemy at a time, they hoped to make peace with Samori while they conquered Mahmadu Lamine, and the Tukulors. In 1886 Samori and the French signed a treaty. To show his faith in French good intentions, Samori allowed them to take his favourite son on a visit to France. But many people in France disliked the treaty, as being too favourable to Samori. A French mission was sent to Samori's capital at Bissandugu, and he signed a further agreement accepting a French protectorate. Here is a contemporary drawing of their meeting.

A French mission visits Samori's capital at Bissandugu

Samori probably understood this agreement to mean that he would not sign any treaty with another European power. He undoubtedly expected French support in his own internal wars, such as the attack on Sikasso. But instead, the French began to encourage a series of revolts within Samori's own territories. Many, though not all, of his subjects joined in, exasperated by his recent edict compelling conversion to Islam, and probably, too, by the financial burden of his wars. Later, the French also supplied arms to his enemy, the ruler of Sikasso. Samori had to give up the seige of Sikasso in order to concentrate on the systematic re-establishment of his authority in his own territories, in which he had succeeded by late 1889. He proposed an anti-French alliance to the Tukulor:

> If you continue to make war on your own, the whites will have no trouble in defeating you. I have already undergone the experience in trying my strength against them. Let us therefore unite. You will hit the French from the North, I will harrass them in the South, and we will certainly manage to get rid of them.

The Tukulor did not take up the offer, probably because they thought that Samori's expansion to their immediate south was as much a danger to them as French aggression. It was only after his own power had been effectively destroyed that Ahmadu, belatedly, began to seek an alliance.

The French invasion 1891–2

In 1891–2 the French made a determined attempt to invade Samori's empire. Samori, for his part, had made careful preparations, buying up supplies of rifles, and reorganising his army. Henceforward his army consisted of a much smaller body of men, which was much better organised and trained. He had twenty companies averaging 150 men each, half of whom had modern rifles. They were trained with the help of western-trained soldiers, who were prisoners of war, or deserters. Some of them seem to have thrown themselves into the conflict in a spirit of real African patriotism. But he realised the fundamental inequality of the struggle, which he tried to delay by diplomatic means. He accordingly offered the British a protectorate, which the officials and Creoles of Sierra Leone were very eager to accept, but the British could not disregard France's treaties without running the risk that France would disregard their own. The resistance of his state was weakened, too, by the aftermath of the Great Revolt, for its suppression had meant much destruction and loss of life.

In 1891 after the fall of the Tukulor capital of Segu, the French invaded Samori's empire. The sofas resisted their advance with heroic courage, suffering heavy losses in the process. But they were unable to halt the French advance. The French reached Samori's capital, Bissandugu, and built a fort there. But having apparently conquered, they found themselves in the middle of a desert. In his grim determination to avoid foreign conquest at all costs, Samori had followed a scorched earth policy. (It is one of the relatively few examples, in West African history, of that total war which has been so characteristic of international conflicts in our own time – the Russians followed the same scorched earth policy in the face of the German invasion during the Second

World War.) As the enemy advanced, villages were destroyed, and the population withdrew, taking all the food with them. The French had to send convoys to Kankan for provisions, and these convoys had to fight their way there and back in the face of guerilla warfare by Samori's forces. The French were forced to withdraw, leaving behind them several besieged garrisons. Samori had won a kind of victory, but at terrible cost to his soldiers and his homeland.

The great move to the east

It was now clear to Samori that the most heroic efforts to stop the French advance had failed, and that he could not continue indefinitely to defend his homeland by destroying it. Instead he decided on a plan of breathtaking magnitude, which he was to carry out with superb tactical skill; that is, to withdraw from his homeland and build a new empire further to the east, far from European aggression. In 1892 he and his people began a systematic retreat to the east, still following a scorched earth policy. He made no further effort to prevent the French conquest of his former territories, and in 1892-3 the French quickly overran vast territories formerly under his command, reaching the frontiers of Sierra Leone. As he moved further east, he left behind him the boundaries of Liberia as well, thus cutting himself off from external supplies of arms and ammunition. (In any case, supplies of modern weapons to African rulers had been banned by an international convention in 1890.) His armies now concentrated on conquering new territories further east.

By 1894 he was established in what is now the northern part of Ivory Coast. The French concentrated on conquests in the Niger area. His armies pressed further east, conquering the Abro state, with its capital at Bonduku, and western Gonja. But his

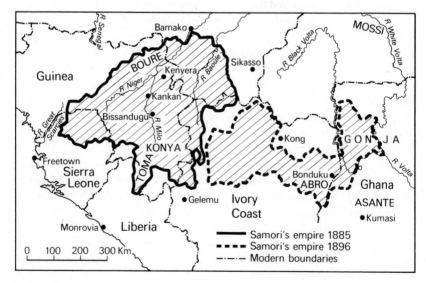

Samori's Empires

conquests brought him once more into conflict with expanding European imperialisms. His territory in northern Ivory Coast created a barrier between the French settlements on the coast and their possessions in the western Sudan, and thus threatened to hinder their grand design of building up a vast continuous block of territory as French West Africa. Moreover, his conquests had brought him to what is now Ghana, where the British had recently conquered Asante, and were eager to establish their rule over as much territory further north as possible. He tried desperately to play the foreign powers against each other, but in vain. Ironically, his old enemy, Sikasso, had by now a new king who was resolved to oppose the French. Sikasso fell to the French in 1898. Now his new empire was surrounded by French and British territory. There was nowhere left to flee.

Since he could no longer withdraw, Samori embarked on a last conflict with the enemy. At the time the French were besieging Sikasso, Samori was besieging the French forces in the wealthy city of Kong. In July 1898 his massed army won a great victory over the French, at Owé. He then began a final retreat, now retracing his steps and moving west with his army, hoping to reach Toma, in Liberia. In the end, he was defeated, not by the French, but by the forces of nature. In forested mountainous country, in the rainy season, his troops were hit by famine. Hardly any of them were left when a French detachment captured him in September 1898. He understood that he had been promised a quiet retirement in his homeland, Konyan, and when he learnt that he was to be deported to Gabon he tried to commit suicide. He died there, of pneumonia, two years later, at the age of seventy.

Samori's achievements

In many respects, Samori is a controversial figure. About some aspects of his career, however, there is complete agreement. His masterly gifts as a strategist and military tactician have never been questioned, and were fully recognised by the French and British at the time. Both French and British observers called him the African Napoleon, comparing him with one of the greatest generals in European history. (Perhaps African historians should call Napoleon the European Samori!) Similarly, all commentators recognise his commanding abilities as a ruler and organiser, which were so clearly shown in the stupendous task of transferring an entire empire from west to east. It is generally agreed that he won his soldiers' wholehearted devotion, partly by his personality, partly by his genuine concern for their welfare, which showed itself in many ways; the wounded were well cared for, the dead decently buried, the disabled were helped to return to civilian life, with suitable employment.

Historians disagree about the sincerity of his attachment to Islam. Some, like the present writer, regard him as a genuinely devoted Muslim who did as much as possible for the spread of his faith and in fact helped to spread Islam over large areas. Others believe that he adopted Islam simply as a suitable ideology to unite his empire, and should be regarded mainly as a military figure.

They disagree, similarly, about how he was regarded by his subjects, and how his rule affected their lives. Here it is clear that we must distinguish between the earlier empire in the west and the later empire in the east. In the earlier empire, he undoubtedly appeared as a focus of Dyula, and Mande, nationalism. His rule offered real benefits. It brought an end to the continuous conflicts between small-scale states, and prosperity to long distance trade. His adoption of Islam undoubtedly appealed to Muslims. But the Great Revolt of 1888 shows clearly that there was some dissatisfaction with his rule. This was partly because of his attempt to force his subjects to become Muslims, and partly because of the financial and human burdens created by his wars of expansion. But the revolts failed; it seems likely that if Samori's regime had continued without external disturbance, it would have brought its people real benefits, and would have helped to create a Mande nationalism. This is what a French visitor thought, in 1887:

> There is no doubt that this organisation which Samori has created and put into effect represents considerable progress . . . From the point of view of civilisation, the good results of his system should become apparent in a few years time, if institutions conducive to peace and the development of resources prove capable of lasting in this unhappy country. Every village can appreciate its new well-being and relative security . . .

But of course his empire was not left undisturbed. He resisted the French invasion of 1891–2, at enormous cost in terms of the welfare of his people, who suffered terribly from his scorched earth policy. His great move to the east, likewise, caused an inconceivable amount of destruction and suffering, because of the same scorched earth policy. It has sometimes been claimed that Samori caused more suffering to the African peoples concerned than the French did. On the other hand, it must be remembered that the migration was forced on him by the French. He had to migrate or surrender. Whether a ruler is justified in paying such a high human cost to avoid surrender to a foreign power is a matter on which individual opinions will differ, but it is certain that other statesmen, at other times have been willing to pay the same price.

Once Samori's empire shifted eastward, however, it lost the basic core of Malinke patriotism. It no longer had any connection with the Dyula revolution. To the people of Abron or Gonja, Samori was a foreign conqueror who was imposing his rule by superior military might. The sheer independent existence of his empire had become Samori's primary goal, an end in itself. He had moved very far from the statesman who had worked for a situation when a solitary woman could travel safely to Freetown . . .

We have had occasion, repeatedly, in this book, to examine the way in which nineteenth-century West African statesmen practised 'selective modernisation', choosing those elements from western society which their state could profitably use, and rejecting others. In a sense, Samori was one of the great modernisers. Circumstances meant that his modernisation took place wholly within the military sphere; it is impossible to know what other channels it would have taken, without French military aggression.

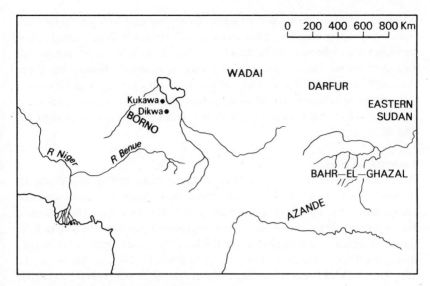

The Central Sudan in the nineteenth century

Fighting empires: 2) Rabih

Twice, in the nineteenth century, Borno came under the rule of an outstandingly talented ruler of foreign or partly foreign origin. El Kanemi was born in Libya of a Fezzani mother (see page 37). Rabih had no original connection with Borno at all, but his whole career illustrates the close links which bind the Lake Chad area with the central and eastern Sudan. Rabih (1840–1900) was born in a village north of Khartoum. He served for some years in the Egyptian army, modernised by Muhammad Ali, and then returned to the Sudan. He became a commander in the private army of a rich slave and ivory trader called Zubeir. Zubeir ruled an area called Bahr el-Ghazal, but was nominally subject to the government of Egypt. On a visit to Cairo, the over-mighty subject was placed in detention. Rabih then served Zubeir's son, Sulayman, until he in his turn was defeated, and slain by Egyptian forces in 1879.

Rabih succeeded to the leadership of what was left of his forces and built them into a powerful army. He set up his own military state in Bahr el-Ghazal, raiding north towards Darfur, and south towards Azande. Gradually, he became convinced that the rising tide of British and Egyptian authority in the Sudan was making his position there impossible to maintain. Rather in the spirit of Samori's migration to the east, he decided to lead his forces deep into the central Sudan, far from foreign influence. His progress was greatly aided by the fact that, with the exception of Wadai, most of the states in his path were small-scale, divided, or both.

Rabih was a disciple of Muhammad Ahmad, a remarkable religious teacher from the (eastern) Sudan who led a great revolt there from 1881 on. He claimed to be, and was thought to be by his followers, the Mahdi, the Rightly Guided One, sent by God to restore the world at a time when evil appears triumphant, and who will 'fill the earth with justice even as it has been filled with injustice'. He died in 1885, creating a great problem for his followers, for the Mahdi was supposed to be immortal. But Rabih's followers continued to wear the Mahdist uniform and carry the Mahdist flag. Rabih remained true to this faith to the end, and after his death a flag with Mahdist inscriptions was found in his tent. His Mahdism had the effect of strengthening the hostility of Wadai and the Sokoto caliphate, both of which rejected the pretensions of the Mahdi.

Conquest of Borno

As he advanced further to the west, he came into inevitable conflict with Wadai. Its strategic position on the trade routes to North Africa made it of great economic importance, and its overthrow would have given Rabih's new empire the economic base it needed. He conquered some southern provinces, but was only able to hold them with difficulty, in the face of Wadai hostility. Moving still further west, he conquered Baghirmi in 1892. Baghirmi appealed to Borno for assistance, but in vain. In 1893 Rabih invaded Borno. The Shehu of the day was weak and irresolute, and Rabih overthrew him without much difficulty. At the eleventh hour, the Borno nobility chose a more warlike member of the royal family, Kiyari, to lead them. Kiyari came near to victory, but Rabih's forces rallied, and won the day. Kiyari and his three brothers refused to flee, and stayed on the battlefield, hurling defiance at the invader, until they died.

Although a conqueror, Rabih was surrounded by enemies. Wadai remained bitterly hostile, cutting off the trade routes which ran through it from Borno until his death. His slaughter of many north African merchants, when he captured Borno, again disrupted trade totally for a time. Sokoto rejected all overtures of peace, fearing his reputation as a ruthless and treacherous conqueror and enraged by his alliance with Hayatu, a member of the Sokoto ruling family who followed the Mahdi. For seven years Borno endured what was in effect an economic blockade.

Rabih built a new fortified capital at Dikwa. On the next page is a picture of the gate of the city.

Borno tradition remembers his rule as grasping and destructive. A French appointed Shehu said after his death:

> For eight years we have been under the affliction of Rabih and his two sons. May God curse them both. When Rabih, the accursed, came to us with his people, the Turks, they took and killed a number of our people, pillaged our crops, destroyed our houses and massacred our men . . . They seized our women and made us slaves. He authorised the killing of members of our family numbering over forty souls from among our uncles and our people, our brothers and the sons of our maternal uncles and others.

This is, of course, the voice of the dynasty he conquered, but there is much other evidence of the greed of his soldiers and the disastrous decline in agriculture which led

The gateway to Rabih's capital of Dikwa

to the speculation that he would have to leave Borno in search of food. So greatly was he hated in the central Sudan that messengers coming from the east went in danger of death because they were fellow countrymen of Rabih. In 1896 there was an unsuccessful revolt in Borno. His very success as a conqueror created for him internal opposition and external enemies. A man from Zinder in modern Niger said, 'Rabih is surrounded by antagonistic powers and hemmed in Borno like a bird in a cage'. In the event, however, Rabih was overthrown not by his African enemies but by white colonialism.

Conflict with the French
The Lake Chad area was of key strategic significance to British, French and German imperialists. The French attacked Rabih on three sides and after fighting several pitched battles, Rabih was killed in combat in 1900, a classic example of one who lived and perished by the sword. His sons continued the struggle for some months afterwards. One of them, indeed, was nearly recognised by the British as Shehu when they took over the area, but he too was killed in battle.

Rabih's achievements
Like Samori, Rabih is assessed by different scholars differently though all agree that he was an outstandingly gifted general. One scholar writes, 'His twenty years' career of rapine and slaughter is important only in so far as it accounts for the final ruin of the Lake Chad region'. A Nigerian historian observes with justice, 'Doing nothing intrinsically different from what his European rivals were doing to African countries, he stands condemned in the view of the latter largely by reason of his failure'. But as

with Samori, it is impossible to tell the impact that his government could ultimately have had because, like Samori, his energies were consumed first by conquest and then by the struggle against colonialism. During his brief seven years of rule, his capacity for independent action was greatly restricted by the economic blockade imposed by his neighbours.

One of the Frenchmen who overthrew him, Emile Gentil, assessed him with considerable sympathy:

> One cannot help feeling a certain admiration for him . . . Death, fortunately, prevented him from fulfilling his ambitions. Yet they were not without a certain greatness, if one may judge by his actual achievements in Bornu. As soon as the country had submitted, the new Sultan set about the task of reorganization. He quickly realized the extreme weakness of the ruler's position – an outcome of the Bornu feudal system, balancing the chiefs' power against the king's, and thus creating a number of states within the state. But he saw also that he, as a new-comer, could not himself undertake the direct administration of a country whose language and customs were unfamiliar to him and his followers. He therefore left the local chiefs in charge of their various districts, so as to provide a liaison between people and ruler; but made them subordinate to his own chief officers, who took his orders, and whose reliability he ensured by keeping them near him. In fact, he replaced the old feudal government by a sort of military dictatorship. He organized taxes, demanding from each district a regular fixed sum, of which he took half himself, leaving half for the military and administrative chiefs to share. His own revenues do not seem to have been spent simply on pleasures and luxuries. He carried out a plan for a public exchequer, to cover the maintenance of his troops, organized in companies of from 150 to 250 musketeers, the erection of healthier and more comfortable buildings, and the storing of provisions with a view to future campaigns.

Resistance in small-scale societies: 1) Ivory Coast

As we noted in the case of the Igbo, the colonising powers often found it much more difficult to conquer small-scale societies, which resisted village by village, than they did to conquer much larger unified states. One remarkable example of this is the resistance which the small states of the coastal areas of Ivory Coast, such as the Baoulé, showed to French rule for many years. This resistance was only crushed, in the end, by protracted and brutal warfare.

The colony was established in 1893 and French control seemed well established by 1900. But the areas effectively occupied were very limited: 'Elsewhere, there are only a few isolated posts under siege', and there was constant hostility, especially among the Baoulé. The Africans, wrote a Frenchman, 'Continued to consider us as much as ever as intruders, reckoning that they were less wretched before our arrival'.

In 1908 Angoulvant became Governor of the colony and began a policy of systematic military conquest. In 1910 there was a revolt along the railway line, which was a protest against forced unpaid labour and the confiscation of firearms. (To make matters worse, the people had recently paid a tax on firearms.) After the revolt Angoulvant was sent reinforcements from Senegal.

> The villages taken were burnt down. No pity was shown to prisoners. The severed heads were put up on poles by the railway stations or in front of the huts in the villages.

Repression continued. All firearms were confiscated and this was a serious matter to the forest peoples who treasured them for hunting. Many chiefs were deported, often being sent to the 'dry guillotine' of Mauritania. Taxes were imposed retrospectively, forced labour and porterage were exacted, and the forest peoples were resettled from their many little communities into new villages near the road, so that they could be easily controlled by the French. After years of military action, Angoulvant left Ivory Coast in 1916, promoted to a Governor-Generalship. A French general, who served in the same area, called him 'A fanatical politician, who used his knowledge to feather his own nest, and attended cynically to his own interests while haphazardly looking after those of the colonies'.

There are many parallels between resistance to the French in Ivory Coast and to the British in south-eastern Nigeria. In each case, there was an enormous difference between the combatants, the colonial power being opposed by little villages or village groups. But despite this, these small-scale societies resisted for years on end, long after empires such as Samori's had fallen. In each case, resistance fed on the sufferings created by colonial rule, especially forced labour and porterage, and the confiscation of arms, which had represented a major economic investment.

Resistance in small-scale societies: 2) Bai Bureh

Another outstanding example of resistance in small-scale states is the rising headed by Bai Bureh, the ruler of a little chieftaincy in Sierra Leone, who led a number of allied states in the guerilla struggle which we shall consider here. In terms of his resources, and the size of his state, his military achievements were comparable with those of Samori.

In an earlier chapter, we studied the foundation of the Colony of Sierra Leone, in a restricted area around Freetown. As time went on, the Creoles were very anxious that the area under British control be extended, to safeguard their commercial interests in the hinterland. But the mid-nineteenth century was, on the whole, a period when British thinking about colonies was dominated by the desire for economy and the limitation of colonial responsibilities. The opportunity was lost, and in the end the French gained large areas which had been within the commercial range of Sierra Leone.

From the 1870s on the British began to extend their authority over the states of the interior. Since their object was simply to exclude the French, they only sought at first to exercise control over the external relations of the states. The chieftaincies concerned welcomed the British as allies against their enemies, or potential enemies, such as Samori.

In the late 1880s and early 1890s, however, colonial rule came to encroach increasingly on their lives. The hinterland was declared a Protectorate in 1896. One of the aspects of colonial rule which caused much resentment was the Frontier Police, who often exploited their position, tyrannising the people and plundering their property. (One finds the same kinds of complaints against soldiers, police, and court officials in, for instance, southern Nigeria, and it created bitter discontent there as well.) When the Protectorate was created, the chiefs lost most of their traditional say in judicial matters. As one of them put it, 'The king of the country, however small he be, who cannot settle small matters is no longer king'. The final factor which was to drive them to revolt was the decision to impose a tax on their houses.★ The key objection was probably not the financial burden involved, though complaints were made about this too, but the implication that they did not have absolute possession of their very homes. It seemed that they were, in some sense, paying rent for them. Both the Creole trading community and the local press sympathised with their viewpoint.

At first the chiefs of the Temne area, Bai Bureh among them, tried peaceful means of protest. They petitioned the colonial government. A deputation spent some time in Freetown for the purpose. When their protests were unheeded, they had no other way open to them but submission, or violence. The House Tax became the climax and symbol of all their grievances. The British governor of the time, Sir Frederic Cardew, came in time to see this clearly.

> The true causes in my opinion . . . are the desire for independence and for a reversion to the old order of things. It is practically a revolt of the Chiefs whose authority has been lessened and whose property has suffered through the abolition of slavery. They are sick of the supremacy of the white man as asserted by the District Commissioners and Frontier Police . . . On top of it all, comes the house tax which is the last straw that breaks the camel's back and hence the revolt.

Bai Bureh

Bai Bureh is the name by which historians normally refer to the Temne chief who led the revolt against the House Tax. In fact, Bai Bureh was his official title as chief of Kesseh. Before he became chief, he was known as Kebelai. He belonged to a caste of professional warriors, who played a very important role in Temne society. Temne war chiefs would recruit these celebrated fighting men, over a large area, to take part in a war. Kebelai was celebrated for his courage and strength. He graduated from

★ The tax was in fact called the Hut Tax – an indication of the disparaging way the Europeans of the day viewed all things African.

warrior to war chief, and was one of the henchmen of a Muslim ruler, Bokhari, who fought a jihad-type series of wars in the area, between 1865 and 1885.

In 1886, after Bokhari's death, Kebelai became the ruler of the small state of Kesseh, on the banks of the Small Scarcies river. One of his predecessors had already signed a treaty with the British; this provided him with a tiny stipend of ten pounds a year, and obliged him to let the British arbitrate in any disputes with his neighbours. Bai Bureh, as he had now become, did in fact take part in such a conflict, but he escaped from British custody when they tried to capture him. A little later, oddly enough, he was fighting as the ally of the British. They were trying to capture a Susu stronghold on the Small Scarcies. After two unsuccessful attempts, they took it with Bai Bureh's help.

In February 1898 the British tried to collect the House Tax at Port Loko, not far from Bai Bureh's capital. The people refused, and Bai Bureh was blamed for this. Troops were sent to arrest him. Bai Bureh's men easily turned them back, jeering at them. This led to the first shots of war, in which the other Temne states came to the aid of Bai Bureh.

Bai Bureh realised that the trade guns with which his men were armed were no match for modern rifles. Accordingly, he resorted to guerilla warfare, attacking the British column, with its large, slow moving, train of carriers, as it moved along the forest paths. He cleverly adapted his people's traditional skill in building fortifications. The Temne towns were surrounded by elaborate stockades, made of logs and boulders. They were so strong that they could shatter the shells of seven pound guns, and

Bai Bureh after his capture

the people were so expert in their construction that a stockade around a whole town could be built in a day. Now, his men built barricades across the forest paths. As the British forces (largely black West Indians) stopped to demolish them, they were attacked by invisible snipers from the bush. He set up an excellent system of intelligence. His men mingled with the British forces' carriers, and watched their movements, unseen, from the bush. To suppress the rising, six companies of the West India Regiment systematically destroyed the villages of the area. The same technique was used against the Igbo, and the peoples of the Ivory Coast.

Even when the rising had been put down, Bai Bureh remained at large, although there was a £100 reward on his head. Finally, he was captured by a British patrol, after twenty-three weeks in the bush. After a period of exile abroad, he was allowed to return, ageing and ill, in 1905, to spend the last three years of his life in his native land.

The British felt real admiration for the soldierly qualities of Bai Bureh, and his followers. In the words of one officer of the Frontier Police:

> But even in their very fighting they betrayed such admirable qualities as are not always to be found in the troops of the 'civilised' nations. They loved their chief, and remained loyal to him to the very last, whilst they understand bush-fighting as well as you and I do our very alphabet!

Secondary resistance

The House Tax War is an interesting example of a type of struggle which historians have called secondary resistance. This has several characteristics. It takes place, not in response to the initial imposition of colonial rule, but afterwards, when its effects have become apparent. It succeeds in uniting many previously disunited states. We noted another example of this type of struggle in the Ekumeku risings among the western Igbo. There are other, very large-scale examples from other parts of Africa, such as the Maji Maji war of 1905, in which people of southern Tanzania tried to expel the Germans.

The Mende war

Bai Bureh's rising among the Temne inspired another movement, further south, among the Mende. While Bai Bureh's war was still in full swing, the Mende broke into revolt as well. Their rising was different from that of Bai Bureh in several important respects. Bai Bureh fought a limited war: he concentrated on attacking enemy soldiers, and left missionaries, for example, unharmed. (Only one missionary was killed, and that was by mistake.) The Mende, however, attacked all the Europeans and Creoles, missionaries and traders, in their midst. It was a total attack on all who had adopted European ways, and was inspired by a variety of grievances, including the House Tax, the oppression of the Frontier Police and a sense of being exploited by Creole traders. Altogether, hundreds of people were killed.

People in Freetown were terrified, awaiting a Mende attack. But the attack did not materialise, and the Mende were much more easily defeated than Bai Bureh's followers.

The rising had been organised by the powerful Poro society. It lacked a general, like Bai Bureh, or Samori, to plan overall strategy, and the Mende fought, and were defeated, in isolated bands. Their weapons were even more inadequate than those of the Temne. The Temne fought with trade guns. Many of the Mende fought with matchets or clubs.

The rising is called the Mende war, but numerous non-Mende took part, among them Vai, Loko, Susu, Bullom and Temne. Many of the insurgents were tried for murder, and ninety-six were hanged.

The unconquered heart

There is no point in time at which we can pause and say: by this time, the conquest of West Africa is complete. In the 1920s, the Portuguese in Guinea-Bissau and the French in Mauritania still controlled uneasy islands of alien power in the midst of a sea of unconquered territory. The history of the colonial period, as we shall see, is very largely a history of various forms of resistance, such as peasants' risings, urban 'riots', strikes, and more or less anti-European religious revivals.

In a number of instances, traditional rulers invoked the assistance of their traditional gods. The Ijebu of southern Yorubaland had fought bravely against the invaders; in 1907 their ruler, the Awujale, was still trying to expel them by ritual and religious means. Earlier, the ruler of the Mossi of Upper Volta had tried the same techniques, also in vain, seeking the same ends.

European critics of colonialism

It would be wrong to give the impression that all Europeans were agreed on the value and moral acceptability of colonial conquests. Just as some Africans collaborated with the invader and some resisted him, some Europeans were enthusiastic supporters of empire and others were equally outspoken in their condemnation of it. In the middle of the nineteenth century, many Englishmen opposed colonies as troublesome and expensive. At the end of the century, when the British Empire was an accomplished fact, an Englishman called J. A. Hobson wrote an enormously influential book called *Imperialism: A Study* (it was published in 1902). Briefly, his argument was that imperialism went together with social injustice at home. Too few people held too large a share of the wealth of the country: there was more opportunity for them to invest their money profitably in overseas markets than at home. Hobson suggested that if the distribution of income were more equal, higher living standards would create a more profitable market in the home country. 'Imperialism is the fruit of this false economy; "social reform" is its remedy'.

The chief Marxist interpretation of imperialism was made by V. I. Lenin, whose argument was broadly similar to that of Hobson. In general, European socialist thinkers tended to see colonial conquest abroad and social inequality at home as different aspects of the exploitation of the poor by the rich. But there were many critics of colonialism who were not particularly socialist at all. These included a number of journalists and writers who attacked specific colonial abuses, such as the dreadful conditions in the Belgian Congo (more precisely, King Leopold's Congo). A Frenchman who was not a socialist published a book in 1911 called *Colonial Crimes* in which he said:

> I had this dream: at last there existed on this earth justice for all subject races and conquered peoples. Tired of being despoiled, pillaged, suppressed and massacred, the Arabs and the Berbers drove their oppressors from North Africa, the blacks did the same for the rest of the continent.
>
> And, forgetting that I was French – which is nothing – I remembered only one thing: that I was a Man – which is everything – and I felt an indescribable joy in the depth of my being.

7

The Colonial Experience I

Patterns of colonial government

Once colonial governments were actually established, the colonial powers found new allies. In the period of conquest the opposition had been led by traditional rulers, although many of these, such as Ja Ja and Samori, were in fact themselves new to positions of authority. The colonial powers had formed in the nineteenth century a kind of uneasy alliance with the educated elite, who were often given high posts in the civil service and a say on the legislative councils. Educated Africans viewed colonial conquest with profoundly mixed feelings. On the whole they tended to see it as necessary for the formation of a compact nation state overriding tribal boundaries and for the spread of 'civilisation' and Christianity. They sometimes protested against specific brutalities but seldom gave the resisters practical help. Sometimes they revealed misgivings as to the quality of alien 'civilisation'. 'Have they not proposed to open up the country with Rum and Gin and Ammunitions of War?'

Once colonial rule was established, the pattern of alliances changed dramatically. The European colonisers and 'traditional rulers', whether of recent or ancient origin formed a marriage of convenience. Indirect Rule, as the new system was called, was the cheapest and simplest way of governing vast areas, for it meant, in theory at least, using forms of government that were there before. Meanwhile, the elite were crowded out of the position they had once enjoyed and instead became a threat to the careers of white officials. The policy of excluding them from the local government of most of the colony was justified by white officialdom on the grounds that the educated elite of the coastal area neither cared for nor understood the 'real Africans' in the interior. Interestingly enough, the elite sometimes accepted this analysis. Chief Obafemi Awolowo said in a book published in 1947:

> Given a choice from among white officials, chiefs and educated Nigerians as the principal rulers of the country, illiterate man today would exercise his preference for the three in the order in which they are named. He is convinced and has good reasons to be, that he can always get better treatment from the white man than he could hope to get from the chiefs and the educated elements.

The frustration of the educated classes at being excluded from the alliance and from positions of power was one of the most powerful forces behind the nationalist movement. By the late 1940s both the British and the French were forced to re-define their alliances once again and they began to work with, and hand power to, the educated group which they had for so long condemned.

From the perspective of 1976 the colonial experience appears a very brief one. In 1900 many of the areas enclosed within the new colonial boundaries had never been visited by a European. As late as 1918 in some areas, colonialism was still being opposed by force of arms. After 1945 the tide of imperial authority was on the ebb. Many West Africans were born before the European conquest and lived through the whole period of colonial rule and then again under an autonomous African government.

But in the brief heyday of colonialism – between, perhaps, 1918 and 1945 – both Europeans and Africans tended to think that colonialism had come forever, if not for good. On the rare occasions when officials contemplated the end of their regime, they saw it as being hundreds of years in the future. Africans inevitably often came to think so too. An Igbo chief once asked a government interpreter if there was any way of getting rid of the white man. He replied, 'Impossible. The white man has come to stay as long as men lived'.

The discussion which follows concentrates, in the main, on French and British West Africa. Germany's solitary possession in West Africa★ – the slender strip of territory which was Togoland – was divided between France and Britain after the First World War. Portuguese Guinea, a tiny triangle of territory which is largely mangrove swamp, will be discussed in the context of nationalism.

The study of French and British systems of colonial rule reveals different types of practice, and a number of theories elaborated to justify the practice, for, as frequently happens, the theory was often developed to justify the reality.

Assimilation
The practice of assimilation rested upon an ideal to which Frenchmen have had, in theory at least, a strong commitment since the Revolution of 1789 – the idea of the equality of men. In the context of colonialism, it meant that subject people should be treated as if they were Frenchmen and encouraged to become as much like Frenchmen as possible. This concept was preserved in the expression used to describe France's overseas territories, *France d'Outre Mer*, Overseas France.

The ideal of assimilation was relatively easy to put into practice as long as France's West African possessions were confined to a cluster of small settlements on the coast of Senegal, whose inhabitants had a fairly high degree of exposure to French culture. The right of electing a Deputy in the French Assembly, and the more fundamental right of citizenship, were held by the members of the four communes (townships) of St Louis, Dakar, Rufisque and Gorée. They also enjoyed a considerable measure of

★ This study, for historical and geographical reasons, excludes Cameroun and Chad, which were part of French Equatorial Africa during the colonial period.

local government, electing their own Mayors and Town Councillors as well as a General Council* which was the equivalent of a provincial legislature in France.

When French rule expanded over the vast area of French West Africa, the doctrine of assimilation became more difficult to put into practice. The numbers involved were vastly greater: if the people of French West Africa had been able to send deputies to Paris in proportion to their numbers, the Africans would have outnumbered the Frenchmen! Moreover, as they came into contact with Africans who had, in fact, very little contact with French culture it seemed less practicable to treat them as Frenchmen.

What actually happened was a compromise. The inhabitants of the four communes kept their rights of citizenship. In all the rest of French West Africa, it was possible, but very difficult, to obtain the same right, after 1912. The applicant for citizenship had to have one wife only, to read, write and speak fluent French, to have done military service, and to have worked for the French for ten years. By 1939 only 500 had obtained it outside the four communes, though there were at least 15,000,000 people in French West Africa.

The strengths and weaknesses of assimilation

The policy of Assimilation had its strengths and weaknesses. On the positive side, the French tended to regard the *assimilé* with a genuine acceptance, which contrasted with the distrust and contempt the British, in the colonial period, often displayed towards the educated. The *assimilé* tended, too, to speak and write French with a perfection that his English-speaking counterpart seldom approached. (This is still true of Francophone Africans.) The price he paid for this was isolation from his own cultural background.

More important, Assimilation created a tiny area of relative equality, and a vast area of inequality. The Subjects, as all the other West Africans in French colonies were called, had hardly any rights at all. The same thing was true of the territories ruled by Portugal; in West Africa represented by the tiny area of Guinea-Bissau. It has been estimated that by the 1950s, the *assimilados* comprised one-quarter of one per cent of the population of Guinea-Bissau. Ironically, many of the inhabitants of Portugal itself were illiterate peasants who would not have qualified as *assimilados*!

Indirect Rule

Nearly all of West Africa was governed by a system called Indirect Rule. It is a great pity that when so many of the really exciting and interesting questions about the impact of colonialism on African societies remain unanswered, or even unasked, so much of the energy of historians who have actually studied the colonial era has been absorbed by the less interesting question: does the government of this area or that

* In 1920 the General Council was replaced by the Colonial Council. Twenty chiefs from the rest of Senegal were added to the original twenty elected Citizens. Since the chiefs depended on the French for their position, this in practice lessened the body's independence.

conform to an abstraction called Indirect Rule? We shall now look at the forms it took, and see how significant the differences between them really were.

Classic Indirect Rule

The practice of Indirect Rule, which simply means ruling through an African ruler, existed early in the nineteenth century. On the Gold Coast in the 1830s Maclean exercised an advisory role among Fante chiefs. From 1854 on, disputes in the Niger Delta were settled at a Court of Equity, where Africans and Europeans sat together, and decisions were reached by majority vote. But the full development of the theory and practice of Indirect Rule took place in northern Nigeria, under Lugard's leadership, until 1906, and after 1912.

Lugard and his successors decided to rule through the emirs. This decision was taken partly because of a genuine esteem for their government (unfortunately the same esteem and understanding were not extended to the political systems of the Tiv, Igbo or Ibibio). It was partly also because of convenience; British officials were few in number, and expensive (they expected high salaries and pensions, and frequent home leave). Indirect Rule was much cheaper than an expansion in the number of white officials. The emirs were allowed to levy taxes and to run their own law courts and prisons. After 1904 they paid a quarter of the taxes collected to the central government. Later this practice was further developed into a system of Native Treasuries. The emir stood at the summit of a hierarchy with District Heads and Village Heads at the lower levels.

As time went on, Lugard's successors became increasingly extreme in their devotion to Indirect Rule. They developed a sense of romantic attachment, which was in part sheer snobbery, a reverence for emirs simply because they were aristocrats. 'They enjoyed playing polo with princes'. One finds exactly the same attitude among British officials who worked in the princely states in India. They came to see their task as one of protection and preservation, and not of development. They sought to shield the aristocratic Islamic society of the north from what they regarded as harmful external influences, such as western education. (Often they were more conservative than the emirs themselves. In 1937 the Emir of Hadejia wanted to appoint an able man to his council. The British official concerned objected because the man was of slave origins! The emir pointed out that times had changed, but the official did not lift his veto.) In doing so, they entirely went against the only reasonable justification for colonialism, that it hastened the process of modernisation. New recruits who realised this and pointed it out were blocked from promotion, or 'banished' to the less favoured Middle Belt! When, with the success of the nationalist movement, the modern world broke in anyway, the north's long lack of contact with western education had placed it at a tremendous disadvantage.

The theory of Indirect Rule often led British officials to turn a blind eye to what they themselves regarded as abuses. In the words of Charles Temple, Lieutenant Governor in northern Nigeria from 1914–17, and an enthusiastic supporter of the system:

To put this policy into effect means first of all that you must shut your eyes, up to a certain point, to a great many practices which, though not absolutely repugnant to humanity, are nevertheless reprehensible to our ideas . . . You must have patience with the liar though he lies seventy times seven; you must at times have patience with the pecculator of public funds (a hard pill this to swallow) . . . You have to make up your mind that men are not all equal before the law and cannot so be treated. An important Chief must not be made to work among a gang of felons from the common herd, even though his crimes be far blacker than theirs . . .

A future Governor of northern Nigeria* made much the same point in the early 'forties. He recalled later:

. . . there was a chief of Niger Province who represented all that seemed to me objectionable in a ruler. As a judge he was venal, as an administrator he was extortionate, his word was valueless, and his fingers were forever sticky with other men's honey . . . But when I made my case to my Chief Commissioner, he replied, 'What . . . Depose a Second Class Chief? Heav'n forfend!'

It is strange that at a time when social, economic and political inequalities were gradually being reduced in Britain, the British kept such inequalities alive in the western Sudan.

Despite the system of Indirect Rule, and the apparent lack of direct government, colonial rule did change political realities in a fundamental way. Before the advent of colonial rule, the ruler was responsible only to his people. If his rule became unacceptable to them, he could be deposed. Most, if not all, African states had, as we have seen, an elaborate structure of checks and balances, to prevent the ruler becoming too powerful. Colonialism disrupted this delicate mechanism, for the continued status and power of the chief depended not on his being acceptable to the people he governed, but upon his being acceptable to his white overlords. Often he was forced to pursue policies which were highly unacceptable to his people, in order to please the white officials. (The very word 'chief', so common in colonial literature, shows how the traditional ruler's status had been weakened, for it was applied to many rulers who in pre-colonial times had been regarded as kings, and were described as such in French and British treaties.)

Fewer important emirs were deposed under the British than in pre-colonial times. British support could thus keep an unpopular emir in power. There was a limit to this process, however, for if a ruler became too unpopular, he was less useful to the colonising power. The British presence often encouraged traditional rulers to continue to practise corruption and injustice. But this does not, of course, imply that all traditional rulers were corrupt. Some rulers were corrupt, including, interestingly enough, some men of outstanding administrative ability. The full range of possible attitudes

* B. Sharwood Smith.

can be seen in the careers of two successive Sultans of Sokoto – the corrupt and unpopular Muhammedu, whose career ended in deposition, and the 'devout and upright Hassan', who succeeded him in 1931 and reigned until his death in 1938. Ja'afaru of Zaria (1937–59) was another traditional ruler of outstanding qualities, as was Yahaya of Gwandu (1938–55), the north's first western-educated emir.

Yahaya indeed deserves a little further mention. The product of Katsina College, he nearly became a Christian. This would have cut him off from any hope of becoming emir, and thus shows his deep religious sincerity. (An interesting comment on the times is that the prospect of his becoming a Christian alarmed the British much more than it did his brother, the Emir of Gwandu, and the mission which had influenced him also discouraged him from conversion.) He was an outstanding District Head, who drove himself round in a small car, without any of the pomp and large entourage which characterised others in his position. After he became emir, he continued in the same personal simplicity, combined with 'a deep compassion for his fellow man' and a sympathy for progressive ideas.

> His features, in repose, were those of a spiritually dedicated man; yet, in conversation, when pleased or diverted, a swift smile of great charm would come readily to his lips.

When corrupt UAC clerks defrauded the peasants, he compensated the victims with money from Native Authority funds.

Modified Indirect Rule

A lively debate has gone on among historians as to whether the form of government which was established in south-eastern Nigeria should be called Direct or Indirect Rule. It depends, of course, on how you define Indirect Rule. It was certainly Indirect Rule in the sense of being rule through African chiefs, but not if Indirect Rule is defined as retaining traditional forms of government.

In south-eastern Nigeria, among the Igbo, Ibibio and Ogoja peoples, the British found a large number of small but complex village democracies. For many years they had no real understanding of their workings. They were, in any case, unsuited to the needs of a modern bureaucratic state for at least three reasons – their small size, the very large number of people involved in decision-making, and their heavy reliance on supernatural sanctions (it is hard to imagine the British running a system which included secret societies and oracles) and these lost much of their force anyway as the spread of Christianity weakened traditional religion. But because the British took it for granted that Africans were ruled by chiefs, they ended up by creating chiefs where none had previously existed.

The British established a series of Native Courts. Those who sat on them received Warrants, and were known as Warrant Chiefs. Since they not only tried court cases but also controlled forced labour, they became extremely powerful. How were they chosen? Some were men who had previously been wealthy and influential (often through slave trading). Sometimes the first man the British met in a village, the one who first came forward, was made a chief. Distrusting the British, the elders some-times put forward one of the community's least esteemed members, to see what happened to him.

The Warrant Chiefs soon became wealthy, corrupt, and highly unpopular, partly because their office was not a traditional one, and they had no precedents to guide them. They became notorious for the sale of justice, and for using forced labour for their own ends. When one of them was questioned about this in the 1960s, he replied, 'to grow fat an insect must feed on other insects'. Finally, in 1929–30, there was exten-sive rioting among Igbo, Ibibio and Delta women, which tradition remembers as the Women's War. This was occasioned by rumours that women would be taxed, but was also the expression of many grievances, among them the exactions of the Warrant Chiefs. This forced the British to change the system, but a heavy price was paid. According to official casualty lists, fifty-five of the women were killed, and fifty wounded.

The difference between Indirect Rule in south-eastern Nigeria and in the north was one of degree, not kind. In both, the African ruler was given a large say in local government; in both, a radical departure was made from tradition, for the African ruler's chief concern was to stay acceptable to the European overlord. In each case, the elaborate system of checks and balances which existed previously was destroyed; both produced a number of instances of oppression and misrule.

Although the British did not transfer their officials as often as the French did, their officials' frequent ignorance of local languages increased the power of the Africans in authority. Few indeed were the officials who mastered the complex tonal languages of southern Nigeria. In the north, a knowledge of Hausa was essential for promotion, but an official who spent his whole career in the north recalled that he learnt Hausa with difficulty in a Kanuri-speaking area: 'At various times I started to learn Shuwa Arabic, Tiv and Fulani but in every case before I got far, I was moved elsewhere', and then he was posted to Idomaland!

Association

In the vast expanse of French West Africa, outside the privileged Four Communes, the French, like the British, ruled through African chiefs. The term for this was *Association*. As with the Warrant Chiefs, scholars disagree as to whether this should be called Direct or Indirect Rule.

Position of the chiefs

There were some very real differences between chiefs under French and British juris-diction. The chief in French territories had much less power. He had very little legal jurisdiction – none in criminal cases – and unlike his British counterpart, he controlled neither police nor prisons. He collected taxes, but had to hand the whole sum over to the government, which paid him a small salary. His British equivalent used part of the taxes he himself levied to finance his own administration, to which he appointed the personnel. In general, the French chief did all the unpopular work of administration for the French, such as levying taxes and conscripting workers for forced labour and soldiers for the army. His salary was so small that he was almost obliged to add to it by corruption, which increased his unpopularity, and his vulnerability, for the French could always dismiss him for corruption.

Sometimes great traditional rulers were made Paramount Chiefs (*Chefs Supérieurs*) but in general the French were less inclined than the British to select members of traditional ruling houses. Sometimes, instead, they chose retired soldiers, clerks, or even cooks, who spoke French and were familiar with French ways. Very often they followed a deliberate policy of reducing the power of great traditional rulers; thus the Almamis of Futa Jallon★ were reduced to small cantonal chiefs.

One should not exaggerate the contrast between French and British policies with regard to chiefs. If the French destroyed the power of the kings of Dahomey, and the Almamis of Futa Jallon, the British abolished the office of Asantehene from 1900 to 1935. And even the French levelling policy did little to undermine the great power of the traditional ruler of Mossi, the Mogho Naba; when his power was at last challenged, it was by Voltaic nationalists. The British did not always keep to their policy of choosing traditionally acceptable rulers; in 1933 they imposed Gbelegbuwa II, an educated Christian, over the Ijebu of Yorubaland. Because by traditional standards he was not eligible for the position, he was never acceptable to his people; he suffered great difficulties and was kept in power only by British backing.

French West Africa was divided into 188 *cercles*, each of which was under the French equivalent of a Resident. These *cercles* were divided into 2,200 *cantons*, often located deliberately across tribal boundaries. The key figures in local government were the cantonal chiefs, each of whom had on average twenty-four village chiefs under him.

In general then, the French chief had fewer powers than his British counterpart. He was dismissed more readily, he was less likely to be a traditional ruler in his own right, he had less freedom of action in his relations with white officials, and he was less likely to be acceptable to his own people. The differences have often been attributed to the fact that the British came from a monarchy and had a weakness for tradition, pageantry, and, indeed, kings. France was a Republic, committed at least in theory to Liberty, Equality and Fraternity. This egalitarian principle tended to undermine the role of traditional rulers. But it did not tend to introduce equality. The vast mass of Subjects in French colonial Africa enjoyed neither liberty, equality nor fraternity.

Position of subjects
Outside the privileged islands of the Four Communes, the Subjects were distinguished by the multiplicity of their duties and the fewness of their rights. They paid taxes and were frequently coerced into forced labour. They did military service. They could neither publish newspapers nor form political parties, nor join trade unions.† One of

★ In pre-colonial times, two rival ruling families took it in turns to provide the Almami, for two years at a time each.
† Until 1944.

their most hated disabilities was the *indigénat* which entitled the French administrator to imprison an African at his discretion for offences which were so loosely defined that they could easily be made to fit any case at all. After 1940 the time of imprisonment was limited to four days, but there were no safeguards against re-arrest.

Some observers have seen related contradictions in both the British and French forms of local government. The British relied on chiefs, but their educational system created a large western-educated elite whom they employed in western style bureaucracy. The whole handover of government to the nationalists could only take place if such an elite existed. The French were advocates of assimilation, but regardless of consistency, they were prepared to extend it only to a tiny group and even this group reacted violently against the loss of identity which assimilation implied, and developed in reaction the philosophy of negritude.

Direct administration

In colonial capitals, such as Lagos or Freetown, or in new townships, such as Kaduna, there was no attempt to rule through chiefs. Freetown had an English type of elected local government, headed by a Mayor, and we have already noted the municipal institutions of the Four Communes. Elsewhere, Africans had no say in the government of the townships in which they lived, except in cities like Lagos which sent members to the Legislative Council. The Legislative Council, however, really belongs to the institutions of central government, which we shall now consider.

Central government

The French colonies

A glance at a map of colonial West Africa shows one of the key differences between French and British colonies. French West Africa formed one continuous land mass.

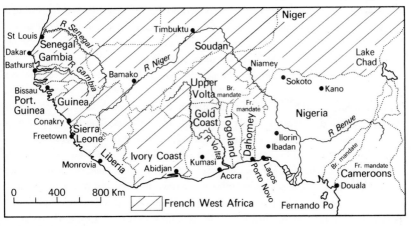

Colonial West Africa

Despite its vast extent, it could thus be regarded as a single unit. This tendency was encouraged by the background of the French themselves, who have always had a preference for highly centralised institutions. The boundaries of the individual French colonies changed from time to time (Upper Volta was created in 1920, portioned among its neighbours in 1932, and recreated in response to local pressures in 1947), but the unit of French West Africa was constant.

At its head was the Governor-General of French West Africa, with his headquarters at Dakar, in Senegal. He exercised supreme authority over the lieutenant governors in the individual colonies, including the governor of Senegal, with his headquarters at St Louis. The Governor-General had a very wide range of powers. He alone could communicate with the Minister for the Colonies (that is, he alone could express his views on major policy matters to the French government). He controlled the customs revenue, which he shared out among the colonies, and even controlled the appointment of most civil servants. His powers were, however, limited in practice by the vast area he governed, which meant that the attention he could give to each area was small. This meant that the local official did, in practice, have considerable freedom. In theory, the Governor-General had to implement laws coming from Paris; in practice, this was sometimes delayed for years. In the formation of policies in the metropolitan government, the African had no voice. In the words of a governor:

> There is no native counterweight to administrative influence. The natives are deprived of representation in France. On the other hand, the influence of the settlers and the businessmen, and especially that of the big companies, is frequently felt in Paris . . .

The Governor-General had an advisory council, the Council of Government, where the overwhelming majority were French officials. The governors of the colonies also had advisory councils, but since they nominated the members in the first place, these were unlikely to create difficulties for them. African interests were expressed most effectively by the single Deputy sent by the Four Communes to the French National Assembly, and by the Council General of Senegal which not only provided one member of the Governor-General's advisory council but was also able to veto the Senegalese budget, a right of which, on occasion, it made good use.

A law passed in 1924 meant that French officials could not serve two consecutive tours in the same colony. This was a backward step. In the early twentieth century, some Frenchmen had become real authorities on the language, history and culture of the areas where they worked. After 1924 they had much less opportunity of understanding local languages, or conditions generally, than their British equivalents. Even more than in the British colonies, much power ended up in the hands of the interpreters, through whom they communicated with the world around them. It was said in the 1930s that 'Circle police, interpreters or secretaries are nearly always the true chiefs of the country'. This power diminished as time went on and more people learnt French. In both French and British colonies, too, the pressure of paper work tended to divert the attention and energies of local officials from local realities.

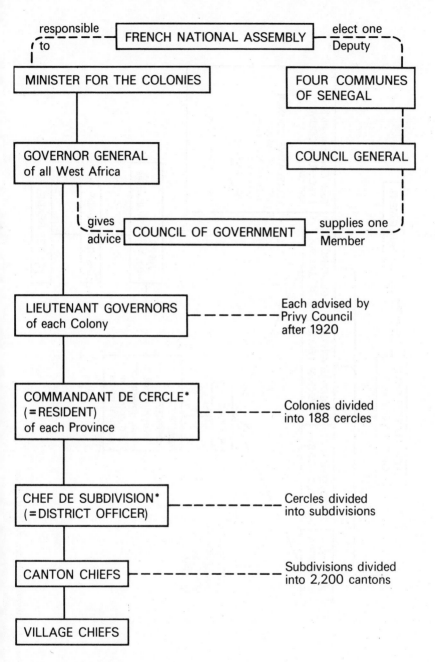

* nearly always white officials

The structure of Government in French West Africa

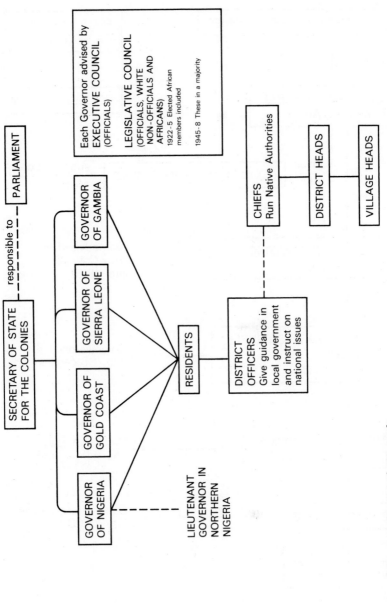

The structure of Government in British West Africa

The English colonies

The colony was the area around Lagos, Freetown or Bathurst. In the Gold Coast, it was larger, embracing the whole coastal area. Inhabitants of the colony area tended to regard their rights as 'British citizens' with jealous pride, not unlike the Citizens of Senegal. A nationalist like Herbert Macaulay, indeed, agitated not for independence, but for fuller implementation of the rights of British citizens, such as not being taxed without being represented.

The four colonies could communicate with each other only by sea, or by crossing French territory. Therefore it was less practicable for them to form one united administration. The attempt was actually made on several occasions in the nineteenth century, in the 1820s and in the 1860s, but it did not succeed. Interestingly enough, the same kind of sentiment persisted in one of the early nationalist movements – the National Congress of British West Africa. But from the late nineteenth century, the four British colonies were each linked directly with the appropriate British minister in London.

Each of the four Governors had two councils, to advise him – an Executive Council, comprising British officials, and a Legislative Council, which made laws with his assent. The Gambia acquired a Legislative Council in 1843, the Gold Coast in 1850, Lagos in 1862 and Sierra Leone in 1863.* These councils consisted partly of British officials, and partly of non-officials, who were drawn from among British merchants and missionaries, and educated Africans. Although they were nominated by the Governor, they were not his tools, and these African members often used their position to subject the government to searching criticism. Sir Samuel Lewis who died in 1903 was noted for this in Sierra Leone, and so were Sapara Williams, in the early twentieth century, and Dr C. C. Adeniyi-Jones at a later date (1926–38) in Nigeria. Since Africans were always in a minority, they could do little more than criticise, but even so they looked on their role as the nucleus of self-government, as it had been in white settler colonies. But in Nigeria, for a time, representative institutions actually went backwards. The educated elite disliked the division of Nigeria into Northern and Southern Provinces and strongly advocated the unification of the country and the extension of western education to the north. But amalgamation when it came – planned by Lugard in 1914 – retained the north/south division. The Legislative Council, which had legislated for all southern Nigeria since 1906, was now confined to Lagos. A Nigerian Council was established, but since this was purely advisory with no real powers at all, it died a natural death.

To strengthen the African voice in the government of their own land, several steps were necessary. First, some or all of the African members must be elected by African electors, to emancipate them from their dependence on the governor's nomination, and to ensure that they really did speak for the people. (Colonial governors always tried to claim that the urban elite had no knowledge of or sympathy for the rural masses.) Nigeria in 1922, Sierra Leone in 1924 and the Gold Coast in 1925 underwent

---

* Before this, Sierra Leone had a combined Executive and Legislative Council.

constitutional changes which provided for elected members.* These were directly elected in a few major townships by a small electorate, and by chiefs elsewhere. The early nationalist movements concentrated largely on trying to expand this tiny foothold of democracy. Four out of forty-six in Nigeria were elected directly, three out of thirty in the Gold Coast, and three out of twenty-one in Sierra Leone. They could criticise, and ask questions, but not reject laws. In Nigeria, the North, which was largely governed by decree, was outside its scope except in financial questions.

The next stage came some twenty years later, when the elected African members became the majority. This change was introduced in 1945 in Nigeria, Gambia and the Gold Coast, and three years later in Sierra Leone. This did not mean that these colonies were now self-governing, however, because the Legislative Council did not control the executive. This was controlled by the Governor, who was responsible not to the Legislative Council, but to the Colonial Secretary in London, who in his turn was responsible to the English parliament. What in fact existed in such a situation, then, was representative, not responsible, government (i.e. the Legislative Council represented the people, but the executive was not responsible to it). Both the British and the West Africans saw it as a half-way post on the way to full self-government. A further step was taken when African members were placed on the Executive Council during the Second World War, but this was less of a breakthrough, because the Executive Council in practice enjoyed little independent authority.

Individuals

We have looked at the formal structures of colonial government. In some ways a more interesting question is: what kind of Europeans joined the colonial service, what were their motives and their attitudes? European culture was, of course, embodied in individuals whether they were administrators, missionaries, or traders.

In the early days of colonial rule (before the First World War) it was difficult to recruit Europeans for West Africa at all (the Indian Civil Service was more prestigious and better paid, and West Africa still had a reputation as the White Man's Grave). Some officials had served in the Boer War, or came from open-air occupations in foreign lands such as tea planting or cattle ranching. Some were seeking an escape from financial problems or personal unhappiness in England. A distinguished early colonial administrator in southern Nigeria went there at his own expense, because he was involved in a divorce case. Later, the African colonial service became an established career pattern. It was often a suitable career for demobilised officers after two world wars, or in the depression years, the only career that seemed available (a nineteenth-century English radical called the British empire 'a gigantic system of outdoor relief for the British middle classes'). Recruits were almost invariably middle class – there was a considerable element of snobbery in their selection, and a candidate whose father was an engine driver was turned down. Many were attracted by the prospect of change,

* Not till 1946 in the Gambia.

adventure and an outdoor life. There were officers who resigned when posted to an area where they could not keep horses.

In the annals of European administration in West Africa, as in any human society, one can find cruelty and kindness, a spirit of service and self-seeking ambition. The basic indictment of colonialism is certainly not that its officials were worse than other men.

The basic criticism of colonialism is concerned not with individuals but with structures. It made one group of men the unquestioned totalitarian masters of a country which was not their own, just because they were white. They used the slender resources of the country to give themselves a level of income and privilege – pensions, home leaves – to which the people of the country could not begin to aspire. An African, even if he was more highly educated than the Europeans, was forced to accept a subordinate role. Because they governed the country, they took it for granted that the economy must function in the interests of the metropolis. Both French and British officials admitted this.

In the words of a British official in Nigeria: 'We don't go out to their countries with entirely altruistic motives, no one does. We have our own country's interests to serve . . .'

A French administrator wrote in words we have already noted: 'If we condescend to be frank with ourselves, we are forced to admit that it is not altruism that leads us to Africa, at least not as a nation'.

Summary

In the colonial era, the colonising powers and African chiefs made a mutually advantageous alliance. The Europeans would never have governed Africa with white officials alone; many factors prevented it, including lack of adequate finance and their frequent ignorance of local languages.* The chiefs for their part retained at least something of their lost authority. Some scholars are very concerned with whether any given chief would have been traditionally entitled to rule or not. In fact, the position of the chief was fundamentally changed by colonialism, which imposed an overlord above him. His success depended on his acceptability not to his people, but to the white official. In his relations with his people, he often became more powerful than before. The might of the colonial state could protect him against his opponents, and colonial rulers seldom preserved, or even understood, the elaborate system of checks and balances which had existed before them.

The challenge to the chiefs came not from the colonial rulers, but sometimes from the masses they governed, and ultimately and more effectively, from nationalism. As in so much of the nationalist movement, self-seeking and genuine concern for the

---

* This varied from place to place. British officials in northern Nigeria spoke Hausa, and sometimes Fulfulde or Tiv as well. Officials in southern Nigeria mastered local languages seldom – as did French officials.

national welfare were inextricably mixed. On the one hand, the nationalists genuinely regarded the authority of, in the main, uneducated chiefs, as unprogressive, and criticised the frequent oppression and corruption of their regime. On the other, they were eager for more career opportunities. The ambitious elite of Lagos longed to be Residents, or at least District Officers. Lawyers particularly resented their exclusion from most of Nigeria's courts. They were only allowed to practice in the Colony; everywhere else, the judicial process rested in the hands of the legally unqualified.

When the nationalist movement gathered momentum in the late 1940s, the educated elite finally gained the initiative as against the alliance between chiefs and colonialism. It is, in a sense, surprising, that except in Sekou Touré's Guinea, the chiefs weathered the storm as well as they did. They did so, partly because they saw the changing shape of the times, and moved accordingly, partly because most nationalists were afraid of the popular opposition which would develop if there was an outright attack on the chiefs, and partly because there were in fact many links between the two groups. Many of the educated were the relations of chiefs. Many legitimised their success by taking chieftaincy titles – like Houphouet-Boigny, Awolowo, and Azikiwe. In the heyday of colonialism, the Emir of Kano gave financial support to Ladipo Solanke's radical West African Students' Union. When Nigeria became independent, the political party which had the largest number of seats was the one dominated by northern traditional rulers and their officials and relations.

Social and economic change

> We have been oppressed a great deal,
> we have been exploited a great deal, and we
> have been disregarded a great deal.
>
> The Arusha Declaration, Tanzania.

In the last section, we looked at a fairly limited and formal aspect of colonialism – the structure of government. In this section, we shall study a much larger and more complicated question; how much did society really change during the colonial period? In understanding the answer to this question, we should begin by making several points clear.

1 Not all the changes which occurred during the colonial period were the work of colonial governments. We shall need to look at how colonial policies really affected people's lives, but in many ways the role of government was extremely limited. It was more like a referee, or a 'keeper of the peace', than a transformer of society. In economic history the really important turning point is the early nineteenth century, and the basic pattern of economic life established then continued – the export of primary products, such as palm oil, produced or gathered by peasant farmers, and an import-export system dominated by a small number of very rich and powerful expatriate firms.

2 People now tend to criticise colonial governments for having done so little to develop West Africa, and there is some truth in these criticisms. One should never forget, however, that colonial policies must be judged, both in terms of the policies and ideals which prevailed in Europe at the time, and in the context of the conditions that prevailed there. It would be a mistake, for instance, to blame colonial governments for not carrying out, in the 1910s, ideals, such as the welfare state, which only became generally accepted in Britain in the 1940s. More basically, the whole colonial experience occurred at a time when Europe itself was going through a whole series of unprecedented crises – the First World War, 1914–18 (more accurately, a European Civil War), the Great Depression, which began in 1929 and overshadowed much of the 1930s, and the Second World War, 1939–45. Even had colonial officials been enthusiastic for economic development, the resources of the metropolitan countries were absorbed by this chain of crises. (As we shall see, there were some bold plans for development in the inter-war years, which were stifled by lack of finance.) When things improved in the late 1940s in Europe, there were dramatic improvements in the colonies as well.

3 It is important to realise that the impact of colonialism changed in many ways as time went on. In the heyday of colonialism, colonial rulers tended to exalt and glorify their role as bearers of peace and 'civilisation', and glossed over its violent and unjust aspects. In a reaction against this, some modern writers seem to see nothing good about colonialism at all, and have built up a terrible case against it, citing cruelty, exploitation and oppression of all kinds. But it is essential to realise that the impact of colonialism changed over time. The so-called 'villages of liberty', as we shall see, were clearly oppressive, but the institution was confined to parts of French West Africa; and died out between 1905 and 1910. To pick out the worst brutalities and injustices of the colonial era from many different times and places, such as the plundering of the bloodthirsty Voulet and Chanoine, and use them to build up a complete case against colonialism is as unjust and misleading as the 'peace and civilisation' theories of colonialism's supporters.

4 There is no subject covered in this book (except, perhaps, the slave trade) where scholars are in such complete and utter disagreement. When we come to analyse the impact of colonialism, the interpretations are often flatly contradictory. Some believe that the metropolitan countries enriched themselves at the colonies' expense, others that the metropolitan countries spent more on the colonies than they gained. It is possible to 'prove' either proposition, depending on how the figures are compiled. Statistics give to most economic discussions an air of authenticity.

Labour migration is another example of how verdicts can differ. Some historians see this as cruel and oppressive. Men are forced by tax demands, or poverty, to leave their families and work for low wages far away. This in its turn encourages other evils (lack of manpower on the home farms, prostitution in the cities, and so on). Other historians see labour migration as a rational way of applying labour to resources. Men thus leave areas lacking in resources, and work in areas where labour is scarce. They see it, too, as a rational way of combatting rural underemployment (if men migrate in the farming 'off-season', it gives them employment when there would otherwise be little to do).

Another area of disagreement concerns West Africa's increasing dependence on food imports. Many historians see the way in which Senegal, for instance, exports cash crops but imports food as an evil. To others, it is progressive to specialise, and the imports of, for instance, foreign rice are a sign of improving standards of living.

Yet another example can be found in the import of foreign textiles. Some historians lament the decline of indigenous textile industries; others say that the imports of abundant and fairly cheap cloth raised the standard of living and brought real benefits to the people. (The same difference of opinion can be found in discussions of iron imports – and the now dead craft of the West African iron smelter.)

In many ways, therefore, it is much easier to condemn, or support colonialism completely than to pick one's way through the conflicting evidence and try to build up, as it were, a colonial balance sheet. This is what this book attempts to do. It is important to realise that it is one historian's individual balance sheet, which some scholars would consider too favourable to colonialism, and others, too critical of it.

The colonial era is often divided into three phases: the period to 1918, which one might call the era of conquest; 1918–45, the era of 'classic' colonialism, which could justly be called the era of stagnation; 1945–60, the era of change.

The era of conquest, to 1918

It was in the era of conquest that the oppressive and violent face of colonialism was seen most clearly. The 'pacification' of West Africa was accompanied not only by much loss of life but by much destruction of property. If a village was thought to be unco-operative, and this could include refusal to supply carriers, or even a sheer mis-understanding, the houses were destroyed, the accumulated food (yam barns or granaries, and domestic animals and poultry) taken, the crops in the fields destroyed, and even trees of economic value cut down. Guns were confiscated and destroyed in vast numbers, which affected the people's ability to supplement their diet by hunting.

To these losses and uncertainties were added the diversion of manpower from agriculture to porterage and forced labour. It was sometimes so hard to recruit carriers that innocent men were kept in gaol until their services were required. The loads, largely luxuries for Europeans, were so heavy that some of the carriers died of exhaustion. In many areas, the imposition of taxation creamed off part of the income of communities already living near the level of subsistence.

In the 1930s a village group near the boundary between northern and southern Nigeria summarised its history for the benefit of a British official:

> The history of these villages from the earliest days to the present time consists of certain definite land-marks, which may be summarised as follows:

1 The founding of the village by a traditional ancestor.
2 Petty raids by surrounding towns, of which there are no details.
3 The coming of the Government in the person of a white man nicknamed Otikpo, the Destroyer.
4 The Influenza (1919).
5 Railway Construction Labour (1921).
6 The Ochima Patrol (1924).
7 Taxation (1928).

He commented, 'With the exception of 1, the list may be said to comprise from the local inhabitant's point of view, a series of public disasters of the greatest magnitude'.

This account presents, in miniature, the image which advancing colonialism presented to West African communities.

In 1913–14 there was a catastrophic famine in the western Sudan. This was caused essentially by drought and consequent poor harvests, which were not, of course, the fault of the colonial governments, but its impact was worsened by the burden of taxation and forced labour. In one part of Soudan, near Massina, twelve people died each day for weeks on end in a single village, and the survivors lived on leaves. A French colonist in French Equatorial Africa described the situation in Wadai:

> During the famine of 1898–99 the Sultan fed his subjects; in 1914, you let them die . . . there were no passes before; no hunting permits; no villages forced to live on the rocks, far from wells because the road passes that way . . . The old subjection was easier than this. When we came, how many large villages were there, rich in cattle and in reserves of millet? They have dwindled and disappeared.

In northern Nigeria, food was so scarce that it actually paid European firms to bring back the groundnuts they had exported to the Niger port of Baro and re-sell them to the farmers. A British official wrote:

> The gaunt ghost of famine stalked abroad through Kano and every other part. The stricken people tore down the ant-hills in the bush to get at the small grains and chaff within these storerooms. They wandered everywhere collecting . . . grass burrs . . . to split the centre pod and get the tiny seed . . . They died like flies on every road.

In 1914 the First World War broke out. Many West Africans were to die in it, in a conflict which was not their own. In 1919 the influenza epidemic struck West Africa with such catastrophic effect that many village communities still date events as 'before' and 'after' influenza.

The years of stagnation, 1918–45

This was the classic age of colonialism when policies might be summed up in the French word *immobilisme*. The lack of change was partly due to the international crises of a world-wide depression and the Second World War. It was the heyday of

Indirect Rule, which had the twin advantages of being cheap and conservative. In the depression years, the prices for imported goods rose. The prices for exported goods dropped steeply. The big expatriate firms continued to make a profit. In 1934 UAC made well over six million pounds profit, and paid a dividend of fifteen per cent on ordinary shares. In 1930–1 famine struck again in Niger, Upper Volta and northern Nigeria. It was due this time to locusts and many parents sold their children into virtual slavery to ensure that they would be fed.

There were some striking exceptions to the policy of *immobilisme*. Guggisberg, the Governor of the Gold Coast, introduced an ambitious ten-year development plan in 1919. It was to be financed from the colony's own resources and had, in the event, to be halted for lack of funds. But it had some positive achievements to its credit, notably the building of a deep-water harbour at Takoradi. In 1921 the French Minister for the Colonies, Sarrault, introduced an ambitious scheme which was explicitly designed to compensate France for her losses in the war and in Russian investments. 'We must make the colonies provide all they can of their considerable resources to *restore the home country*.' Again, the necessary finance was not forthcoming.

One ambitious scheme which was implemented concerned the Niger Office. This was originally a scheme backed by French cotton manufacturers to grow cotton by means of irrigation in the so-called inland Delta of the Niger, in what is now Mali. The scheme was later expanded to include rice cultivation, which would, it was hoped, supply the needs of Senegal, and improve nutrition generally. It was an ambitious project, which aimed to create an island of prosperity in an area of semi-desert. But in the fifty odd years which have elapsed since work started in 1924, it has been plagued by technical shortcomings. Although it was set up at vast expense, the yields have been much less than was hoped for, and irrigation has had a very bad effect on the structure of the soil. This could have been foreseen and prevented by means of pilot projects. In the inter-war years, the settlers lived under conditions which have been compared with a concentration camp, and to this day it has proved unattractive to local people, and most of the settlers have had to be brought from far afield. In 1931 the French made another development initiative – the Great Colonial Loan – which was largely swallowed up by the Niger Office and left a damaging legacy in its heavy rates of interest.

In 1929 the British passed the Colonial Development Act, intended to reduce unemployment in England by stimulating exports. British West Africa was allocated half a million pounds, but half of this totally inadequate sum went to help an ex-patriate mining firm. A further Act was passed in 1940, but it had little effect because of the Second World War.

These few development initiatives were little more than ripples on the surface of an unchanged sea, and observers of rural life described with one voice the picture of *immobilisme*. A visitor to Guinea in 1932 said: 'During this rapid tour I gained the impression that this region, which I visited in 1905, has not made any progress'.

A French professor, who was studying groundnut cultivation in Senegal in the 1930s, wrote:

Everything in tropical Africa has evolved; there are railways and roads that can be used by cars for most of the year . . . But Senegalese agriculture has not evolved – the methods of cultivation are still as primitive, the insects and parasites take a high tithe from the harvest, for the want of measures that are relatively easy to take.

While some money trickled from Europe to Africa in the form of loans, just before the Second World War money began to flow in the other direction through the operations of the Marketing Boards, which the British established in their colonies. In theory, these were supposed to stabilise the price of, for instance, cocoa, by keeping part of the peasant's price for his product in good years and subsidising prices with it in bad. In fact, the Marketing Boards fixed prices at levels much lower than were being paid for the products in the world market, and the profit which they made each year was kept in Britain to increase her banking assets. In effect, the West African peasant helped finance Britain's war effort. This difference between world prices and the price paid the peasant continued after the war. In 1953 cocoa growers were paid £28,000,000 for cocoa which was sold for £74,000,000. The surplus in due course was spent by an independent Ghana (in the case of Gold Coast cocoa) and the day of redistribution among the peasants never came.

The Second World War had both good and bad effects on West Africa's economic life. It created an extreme shortage of consumer goods, but demands for West Africa's primary exports soared, and the lack of shipping space and of consumer commodities encouraged local industrialisation. For many years, the groundnuts of Senegal had been exported in their shells and processed in France and proposals to process them in Senegal made little headway against French shipping and groundnut factory interests. During the war, lack of shipping and desperate shortages forced a change.

The years of change, 1945 to independence
After 1945 the nature of the colonial presence changed greatly. In the post-war years, economic and political change were closely linked, and we shall look at the years of change more closely in our discussion of nationalism. Briefly, the change was due partly to the booming price for West Africa's exports and a tremendous expansion in their quantity, which earned a substantial surplus for development. For the first time, the metropolitan countries began to invest substantial amounts of their own capital in West Africa. The British Colonial Development and Welfare Fund and the French FIDES (Investment Fund for Economic and Social Development) played basically the same role. Some of the money was used wastefully, for instance, in importing furniture for schools in French colonies which could easily have been made locally, or in a disastrous scheme for egg production on the Gambia. They have also been criticised for concentrating on social services such as health and education rather than on economic development, such as agriculture and industry, which was necessary in the long run if social services were to expand or even continue. But perhaps the key factor was that West Africans themselves were regaining a real say in their countries' destinies.

The buying power of West Africa's exports 1900–60

This chart indicates the changes in the quantity of imports that could be purchased by a given unit of exports. Incomes of West African countries depended on this, plus the quantity exported.

Period	Causes of change	Change in buying power	Effects
1900–1913	Imposition of colonial rule	Steady improvement	1. Made colonial rule more acceptable. 2. Helped to finance railways. 3. Encouraged more production of exports.
1914–1919	1. First World War made imports scarce and expensive. 2. Exports suffered because some European markets closed, and shipping difficult.	Decline	
1919	Post-war boom	Brief improvement	

Period	Cause	Trend	Effects
1920–1921	Collapse of export prices	Decline	1. Small firms suffered – big combines formed. 2. African disillusion with colonial rule.
1922–1929	Introduction of motor lorry meant new areas opened up for production of exports.	Slight improvement	
1930–1944	1. World depression. 2. Second World War cut off European markets. French West Africa blockaded.	Decline	1. Colonial governments unwilling and unable to invest in development. 2. African discontent contributed to growth of early nationalist movements.
1945–1960	1. Revival of European demand for tropical products. 2. Raw materials required for war in Korea.	Improvement	1. Great increase in public and private investment. 2. Growth of manufacturing industries. 3. Increase in agricultural production. 4. Confidence and economic strength for nationalist movements.

There was an expansion of industrial capacity, which was to progress still more rapidly after independence was achieved. At first, this concentrated on processing exports, for instance, shelling groundnuts, and on manufacturing goods which would otherwise be imported such as textiles, soap, beer, cement and so on. As export earnings expanded and the buying capacity of West Africans increased, this kind of import substitution appeared an ever more attractive outlet for foreign investment.

But if one turns again to rural life, one is still confronted with an almost unchanged scene. A report in 1949 on French West Africa said 'it can be said that the people in the whole territory lack balanced nutrition; and this is a permanent state'. Another French visitor said at much the same time:

> The daily ration of an adult might even go down to 208 calories* per day, not during famines but simply at times of shortage. So great was the surprise of the personnel in charge of these calculations in France that they suspended their work, believing it an error on our part. There was no error.

When colonialism had come and gone and Nigeria had been independent for seven years, a scholar† made a detailed study of a Hausa village, which was only nine kilometres from the major city of Katsina. She discovered that the changes which colonialism had brought were few indeed, and they were not all by any means in a modernising direction (it appears that the practice of keeping rural Hausa wives in purdah, for example, developed during the colonial period). This is how she described the village:

> Farm-tools (other than the oxen-drawn plough which is a most important innovation) are still made by local blacksmiths. The donkey is mainly used for transporting crops, manure and trade goods – there are no carts. Houses, granaries and domestic wells are of traditional construction, there being only a small usage of manufactured (as distinct from local) cement. There is no piped water, modern sanitation, electric light, telephone or post office in the *gari*. Despite the establishment, as long ago as 1946, of an excellent primary school, which has recently enabled many young men to enter higher education and to take up jobs in the modern sector, there is a fairly low level of literacy in Hausa and English . . . Apart from the single mechanical grinding mill (which is apt to fall out of order for long periods), and the fifteen (or so) groundnut decorticators which are mainly used for shelling nuts destined for export, food processing methods are as laborious and time-wasting as ever, mainly involving the hard grindstone and the pestle and mortar . . .
>
> The introduction of the lorry has greatly reduced the risk of famine . . . It cannot be taken for granted that (the risk of famine apart) general life expectancies are higher than in former times. Certainly smallpox is controlled by vaccination and leprosy will soon be a scourge of the past; but if the incidence of acute rural

* Normal calorie requirements are about 2,000.
† Dr Polly Hill.

poverty is higher than formerly, death-rates might have risen. Certainly, most Batagarawa citizens receive no modern medical attention before they die . . .

Government and society

Most modern studies of colonial government emphasise its extremely limited aims and role. Like a policeman or a referee, its primary concern, like that of the African governments which preceded it, was to maintain order. Many of the most fundamental changes, such as peasant cultivation of export crops, began before the colonial period or developed independently of government initiatives. Nevertheless, there were some areas where colonial governments did have a real impact on men's lives, and it is these that we must now consider.

How colonial governments were financed

It was a basic demand of colonial government that the colony must be self-financing. This meant, in fact, that the whole weight of financing a colonial administration and of developing roads, railways and so on rested upon the peasant farmer rather than on the big expatriate firms which, as we shall see, made fortunes in West Africa and benefited directly both from 'law and order' and from the building of roads and railways. Even if a colony borrowed money, both the loan and the debt servicing charges had to be re-paid from its revenues. In Nigeria, in the 1930s, one-third of government revenue went on interest and loans repayment.

Indirect taxation

Colonial governments extracted taxation or its equivalent in services from their subjects in a number of different ways. Indirect taxation, which took the form of duties levied on imports and exports, was an important source of revenue. It had several disadvantages, the most important of which was that it weighed equally heavily on everyone, whereas income tax is graduated according to income: the more you earn, the more you pay. It had other implications too. It meant that much of the income of the colonial government depended on the bulk of its external trade. If there was a trade recession, its income shrank. It could not easily reduce its expenditure to match (many items like salaries or interest payments on loans could not be reduced).

Direct taxation

The imposition of direct taxation caused much resentment in many places, especially where there had been no local tradition of taxation. We have already seen the House Tax War in Sierra Leone in 1896, and the Women's War in south-eastern Nigeria in 1929, which was very largely a protest against direct taxation. Nobody likes paying taxes anywhere in the world. Some West Africans were ready to go to war about it for two reasons; first, they regarded it as a rent on their land or property, which infringed their absolute ownership, and second because it brought very few visible benefits in return. As an elder in south-eastern Nigeria said: 'The government promised us development; but tell me what development there is in Umulolo today after more than thirty years of taxation?'

The numerous memoirs written by officials who worked in northern Nigeria show that they spent much of their time travelling round the countryside making tax assessments. Because of the hardships they endured, they prided themselves on their activities. It seldom occurred to them that their arrival was, to a village, very rightly, a source of alarm since it meant that the villagers had to make cash payments for which they received nothing in return. For the British, it became very much like a sport to pursue Fulani pastoralists round the countryside to count their cattle. 'It was very much a game, relieved the tedium . . .' To the Fulani the 'game' was in deadly earnest. It meant that some of their cattle had to be sold to pay the tax on the others. A British official admitted, that 'with so little to see physically in return, it was hard to make an impression on the widely held belief that tax was a tribute and went into the pockets of those collecting it . . .'

Forced labour

Forced labour was essentially a tax paid in work rather than in money. Forced unpaid labour was most extensive in the French colonies. In addition, both British and French colonial administrators often exacted forced labour – sometimes paid, sometimes unpaid – not only for public works, such as roads and railways, but also for a variety of other purposes which those involved would not have seen as benefitting them. These included building houses and sports facilities for expatriate officials, army barracks for the soldiers who would suppress 'risings', and prisons. Compulsion was used to provide labourers for European plantations on the Ivory Coast. White settlers called them 'banana machines', referring to the food they were given. Sometimes workers had to travel 800 kilometres at their own expense to their place of work.

These hated impositions were only abolished in 1946. In that year, Houphouet-Boigny said:

> One has to have seen these used-up workers, skeletons covered with sores, wandering or in the fields . . . One has to have watched the distracted flights from the village chiefs or canton chiefs into the bush; one has to have read the eyes of planters forced to abandon their own land to work for starvation wages . . . one has to have seen the recruiting agents, the modern slave traders, crowd people heedlessly in trucks, exposed to all climates, or pack them into baggage cars like animals . . . to understand the drama of forced labour in Ivory Coast.

In British colonies, forced labour was exacted most extensively in areas which did not pay direct taxes. It gradually died out in the 1930s. As in the French colonies, it was extremely unpopular, especially since chiefs often misused the labour for their own purposes. Since the educated tended to be exempt, it was a particularly unjust kind of taxation, falling most heavily on the poorest and most vulnerable section of the community.

African carriers receiving their loads

Service as carriers was a particularly unpopular form of forced labour. It was, of course, most common in the early colonial period, but continued into modern times in areas which lacked modern forms of transport. Some carriers were professionals, but many were reluctant conscripts. Heavily burdened and defenceless, they were often killed in colonialism's wars. Some were even shot by their employers when they tried to escape. Some died of exhaustion. Others had their health permanently wrecked as they limped along on damaged feet with twenty-three kilogram boxes of luxuries for white officials. A European official in Ondo in western Nigeria wrote in passionate protest in 1915:

> I have evidence that, in the past, men have almost invariably been compelled to serve as carriers . . . These messengers used to enter private houses and, I am assured, extort money from persons either ill or otherwise incapacitated from serving as carriers. On all sides I hear charges of extortion and oppression . . .
>
> It is possible, also, that harsh treatment in the past may have caused an added distaste for such work. An English officer has recently told me in confidence, that he has known of instances of carriers being put in prison for three or four days at a certain station to prevent them from going away, when they had been secured . . .
>
> To me, the system of forced labour is most repugnant. To compel a free man, by fine or imprisonment, to carry a tent or a hammock is, I submit . . . illegal. The system is, I think, vicious and cowardly, since it operates only against a certain class – the most illiterate portion of the Community. I believe that the system is widely practised throughout the Protectorate, and that it is responsible for much of the oppression and unrest one hears about. ·

227

The compulsory cultivation of export crops which was common in French territories was closely allied to forced labour. There was much compulsory cultivation of cotton, an essential raw material for French industry. Angoulvant (see page 195) introduced compulsory cocoa cultivation into Ivory Coast. (The people watered the plants by night with warm water to ensure failure – just as at Asaba on the lower Niger the people boiled cotton seeds before they planted them, to foil the hated Royal Niger Company's plans for cotton plantations.) There was compulsory groundnut cultivation in Upper Volta, leading a famous French administrator to complain, in a book published in 1931:

> Already the railway 'machine' of the Ivory Coast . . . used up bearers. And now see how a groundnut 'machine' came to gnaw away at the very heart of the country . . . And the country was tired, stupefied by forced labour on the routes and compulsory crop cultivation.

The more closely one examines the sources from which much of the history of colonialism must be written, the more instances one finds of oppression and injustice. In 1920 a doctor visited the government gaol in Awka, in south-eastern Nigeria. He reported:

> There are no means of ablution within the Prison. Prisoners never get meat or fish in their diet as it is practically unobtainable . . . There is a death rate of 222 per thousand . . . I saw two prisoners with intractable ulcers on their buttocks, the unhealed effects of flogging administered by the Native Court some three weeks previously . . .

The end of slavery
In constructing a colonial balance sheet, one may find that the evils of forced labour are counter-balanced by the end of another form of forced labour, domestic slavery. In the long run, the general effect of colonial rule was that domestic slavery withered and died.* Former slaves were free to move away from their homes and start new lives elsewhere. Often they became more successful and prosperous than their former masters.

In the first phase of colonial rule, however, the French and British were not nearly as anxious to free domestic slaves as one would expect from nations which had agitated for a century over the evils of the slave trade. Their alliance with traditional rulers made them reluctant to threaten one of the traditional sources of their wealth. They feared, moreover, that the emancipation of the slaves would endanger law and order, for in parts of the western Sudan many observers believed, perhaps wrongly, that slaves formed between quarter and half of the total population.

For a time, both the British and the French followed a half-way policy. Slaves were not automatically emancipated, but masters could not recapture slaves who ran away,

---

* But instances of pawning and kidnapping children have continued into modern times.

as many did. Until the first decade of the twentieth century, both the French and the British often entered the slaving business themselves by rewarding their soldiers with slaves, or turning a blind eye when they enslaved their prisoners. The French, for a time, put escaped slaves in so-called 'villages of liberty' where instead of working for an African master they were forced to labour for the French. If they escaped, they were pursued, brought back and punished. Conditions were so grim that if a community refused to pay its taxes, one of its children was placed in a village of liberty to coerce it into doing so. Here is a picture of one of them.

A village of liberty

The institution died out between 1905 and 1910.

These abuses and injustices were of course temporary. On the whole the slaves became free gradually and peacefully. The transport revolution helped, by limiting the need for head porters and canoe paddlers. Some societies still remember which individuals are of slave origin. This is both an unhappy relic of past injustices and historically untrue – for if one takes the enquiry back far enough, all families are originally free.

How colonial revenues were spent

In both French and British colonies, nearly half of the wealth created by the labours of African peasants went on the salaries and pensions of a tiny minority of white officials, who formed a little island of privilege in a vast expanse of rural poverty. There are cases where one European was paid as much as all his twenty-five African assistants put together. The African peasants who paid their pensions worked until they died, or until they could work no more, when, if they had no children able and willing to support them, they faced a terrifying future of absolute destitution.

Not much government revenue was left, once salaries, pensions, interest and loan repayments had been deducted. In 1914 in French West Africa the amount available for post and telegraph services, public works, education and health was 'about half the sum which the city of Paris devoted to the upkeep of its streets and boulevards'.

Education

In 1918 the Nigerian government devoted one per cent of its revenue to education. In its own official reports it described the educational system as totally inadequate. In the British colonies, and to a lesser extent in the French colonies, most of what education was available was provided by Christian missions and real educational expansion only began in the late 1940s and 1950s, as the colonies moved towards self-government. In the inter-war years, colonialism needed Africans educated to a limited level to act as clerks, storemen, primary school teachers and so on. But white officialdom had no desire to educate Africans to a level which would render its own role unnecessary.

Health

Health services were similarly inadequate, and what existed was primarily for Europeans. Nigeria in the 1930s had twelve hospitals for 4,000 Europeans and fifty-two hospitals for 40 million odd Nigerians.

It is difficult to know how much health conditions really improved during the colonial period. The population undoubtedly expanded greatly and this is usually explained in terms of improved health services. But health services were almost non-existent in rural areas and the benefits brought through vaccination against diseases like yellow fever and smallpox may have been counter-balanced by the damage done by imported diseases. These probably included tuberculosis, first identified in French West Africa in 1880, and plague which was first noted in 1899 and which became endemic in Senegal until about 1940, though fortunately without spreading elsewhere. Syphilis, which reached West Africa in the era of the slave trade, is thought to have spread through labour migration, which separated men from their families and encouraged the growth of prostitution. High child mortality rates, often of fifty per cent or more, continued, often linked with inadequate nutrition. In the western Sudan, epidemics of cerebral spinal meningitis were a regular feature of the dry season. There was a village in Zaria Province, in the 1950s, which 'was known as the village of the blind. Every male in the community became blind in adult life from prolonged contact with the *simulium damnosum* fly*'.

Economic growth

Almost nothing was done to develop the economy either by improving the productivity of agriculture or by encouraging industrialisation. What research was done in

* A fly which brings a disease which causes blindness.

agriculture concentrated exclusively on export crops. It was not until West African states became independent that serious attention was devoted to improving the food crops on which the people's nutrition depended. Much money was wasted, as we have seen, on a small number of disastrous ventures into farm settlements and mechanised agriculture. The experiences of the Niger office have parallels elsewhere, for example, in an unsuccessful attempt by SCOA to cultivate groundnuts mechanically in Senegal and an absurdly unsuccessful scheme in the late 1940s to produce eggs on the Gambia. In general, African farmers have been helped, not by mechanised and highly capitalised projects, but by improved varieties of seed, fertiliser and pesticide and research into plant diseases.

The transport revolution

One of the most important changes which colonialism introduced could be called the transport revolution – the construction of roads and railways. Most people consider that these established an essential infrastructure for all further economic development. Critics point out that they were paid for entirely by the African peasant and not by the expatriate firms which profited so much from them. Roads and railways were constructed for two main reasons: to strengthen the government's control over her subject peoples and to facilitate the export of her primary products. Here is a modern map of West Africa's railways.

It shows clearly how the colonial powers had no interest in developing trade between different parts of West Africa. Each railway was simply designed to link the colony's port with its economic hinterland, a visible symbol of one of the key economic facts of colonialism: that each colony was linked more closely to the metropolitan

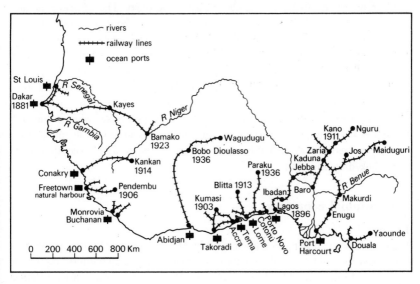

West African railways

French railway construction

power than to its African neighbours. Because they were built with different gauges, it is now impossible to unite the different railways into a single system.

Most of the railways were built before 1914. In the 1920s their role was partly undermined by motor lorry transport which was developed largely by African businessmen.

The building of roads and railways ended West Africa's economic dependence on head porterage and its limited number of navigable rivers. The efficiency of these pre-industrial methods of transport should not, however, be underestimated; for a time the Lagos–Ibadan railway was unable to compete successfully with canoe transport on the Ogun river. The changes in transport emancipated countless numbers of canoe paddlers and carriers but, as we have seen, many of the roads and railways were built by forced labour in an atmosphere of bitter resentment. In the early days of colonialism, corrupt profiteers sometimes made fortunes in railway construction. When the Dakar–St Louis line was built 'hardly had one year passed when the mounds of sand began to crumble everywhere, leaving the rails suspended in mid-air; the sandstorms overthrew the hub, the wooden beams were gnawed by insects, the engines were choked up with dust'.

The colonial economy

Exports

In some ways, the true turning point in West African economic history, in the years covered by this book, took place in the early nineteenth century when the slave trade declined and was replaced by 'legitimate' trade. The basic pattern was then established of the export of primary, mainly agricultural, products in return for manufactured goods. As time went on, new export crops, such as cocoa, were developed but the basic pattern persisted. In the nineteenth, as in the twentieth century, agricultural exports were produced almost entirely by small independent peasant farmers.

Groundnuts

In the colonial period, the major exports of the nineteenth century, groundnuts and palm products, remained important. Senegal remained a major groundnut producer, but the area under cultivation increased steadily as groundnut production followed the railway. So much land was used for the cultivation of groundnuts that Senegal, which had once been self-supporting in food, now became heavily dependent on imported food, especially Asian rice. The groundnut economy developed, not because Senegal could grow nothing else – modern agricultural scientists have listed many products which could be grown more profitably in its different areas – but because Europe needed large quantities of vegetable oils. Every year the groundnut growers endure what is called the 'hungry season'. A modern scholar writes of 'the overwhelming dependence on the peanut as the sole cash crop which engendered a life cycle of indebtedness and penury, relieved only by a reckless splurge of spending following the harvest'. The French have a special word to describe it, *l'arachidité*.* During and after the First World War, northern Nigeria, especially the Kano area, became a major groundnut exporter, again a direct consequence of railway construction and of the enterprise of Hausa traders, who offered the farmers guarantees. By the 1950s, Senegal and Nigeria together produced seventy-five per cent of the world's groundnuts, each in equal amounts.

Palm products

Palm products made up half the value of British West Africa's exports at the beginning of the colonial period. By the 1950s this had shrunk to fifteen per cent, not because the export of palm products declined, but because other export commodities expanded. The passage on page 235, shows how the patterns of international trade appeared to the palm oil producer. Most of French West Africa's palm products came from Dahomey (Benin). It has always been Dahomey's (Benin's) major source of revenue, one totally inadequate for the country's needs.

Coffee and cocoa

Coffee and cocoa had been produced in small quantities in the nineteenth century but first became of great importance in the twentieth. The establishment of the Gold Coast cocoa industry will always be linked with the name of Tetteh Quarshie (1842–92), an illiterate blacksmith from Christiansborg who brought cocoa seeds from Fernando Po in 1879 and established a cocoa plantation in Akwapim. His claim to have first brought cocoa to the Gold Coast has been challenged, but although Christian missions had experimented with it on a small scale earlier, it was Quarshie's example which led

* Based on the French word for groundnut, *arachide*.

African farmers to tackle cocoa cultivation seriously. In the Akwapim area, farmers left their homes and settled on virgin land, expressly in order to grow cocoa. This shows what nonsense it was when colonial administrators claimed that the African peasant was feckless and lacking in foresight, for a cocoa tree takes fifteen years to mature. Where lack of transport hindered the export of the crop, the growers banded together to build roads and bridges.

The Gold Coast first exported cocoa in 1885. By 1911 she was the world's leading producer. Cocoa cultivation in western Nigeria developed at much the same time as groundnut production in Kano, and by the 1950s comprised twenty per cent of Nigeria's exports.

The history of cocoa and coffee growing in the Ivory Coast is one of the most striking examples of the way in which African peasant agriculture was more productive and efficient than expatriate-run plantations. The French colonial government put the full weight of its authority behind the white planters, supplying them with forced labour and giving them great economic privileges during the Second World War. In 1946 forced labour was abolished. The results were dramatic. In a few years time, the expatriate plantations had fallen by the wayside but African farmers were producing export crops in such volume that Ivory Coast had become one of France's richest West African colonies.

Rubber

In the years before the First World War there was a short lived but frantic rubber boom in southern Nigeria and Guinea. The invention of the pneumatic tyre in 1888 created a tremendous industrial demand, but after 1910 Asian plantations began to produce *hevea* rubber with which the wild liana rubber of southern Nigeria and Guinea could not compete. Rubber became important again in the West African economy, as we have seen, after Liberia made a huge land grant to Firestone in 1926. Ironically, the only independent nation in West Africa became the only one where expatriate plantations were established on a really large scale.

The role of the peasant

The overwhelmingly important role of the peasant producer in West Africa makes a striking contrast with the history of colonies such as Kenya or the Belgian Congo where Africans became labourers on European farms or plantations. Books about colonialism in West Africa have often praised the British, in particular, for this,★ assuming that the aim was to protect the peasant farmer from external exploitation. But if they were excluded as a matter of principle, it is difficult to see why this same principle did not extend to mining, which was almost entirely in expatriate hands and which employed no technology more elaborate than baskets and picks. The real reason was that African peasant production was more efficient and successful than the plantation, and had been seen to be so long before colonialism was established. Since

★ There were, as we have seen, some European plantations on the Ivory coast.

wages were very low, this shows that the African peasant was in fact grossly underpaid for his own and his family's labour. It was possible to underpay him because his family supplied most of its own food.

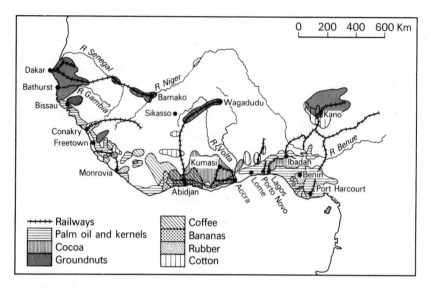

The Atlantic export economy in the mid-twentieth century

One consequence of the expansion of commercial agriculture was the growth of increasing class distinctions between richer and poorer peasants. A historian of East Africa describes the colonial period as 'the age of improvement and differentiation'. A brilliant woman economist, Dr Polly Hill, has described it in great detail among the cocoa growers of Ghana and the groundnut farmers of northern Nigeria. Some peasants came to own a larger amount of land and employed hired labour; others owned too little land or no land at all and were forced to migrate in search of work. A pattern of labour migration, when impoverished peasants, or those living far from the areas where export crops were grown, left home in search of work, developed in the colonial period. Thus men such as the Mossi of Upper Volta were forced from their homes by the need to earn money to pay their taxes. The map on page 236 shows how extensive the practice had become by the end of the colonial period.

The peasant producer was very much at the mercy of fluctuations in the world prices of primary products, over which he had no control. He was at the mercy of a world-wide change in trade which has taken place throughout this century, in which prices of primary products have declined relative to the cost of imported goods. When prices improved, the surplus was creamed off by the Marketing Boards. Whether prices were high or low, the small number of expatriate firms which controlled the export trade continued to make substantial profits. In 1945–6, for example, in the French West

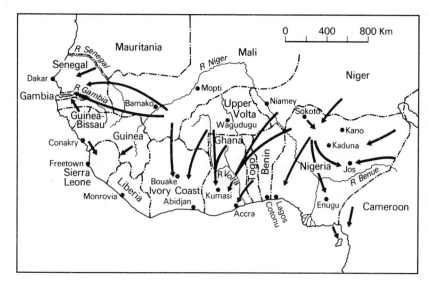

Patterns of labour migration

African colonies, the producer was paid one-quarter of the final selling price of his coffee and bananas. We need to deduct the cost of transport, roasting in the case of coffee, and losses en route. It is extremely unlikely to amount to seventy-five per cent.

Minerals
Mineral exports, though much less important than they were to become in the 1960s, had some localised importance. They included tin and other minerals from the Jos

Tin mining on the Plateau, Nigeria

Coal mining at Udi, Nigeria

plateau in Nigeria, and small amounts of gold, diamonds and manganese from the Gold Coast. In the 1950s Sierra Leone became an important exporter of diamonds. As in agriculture, the small African producer was often more efficient than the expatriate firm. The Sierra Leone government tried in vain to protect the mining companies against individual African prospectors, to whom it was ultimately forced to grant licences. In French West Africa in 1928, individual African gold prospectors produced 200 kilograms of gold, the European firms 56 kilograms. As in agriculture, the technological level of mining remained extremely low so that it did not build up any reservoir of skills in the community.

Some traditional forms of mining were unable to compete with imported raw materials and vanished altogether. The classic example of this is the now vanished craft of iron smelting, once very widely practised in West Africa. Some Saharan salt-mines continue in production because they cater to local tastes, but many others have vanished, such as the once famous salt-mines of Uburu in eastern Nigeria which had been mined by an exclusive guild of women producers and which had a brief revival during the Nigerian civil war.

Assessment

The economic situation we have described, where primary products are exported and manufactured goods imported was a clearly disadvantageous one. The real profits of the transaction are made in the industrialised country, where value is added to the raw materials by industrial processing and where an important pool of skills is gradually built up in the society. The shareholders in the big French and British companies which dominated the export and import trade made large profits, while the Dahomean

(Benin) peasant who climbed the rough trunks of the oil palms lived and died in poverty.

There were other disadvantages. West African countries were a few out of many suppliers of, for instance, vegetable oils. Groundnut oil and palm oil competed with each other and with oil extracted from copra, cotton seeds, tallow and other substances. They were entirely dependent on the external market. If the external market ceased to need their products, as actually happened in the case of West African dyewoods and gum, or could obtain them more cheaply elsewhere, as with liana rubber, there was little the producer could do about it. An agricultural economy was very much at the mercy of natural forces. Drought could ruin the groundnut crop, or swollen shoot disease the cocoa crop, with catastrophic consequences if the area had become dependent on imported food. This basically disadvantageous relationship was made much worse in the colonial period by the fact that one of the trading partners ruled the other, and inevitably used this situation to defend its own economic interests.

Historians have tended to focus on the export trade, to the exclusion of the subsistence economy. But it is essential to realise that throughout the colonial period and beyond it, the typical village community was very largely self-sufficient. It grew its own food, produced its own beverages such as palm wine or millet beer, spun and wove at least some of its own cloth, made its own pots, and tools, and constructed its buildings from local materials. In certain areas, inter-regional trade remained of great importance, especially the trade between the forest zone and the western Sudan in kola, cattle and dried fish.

Imports

West Africa imported a wide variety of consumer goods. Among these, cloth was very important. This had the disadvantage of undermining local textile industries (which survived mainly as producers of expensive luxury cloth and dress for ritual occasions) but undoubtedly benefited the peasant consumer. As we have seen, some colonies came to rely heavily on food imports such as rice and sugar. This made the colony dangerously dependent on external trade. Most historians regard this as an evil, but it has its defenders who regard it as a natural consequence of increased agricultural specialisation and of urban growth, and possibly as a sign of rising standards of living. Firearms, a major import in the nineteenth century, declined in importance, mainly because of government controls and high duties. Imports of alcoholic drinks formed a smaller proportion of total trade but remained important. In 1953 8 per cent of Ivory Coast's imports and 9.6 per cent of Dahomey's imports consisted of drink. A French economist laments, 'Alcoholism was the first "gift" presented to Africa by Europe.' When local industries were set up in the 1950s and later, breweries were prominent among them, absorbing much capital which could have been better used.

From the late 1940s onwards, capital goods imports such as machinery, motor vehicles and industrial raw materials, became more important in the richer colonies partly as a side effect of industrial growth. Critics point out that industries which are dependent on imported inputs have not made a real step towards self-sufficiency.

The expatriate firms

The import and export trade, mining, banking and shipping, were dominated by a small number of large expatriate firms. In theory, the economy was one of free trade. In practice, it was a monopoly, dominated by a small number of huge combines.

> The unrestricted play of market forces
> Yields the best allocation of resources
> This faith we stick to, since it favours us . . .

There was a striking tendency for the richer and more successful firms to absorb all others until by the 1930s between two-thirds and three-quarters of all West Africa's overseas trade was in the hands of three huge combines. Two of them were French – the Compagnie Française de l'Afrique Occidentale and the Societé Commerciale de l'Ouest Africain. But the biggest of all was British, the United African Company, which handled almost half of all West Africa's trade in the 1930s. This diagram shows how a long series of mergers finally led to the creation of this economic giant.

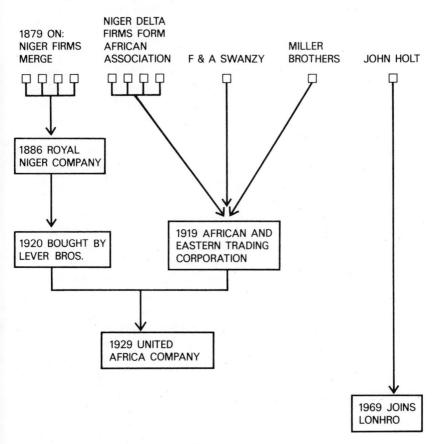

Development of the monopoly system (After Ofonagoro)

The first step was taken on the Niger, when Sir George Goldie succeeded in uniting the various British firms competing there. This competition, of course, benefited the African for they strove to see who could offer the most favourable prices and attractive goods. In 1886 the company in which all these firms had merged obtained a charter to govern as the Royal Niger Company. It used this to establish a monopoly which enabled it to offer what prices and goods it liked. It lost its charter in 1900, receiving an enormous compensation from the British government, but it continued to play a dominant role in Nigerian trade. Ultimately it became merged with many of the other firms engaged in Nigerian trade in the gigantic Unilever combine. John Holt was an important firm which stayed out, but it too, joined another giant combine, Lonhro, in 1969.

There was the same tendency to combination and monopoly in shipping and banking. Shipping services to British West Africa were in the hands of Elder Dempster, the fortunes of which were founded by Sir Alfred Jones. To avoid competition, the firm made special arrangements both with the combines controlling the import-export trade, and with its German rivals. French shipping to West Africa was dominated by two big firms (they did not compete with the British line, as they plied different routes). The banking system of British Africa was largely in the hands of the Bank of British West Africa, founded in 1894, by the same Sir Alfred Jones. It kept a near monopoly until 1926, when another British bank, Barclays, arrived on the scene. Banking in the French colonies was dominated by the Banque de l'Afrique Occidentale.

Even at the time, European colonial officials were uneasy at the huge wealth and power of these commercial giants, which enjoyed a revenue much greater than that of their own governments. They realised that monopoly and price fixing agreements lowered the prices offered to the peasant and reduced the quality of the goods he was sold. They realised that the expatriate control of credit made things difficult for the emerging African businessman. That is why the Nigerian nationalist, Nnamdi Azikiwe, for instance, founded the African Continental Bank. Most of the expatriate firms came to West Africa with little capital. John Holt, the founder of the great business which bears his name, came to West Africa with a salary of £100 a year. Their wealth was really created by the labour of the West African peasant.

Expatriate officials realised this. They were aware, equally, that not only was wealth concentrated in a few hands but that much of it was sent abroad to enrich foreign investors. In 1951 an official document pointed out that about half the earnings of the Gold Coast's irreplaceable mineral wealth, consisting of gold, diamonds and manganese, had been sent abroad.* Colonial governments did nothing about these things because of the strong belief in *laissez faire*. This is a doctrine which maintains that the natural workings of the market, left to its own devices, would ultimately produce a result beneficial to everybody. 'Private profits mean public benefits'. What really happens under *laissez-faire* is that the rich get richer and the weak and helpless go to the wall. This is basically what happened in West Africa.

* In 1949, taken as a typical year.

The West African businessmen

Although the heights of the economy were commanded by expatriate firms, some Africans did manage to achieve a wealth which was substantial by any standard, although it does not bear comparison with the vast resources of the great expatriate firms. Many, too, attained a more modest prosperity in retail trade; the expatriate firms controlled the import business, but much, though not all, retail distribution was in African hands. Africans who succeeded in business typically gained their initial capital and experience with expatriate firms. An example of an entrepreneur of the earlier period was J. H. Doherty of Lagos, who died in 1928. He started as a clerk, and entered business with £47 capital. He built up a chain of stores which brought him and his family great wealth. A later instance was Louis Philip Ojukwu, an Igbo,who entered the transport business in 1937. He is an example of a businessman who made his wealth by wisely entering sections of the economy in which expatriates were not seriously involved. In the forties he built up a large fleet of lorries, and amassed a great fortune.

Historians interpret the careers of such African businessmen differently, the differences resting ultimately in differences in their own political views. Some, the majority, regard their careers as triumphs of African ability and enterprise. Others regard them basically as joining hands with the expatriate firms to consume the wealth created by African peasants and workers.

The Lebanese

We have already had occasion to mention the Lebanese* community in West Africa, in our account of Sierra Leone. They arrived in West Africa almost by accident. They had hoped to emigrate to America in an attempt to escape the poverty of their homeland. Instead, many were routed to West Africa because they had too little money for the fare to America, could not meet the health requirements or lacked the necessary documents. The Lebanese were willing to endure any hardship. By the most grinding economy and hard work, they built up a little capital, and forced their way into produce buying and retail distribution. Whereas the British and French firms dominated the heights of the economy, the Lebanese came to have a firm grip on much of it at the middle and lower levels. A few outstandingly successful individuals even challenged the Europeans' control of the import-export trade, as when Saul Raccah broke into the groundnut exporting business at Kano in the 1930s.

The Lebanese faced many difficulties, comparable, in many ways, with those faced by Indians in East Africa. Europeans looked down on them. Africans resented their economic power and prosperity. But they had been forced out of their homelands by poverty. If they are to be criticised, it is the same basic criticism which applies to the expatriate firms and the successful African merchant – that they wer : part of a system which enriched European businesses, but which did nothing to end the poverty and dependence of West Africa.

* There were also smaller communities of Syrians and Greeks.

The growth of cities

One of the most dramatic aspects of the history of the colonial period was the mushroom growth of urban centres. Some of these were entirely new built as the result of an administrative decision, like Kaduna, or Niamey. Others had already existed in pre-colonial times, like Kano and Ibadan, but expanded still more in the colonial era, until, in many cases, the immigrants came to outnumber the original inhabitants. Often, to cope with the strains and difficulties of urban life, the immigrants grouped themselves into voluntary associations. The uniting factor in these was usually the town or village of origin. Urban life brought people from different tribal backgrounds into close contact and the competition for jobs and housing often intensified a spirit of ethnic rivalry. Urban growth, which continued at an accelerated tempo in the independence era, outstripped even such basic amenities as water and sanitation services.

Wage employment

The growth of cities was closely linked to the growth of wage employment. Most immigrants to the city came in pursuit of employment (or of other sources of livelihood such as improved trading opportunities). As time went on, the demand for wage employment often exceeded the supply – a situation which has become much more acute since independence. 'Applicant' has become the recognised description for a large class of people, who are unable to find work, and who depend on their relatives for support, but who are nevertheless unwilling to return to the hardship and monotony of rural life.

By leaving the village for the town, and entering paid employment, the mental horizons of the individual were greatly widened. He had better access to western education, or his children did. He was likely to buy and read newspapers or, in more recent times, to own a transistor radio. Those who moved to the cities were those who were most exposed to change, and who were in the best position to take a hand in initiating change. More research still needs to be done into the history of popular attitudes, and the real location and strength of support of nationalist movements, but it seems fairly clear that the core of articulate and conscious support for independence movements came from urban workers, clerks, teachers and so on.

Although the growth of cities was so striking, the total proportion of West Africans involved in the modern sector was very low indeed. By the early 1960s it was estimated that the population of West Africa was about 88 million, and that only 2 million of these were in wage employment.

In all West African countries, the Government was the main employer, a fact which sometimes tended to damp down political nationalism. By international standards, wages for the unskilled and manual workers were very low (a factor which inflated the profits of the expatriate firms.) Colonial administrators, and the African elite who took their place, enjoyed salaries geared to conditions in Europe. In some ways their conditions were and are more favourable. For example, an English university teacher does not have subsidised housing, a car loan, or a car allowance. African manual workers received only a tiny fraction of the income of their English, French or

American counterparts, for their wages were linked to African rural incomes. The result was a great gulf between the standard of living of the foreign and local educated elite on the one hand, and the urban workers and peasant farmers on the other. In 1964 a Nigerian government inquiry showed that £16 a month was the minimum amount needed to support a Lagos labourer, his wife, and one child at a level 'which allowed no margin for anything other than the essentials of existence '– and that such a worker (who in practice often had more children to support) earned less than £100 a year in Lagos, and less than £70 a year in Kano. Since then, wages have risen, but inflation has repeatedly cancelled out the gains.

8

The Colonial Experience II

Civil war in the mind

A famous thinker in eighteenth-century France said that his generation suffered from a civil war in the mind. One of the most characteristic aspects of the colonial experience was this kind of civil war in the mind – the troubling conflict between traditional values and western materialism and individualism, between pride in one's own culture, and the attacks launched on it both by the missions and the Europe-centred education system. There was the need to choose between the demands of the two mutually intolerant world religions of Christianity and Islam (there were, of course, other options such as keeping to traditional religion, or giving up religion altogether but in practice the educated found neither attractive). These conflicts did not only exist at a very abstract level; they meant a constant series of practical choices. Should a man take more than one wife, which meant more children, and status in the traditional community, but perpetual second class citizenship in the mission community? Should he spread his resources thin among as many of his kin as possible, as traditional society expected, or concentrate on the education of his children, and his own financial security and material comfort, in the fashion of the western world? If he was sick, should he go to a hospital, a traditional herbalist/diviner, or both?

Two points must be made clear at the outset. What was new about colonialism was the *rapidity* of change, and the *multiplicity* of choices. We saw in the first part of this book, how fast the rate of change was in nineteenth-century West Africa. This was true in the sphere of ideas, as elsewhere. We have seen the rapid spread of Islam, and development of the restricted but intensive pockets of Christian mission influence. It is less well known but equally true that changes were also taking place in traditional religions; for instance, members of trader communities, who often left their homes, were tending to emphasise the supreme God (because the local shrines and cults of their home area could not be conveniently worshipped away from it).

The second point is that this kind of civil war in the soul was experienced most acutely, perhaps exclusively, by the western educated. The rural masses were much less exposed to change, their crisis was one of economic survival, not of identity. In a sense, the crisis of identity, which produced theories such as negritude (see page 276) was the luxury of an elite group, which was most intensely exposed to western influences, and which was sufficiently removed from the grim struggle for existence to have leisure for thought.

The problem of cultural identity was felt most acutely by the first generation to be seriously exposed to western education (and often, though not always, to Christianity). For such men, both the old and the new world were living realities and they were obliged to find a way of living with both. They had to distinguish between the essentials of Christianity and the cultural ideas which were introduced along with it in West Africa. Each followed his own path. D. B. Vincent, a Yoruba from Ekiti, was the leader of the Native Baptist Church. He changed his name to Mojola Agbebi and wore the agbada even in freezing North American winters. He called Christianity 'the grandest and greatest revolution that has ever affected humanity', but was led by his intense cultural patriotism to defend cannibalism and human sacrifice.

The same confusion was very clear in political attitudes as well. Sometimes the elite spoke critically of colonial conquest and colonialism. Sometimes they spoke of British rule in words which today seem surprisingly favourable. Thus in 1925 it was said, 'Nigeria has only one AIM, only one THOUGHT, and only one DUTY and that is Loyalty to the Throne and person of the King-Emperor'.

Many of the elite felt a sense of loss at their increasing distance from their cultural heritage. In British colonies especially, their confidence was cruelly undermined by the way in which the British, whom in many respects they tried so eagerly to be like, rejected them. A British visitor observed in the thirties, 'Few white people have a good word to say for the educated Africans . . . Their failings and absurdities are one of the stock subjects of conversation among people in West Africa'. Tragically enough they came to repeat this very condemnation, criticising their own mimicry of the Europeans.

This loss of self-confidence often went hand in hand with a tendency to romanticise and idealise village life. This attitude is still not dead. There is a striking example in a recent book by an eminent Nigerian historian:*

> Without regretting it at all the 'pagans' have consistently refused to come to terms with the history of modern Nigeria. And it would be a mistake to think that, because they have refused to join the ranks of the educated elite collaborators, they are less happy than we are. Spiritually the 'pagans' are the richest . . . Their whole being is completely absorbed in worship, prayer, singing and propitiation . . .

The present writer's interpretation is an entirely different one. Most villagers have not refused to join the modern world but have never been given the chance to enter. Rural Africa's life is still darkened and saddened by ill health, much of it avoidable, by high child mortality rates and chronic economic insecurity. Its anxieties may be

---

* Professor E. A. Ayandele.

different but they are equally real, as studies of mental health in rural areas show. The unseen world may appear less benevolent than dangerous. Where natural explanations for misfortune are imperfectly understood, the belief in witchcraft often flourishes, poisoning personal relationships with a cloud of suspicion and fear. Some of the elite, indeed, have lamented the yawning gulf between the rural masses and modernising change. Henry Carr, who died, aged over eighty, in 1945, was a remarkable Nigerian intellectual and civil servant. He wrote movingly,

> Change all round
> O those who changed not
> To think is to live
> To change is to live

The spread of Islam

The spread of Islam in the colonial era was much more rapid than that of Christianity, though historians have often concentrated on the latter (perhaps because many of them come from a Christian/western background, and missions have a prominent place in the French and English records).

One authority has claimed that Islam spread more rapidly in the fifty years of colonial rule than in the thousand years preceding it. All such estimates can be only rough approximations, but in the 1950s it was claimed that thirty-four per cent of West Africans were Muslims, and only four and a half per cent Christians.

Reasons for expansion

Different reasons have been given for this expansion. Islam, of course, had been established in the western Sudan for centuries, and had made considerable progress further south, as we saw in an earlier section of this book. The turning point in the spread of Islam in Senegal came in 1864, with the conversion of Lat-Dior. This century, Islam has continued to expand in the Senegambia, in Guinea and Sierra Leone, and among the Vai of Liberia and the Yoruba of western Nigeria

The Mossi of Upper Volta, who had previously resisted Islam, became much more receptive in the colonial era. In Ghana, Togo and Dahomey, Muslims were found either in the northern areas, or among groups of northern immigrants to the south (these last were sometimes so numerous that, strangely, Kumasi and Accra became Ghana's largest Islamic centres).

British officials in northern Nigeria, although themselves at least nominally Christian, positively discouraged the introduction of Christian mission work, and mission schools. They had a romantic devotion to the Holy North, a desire to keep it protected from the winds of change. Islamic rulers were treated with much more respect than non-Muslim ones. It has been said that 'All who in any way had dealings with the administration in regions like northern Nigeria found it politically and socially expedient to profess Islam'. States such as Argungu, which had resisted Islam in the past, were converted to Islam under the British.

Both the British and the French always feared the revoluti
Muslim world. The French, in particular, feared the possibility (
ment which would unite North and West Africa, and the near
they could to discourage their Muslim subjects from studying
abroad, in Egypt and elsewhere.

Like the British, however, the French were eager to ally wit
did not threaten their interests. The famous Senegalese religiou
his fellow Muslims in prayer for French success in the First World War. In return, the
French financed the publication of some of his theological writings. Initially, they
persecuted the founder of the Mouride movement. Later they realised its economic
usefulness to them in expanding groundnut production, and changed their attitude
entirely.

It is possible that Christianity was so closely identified with the colonial regime that
some men became Muslims out of patriotism (though the favour which colonial
rulers showed to Islam casts doubt on the suggestion). Certainly, in some communities, social and ethnic divisions expressed themselves in religious terms. The Creoles of
Freetown tended to be Christian, and immigrants to the city, Muslim. In Lagos, the
situation was reversed – immigrants tended to be Christian, the original Lagosians,
Muslim.

But the real reasons for the spread of Islam must be found in considerations more
fundamental than the policies of colonial powers. Islam was spread by Africans;
Christianity on the other hand was closely associated with western cultural ideas. The
Christian churches expected a convert to renounce all his wives but one, and go
through a long course of probation and instruction. To be a Muslim, one needed only
to make the basic statement, 'There is no God but God and Muhammad is His
Prophet', and a gradually deepening knowledge of Islamic faith and practice could
follow slowly. Muslims tolerated a certain amount of continuity with past beliefs. As
a distinguished Malian Muslim has said, with regard to amulets: 'When a child is
small, we give him milk; the meat will come later. Charms bring peace to the heart.
Islam tries to ennoble them by lending them God's name'.

Scholars differ in their interpretation of how Islam was spread. Some have emphasised the role of travelling traders. Certainly, many have been converted to Islam by the
example of the ordinary believer, impressed by his dress, his dignified bearing and
religious conviction, his fidelity to prayer, fasting and almsgiving. More recently,
more stress has been laid on the role of the cleric, or marabout – some of them learned
theologians, some of them men of limited scholarly achievements. A Malian doctor
has said that Islam spreads 'thanks to the courage, thanks to the abnegation, of these
humble marabouts, anonymous apostles who follow the difficult trails with their sack
of provisions and their book'.

One of the most striking characteristics of Islam in twentieth-century West Africa,
as in the past, has been the importance of the sufi orders. As among Christians, only a
tiny minority of Muslims become mystics, but all Tukulor, for instance, tend to be
Tijani, because of Al Hajj Umar. The Tijaniyya and the Qadiriyya remain the largest

rders. The Tijaniyya seems to have a greater impact on individual lives – ..orthern Nigeria, the Tijani are something of a religious vanguard, practising religion with fervour and exactitude.

Muslim responses to colonialism

We have seen that in the nineteenth century, Islam was often linked with a strong interest in innovation and the mastery of western skills. In the twentieth century, the deliberate policy of colonial governments tended to exclude Muslims from these worlds. In the words of a famous administrator, who prided himself on his love for northern Nigeria, Indirect Rule 'certainly did not admit the institution of schools where young natives are to be taught to read and write in English, and, as a corollary, European habits and customs, because practically every young native who has passed through a school is divorced from his own people'. Western education became largely, though not entirely, the preserve of Christian missions, and Muslim children tended to be educated in Quranic schools, which paved the way to no career except Quranic education (or work in northern Nigerian local authorities). When the Nigerianisation of the senior civil service began in the late 1940s, northern Nigerians were at a great disadvantage, which, in its turn, created strains in a democratic political system.

In general, in the colonial era, West African Islam tended to become conservative and inward-looking. (It should not, however, be forgotten that a considerable number of those Muslims most opposed to alien rule had migrated, at the beginning of the century, to the eastern Sudan.) Gradually it became apparent that a Quranic education which taught literacy in Arabic, but not French or English, excluded its pupils from positions of advantage in the modern world. Just as the conflict with the traditional norms of African religion created a crisis of identity for the Christian churches, the conflict between their inherited tradition and the need for adjustment to the colonial situation created a crisis of identity for West African Muslims. They responded to this in a number of different ways.

Hamallism and the Mourides

One response was the militant, and sometimes unorthodox, path of Hamallism, which we shall look at briefly in a later chapter (see page 273). Another was the specifically Senegalese, and Wolof, path of the Mourides, who number over half a million.* Some radicals criticise the Mouride brotherhood as a form of economic exploitation. The voluntary unpaid labour of bands of disciples, and the 'Wednesday fields' of the less totally committed, maintain the marabouts in wealth and luxury, with their large cars, and combination safes, and, on occasion, a liking for liquor. Defenders of the

---

* It is interesting to note that the million-odd Senegalese Tijani outnumber them, and that there are 300,000-odd Senegalese Qadiri.

system say that it gives a measure of economic and psychological security to its followers, which are of value in an age of rapid dislocation and social change. A Mouride would add that it gives believers the eternal and incomparable joys of Paradise. Here is a picture of their great mosque at Touba, the visible symbol of their unity and strength.

Touba Mosque

The Ahmadiyya

The Ahmadiyya is a particularly interesting Islamic movement which arose as a specific response to the challenge of Christian missions and western education. It is not a brotherhood but a sect – which Sunni Muslims regard as unorthodox – and in 1973 the Saudi Arabia authorities forbade its members to go on pilgrimage.

The founder of the Ahmadiyya was a Punjabi from India, Ghulam Ahmad, who died in 1908. He claimed to be a Prophet (a claim totally unacceptable to an orthodox Muslim) and his movement modelled its organisation on that of a Christian mission, with professional missionaries, schools and publishing houses. The Ahmadiyya reached West Africa during the First World War. Its first converts – still its largest group of supporters – were the Muslim Fante. In Nigeria, where the movement was long dominated by Indian missionaries, it played an important role in establishing schools with western-type curricula among Muslims. It never obtained a large following, and the exclusion of Ahmadis from the pilgrimage to Mecca in 1973 led many Nigerian adherents to revert to orthodoxy.

The Ahmadiyya brought together western education and Islam, but at the cost of heresy. Some Nigerian Muslims sought the same end of mastery of western education, while remaining within the limits of orthodoxy. They founded a number of educational societies, such as the Jamaat Nasril Islam, and the Ansar-ud-Deen. After Nigeria became independent, attitudes towards western education changed fairly rapidly among Nigerian Muslims. The network of secular schools in the north expanded with tremendous rapidity, and were attended by ever increasing numbers of Muslim children.

The spread of Christianity

Although, as we have seen, it was greatly overshadowed by the expansion of Islam, Christianity nevertheless spread very rapidly in the colonial era. It made practically no headway in areas where Islam was well established and was most successful in the coastal areas, such as southern (especially south-eastern) Nigeria, southern Togo, Dahomey (Benin), Gold Coast and Ivory Coast. Even today scholars disagree as to how thoroughly Christianised these areas really are. Census returns show that seventy per cent of the people of southern Ghana and fifty-nine per cent of the people of southern Nigeria say that they are Christians when asked. But a distinguished Nigerian historian writes, 'Until this day, by far the majority of unlettered Nigerians outside the Islamic areas remain pagans'. A brilliant English scholar, who has spent much time in southern Nigeria, writes, 'African Christianity in such areas as southern Nigeria presents as much social penetration as Christianity almost anywhere'.★ This is an interesting example of how scholars can disagree even in describing the world that they see around them, let alone what happened a hundred years ago (the present writer agrees with the second view).

Reasons for expansion

Different explanations have been given, none wholly satisfactory, of this movement to Christianity. One interpretation stresses the support, power and prestige of the colonial government, but these factors did not lead to the conversion of Indian Hindus, or the Muslims of the western Sudan. Often, indeed, colonial officials seemed to favour Islam rather than Christianity. Many French officials had a strong prejudice against the Church and were very suspicious of any apparent extension of its power.

A more persuasive explanation stresses the missions' role in western education, which in many areas amounted to nearly complete control, and which enabled them to influence the minds of the young at a crucially impressionable age. A very large number of West Africans now and in the past have said that their adherence to Christianity was due to attendance at a mission school.

A more abstract and complicated but very interesting argument points out that African religion was extremely local in character. The High God tends to be remote,

★ E. A. Ayandele and J. D. Y. Peel.

and religious life centres in practise around local spirits, honoured in local festivals, their cults dominated by a local priest or diviner, and linked with local physical landmarks – a sacred hill or cave or spring. A man who left his village and went to live in Accra or Freetown would find it difficult and perhaps unattractive to keep up such practices. Even within the context of traditional religion, groups such as traders, who spent a lot of time away from home, and from the local surroundings of their religion, tended to give increasing emphasis to the High God. Islam and Christianity were both religions which laid their whole emphasis on that same High God and it is significant that some communities such as the Ijebu of southern Yorubaland, gave an enthusiastic welcome to both Christianity and Islam.

Problems created by Christianity

The spread of Christianity created problems which had already been experienced in the nineteenth century by the Creoles of Sierra Leone and others. These concerned the tensions between African traditional culture and Christianity, which was brought to West Africa along with its strongly European cultural background. The first Christians, like the missionaries themselves, tended to identify the various aspects of this cultural background, such as European dress and European given names, with Christianity. Others, even in the nineteenth century, tried to think out the best relationship between their new faith and their own historical heritage. One fervent nineteenth-century Yoruba Christian was so anxious not to deny his heritage that he defended cannibalism and human sacrifice! (See page 245.) But the answer was clearly not to reject the African inheritance as a whole, or to accept it as a whole, for most traditional African cultures included elements unacceptable to any Christian conscience. What was needed was a search for a way to bring together the best aspects of traditional and Christian beliefs. This search is perhaps the most striking aspect of twentieth-century West African Christianity.

The conflict which so often existed in the individual heart and mind can also be seen in whole communities. Some Christian converts were drawn from the outcasts of society or were slaves. These converts, because of their superior education, or simply because of their belief in the brotherhood of man, found themselves in conflict with traditional chiefs who had everything to gain from preserving the traditional state of affairs unchanged. Many converts were young and found themselves in conflict with their elders. Some communities were bitterly divided on denominational lines – Catholic against Protestant.

An important area of tension developed over the career structure of the church. Just as the elite in general were dissatisfied over their exclusion from the top positions in the civil service, African clergy were frustrated by their exclusion from the highest positions in the churches. When the great Bishop Crowther died, a European succeeded him, and in the colonial period, the highest position an African could achieve tended to be that of Auxiliary Bishop, or Half-Bishops, as they were called disparagingly. This conflict over authority led to the creation of a whole series of independent churches between 1888 and 1920. These are generally called the African churches.

They broke away mainly because they desired church self-government, and their teachings and practices were much the same as those of the parent churches, though they tended to permit polygamy. In Nigeria, they included the African Baptists, founded in 1888 through a split from the American Baptists; the United Native African Church (1891) and Bethel Church (1901) founded through a split from the C.M.S. and the United African Methodists, 1917, formed through a split from the Methodists. In practice, they tended to lead a settled congregational life, very much like that of the mission churches.

The prophetic churches
The most remarkable examples of successful evangelical work came neither from the mission churches nor from the so-called 'African Churches', but from a series of remarkable prophetic movements. The three most important of these were:

1 The work of the Prophet Garrick Braide, which began in 1912 and ended with his imprisonment in 1916 (he later died in prison).

2 The work of the Prophet William Wade Harris in Ivory Coast, Liberia and the Gold Coast, which began in 1912, reached its height in 1914–15, and continued on, though with diminishing impact, until his death in 1929.

3 The Aladura movement in western Nigeria. This began during the influenza epidemic of 1918–19 and made its greatest impact during the Great Revival of 1930.

Garrick Braide
Braide was a simple Kalabari fisherman from Bakana who was converted to Christianity (C.M.S. version) as an adult. After he had been baptised and confirmed he devoted himself to prayer and fasting. He became a celebrated evangelist and faith healer. People flocked to hear his message and other evangelists, inspired by his example, carried his teachings far and wide. He insisted on the complete rejection of traditional religion and the destruction of charms, 'idols' and so on. He forbade liquor but permitted polygamy. As time went on, the church of which he was a member became increasingly uneasy about his influence. British traders and officials were unhappy about the dramatic drop in revenue from liquor imports. Accused of fermenting opposition to the colonial government, he was put in prison and later died there. Some of his followers founded their own church but most of those he influenced joined various established churches. He could well be called the John the Baptist of south-eastern Nigeria.

William Harris
William Wade (pronounced Waddy) Harris was a Grebo from Liberia. He was originally an Episcopal catechist and teacher, who first came into the limelight through his participation in a political movement. As part of the Kru-Grebo attempt to replace Liberian Settler rule with British government, he pulled down the Liberian flag flying in Monrovia and replaced it with the Union Jack. For this, in 1909, he was imprisoned.

In prison, he underwent a great religious conversion. When he came out his wife died of grief, thinking he had gone mad. Henceforward he saw himself as a Prophet, called by God to lead, not a political revolution but a religious one, to win men from paganism to Christianity. He wore flowing white robes and carried a cross. A Gold Coast lawyer wrote, 'He is a dynamic soul of a rare order . . . It seems as if God made the soul of Harris a soul of fire'. When he died, a Catholic paper which had been consistently hostile to him wrote, 'He demanded nothing, accepted nothing'.

His teachings were astonishingly similar to those of Braide. He condemned liquor but permitted polygamy. He insisted on the destruction of all pagan charms and images. Like Braide, and unlike the mission churches, he gave baptism to all who sought it, without insisting on a long course of instruction beforehand. It has been suggested that this appealed greatly to potential converts, who felt otherwise that they had abandoned the protection of traditional deities without immediately obtaining the spiritual protection of baptism. His ministry had a tremendous impact, especially in the Ivory Coast where, as we have seen, the unsettlement, destruction and distress caused by Angoulvant's 'pacification' had perhaps paved the way for a prophetic figure of this type. He was thought to have miraculous powers, to make the rain fall, to heal the sick and insane, and to expel evil spirits. Backsliders died mysteriously. In the end the French became so nervous about his influence that they deported him in 1915.

He did not try to found a new church, though some of his followers did this. He urged the converts to follow the teachings of the missionaries who would come after him. He said that they would recognise them by the central role of the Bible in their message. For some years the villagers waited. They built churches, sheltering large Bibles which they could not read. In the end some of them formed an independent church. Some became Catholics and others Methodists. Like Braide, Harris converted an enormous number of people to Christianity and paved the way for the older mission churches.

Aladura movement

'Aladura' is a Yoruba word meaning the people of prayer. It refers to a whole series of churches founded by a number of prophetic figures from 1918 on. Like Braide and Harris, they emphasised the destruction of traditional religious images. On the next page is a picture of the destruction of charms at the 1930 revival in Ilesa (it shows a famous Aladura prophet, Joseph Babalola, in a long white gown).

The main Aladura branches today are the Christ Apostolic Church, the Seraphim and Cherubim, which is itself split into many branches, and the Church of the Lord, Aladura. All of these emphasise the importance of prayer and its power to win blessings from God, including this-worldly blessings such as good health or examination success. In this, they are in the spirit of traditional African religion, which also offered this kind of benefit. The Aladura churches differ from each other in some details. The Christ Apostolic Church forbids its followers to use western medicine. They are

The Prophet Babalola during the 1930 revival

expected to rely entirely on God for healing. The Cherubim and Seraphim are characterised by their distinctive robes and their emphasis on visions.

New Christian churches tend to be founded as a re-affirmation of one aspect or another of Christ's teachings. The Aladura churches emphasise the Christian teaching of the importance of prayer, and the need for its persevering practice.

Much of the effective Christian evangelisation of West Africa, then, was carried out by West Africans. This was equally true of the mission churches, where expatriate clergy were few and far between. The expatriate Catholic priest, for example, was essentially the supervisor of twenty or more parishes whose day to day religious leadership was in the hands of African catechists. These catechists, as yet little studied by historians, were often men of exemplary religious devotion, and did the real work of planting and fostering Christianity in the villages, as they still do. But the African role in Christian evangelisation of West Africa this century has not always been generally appreciated. Every Nigerian schoolchild has heard of Bishop Shanahan; few, indeed, have heard of Garrick Braide.

Some scholars have seen the prophetic churches as a form of protest against colonial rule. There were, indeed, elements of this – Braide said that the rule of the white man would soon end – but their basic concern was not with politics, but with religion, with the winning of individuals from traditional religion to Christianity, the pattern of a Christian life, and its eternal reward.

Western education

It would, of course, be a great mistake to equate 'education' with 'western education', and write as if both developed from small beginnings in the twentieth century. All traditional societies had their own systems of education, which were primarily vocational and moral. Children learnt farming techniques, and a variety of other skills, which might include fishing, blacksmithing, spinning and weaving, or pottery making, depending on the area, and the sex of the child. Islamic West Africa, as we have seen, had a vast network of Quranic schools. A gifted pupil could go on to further studies, travelling from scholar to scholar – as European students did in the Middle Ages. A knowledge of Arabic opened to him the whole world of international Islamic learning. The Vai of Liberia taught their own alphabet in their own schools, and the Efik, in the eighteenth century, perpetuated the knowledge of reading and writing, which some of them had mastered in England, in the same way.

Here, however, we are concerned with western education. And it was western education which was of crucial importance both to the individual and to society in the colonial era. To the individual, the western educational ladder offered a prospect of a transformed earning power, and life style, which neither the traditional educational structure, nor Quranic education, could provide.

The history of the educational system of the colonial period is essentially the history of the interplay of three forces. The first was that of Christian missions. They had established a number of pioneering schools in the nineteenth century. The Wesleyans set up a school in the Gambia in 1826, and one in Nigeria in 1842. Both the C.M.S. and the Wesleyan Methodists engaged in educational work in Sierra Leone, which was the most favoured, in this respect, of the British settlements. But the growth of schools was limited by lack of funds, and sometimes, though not always, by parents' unwillingness to send their children to them.

In the colonial era, these last two factors changed abruptly, to some extent at least. It was impossible for a colonial government, or the big foreign firms, to function without a large number of literate and numerate local personnel. To recruit clerks, storemen, artisans and schoolteachers from abroad would be impossibly expensive. The government, in British colonies, rapidly reached an understanding with the missions. The missions provided a relatively cheap and efficient educational service, in return for government subsidies. They welcomed the opportunity to influence the minds of the young, and government subsidies rescued many a mission from poverty. In the French colonies, there were no subsidies to mission schools, in West Africa at least, because of the separation of church and state in 1905.* In spite of this, missions retained a dominant role in Dahomey (Benin) and Senegal especially.

As it was apparent that western education led to positions, such as teaching or clerical work, which were both better paid and less laborious than farming, an insatiable demand for more schools was created, which, in the colonial period, in many areas,

* Despite this, subsidies continued in some other French colonies.

far outstripped the supply. This led to the widespread establishment of unofficial schools, sometimes of poor quality. In response to criticism it was claimed that any education was better than none.

In 1939 it was estimated that twelve per cent of school age children in Nigeria attended school. The position was worse in the French colonies. Ten years later, in 1949, it was estimated that in French West Africa about six per cent of school age children attended school. The educational situation was in fact worse than these figures suggest for the very high drop out rate meant that many children left school with little real command of western skills. Various factors explained this drop out rate, among them the difficulty of study in a foreign language. In Senegal as late as 1960, fewer than a third of primary school entrants completed their course successfully.

The inadequate amount of money provided for education was the direct consequence of government reluctance and shortage of funds. In Nigeria, in 1924-5, exactly 1.8 per cent of total expenditure went on education. By 1951–2 when Nigerians began to have a say in their own government, it had risen to just under 17 per cent. In the years just before independence, educational expenditure swung to the other extreme. The Regional Governments in both eastern and western Nigeria devoted as much as 40 per cent of their budgets to education, partly out of a genuine desire to spread opportunity more widely and partly in response to the insistent demands of the electorate. They both tried to abolish school fees, but it proved financially impossible to sustain the experiment (the same was also true of Ghana). However well-intentioned this colossal expansion in education was, it had the effect of diverting money from industrial and agricultural development which might have provided more jobs for the newly-educated. Rapid educational expansion took place partly at the cost of quality. When Nigeria and Ghana became independent, half their primary schoolteachers were untrained. Some had outstanding qualities of intellect and character which compensated for this, but to outside observers the system often looked very much like the blind leading the blind.

Criticisms of colonial education

In recent times the educational system of the colonial period and mission education in particular have often been criticised for having a literary rather than technical and vocational bias and teaching its products to despise manual work. These criticisms are unjust. The pattern of education which developed was a response to the structures of available career opportunities and the demands of those who were being educated. There was a great demand for the literate and numerate in a developing bureaucratic state and in the modern sector of the economy. Villagers had no desire for their sons to be taught manual work which they could be taught equally well at home. For them, the whole point of seeking a western education was to escape it.

The preference for white collar rather than blue collar work was due to two factors. First, clerks were paid more money for less work than carpenters, let alone gardeners. Secondly, Europeans, who frequently spoke of the virtues of manual labour throughout the colonial period, have never, in West Africa, shown the slightest inclination to demonstrate these virtues in their own lives, so that there was an even wider than customary gap between teaching and example. When a Commission in the 1920s advocated greater stress on vocational and agricultural education, West Africans opposed it vehemently, fearing that it would limit their career prospects. When schools and missions did run farms, they were often less efficient than those of the villagers around them. Furthermore, they used students' labour in a manner which looked very much like the forced labour which the Government exacted. It is interesting to notice that when vocational training did expand rapidly in the 1950s and 1960s, it did so not through government or mission initiatives but through a system of private apprentice-ship very much like that of pre-colonial times.

A juster criticism of the educational structure of the colonial period is that it alienated pupils from their own culture. They wrote essays on 'Snow' and 'Walks in London' rather than about the world they actually knew. It was said that if a class in British West Africa were asked to sing a song of their choice, it was likely to be the British Grenadiers. The most extreme form of this kind of absurdity was found in an often-quoted text book in French West Africa: 'Our ancestors were the Gauls. They had red hair and blue eyes'.

Higher education

The lack of educational opportunity was felt most acutely at the higher levels. Until the post-war period, the only provision for university education in West Africa was Fourah Bay College in Sierra Leone, which was limited to arts and theology, and struggled on in the face of financial and other difficulties.

Each colony tended to have one or two star institutions which absorbed a large amount of available finance and which were proudly displayed to admiring foreign visitors but which were pathetically inadequate to the demand. In French West Africa, the Lycée Faidherbe at St Louis, and the William Ponty Normal School in Dakar, took 50 to 80 boys a year, who became teachers, or medical assistants and so on. There were two professional schools in Dakar, and a veterinary school in Bamako. In the Gold Coast, the government established Achimota College in 1924. In Nigeria, Yaba Higher College in Lagos began as a medical school in 1930 and opened fully four years later. It was a good example of the way in which the colonial educational system was designed to keep Africans in a subordinate role, for only a quarter or less of those who applied were admitted, and of the few chosen, some were discarded every year. After a course of study which lasted longer than the equivalent degree course elsewhere, the students were awarded not degrees, but diplomas, and became not doctors and engineers, but medical assistants, engineering assistants and so on – though Nigerians abroad had no difficulty in qualifying as doctors, lawyers, etc.

In the post-war period, facilities for higher education expanded dramatically. In 1948 the University of Ibadan was founded, soon to acquire an outstanding inter-national reputation. More generous scholarship schemes enabled increasing numbers of West Africans to study abroad. In 1950 an Institute of Higher Studies was estab-lished at Dakar, which became a full university in 1957.

Opportunities for the educated

By the time the states of West Africa became independent, the inadequate provision of secondary schools had created a bottleneck in the educational system. In western Nigeria only six per cent of those who left primary school in 1960 were in secondary school by 1961. In the 1960s there was a tremendous expansion of secondary schools but since it was impossible to expand employment opportunities equally rapidly, it contributed greatly to the problem of educated unemployment. At the beginning of the colonial period, the primary school graduate could be assured of clerical work. By the depression years, this was no longer the case and by the 1960s, many secondary school leavers found themselves unemployable. An educationalist★ who has worked for many years in Ghana describes the situation in these words:

> Education . . . was rapidly becoming subject to the law of diminishing returns. Clerical and store-keeping posts in government and commerce were limited and soon filled, but the education machine still went grinding on as before, turning out increasing quantities of people fitted for repetitious duties of a clerical kind but of whom only a relatively small proportion could be employed. Despite the patent fact of growing unemployment among a large proportion of the products of such education, each learner in the school hoped that he would be among the lucky few to win the glittering prize of a lucrative post, status, security, and the opportunities of urban living. The schools thus became hot-beds of competition in which were sorted out only a few pupils who would enjoy privilege by escape from the hard economic, social, and political facts imposed by environment.

The salient fact about the educational system in the colonial period – and still, to a lesser extent, today – was the lack of opportunity, the vast expanse of potential talent which was never exploited. Occasionally, in the records of colonialism, one of these untaught unrecognised men of great ability emerges. A man called Tasuki, 'usually in pain from a complication of diseases', showed a great talent for bridge construction in colonial Borgu:

> When I arrived, the pulleys had not come but the first trestle was up. Tasuki had invented all by himself and for this one job, the compound lever, the multiple pulley and several new devices never seen before and probably never used again.

Alien wars

In an earlier chapter, we saw how the conquest of West Africa was carried out largely by African soldiers. Nigerians fought in the Asante campaign and the Senegalese conquered the western Sudan for France. It is one of the sad ironies of West African history that even while some West African peoples were still fighting and dying in the attempt to resist colonial rule, other West Africans were fighting and dying for the

★ John Wilson.

same colonial conquerors, not only in Africa but in alien battlefields far away. 'Imperialism makes its victims its defenders.'

Probably the first occasion when West Africans fought abroad was in Madagascar in 1828. African soldiers took part in the Crimean War, and the Franco-Prussian War of 1870. They fought in Central America, in Mexico and Guyana, and also in Morocco in 1908.

The First World War, 1914-18

The impact of the 1914-18 war, however, was incomparably greater, especially in Francophone West Africa. It has been estimated that 211,000 soldiers were recruited in Francophone black Africa and that of these, 163,952 fought in Europe. According to official figures 24,762 died, but since this excludes those missing in action the estimate is certainly far too low. The impact on the French colonies was the greater because, as we have seen, they were already weakened by the human losses and destruction of 'pacification' and, more recently, by a disastrous famine. Compulsory military service had been introduced in 1912, a good example of the way in which Subjects had the duties of Frenchmen but not their rights. From 1915 on, resistance to military service intensified, as the wounded and mutilated began to return and as it became obvious that no adequate provision was made for the families of absent soldiers. There was a major rising in Soudan which spread to Upper Volta. The Tuareg rose in a war against French authority and in 1916 there was a rising in Borgu and in other parts of Dahomey. Whole villages hid in the bush to avoid conscription and thousands of young men crossed the border into British colonies. Some even mutilated themselves. Towards the end of the war, when the supply of soldiers seemed to be drying up, the French sent the Senegalese Deputy, Blaise Diagne, on a recruiting campaign. He did this in turn for promised concessions, some of which were granted in due course, and others not.

The impact of war on the British colonies was much less serious. Their population was greater and the numbers recruited much lower. They took part with the French in the conquest of Togo and Kamerun. Both these campaigns were essentially wars between two bodies of black troops with a handful of white officers. Togo, which was strategically indefensible, was easily taken, but the conquest of Kamerum meant a tough campaign of three years. After it fell, West African troops and carriers were sent to fight the Germans in East Africa. Five thousand carriers were sent from Sierra Leone, and over a thousand Nigerians and Ghanaians were killed or died of disease there, relatively small numbers in comparison with those of Francophone Africans.

For those who escaped injury and death, the war was sometimes an avenue of social mobility. In the French colonies, chiefs often recruited slaves and the rejects of society. They came back with pensions, to a position of relative privilege and some became chiefs in their turn. But on the whole it is difficult to see what advantage the war brought to West Africa. In the French colonies, it led to the introduction of a compulsory three-year period of military service.

African soldiers in Europe during the First World War

The Second World War, 1939–1945

Most modern historians consider that the First World War was unnecessary, the tragic consequence of a series of blunders and misjudgements. The war not only solved nothing, but directly paved the way to the Second World War, by the unjust treatment of defeated Germany which followed it. Practically all historians, on the other hand, whatever their political views, see the Second World War as a struggle in a just cause against German Fascism and racism. This view inevitably colours their interpretation of its impact on West Africa. But it is still certain that West Africans died in a war not their own.

French West Africa

As soon as the war broke out in 1939, France began the large-scale recruiting of African troops which she had practised in the past, and within a few months, 80,000 had been sent to Europe. But in June 1940, the picture changed dramatically. France was invaded by the Germans and surrendered. Now, northern France was directly ruled by Germany, and in the south of France, a French government, known as Vichy, was set up in collaboration with the Germans. Not all Frenchmen accepted this, however. Some continued to fight against the Germans as best they could, in their own country, and in exile, General de Gaulle set up the Free French Government.

Batteries at Dakar being manned by African soldiers

The French officials in Africa were faced with an extremely difficult decision as to which Government to support. Equatorial Africa opted for the Free French – the decisive initiative was taken by Félix Eboué, the black Governor of Chad, who came from French Guiana. De Gaulle established his headquarters in Brazzaville, the capital of French Equatorial Africa. He said later that Africa gave France 'her refuge and the starting point for her liberation'.

The white officials in French West Africa, on the other hand, decided to support Vichy France. Boisson was appointed Governor-General, a man who had lost a leg in the First World War, fighting against the Germans. Historians interpret his role differently. Some regard him as a traitor, others think that he was trying to keep French West Africa neutral until it could join the Allies in fighting against Germany. It is clear that Africans had little say in the matter either way. A Camerounian recalls movingly,

> I remember, as a child, seeing Camerounian men being conscripted by non-Camerounian Bambara soldiers. Some hid in the bush. Many others who were taken away clearly went against their will, not because they didn't want to fight against Nazi Germany and on the side of France, but simply because they couldn't be bothered one way or the other . . .

It wasn't Africans who vacillated between the Free French Movement and the Vichy regime. The right even to vacillate was denied them because, although French forces had been defeated in France, French-speaking Africans were still a colonised people.

Historians differ in their estimates of Vichy's impact on West Africa. Some emphasise its racist and authoritarian aspects – the Citizens lost their cherished privileges and a few Africans were shot for helping the Free French. The King of Abron and a large entourage left Ivory Coast for the Gold Coast, and the King of Porto Novo committed suicide when imprisoned for aiding the Gaullists. Others believe that these isolated episodes of resistance have little significance – the Abron migration, for instance, was probably caused by local political factors. Neither racism nor authoritarianism were new in French West Africa and for the masses, probably, life continued much as before. In some ways French West Africa even benefited from Vichy rule, as shortages in Europe forced up the price for her exports.

In November 1942, when German victory no longer seemed as likely as before, French West Africa transferred its support to de Gaulle and the Free French. Once more, Francophone West Africans travelled to alien lands to fight in alien wars. There were a hundred thousand black soldiers in the Free French armies, at one stage more than half their total numbers. In their desperate need for raw materials, the Gaullists imposed extremely heavy burdens on West Africa between 1943 and 1945. Their demands were so excessive that sometimes villages were compelled to buy what was demanded, and resell it to the government at a loss. The artificially high prices of German-ruled Europe fell abruptly to the lower level common in the rest of the world. In 1944 African opinion was shocked by the grim tragedy of the Tiaroye massacre, when released African prisoners of war mutinied in support of pay demands and were shot down by French officers, so that forty Africans who had risked their lives for France lost them at French hands.

Despite all this, there were real long term gains. Ultimately, African hopes were more likely to be realised under French or British rule than under the racist regime of the Nazis. Even if only for propaganda purposes, the Gaullists were forced to show that they were better colonial rulers than Vichy. Hence the significance of the New Deal promise at Brazzaville . . . (see page 288).

British West Africa

The impact of the war on British West Africa was less dramatic, though many English-speaking West Africans, too, fought and died on distant battlefields. The West African Frontier Force increased its strength to 146,000 men, who were, in theory, though not always in practice, volunteers. Despite the unaccustomed cold and high altitude, they played a major role in defeating the Italians in Ethiopia. West African carriers and soldiers played a key role in the Burma campaign against the Japanese between 1943 and 1945. In strange surroundings, they fought with a courage that won the praise both of their British officers and their Japanese opponents. A Japanese wrote in his war diary:

The enemy soldiers are not from Britain but from Africa . . . they are not afraid to die, so even if their comrades have fallen they keep on advancing as if nothing had happened . . .

We have already noted the way in which the accumulated surpluses of the Marketing Boards contributed financially to the British war effort. In addition to this, governments, communities and individuals voted over £900,000, although most of their people lacked hospitals, schools, good roads and even pure water. It was suggested that the contributions were raised by force, but the Sultan of Sokoto wrote to *The Times* to deny it.

In British West Africa, as in French West Africa, the rural masses probably knew and cared little about the issues at stake. Both the traditional and the modern elite, in their attachment to the British cause, showed that affection for the metropolitan power which always existed side by side with resentment and criticism.

In the long run, the significance of the war, both for French and British colonies, was tremendous. It appears now the clearest watershed in their whole colonial history. It was followed by an era of militant nationalism and more generous financial resources, and by changed attitudes both in the colonies and the metropolitan countries, which were soon to sweep away colonialism for good.

A colonial balance sheet

All historians will probably agree that the only criterion by which a government can be judged is whether it makes the governed worse off or better off. In the context of colonial rule, as elsewhere, this is not easy to establish. Some categories of individuals were clearly better off, such as the new chiefs, the teachers, clerks and interpreters, the successful cash crop farmers, the many individuals whom colonial rule rescued from slavery and the ultimate form of social oppression, human sacrifice. It ended the almost infinite suffering caused by traditional magical and religious beliefs and prohibitions, to groups such as the old women accused of witchcraft, or, in some societies, twins and their mothers. Some were clearly worse off, such as those who were mutilated or killed resisting colonial conquest, or in foreign wars, those who worked on unpaid road construction with their bare hands, since tools were not provided, those who, to pay their taxes, had to leave their homes and work for low wages far away. And one should note that even those who appeared to be better off, such as the new educated elite, had to grapple with problems of identity and divided loyalties. An old Nigerian, whom the writer once questioned on this subject, said, 'we were more progressive but we were not happier'.

Each individual who lived under colonial rule would have drawn up a slightly different balance sheet. The many creative artists of the colonial period, especially the sculptors, often, though not always, anonymous, give us striking images of their own perceptions of change. Here are a few examples – a very fine ivory carving of a cyclist, a merchant in a hammock, a teacher with a book.

Images of the colonial presence

Here is an assessment made by one of the many women of south-eastern Nigeria who took part in the Women's War of 1929. They would not normally have been asked their views at all. They had the chance to put them on record only because the colonial government had been alarmed by the threat to 'law and order'. They were not in any way those most badly affected by colonialism. They lived in the heart of the palm oil and kernel export economy, an area where intense mission concentration meant that western education was comparatively accessible for their children, if not for themselves. But in the colonial balance sheet they constructed, these were out-weighed by administrative oppression and economic injustice.

> Our grievances are that the land is changed – we are all dying . . . It is a long time since the Chiefs and the people who know book . . . have been oppressing us . . . We are telling you that we have been oppressed . . . The new Chiefs are also receiving bribes . . . Since the white men came, our oil does not fetch money. Our kernels do not fetch money. If we take goats or yams to market to sell, Court messengers who wear a uniform take all these things from us.

9

Nationalism before 1939

Colonialism created a situation within which certain possibilities for choice existed. The history of the colonial era is, as we have seen, largely one of African initiatives within this situation. But the range of choices was limited – a peasant could choose to grow cocoa, but not to become a professor of mathematics, and for many peasants, even the cocoa growing choice was not open. In the sphere of educational opportunity, in the civil service and in the churches, the highest positions were closed to Africans.

This chapter studies efforts to change the situation of colonialism, either totally or in part. The pattern that emerges is basically that of two streams which seldom met in the inter-war period – that of elite and urban political movements, and that of localised popular outbursts such as 'riots', peasant risings and strikes. Despite their differences, they had two things in common; they were localised not nationwide, and, in the inter-war period, they sought to modify aspects of colonialism rather than topple the structure.

Early forms of nationalism

We have seen how the tradition of violent confrontation with colonialism continued well into the twentieth century. When grievances seemed intolerable, the tradition of violent opposition reappeared. Thus we have a whole series of 'riots' and risings in southern Nigeria – at many places in Igboland during the First World War, in the Yoruba town of Iseyin in 1914, and in Abeokuta in 1918. In 1915 there was a small rising in Bussa, in Borgu. In 1916 where was a revolt at Donga, in the Benue area, led by a man called 'the Invulnerable One'. In 1927 there were anti-tax riots in Warri and in 1929–30 there were very extensive disturbances among the women of south-eastern Nigeria which tradition remembers as 'The Women's War'. Beginning as a protest against taxation, it escalated into rejection of the whole colonial structure and the demand 'that all white men should return to their country so that the land in this area might remain as it was many years ago before the advent of the white man'. In

1931 there was a peasant revolt in northern Sierra Leone known as the Haidara Rebellion. This grew out of the distress caused by falling produce prices, which made the House Tax appear even more of a burden. A Mouride Marabout from Senegal exhorted the peasants to revolt, and he himself was ultimately killed in battle.

Discontent with the prices for produce sometimes produced a rural equivalent to industrial action, when the peasants tried to force buyers to pay them higher prices by withholding their produce. African palm oil brokers had often used this technique successfully in the nineteenth century. The most outstanding examples in the inter-war period were the three great cocoa hold-ups in the Gold Coast, in 1921, 1930–1, and 1937, which, although unsuccessful, showed remarkable solidarity in protesting against worsening terms of trade.

As the peasants withheld their produce, the workers went on strike. Each of the four British colonies experienced a considerable number of strikes during the inter-war period, such as the railways workers' strikes in Nigeria in 1920 and 1941–2, and the gold miners' strikes in the Gold Coast in 1924 and 1930.

A remarkable figure in what one might call the history of economic nationalism was Winifred Tete-Ansa, of the Gold Coast, who in the late 'twenties and early 'thirties made a remarkable attempt to break Europe's control of the economy. He formed farmers' co-operatives to market their members' produce and set up a bank to make money available to African businessmen. An Afro-American company was set up in the USA to market the farmers' cocoa and to send back manufactured goods in return. It was a remarkably bold attempt to carve out a role for the African businessman in the colonial economy and to win for the farmer a greater share of the fruits of his labour, but all his efforts ended in failure. It should be noted that his aim was similar to that of early political nationalist movements, being less to abolish colonialism than to win for the African a more favourable position within it.

Sometimes protests against colonialism took the form of religious movements. We have already seen how colonial governments feared and suspected prophetic movements – the prophet Harris was deported, the prophet Braide imprisoned. But the primary concern both of these leaders and their followers lay in non-political spheres: the protection of the individual against both known and unknown dangers in this life, and his salvation in the world to come.

Some outstanding patriots concentrated on education. Eyo Ita, who returned to Nigeria with American university degrees in 1934, devoted himself to educational work in what were then the remote areas of Ogbomosho and Calabar. He believed that education must 'make our youth hyper-sensitive to the sacredness of equal social justice'. Much later in the 1950s, he was to lead a small opposition party in the Eastern Region. J. E. K. Aggrey of the Gold Coast spent many years of study in the USA. In 1924 he returned home with two doctorates. He became Vice-Principal of Achimota College, a post he held with outstanding success until his premature death in 1927. He was a gifted and dynamic teacher who summed up his educational philosophy with the words that flies should be caught with molasses, and not vinegar. He wrote in a letter to his nephew, 'To those who have fire I give more fire and to those who have might

I want to give a might mightier than man's. I want to sing a song of hope to the despairing, to breathe the breath of love that will chase away all parting.'

Another type of movement which can be seen as a form of nationalism, can be found in organisations which were political in emphasis, but which concentrated, not on the colony, but on the ethnic sub-division. Examples of this, in Nigeria, are the Yoruba Cultural Organisation, Egbe Omo Oduduwa, which was founded in 1945, and the Igbo State Union founded in 1949.* Another can be found in the long unsuccessful struggle of the Ewe (pronounced Evay) people, divided between the Gold Coast and Togoland, to be united under one government.

Political nationalism in English-speaking West Africa

The Aborigines Rights Protection Society, founded in the Gold Coast in 1897, is generally regarded as 'West Africa's first effective political organisation'. It was formed to oppose a specific government proposal, to classify unoccupied land as crown land, which meant it would belong to the Government, and in this it was successful. Later it intervened, often with success, on other specific issues.

The National Congress of British West Africa

In 1920 a much broader organisation was formed under the leadership of Joseph Casely-Hayford, a distinguished Gold Coast lawyer. The National Congress of British West Africa held its first meeting at Accra, attended mainly by professional men, especially lawyers and merchants. It is interesting to note that just as the ethnic unions were concerned with a unit smaller than the colony, the National Congress was based on a larger unit – the four colonies of British West Africa. Where the Aborigines Rights Protection Society, and a similar Lagos movement led by Herbert Macaulay, had united traditional rulers and the western educated elite, the National Congress excluded traditional rulers, and thus alienated them. A more significant source of weakness was the distance between the movement and popular discontents which could have given it so much more force and vitality. But instead of showing concern for the grievances of the peasants and urban workers, the elite members of the National Congress were concerned mainly with their own exclusion from authority and opportunity. They asked that half the members of the Legislative Council should be elected Africans and that elected Africans should control finance. They opposed discrimination against Africans in the civil service and asked for a West African university. They asked for stricter immigration controls to exclude 'undesirable' Syrians, a request inspired by resentment at the role they had carved out for themselves in the economy. (This tendency to attack a politically weak, economically prosperous, ethnic minority was unfortunately to occur in some later African nationalist movements.) The Congress sent a delegation to England in 1920. The Government paid little

* Other pan-Igbo organisations had existed earlier under different names.

attention to its requests and its failure to win immediate results discredited it. Nevertheless, there was a fairly obvious link between its demands and the changes made by the various colonial governments to the Legislative Councils between 1922 and 1925 (see page 213).

One notable exception to this general picture of disregard for the masses should be recorded. Several members of the Sierra Leone branch of the National Congress raised funds for striking workers – a potential alliance which, significantly enough, caused the utmost alarm to the colonial government.

Legislative Council elections

Wherever there are elections, there is a tendency for political parties to develop to fight them. After the changes of 1922–5 there was a small elected element on the Legislative Councils of Nigeria, the Gold Coast and Sierra Leone. This led to the formation of a number of small political parties which were united less by any particular ideology than by personal loyalty to some dominating personality. In Nigeria, Herbert Macaulay formed the first Nigerian National Democratic Party,* which monopolised the three Lagos seats until 1938. Macaulay could not contest a seat himself as he had been accused of financial irregularities on several occasions, and had served a gaol sentence.

Although the elite had asked for elected members so eagerly, the actual results were, to some extent, disappointing. Energies were diverted from the broad stage of the National Congress to the small world of municipal politics, a world so often torn by petty jealousies and rivalries. Because the elected members were in a minority, they could do little to fulfil the wishes of their constituents, so that, increasingly, many of those eligible to vote did not bother to do so. There was a tendency for the politically active to move ever closer to the colonial government, which was the country's main employer, and the source of honours and privileges. His critics say that Macaulay's party was neither national, Nigerian nor democratic. Nevertheless, some elected members, such as Dr C. C. Adeniyi-Jones of Lagos, did have some effect on government policies through their searching criticisms.

In the Gold Coast, no real political party was formed in these years. In Sierra Leone, politics were dominated by the local branch of the National Congress.

Like the members of the National Congress, politicians such as Macaulay did not seek the immediate end of British rule. They wanted a larger say in government and hoped to influence government policy on specific issues. Like the National Congress, they did not try to ally with the rural masses and the urban workers whose varied expressions of discontent are so striking an element in West African history in the 1930s.

To Macaulay, British rule was basically beneficial, and during the Second World War he appealed for 'allegiance pounds; constancy shillings and loyalty pence . . . For the innumerable blessings of the Pax Britannica.'

* A second party with the same name existed briefly in 1964.

The role of the press

British West Africa had a vigorous press, the history of which goes back to the nine-teenth century. In the colonial period, it fulfilled the same essential function as that of the elected members on the Legislative Councils – that of criticism. Journalism, like law, was one of the few professions the educated elite could pursue successfully outside the confines of government employment. Both, it has been said, thrive on grievances.

West Africans abroad

It is striking that many of West Africa's future nationalist leaders, Senghor, Nkrumah, Azikiwe, Awolowo among them, studied abroad. They obtained the education they needed to challenge white domination effectively, and the fact that they often suffered from white racism while abroad made them far more militant. One of the key institu-tions of nationalism among English-speaking West Africans in the inter-war period was the West African Student Union, founded in London in 1925 by a Nigerian law student, Ladipo Solanke. Solanke himself was a tireless leader who deserves to be remembered as one of the fathers of Nigerian nationalism. He toured West Africa to raise funds for the Union, which published its own journal. He and his fellow members stressed cultural nationalism. They emphasised the greatness of Africa's past, an em-phasis reflected in the title of a book by another leading member, the Ghanaian J. W. de Graft-Johnson, *The Vanished Glory.* Unlike the elite politicians, they believed that West Africans should seek their independence in the near future:

> It took the white race a thousand years to arrive at their present level of advance; to took the Japanese, a Mongol race, fifty years to catch up; . . . there is no reason why we West Africans should not catch up with the Aryans and the Mongols in one-quarter of a century.

The Ethiopian Crisis, 1935

As individuals were sometimes moved to become politically radical by their experi-ence of racial prejudice, one might well say that the whole body of West African nationalism was jolted towards radicalism by Italy's invasion of Ethiopia in 1935. Ethiopia had a very special significance for colonised Africans. It was an ancient Christian kingdom, an island of freedom in a colonised continent. Ethiopia has often been taken as a synonym for Africa and African Christians have always loved to apply to themselves the prophecy of the psalms, 'Ethiopia shall stretch out her hands to God'. The Italian invasion and conquest of Ethiopia outraged the nationalists. One Nigerian even took the name Abyssinia. Nkrumah, who was in London at the time, recalled later, 'At that time it was almost as if the whole of London had suddenly declared war on me personally'.

Panafricanism

We have seen that it was for a long time uncertain which unit nationalists should adopt as the basic of their movement – the ethnic group, such as Eweland, the colony and potential nation state, or the whole of British West Africa. One could take a larger unit still, and stress the essential identity of black men everywhere. This latter movement tended, for obvious reasons, to be dominated by black men from the New World, since having lost their knowledge of their original ethnic origins, black identity was the only choice left to them.

The first Panafrican Congress was organised by a Trinidadian in 1900 and was attended mainly by black West Indians. Like the early African nationalist movements, it tended to be concerned with elite grievances, such as the disabilities of black civil servants. The next Congress was held in Paris in 1919 at the initiative of an outstanding black American leader, William Du Bois, the founder of the National Association for the Advancement of Coloured People, who hoped that the problems of black men would be included in the discussions of the Peace Conference at the end of the First World War. But its resolutions were moderate in the extreme – 'The natives of Africa must have the right to participate in the Government as fast as their development permits . . .' No important English-speaking West African political figure attended this or later meetings, and little attention was paid to it in the British West African press. Later Congresses, in 1921, 1923 and 1927, were even weaker and less influential. It is clear that the Congress movement had very little influence on West African leaders or history.

Marcus Garvey

Marcus Garvey, 1887–1940, the founder of the Universal Negro Improvement Association, was a Jamaican resident in New York who influenced West Africans much more profoundly. Garvey spoke with the authentic voice of black radicalism, a voice which was to become general only in the 1960s. He spoke of pride in black identity and urged black men in the New World to return to Africa and fight for what was their own – Liberia was to be the launching point for this invasion. He founded a shipping company, the Black Star Line, to strengthen the links between Africa and the Afro-Americans.

Like Tete-Ansa, he had a sweeping vision which could not be translated into practice. The Liberian government, which was soon to give such vast concessions to white American capitalism, refused to have anything to do with him. His shipping company was a financial disaster. The elite black leadership in the USA not only refused to have any connection with him but brought criminal charges against him. He was jailed for fraud and then in 1927 deported to Jamaica. He died there thirteen years later, in poverty and obscurity.

But although his life looked like a failure, his impact on West Africans, and indeed on black men everywhere, was tremendous. At a time when colonialism looked permanent and when black Americans were subjected to great injustices, Garvey spoke with a voice which has never ceased to echo. He said that to be an African was a matter for joy and pride, and that black men everywhere should gain their rights by militancy and not by supplication. Branches of his movement were established in Lagos and the Gold Coast. Nkrumah said later that of all the books that he had ever read, the one which fired his enthusiasm most was one by Marcus Garvey. When he died Azikiwe's *West African Pilot* said,

> Marcus Garvey has lived and died, leaving an indelible impression of his footprints on the sands of the time . . . He inspired Africans to regard their black complexions with pride and to develop race-consciousness so as to look forward to a place under the sun.

His influence was not confined to the educated. In northern Nigeria, a young groom was arrested on charges of sedition. 'He had been telling the local pagans . . . that a black king was coming, with a great iron ship full of soldiers, to drive all the whites out of Africa.'

The Youth Movements

A certain pattern occurs again and again in nationalism in the inter-war years. A new party is founded, with a radical programme. Gradually, it becomes more and more acceptable to the powers that be, until newer, more radical, movements spring up, roundly condemning the compromising of their predecessors. These new movements lose their radicalism in their turn and the cycle repeats itself. In the 1930s, a series of new movements sprang up in Nigeria, the Gold Coast and Sierra Leone. They differed from each other in many ways, but each called itself a Youth Movement. This is not because their members were really youths – they were often middle-aged – but because the word 'youth' has often been used in West Africa to symbolise one's rejection of the past.

The Gold Coast Youth Conference was organised by J. B. Danquah, and first met in 1930. It was not a political party, but a discussion centre, which brought together a large number of debating clubs and so on to discuss issues of national importance.

The Nigerian Youth Movement, founded in Lagos in 1934 by a predominantly Yoruba group, was much more dynamic and obviously political. It grew out of the Lagos Youth Movement, which had been formed to protest about the kind of education provided at Yaba Higher College, with its inferior professional qualifications. Some of its members had been active in the West African Student Union. In 1938 it won all three Lagos seats but only three years later it was wrecked by the personal rivalries and dissensions of its leading members. Soon new parties arose which in their turn condemned it as conservative.

A Sierra Leonian, Isaac Wallace-Johnson, organised the West African Youth League in 1938. Wallace-Johnson was an interesting figure, notable as the only major West African political figure of the inter-war years to favour Marxism. This is, in a sense, surprising, for communism had a great appeal to intellectuals all over the world in the 1930s when the Great Depression seemed to reveal the weakness of western capitalism. One would have expected that communism's hostility to colonialism would have given it a great appeal to colonised peoples. That this was not the case in West Africa shows the great influence the colonising countries had on the attitudes of the colonial elite.

Wallace-Johnson had an international background. He had visited London and Moscow, had worked for a communist newspaper in Hamburg, and had been jailed for sedition on the Gold Coast. Himself a Creole, he made a determined effort to include the peoples of the Protectorate and by stressing labour grievances he made a strong appeal to the urban workers. The onset of the Second World War brought his movement to an abrupt end. Wallace-Johnson and his supporters were interned and the Youth League proscribed.

But nearly thirty years later, in 1967, the government of Colonel Juxon-Smith declared that it would follow the 'principles of three eminent Sierra Leone citizens . . . honesty, integrity and nationalism'. One of the three was Isaac Wallace-Johnson.*

Nationalism in French-speaking West Africa

The pattern of nationalist movements in Francophone West Africa, in the inter-war years, was in many ways basically similar to that of the four British colonies. There was an island of fairly intense political activity in the Four Communes, corresponding to the political life of Lagos, Freetown, and southern Gold Coast. There was the frustrated attempts of educated Subjects, who lacked the privileges of the Four Communes, to find political expression, which they did, sometimes by living in France, sometimes by secret and dangerous political activities outside the Communes, especially in Dahomey, Finally, there was a deep current of discontent among the peasants and workers – a potentially revolutionary force which never really merged with the elite leadership, or found concerted expression.

As in the British colonies, popular discontent took many forms. The many thousands of Wolofs who joined the Mourides, the many thousands of Ivorians who followed the prophet Harris, were giving expression, in different ways, to their discontent with the colonial situation. Hamallism was a more clearly revolutionary movement. Its founder, Sheikh Hamallah, who lived in Nioro, was an orthodox Muslim saint – a fervent mystic, living a life of seclusion and austerity. He preached a return to the original practices of the Tijaniyya. The French became alarmed at his influence, and he was deported for ten years, from 1925 to 1935. In his absence, his followers became more militant and less orthodox, and in the 'thirties, and during the Second World War, they were involved in a number of violent incidents. Hamallah was deported again, this time to France where he died in 1943, after a series of hunger strikes. French officials wrote that the movement was 'an attempt towards social liberation . . . expresses the confused and still insecure aspirations of lower class people and those of poorer condition . . . the reaction of an unhappy and hopeless mass'.

Not all opposition movements, of course, took a religious form. We have already noted the widespread risings against French conscription during the First World War.

---

* The other two were Bai Bureh (see page 195) and Sir Milton Margai (see page 288).

The Moors* of Mauritania and the Tuareg remained hostile well into the 'twenties, when Port Etienne (a port at Mauritania's northern boundary) was attacked twice. It is often difficult to draw the line between wars of resistance and what the colonial powers called 'riots'. In 1923 in Porto Novo, there were serious disturbances which greatly alarmed the colonial government, for they combined a whole series of dissatisfied groups, embracing the grievances of Muslims and of the local western educated elite, local dynastic conflicts, and resentment at increased taxes. There were further riots in Dahomey in the 1930s. In 1934 there was a movement among the Bobo of Upper Volta, protesting against the arbitrary seizure of food and stock. It was called 'Nana Vo': 'Nana' means taking without paying, and 'Vo' means end!

There were other forms of protest. Sometimes whole villages changed their positions to escape taxes and forced labour. Thousands fled across the border into neighbouring British colonies.

Until 1937 strikes were illegal, but French West Africans were never afraid to strike. In 1925 there were strikes among the railway workers in both Senegal and Soudan. In the latter case, the troops refused to take any action against them. In 1938 there was a further, more extensive railway strike, which was put down by armed forces, with bloodshed. In 1927, the telegraph workers of Dakar went on strike.

It was the key weakness of the nationalism of the inter-war years that it never managed to ally with these different unco-ordinated forms of protest.

Blaise Diagne and the Four Communes

The Four Communes of Senegal were, as we have seen, a small island of relative political freedom in the vast sea of French West Africa. They were entitled to elect one Deputy to the French National Assembly. Until 1914, this Deputy was always a Frenchman, or métis. In 1914 they elected the first black Deputy, Blaise Diagne, a former customs official who had served in many countries. A Wolof, he was married to a French wife, whom he dearly loved. He organised a political party, the Republican Socialists, and, despite a number of challenges, remained Deputy until his death in 1934. Diagne is a controversial figure, whom it is not easy to assess. He won some real benefits for his people, such as the *loi Diagne*, which guaranteed the political rights of the members of the Communes and their descendants, which had been threatened. But as we have seen, he played an active role in wartime recruitment. Some people think that by doing this he betrayed his fellow Africans, by sending them to die in a war which was not their own. Others think that the men would have been conscripted anyway, and that Diagne did his best, by seizing the opportunity to gain what concessions he could, such as the *loi Diagne*. Certainly, the esteem in which the French held him, and the important posts he was given were in themselves, in a sense, a victory for the black world. That is certainly how he and others regarded it. He was a living demonstration of the truth of the words which Azikiwe later addressed to a fellow

* The Trarza Moors, in fact, Arabised Berbers, who form 75 per cent of Mauritania's population.

Nigerian nationalist, that there was no position in the world which could not be well held by a black man:

> There is no achievement which
> Is possible to human beings which
> Is not possible to Africans.

It was his support, too, that enabled the 1919 Panafrican Congress to meet in Paris.

But as time went on, and he became more and more pro-French, he seemed to become increasingly remote from his own people. He said, 'I am a Frenchman first and a Negro afterwards.' In the 1920s he signed a pact with French commercial interests by which it was agreed that they would support him, and he would stop attacking them. In 1930 he even defended forced labour at an International Labour Office inquiry into the subject. The French rewarded him for his loyalty to their interests. In 1931 he obtained ministerial rank as Under Secretary of State for the Colonies. As he drew closer to the French, he moved further away from his Senegalese constituents, among whom he spent very little of his time. Opposition to him grew, but he did not lose his seat, mainly because of the divisions among his opponents. But after he died, in 1934, his successor as Deputy followed much the same path, of co-operation with the French, with all the rewards it brought.

Diagne's career parallels the pattern of so many parties in colonial British West Africa. They began with a radical attitude but drew ever closer to the powers that be. But in a sense, the political life of the Four Communes was an inspiration to the rest of French West Africa. They saw a society where political associations could be formed, and meetings held. Local and French newspapers circulated freely, and politicians were outspoken in their criticisms both of the French and of each other. This made the rest of French West Africa more conscious of their own disabilities and lack of freedom.

Francophone West Africans abroad

There were a number of Francophone West Africans in France, especially in Paris, in by 1930s. Some were ex-servicemen who had stayed there, and there were others who had managed to find the financial backing for university studies. These came into close contact with radical black intellectuals from the New World, and with the intellectual currents prevalent in Europe at the time – among them, communism. Many of these radical Africans, who looked on Diagne as a traitor to his race, preferred to live in France, and enjoy relative liberty of expression,* to returning to live under the oppression of a colonial government. This was especially true of Daho-meyans, who had no hope of playing a political role in their own country.

One of the most remarkable of these expatriates was a man who only played an important role in politics in the post-war period. He was Leopold Senghor, who was mainly concerned, in the inter-war period, with cultural questions.

* Even this was restricted, the French government feared them, had them watched by police, and hampered the publication of their journals.

Senghor was the classic example of an apparently perfectly assimilated African. He studied in Paris, and became the first African *professeur agrégé*.* After a brief return home to Senegal, he taught in a French college. He even taught French to French workers, in adult education classes. During the Second World War, he fought for France, was a prisoner of war, and took part in the Resistance against the Germans.

But although his mastery of French culture was so complete, he felt a great nostalgia for his African heritage, a sense of lost identity. He and other French speaking intellectuals sought to capture this elusive identity – which he called *négritude*. In 1934 he and a friend launched a magazine called *L'Étudiant Noir*, the Black Student. Later, in 1947, this kind of cultural revival led to the foundation of a celebrated journal called *Présence Africaine*.

Senghor and others thus created what one might call cultural nationalism which was essentially a reaction against the theory of assimilation, which held that the black man would realise his true destiny by becoming more and more French! But there are criticisms one might make of negritude. It sprang, not from a close and constant contact with African culture, but from expatriates lamenting their cultural isolation. The Nigerian playwright, Wole Soyinka, has said that a tiger does not go round proclaiming his tigritude . . . It seems that they developed a concept of the African personality which was oversimplified, and which did not do justice to the intricate complexity and subtlety of African institutions, or culture. Senghor's poems, written in superb French, clearly reflect this kind of image.

Nationalism outside the Four Communes

A privileged minority were able to participate in the political life of the Four Communes. A much smaller minority plunged into Paris intellectual and cultural life and played its own creative role in it. The vast majority of French West Africans lived outside the stimulus of these environments. This hampered, but did not entirely prevent, political activity. As we have seen, they were forbidden to form trade unions and go on strike, but they formed unions under a different name, and still went on strike. A few courageous intellectuals, despite all the restrictions surrounding them, still spoke with a radical voice. Their most outstanding representative was Louis Hunkanrin of Dahomey.

Louis Hunkanrin

Dahomeyans felt their political restrictions particularly acutely, because, after Senegal, theirs was the French West African colony which had reached the highest level in education and which had exported educated personnel elsewhere. Hunkanrin, in the words of a French scholar, 'had a powerful sense of justice, as well as inexhaustible energy'. At first he supported Diagne, but broke with him when he associated himself more closely with the French. He himself never seems to have been tempted to follow the same path. In 1910 when he was only twenty-three years old, he lost his job and

---

* The highest teaching qualification awarded after an extremely tough examination.

was imprisoned. During the First World War, he led a successful protest movement against a governor whose regime was both oppressive and corrupt. The protest succeeded, and the governor was recalled. Hunkanrin fought in the war, in Europe, spent a short time among the Paris radicals, and then returned to Dahomey. He got round the prohibition on political parties by establishing a local branch of a French organisation, the League of the Rights of Man. In 1923 he was blamed for the Porto Novo riots, although he was not present, and was exiled to Mauritania, with a number of other Dahomeyans. Mauritania was called the 'dry guillotine' because so many political prisoners died there, and of the Dahomey contingent only Hunkanrin survived. But his spirit was not broken, and even in exile he kept in touch with his friends, and radical international opinion.

Hunkanrin is now little known, except by historians. He was one of the first Africans to graduate from the teachers training college in St Louis. He could have led a useful, honoured and prosperous professional life. Instead, he sacrificed career, prosperity and even freedom itself in the name of an ideal.

10

Nationalism Triumphant

The forces of change

The collapse of colonial rule in West Africa was as astonishingly rapid and complete as its first establishment (both were substantially achieved in fifteen years – 1885 to 1900, and 1945 to 1960). Suddenly, the experience of the post-war years shattered what an eminent Briton, perhaps with regrets for lost opportunities, called 'the fallacy of indefinite time ahead'. The sudden dramatic change was very largely the result of international factors and the war in particular. The Second World War had a shattering effect on both the major colonial powers in West Africa. France was invaded and conquered, her people were divided into two bitterly hostile groups, each denouncing the other as traitors. Britain came to the very brink of defeat and emerged from the war with a gravely weakened economy and her status as a Great Power permanently undermined. The new super powers were the United States and Russia, both bitterly hostile, for different reasons, to colonialism although both, in fact, had, at different times and places, been colonising powers themselves. The newly established United Nations Organisation provided a forum where grievances could be aired and colonial rulers criticised.

Japan had always been of particular interest to educated West Africans, as a non-European power which had effectively industrialised itself. In 1942 with shattering rapidity, Japan overthrew a whole series of colonial regimes, expelling the British from Malaya, Burma and other smaller territories, the Dutch from Indonesia and the Americans from the Philippines, and controlling French Indo-China by agreement with Vichy.

African soldiers who fought abroad had their illusions about Europeans destroyed for good. In West Africa, the whites had carefully preserved the image of a secluded superior group. The African soldier abroad, in the words of an American scholar, 'could observe the white man as he actually is – stupid and intelligent, cruel and kind, evil and virtuous, filthy and immaculate, irrational and rational'. European servicemen in West Africa often destroyed the superior image equally effectively by their extreme racism and bad behaviour. Some individuals among them, however, sympathised

with the Africans and encouraged nationalist aspirations and F
up a whole series of study groups.

In the metropolitan countries themselves, many were incr
the claims of the colonised. The myth of racial superiorit'
imperial powers the illusion that they were destined to rule
finally undermined by the hard facts of twentieth century histʊ
two World Wars. The Labour Party came to power in Britain with an cₐᵣ
mitment, which was not always realised in practice, to defend the underprivilegeꓒ.

> We in the Labour Party have always been conscious of the wrongs done by the
> white races to the races with darker skins, [said Mr Clement Attlee during the
> war]. We have always demanded that the freedom which we claim for ourselves
> should be extended to all men.

This is a voice which has often been muted, especially when in power. It was muted
after the war by the Labour Party's fear of losing votes by appearing to be responsible
for the disintegration of the British Empire. But it is a voice which has never been
entirely silenced. In France, the communists, even more hostile to imperialism, were
part of the government until 1947.

Most fundamentally, the war had been fought in the name of an ideology, in the
name of freedom, democracy and the self-determination of nations. It had been waged
against German racism and Japanese imperialist aggression. The Atlantic Charter
spoke of 'the right of all peoples to choose the form of government under which they
will live'. (Churchill attempted to exclude the British Empire from this general
principle!)

In a very real sense, too, the West African nationalist struggle was won in India.
Educated West Africans had always taken the keenest interest in the Indian nationalist
struggle, which was finally crowned with success in 1947. In Indo-China, the French
decided to fight to keep their control. After a long and bloody struggle, they lost it
anyway. With the exception of Portugal, the significance of this was not lost on the
colonial powers.

The social conditions of the time increased the popular discontent which past
nationalists had neglected, but which post-war nationalists made use of. Although the
war created a massive demand for raw materials, especially after the loss of the Asian
colonies, it led to a great shortage of imported goods which in its turn resulted in
inflation.

Something of this discontent is reflected in a song which was popular in western
Nigeria:

> I bought okro
> I bought onion
> I bought one penny worth of salt
> But it was inadequate for my soup
> I would send a curse to the white men in Akure

he war, goods gradually became more readily available but buying power
tricted by the Marketing Boards, which syphoned off much of the profit made
e colonies' exports. There had been a great expansion of wage employment and
trade unionism. During the war the number of unions in Nigeria grew from five
to seventy. The rapidly expanding cities had their own social problems with intolerable pressures on accommodation and amenities.

West Africans had been promised a New Deal after the war. Some of them had
died for it. Although things were improving, there was discontent because they were
not improving fast enough. Indeed, it is possible that discontent becomes fiercest
precisely when things improve, when the possibility of change exists, hope makes
one's suffering unbearable. 'Discontent is likely to be highest when conditions have
so improved that an ideal state seems almost within reach.'

But although many books speak glibly about the rise of mass nationalism, it is
important to realise that even when the nationalist movement was at its height, its
popular base was fairly narrow. It included the newspaper readers, union members,
clerks and teachers, but the rural masses, on the whole, were very little involved. Chief
Awolowo said in a parliamentary debate in 1956, 'The generality of the people are not
interested in self-government or in government generally'. A British official★ found
a striking example of this in southern Zaria, after independence.

> We chatted in the evening to the old men, some of whom . . . had never travelled
> further than . . . five miles away. We tested their knowledge of current affairs.
> Kaduna, the Northern Peoples' Congress, the Premier were unknown to them.
> Then one old, old man had a dim recollection of a great overlord from the out-
> side world who had come and gone but no doubt still ruled his domains elsewhere.
> I asked the name, 'Dan Giwa', came the reply, the nickname of . . . the British
> officer who led the 1907 patrol into the hills. I commented to my students that
> Independence seemed to have gone unnoticed among the Kiballo.

The history of post-war nationalism in both English and French-speaking West
Africa falls into two sharply contrasting phases which might be called the era of con-
flict and the era of joint control. The moment when Nkrumah left prison to become
Leader of Government Business in 1951 is a symbolic turning point between the two.
The first phase was marked by militancy and popular unrest – the Zikist movement in
Nigeria, Nkrumah's Positive Action Campaign in Ghana, and the period of strikes,
riots and demonstrations in the Ivory Coast.

In the fifties, the colonial governments began to share power with 'the political
class'. It was certain that independence would come, the only thing still undecided was
the timing, and the form that an independent government would take. New vistas
of opportunity opened up before the elite, glittering careers in politics and the rapidly
Africanising civil service. New universities and more generous scholarship schemes
benefited both potential university teachers and potential students. African business-

★ John Smith.

men profited from the expansion of the economy, from Africanisation policies in expatriate firms, and most of all from the change which meant that Africans now awarded contracts. For a few years at least, 'first comers' had the prospect of far more glittering careers than their counterparts in Europe.* Conflict between African nationalists and white officials gave way to a conflict within the African elite, as to the division of the spoils and, more rarely, the type of society which an independent government should work towards.

English-speaking West Africa

Ghana

The way to independence was first followed by Ghana, and within Ghana the lead was taken by Kwame Nkrumah. Nkrumah is a controversial and in some ways a tragic figure, but he dominated the nationalist movement to such an extent that the late 'forties and 'fifties have been called the age of Nkrumah.

It is interesting that the two outstanding nationalists of British West Africa both studied in America. Nnamdi Azikiwe returned from the States in 1934; inspired by his example, Nkrumah, then a school teacher in southern Gold Coast, decided to do likewise. His experiences there were very similar. He went through many hardships and financial difficulties, and had some bitter experiences of white racism, but he emerged from his studies with great success. Like Azikiwe, he obtained a position in an American university, and could have spent his days in one of the most agreeable of all professions. Instead, like Azikiwe, he chose to devote his life to the struggle against colonialism.

He spent some time in England, between 1945 and 1947, where he became friends with George Padmore, a radical West Indian who had been for a time a communist, and who later settled in Ghana. He was a leading spirit at the 1945 Pan-African congress, held in Manchester. This spoke with a militancy very different from its predecessors:

> . . . we are unwilling to starve any longer while doing the world's drudgery, in order to support by our poverty and ignorance a false aristocracy and a discarded imperialism. We are determined to be free.

Nationalism in the Gold Coast followed a familiar pattern – the formation of more radical parties, which condemned their 'conservative' predecessors but which were themselves soon condemned as conservative by newer, more radical movements.

In the Gold Coast, as elsewhere, the British realised that it was necessary to make some changes to pacify nationalist feeling. The changes, which were introduced in a new constitution of 1946, were, however, quite inadequate to satisfy Gold Coast nationalists. Elected Africans were now a majority on the Legislative Council, but the Legislative Council still had no control over the executive, and only five of the eighteen

---

* This is still true, to some extent.

elected members were elected by the people, the rest were chiefs, elected by chiefs, representing the old alliance between the colonial power and traditional rulers which the western educated had resented so bitterly and so long. To protest against it, a new party was formed in 1947, the United Gold Coast Convention, by the veteran nationalist, J. B. Danquah. Its members were very far from being revolutionaries. They were respectable, essentially moderate, successful professionals and businessmen: lawyers, teachers, merchants and so on. Since their main energies went into their own careers, they decided to appoint a full time organiser. In one of the fateful moments of history, they offered the job to Nkrumah, then in London.

Nkrumah hurled himself into his task, setting up hundreds of branches of the UGCC, and advocating a more militant approach generally. In 1948 there was one of those outbursts of popular anger which had occurred repeatedly earlier in the colonial period, but which had not previously been channelled into effective political action. In protest against high prices, a boycott was successfully organised against European shops. Just at this time, a peaceful demonstration was held by ex-servicemen. Police fired on the marchers. This sparked off massive rioting, in which lives were lost and much property destroyed. The horrified colonial government imprisoned the 'Big Six' of the UGCC for a time and set up a committee of inquiry. This committee recommended that an all-African commission, headed by Mr Justice Coussey, should be set up to draw up a new constitution. All the Big Six were invited, but not Nkrumah.

Meanwhile, there was a growing rift between the UGCC and Nkrumah. They feared his radicalism, his left wing sympathies, and his militancy. Finally, Nkrumah left them and set up a new party, the Convention People's Party, and embarked on a programme of Positive Action in 1951. There were strikes, arrests, police raids. Nkrumah and some of his associates were sent to gaol.

The Coussey constitution was a big advance on the past, but fell far short of self-government. Nkrumah denounced it as 'bogus and fraudulent'. It proposed an all-African Legislative Assembly of seventy-five members, but only five were to be directly elected by the people. Thirty-three were to be indirectly elected, and thirty-seven were to be chosen by chiefs. Eight out of eleven Cabinet Ministers were to be African. But despite these criticisms the CPP contested the election held under the constitution, in 1951, and won an overwhelming victory. Nkrumah himself successfully contested the key Accra Central seat from prison. He was brought from prison to head the new government, not yet as Prime Minister, but as Leader of Government Business. Those who had been to prison proudly wore their prison caps. One who had not, had his own cap inscribed D.V.B., standing for Defender of the Verandah Boys, these being members of the community so poor that they did not have any room to sleep in, and so had to sleep on verandahs.

The years between 1951 and 1957 were years of joint control, that is, years when authority was divided between Nkrumah's government and the British. Nkrumah was in a very difficult position. He had to satisfy the people who had voted him to power with such enthusiasm, and at the same time persuade the British that he was not the fiery communist-inclined demagogue they thought he was. In his relationship with the British, he succeeded very well, and to everyone's surprise he and the British Governor, Sir Charles Arden-Clarke, got on excellently together. Some people think that he achieved this by sacrificing some of his original idealism, and some of his closeness with the masses. He won an overwhelming majority at the 1954 election – seventy-two out of a hundred and four seats – but there were indications that the CPP was moving further away from its popular base. As in other African countries, the benefits of office caused many to forget their original idealism, and the cause of the verandah boys, and concentrate on personal enrichment. The electoral success of the party caused many who had never been idealists to jump on the bandwagon – again, in search of their own interests.

One of the key grievances of an important sector of the population – the cocoa farmers – was the fact that, as we have seen, cocoa prices were booming, but much of the profit was syphoned off by the Marketing Boards. They·wanted a larger share of the fruits of their labour, but this was denied them.

There were certain weaknesses in the era of joint control, which were to become more serious after independence, but these should not obscure the tremendous achievements of those years. The Gold Coast's rapid strides towards independence were an inspiration to the whole of Africa, and a promise of success to other nationalist movements. Nkrumah became a major international figure. The humiliating years of colonial subjugation melted away almost as if they had never been, and the black man began at last to take his rightful place in the world.

There was one more hurdle to cross before independence was achieved in 1957, and this was the factor which was destined to endanger, and almost to destroy, an independent Nigeria – ethnic nationalism. After the CPP's electoral victory in 1954, the year in which the Gold Coast obtained full internal self-government, a number of regionally based parties were founded, the most important of which were based in Asante, the National Liberation Movement, and among the Ewe of Trans-Volta. These regional movements wanted a Federal constitution. There was a long period of open violence in Asante, which persuaded the British to hold yet another election, in 1956. The result was almost the same as before, the CPP again winning seventy-two out of a hundred and four seats. A weak form of regionalism was introduced, and in 1957 the former colony became the first in sub-Saharan Africa to regain its independence. It took as a symbol of continuity with and pride in African cultures of the past the name of the ancient empire of Ghana.

Nigeria

A new political era dawned in Nigeria in 1944, when the first of the three major parties which were to dominate politics until all parties were abolished in 1966 was founded, and proposals were put forward for what soon became popularly known as the Richards Constitution. The National Council of Nigeria and the Cameroons (NCNC) filled the vacuum created by the ruin of the Nigerian Youth Movement. The aged Herbert Macaulay was its President until his death in 1946 but it was dominated by the highly controversial figure of Nnamdi Azikiwe.

Azikiwe had studied successfully in America, obtaining two Master's Degrees and most of the credits for a doctorate. Although he had taught in an American university, in Lagos he was denied even the position of schoolmaster. He turned to journalism and after three years in the Gold Coast, 1934–7, when he narrowly escaped a gaol sentence for sedition, he came back to Nigeria and set up the *West African Pilot*, and a chain of provincial newspapers.

This was West African journalism with a difference. Unlike its predecessors it was a great commercial success, building up a mass readership with its stinging attacks on the colonial government. His fellow Igbo looked on him with an adulation which is difficult to understand in an age more disillusioned with politics. They saw him as a living proof of Igbo capacity, a successful 'been to' to compare with Yorubaland's long lists of lawyers, doctors and other graduates. In his search for popularity, he often appealed specifically to the Igbos, but, at least in the 1940s, his appeal was much wider and he was the idol of teachers, clerks, traders and urban workers throughout southern Nigeria. He was less popular with his fellow politicians, however, who accused him of dividing nationalism with ethnic rivalries, blaming him for the death of the Nigerian Youth Movement. They said that he wished to destroy everything he could not dominate.

Obafemi Awolowo was a highly gifted Yoruba from Ijebu whose career was not unlike Azikiwe's own. There was the same desperate and ultimately successful struggle to attain an education overseas and personal prosperity. In reaction now, he set up a Yoruba cultural organisation in 1945 – the Egbe Omo Oduduwa.

The Richards Constitution was designed to placate nationalist opinion with timely concessions. Instead, the nationalists were outraged, most of all perhaps because it had been introduced without consultation with them. The Richards Constitution gave too little too late. Only four out of forty-four members of the Legislative Council were directly elected. There was a body of chiefs and emirs who were certain to support the government and who in fact welcomed the Constitution. To add insult to injury, when it came before the House of Commons in London, it was given exactly twenty-nine minutes of discussion in an almost empty House.

The Richards Constitution introduced the three Regions★ which were to be retained in all constitutional arrangements until 1966. Later on, Nigerians, with the advantage of hindsight, saw this as a sinister device to enable the British to divide and rule. In fact, it simply preserved administrative arrangements which had been arrived at earlier almost by accident; partly in response to the justifiable fears of northerners that in an independent Nigeria, they would be dominated by the educated elite of the south. In 1947 the future Sir Abubakar Tafawa Balewa, whose image was never one of a radical, startled the Legislative Council by stating that if independence was granted too soon, the north would continue its 'interrupted march to the sea'.

In the late 'forties, the NCNC was Nigeria's only important political party. It therefore, to its great advantage, had a monopoly of effective and vocal protest. In

★ Later, four.

1945 it increased its popularity in the cities by supporting the General Strike. At last the separate streams of elite grievances and workers' discontent, which had remained distinct during most of the colonial period, seemed to have come together. In 1947 the NCNC sent a deputation to England, financed by popular subscription, to protest against the Richards Constitution. Not only was it unsuccessful, but it became involved in sordid squabbles about the misuse of funds, a sad prelude to the cries of corruption which have haunted Nigerian government ever since. Critics pointed out acidly that the same protest could have been made in an air letter costing one shilling. By the late 1940s the NCNC was in temporary eclipse and Azikiwe himself said that he was a dormant – not an extinct – volcano.

The radical interlude

The political vacuum created by the eclipse of the NCNC was filled by a phase of radical agitation which is closely parallel to the phase of Positive Action in the Gold Coast at the same time, and the period of demonstrations, strikes and riots in Ivory Coast from 1949 to 1950. The new radical movement called itself Zikism. It was later to appear that its crucial weakness was that it attached itself to an individual rather than to an ideology. Its leader was a northern radical, the future Alhaji Raji Abdallah, and it also included some leading Igbo ex-servicemen and trade unionists. Like many radical movements, it had a clearer view of what it sought to destroy than of what it sought to build. As its secretary admitted later,

> There was little thought of the detailed organisation of the future State and the motive power of the Movement was the destruction of the old State machine which had become oppressive and repressive.

It was closely linked with a short-lived church founded in Azikiwe's honour. In 1949 some of its members were imprisoned when Abdallah called the Union Jack 'a symbol of persecution and brutality'. In the same year, 1949, a number of striking coalminers in Enugu were fired on and killed. The Zikists responded with Positive Action, in an outbreak of riots throughout Nigeria. The government banned the movement and thereafter it disappeared from view.

It is at first sight surprising that this radical phase evaporated so readily. There are several reasons for this. The era of joint control in the 1950s created very extensive opportunities for able Nigerians. There was an Africanisation policy in the Civil Service and 1948 saw both the foundation of the University of Ibadan and the introduction of an overseas scholarship scheme. Building a career looked more promising than radicalism. But the fundamental weakness of Zikism was that its pivot was not a political programme but an individual. Azikiwe himself shrank from involvement in its revolutionary aspects, leaving the Zikists with a painful feeling of betrayal.

Joint control in the 1950s

It soon became clear, even to the British, that the Richards Constitution was obsolete before it came into effect. In 1948 the unpopular Richards, whom one nationalist called Richards Iron Hand, was replaced by a new Governor, Macpherson. Since his predecessor had been blamed for lack of consultation, Macpherson went to the other extreme and held an elaborate series of constitutional discussions at the village, provincial, regional and finally national level. The final result, the Macpherson Constitution of 1951, was a compromise, and thus widely criticised by leading nationalists. In retrospect its most important provisions were that it retained the Regions and that the north was given as much representation as the other two put together. As Awolowo pointed out at the time, this established federalism without the essential condition which makes federalism workable – the equal size of the component parts.

The prospect of elections, as we have seen, encourages the formation of parties to fight them. Although the NCNC tried hard to preserve its national image and had, in fact, many supporters in the west, it increasingly appeared Igbo-dominated to other Nigerians. In 1949 the Northern Peoples Congress was formed on an explicitly regional basis. Aminu Kano, a northern radical, thought it too conservative and too dominated by traditional rulers. In 1950 he formed the Northern Elements Progressive Union, which gained much support among urban workers but was never a serious threat to the Northern Peoples Congress. In 1951 Chief Awolowo formed the Action Group in the west, again on an explicitly regional basis. Henceforth, each of the three Regions was to be dominated by a single party, closely linked with the majority ethnic group. Each Region contained small minority parties. In the east the COR areas (Calabar Ogoja Rivers) wanted a separate Region as a protection against Igbo domination. So, in the west, did the many different ethnic groups of what later became the Mid-West. In the north, the NPC was challenged not only by Aminu Kano's party but also by the Bornu Youth Movement and by the United Middle Belt Congress. This last was strongly supported by Middle Belt peoples such as the Tiv, who detested Hausa Fulani domination. Each of the three major parties tried to ally with the small opposition groups in other Regions to weaken its opponents and to present a national image.

The 1951 election was the turning point between the era of radicalism and the era of joint control. In the 1950s Nigerian politicians turned their energies from attacks on the government system to seizing benefits within it. In the east, the unpopular system of Indirect Rule was given up altogether, and replaced by the English system of local government. It was a time of economic expansion, with rising export prices. The educated found a world of new opportunities in the civil service and in business. Many enriched themselves corruptly. There was a whole series of disturbing enquiries at the level of local government and at a higher level in 1956.

In the 1950s the British and the nationalists were in basic agreement. The principle of independence was generally agreed on. The only uncertainties remained its date and the exact form that an independent government should take. The key dividing line in the 1950s came to be that between northern and southern politicians. In 1953 a motion was introduced in the central legislature, advocating self-government by 1956. Southern politicians supported it with enthusiasm, but the northerners opposed it, because, in their leader's words, 'the Northern Region does not intend to accept the invitation to commit suicide'. When southern politicians tried to bypass the northern leaders by sending a delegation to the north, ethnic tensions erupted into bloodshed; the Kano riots took place in 1953 when at least thirty-six were killed. The British, alarmed by the riots, and by northern threats of secession, held yet another constitutional conference. This led to the Lyttleton Constitution of 1954, which was fully federal. As a compromise between northern and southern views on the date of independence, the eastern and western Regions gained full internal self-government in 1957. At the centre, Sir Abubakar Tafawa Balewa became Prime Minister at the head of a coalition of all three parties. Two years later, the north too accepted self-government, and in 1960 Nigeria became independent. Like other newly independent countries of the time, she celebrated her independence with great expense and extravagance, inviting large numbers of overseas visitors and entertaining them royally.

Nigeria became independent in what has been called 'a conspiracy of optimism'. By 1960 British officials, with their minds on possible careers elsewhere, were as anxious to go as the Nigerians were for them to leave. This led both parties to gloss over a number of very real difficulties which were to loom ever larger in the years ahead. One was the dissatisfied grievances of the minority groups in each Region, another was the difficulty of operating a federal constitution where one sector was much larger than the rest. The north had been given an absolute majority of seats, so that if it had been unanimous, – which it was not – it could have ruled Nigeria perpetually all by itself.

The shadows of corruption and ethnic violence had already appeared. Still more disturbing shadows lay unsuspected in the future. But, as in Ghana, this should not obscure the very real achievements of the years of joint control, as of the years of independence to follow. There was a tremendous expansion in education and the road network was greatly improved. In the Regions a series of state-owned corporations were established which steadily expanded the nation's industrial capacity. But as in the colonial period, the position of the rural masses remained much as it had been before. As an obscure local history, published in the east in 1960, put it bitterly:

> Government – Eastern or Federal – had never done ANY GOOD THING in Item but never failed to collect rates and taxes even from the poorest church-rat
> ... The Eastern Government remembers that there are people living in this area ONLY when an election comes.

Sierra Leone and the Gambia

In Sierra Leone, the key issue before independence was not so much a struggle between the local people and the British, as a struggle between the Creole community and the rest of the country, known as the Protectorate. In the inter-war period, the nationalist movement had been dominated by Creoles, such as Isaac Wallace-Johnson, whose career we studied earlier. The Creoles expected to continue to play a dominant role in the life of the country, because of their high educational level – in the Protectorate,

90 per cent of the people were illiterate. But their role was coming to be increasingly resented in the Protectorate, especially by the educated. Two especially outstanding members of this educated class were Milton and Albert Margai. They were Mende who became respectively the first Protectorate doctor, and the first Protectorate lawyer.

The post-war constitution, which gave much more representation to the Protectorate than to the Creoles, was bitterly resented by the Creoles, but since they were a minority in the country,* they had to accept their minority position in any democratic form of government. In 1951 the educated elite and the chiefs of the electorate formed the Sierra Leone People's Party, led by Dr Milton Margai. Several Creoles joined it and one of them, Lamina Sanko, took a Temne name as a sign of national unity, but very few Creoles followed his example. In 1951 it won an overwhelming electoral victory. In the fifties, as in Ghana and Nigeria, the British gradually relinquished more and more of their power. In 1957 the SLPP won a further resounding victory.

As in the other colonies, internal divisions arose just before independence. Another Protectorate politician, a trade unionist, Siaka Stevens, formed a new opposition party, the All People's Congress, which drew most of its support from the urban workers. So sharp was its challenge that a state of emergency was declared on the very day when Sierra Leone gained her independence in 1961. The SLPP was still in power, but as events were to show, it was not to keep it for long.

The Gambia was the smallest and poorest of the four British West African colonies. It has a population of only 300,000 and consists of a strip of land on either side of the river Gambia. Its economy depended on groundnuts, and it had received regular subsidies from Britain. Its prospects as a viable independent state seemed doubtful; and its move to independence was largely a question of the British extending to the Gambia concessions already made to the other colonies.

Because of its economic weakness and small size, it was suggested that it should merge with Senegal – a move which both Britain and Senegal supported. The Gambian elite rejected the proposal, partly because of the language barrier, and partly because they preferred an important role in a small country to a subordinate role in a large one.

French-speaking West Africa

The different pattern of their experiences under colonialism meant that the French-speaking countries followed an entirely different path to independence. For a long time, the ideal to which both African nationalists and the French worked was not independence from France, but greater equality for Africans in what was called *France d'Outre Mer*, or Overseas France. A statement made at the Brazzaville conference in 1944 (which, incidentally, no African delegate attended), while it was far from being

---

* Various estimates put them at 25,000, 30,000 and 60,000 in a country of three million.

an accurate description of French practice at the time, was a fair account of the ideal they were working towards. 'In the Greater France there are neither people to set free, nor racial discrimination to abolish. There are people who feel themselves to be French and to whom France wishes to give an increasingly large part of the life and democratic institutions of the French community.'

After the war, a Constituent Assembly was held in France, in 1945, to determine the political shape of the Fourth Republic. Out of a total of 586 deputies, there were six Africans from French West Africa and three Africans and one métis from French Equatorial Africa. On average, one per cent of the population of French West Africa had voted in the election. In the first assembly, the key grievances of forced labour and the *indigénat* (see page 208) were abolished, and all people in the colonies became citizens of Greater France. The findings of the assembly were then put to a referendum, in which only Frenchmen voted. The original aims of Brazzaville were modified, partly in response to a white settler pressure group.

The constitution which finally emerged was a big improvement on the inter-war years, but it was still far removed from democracy. About three and a half per cent of the population of French West Africa had the vote. There was an Assembly of the French Union – which had in the event no real power at all – where French West Africa had twenty-one out of three hundred and fifteen seats. In the National Assembly, the real focus of power, French West Africans elected fourteen out of six hundred and eighteen Deputies. If the various areas of the French union had been represented in proportion to their population, France herself should have provided only three hundred and thirteen Deputies, but even African Deputies did not advocate anything so radical. There was a Great Council at Dakar to vote the West African budget and advise the Governor-General.

The Rassemblement Démocratique Africain was founded at a meeting at Bamako in October 1946 and sprang essentially from disappointment at the final form of the constitution. It included representatives from both French West Africa and French Equatorial Africa (some delegates travelled by lorry all the way from Chad!). Until 1950, it was allied with the French Communist party. The two leading Senegalese politicians, Guèye and Senghor, did not join it, retaining their old alliance with the French Socialist party. It is important to realise that the members were not seeking independence from France, but a greater say within the French community.

The leader of the RDA was Felix Houphouet-Boigny (born in 1905), a Baoulé from the Ivory Coast. He was an assistant doctor (médecin Africain), who later became a prosperous planter and chief. He first came to prominence during the Second World War, when he formed an African planters' union, as a protest against the Government's extreme discrimination in favour of European planters (policies which forced a prosperous group, who were potential allies of the colonial regime, into radicalism). At the end of 1945 he founded the PDCI (Parti Démocratique de la Côte d'Ivoire). He was elected to both constituent assemblies as the representative of Ivory Coast and Upper Volta. The French, following their old policy of allying with the traditional rulers against the nationalists, agreed with the Mogho Naba to put forward one of his chiefs as a rival candidate. An amusing story is told of how this chief went round quietly telling the voters to support his opponent. 'What will I do in that Paris at my age, with my forty-four wives – I don't speak a blasted word of French.' After Houphouet was elected to the National Assembly in 1946, he took the additional name of Boigny, which is Baoulé for 'irresistible force'.

The late 1940s was the period of intense mistrust and antagonism between America and Western Europe on the one hand, and the communist bloc on the other. The RDA-French communist alliance meant that the French Government showed it the bitterest hostility.* Its supporters were persecuted, and sometimes dismissed from their jobs, and elections were manipulated in favour of their opponents. The RDA responded with demonstrations, strikes and boycotts. In 1949–50 their mutual hostility grew to a crescendo of violence which suggests an interesting parallel with events at the same period in Ghana. Many RDA leaders, though not Houphouet-Boigny himself, were imprisoned, and went on hunger strike. Women demonstrated outside the gaol. Cunningly, the RDA attacked the Europeans where they felt it most. Their domestic servants disappeared, and the fruit and vegetable sellers who catered for them went on strike! But there was a basic moderation; there was no attempt at a violent rising on Mau Mau lines, and the scattered white settlers went unharmed. By 1951 according to official figures, which are generally regarded as under-estimates, fifty-two Africans had been killed, several hundred wounded, and three thousand imprisoned. Now there came a dramatic turning point, just as there was in Ghana, when Nkrumah came out of prison to head a Government. Houphouet-Boigny decided that the alliance with the communists was doing his cause more harm than good, especially as the French communists were no longer in power, and abandoned the alliance. But for some radical members of the RDA, it had been based on shared ideals and not political convenience. These protested and were expelled from the party. Among them was Gabriel d'Arboussier, the party's outstanding métis Secretary-General.

, In the elections of 1951, the RDA, gravely weakened by its experiences, managed to elect only three deputies, largely because of French electoral manipulation, for the French officials were not convinced of the reality of Houphouet's break with communism. But in the years that followed, Houphouet-Boigny built up the party strength. In a radical change of policy, he formed an alliance with French business interests and encouraged an in-flow of foreign capital into the Ivory Coast. As the colony became more prosperous, he came to oppose federalism, anxious that the Ivorians should keep their revenue for themselves. In the 1956 elections, which were apparently free from French intimidation, the RDA won nine seats and Houphouet-Boigny was made a member of the French Cabinet, a post he retained until 1959. He gave the French unquestioning support, even on matters such as the invasion of Suez.

The Senegalese had refused to join the RDA. This weakened it and diminished their own political influence, for Senegal, of course, had by far the longest political tradition

---

* The French communists left the coalition government in 1947.

and had some outstandingly able leaders. These lost the role they might otherwise have played, by identifying themselves too closely with the metropolis and its political parties. Senghor entered politics as the protégé of 'Citizen' Deputy Lamine Guèye. He came, however, to identify himself increasingly with the Subjects, partly because Lamine Guèye identified himself so closely with the Four Communes. Like so many figures in West African political history before and after him, Lamine evolved from a 'moderate' into a reactionary – incredibly, he supported the French during the railway workers' strike. Senghor began to build up his own political support among the Subjects. Himself a devout Catholic, he allied with Muslim religious leaders against the Communes and the traditional rulers. In 1948 he founded the Bloc Démocratique Sénégalais, which formed part of the larger grouping, Indépendents d'Outre Mer. (A year earlier he had been a founder of the journal *Présence Africaine*, a landmark in cultural nationalism.) In 1951 the BDS won both the Senegalese seats. Henceforth it was to dominate politics in Senegal but could not compete with the RDA in the rest of French West Africa. Senghor then supported the formation of two republics from the colonies of French West Africa, which were to stay within the French union.

Politics in Guinea were dominated by Sekou Touré, a descendant of the great Samori, born in 1922 of a poor Muslim peasant family. He rose to political prominence through the labour movement and was a devoted trade unionist. He once said:

> Trade unionism is a faith, a calling, an engagement to transform fundamentally any given economic and social regime, always in the search for the best, and the beautiful and the just.

In 1953 he won immense popularity in Guinea, when he successfully led a general strike. At first, the French tried to suppress him, by the familiar tactic of rigging elections, but they could do little against his tremendous popularity. In 1955 he was elected Mayor of Conakry, and in 1956 he became a Deputy. In 1957 he broke with the communist trade union organisation and formed a new federation of African trade unions, the Union Générale des Travailleurs d'Afrique Noire (UGTAN). He did this because he felt that African unions had their own distinctive needs and problems which should not be subordinated to the ideologies and aims of unions abroad. This formation of UGTAN was an important step towards the unity of French West Africa, though history was destined soon to take a different turning.

Economic changes

After the war and the foundation of FIDES (see page 221), the French began to invest heavily in their West African colonies. It has been estimated that between 1946 and 1958 the French provided over 70 per cent of total public investment and over 30 per cent of recurrent civil and military expenditure for these states. This investment and their own poverty greatly restricted their leaders' real freedom of choice. It formed a powerful link to, and a pattern of dependence on, France which a really poor state such as Niger could not ignore. Guinea's experiences in 1958, when she opted for independence and the French withdrew all their technical and administrative personnel practically overnight and even destroyed files and tore out the telephones, brought the lesson home very dramatically.

Like their counterparts in the British colonies, the Francophone elite were understandably anxious to obtain the same salaries and conditions of service as expatriates, and this was gained in 1950. This seemed to them an essential dimension of real equality, but as in the British colonies, the results were disastrous, creating an enormous gap between the incomes and life styles of the elite and the masses, and imposing a heavy burden of salaries which the states concerned were too poor to bear. As we shall see, some French states were to spend over 60 per cent of their income on administration.

The Loi Cadre

The Loi Cadre (Outline Law) of 1956 was intended by the French as a concession to nationalist sentiment, parallel to the ever-increasing autonomy of the four former British colonies, rather like earlier measures, such as the law of 1950 which gave white and black civil servants the same conditions of service, and the Labour Code of 1952 which, among other things, put African trade unions on the same footing as those of France. It was passed against a background of a rising tide of nationalism. Ghana was on the brink of independence, and so was little Togo. Morocco and Tunisia became independent in 1956. The French had attempted to retain empire by force in Algeria and Indo-China, with uniformly disastrous results.

The Loi Cadre provided for each colony a kind of half-way house to independence, exactly the structure of joint control which the English colonies passed through. It gave internal autonomy to each colony. The executive head remained the Governor but his deputy was the leader of the majority party. The elections of 1957 were held under this law. Whereas leaders in the British colonies had on the whole welcomed this kind of arrangement as a stepping stone to independence, the Francophone leaders were divided. They objected, not to the considerable powers left with France (defence, external relations, economic development and the *content* of education) but to the tendency to split French West Africa into its component colonies. Of the leading Francophone West African political figures, only Houphouet-Boigny approved of this division into countries – and it is likely that its introduction was due to his support. He led the minority which welcomed it. He welcomed a breakdown of federal structures because of his reluctance to spend Ivory Coast revenues on poorer states, but most of the Francophone leaders, among them Senghor, Touré and the Soudan (later Mali) leader, Modiba Keita, wanted the Francophone colonies to form a single federation. They felt that if each colony went its separate way they would always be weak and poor and that only a united and compact block could speak to the French on equal terms. This question led to a split in the RDA, which was subsequently papered over. At this point the IOM and the SFIO★ broke away

★ For IOM see page 291. SFIO was the Senegalese branch of the French Socialist party, which Senghor left when he formed the BDS.

from the metropolitan parties. Senghor, who had formerly advocated two republics, now supported one.

General de Gaulle came to power in May 1958 – he was to keep it for exactly ten years – and a new constitution was drawn up for the brand new Fifth Republic. The new constitution made the French colonies autonomous within the French Community. Houphouet-Boigny supported this but other leaders opposed it, not because they disliked the continuance of links with France but because they thought that Francophone West Africa, potentially a strong and united state, was being weakened by being divided. Scholars disagree as to whether this was really a deliberate policy stemming from the fact that small impoverished states would defer much more to French interests than a united French West Africa. The colonies had the option of accepting the constitution or of leaving the French Community altogether. Their heavy economic dependence on France made the latter course a perilous venture. Some leaders, however, decided to do just this. Touré said, 'We prefer poverty and freedom to riches and slavery.' An important factor in his decision was a personality clash with de Gaulle. It is an index of his enormous popularity in Guinea that his lead was followed unquestioningly with a 97 per cent vote for 'non'. Djibo Bakari of Niger supported the same course but was unsuccessful, apparently because of French electoral manipulation. Guinea's vote for independence was immediately followed by an almost total withdrawal of French capital and personnel. In the former Governor's Palace, Touré

> found an absurd scene of desolation: furniture and pictures had all been removed, the cellars emptied, the crockery smashed. The safe was intact – but no one knew the combination. Even the telephones had gone. It was the same all over Guinea.*

It is certain that Touré had not expected such severe consequences of his 'non' vote. Ghana came to her aid with a timely loan, help which some years later, when Nkrumah was in exile, Sekou Touré was to remember generously. In his desperate search for external assistance, Touré turned increasingly to the communist bloc.

The states which had opted to remain within the French Community still hoped to be able to form a federation. A federation was formed to comprise Senegal, Soudan, Upper Volta and Dahomey, but the last two pulled out largely because of Houphouet-Boigny's persistent opposition (landlocked Upper Volta depended on Ivory Coast for its access to the sea and Dahomey feared it would be on the remote edges of a federation centered in Dakar). Senegal and Soudan persevered and formed the Federation of Mali, but it ended in disaster, after exactly two months as an independent state. Its failure was partly due to the problems created by the differences in resources of the two countries, as Mali was much the poorer, and partly to personality clashes and differences in political ideology.† Since federal feeling was so strong, Houphouet-Boigny,

---

* E. Mortimer.
† i.e. Mali's commitment to socialism.

as a concession, formed a loose grouping of Upper Volta, Ivory Coast, Niger and Dahomey, called the Conseil de l'Entente. It has always been dominated by its most prosperous member, Ivory Coast. When the French agreed to the Mali federation, members of the Conseil too opted for independence.

It will be seen that the French colonies' passage to independence was very different from that of the British colonies. They obtained an independence, which they had not sought, almost by accident. What the majority of Francophone leaders had sought was a strongly united French West Africa within the French Community. They had sought this, partly in awareness of their economic dependence on France, partly because of the emotional links which tied so many of their leaders to the metropolis. In the event, the pan-African goal which was to them of overriding importance – French West African unity – was lost and the extreme poverty of many of the states concerned meant that the reality of their autonomy was very doubtful.

Guinea-Bissau

If one looks at the experience of nearly all of West Africa, one has the impression that independence was gained in a fundamentally peaceful way, by political means. This is untypical of Africa as a whole. Colonial powers were not always prepared to withdraw, especially when the governing country was so poor that the colonies played an essential role in her economic life. This was the case with Portugal, where Africa accounted for twenty-five per cent of her income. In other parts of Africa there was a large white settler body who attracted sympathisers in the metropolitan country and acted as a pressure group there. Because there were a million French settlers in Algeria, independence there was only achieved after long and bitter warfare (1954-62). The independence of Kenya was preceded by the bloody Mau Mau struggle, between the white settlers and the Kikuyu, a struggle in which many atrocities were committed on both sides. The presence of many Portuguese settlers in Angola and Mozambique stiffened the determination of the Portuguese to keep these colonies at all costs. At the time these words were written (September 1975), white settlers still remained in control of Zimbabwe and South Africa. In the former, their overthrow is likely before long. The latter will present much greater difficulty, though one has only to compare the size of the populations of white and black Africa to see that it is, in the long run, assured.

In West Africa, only one tiny country has shared the experience of military struggle for independence – a struggle which began in 1963 and was crowned with victory ten years later. This was Guinea-Bissau (sometimes called Guiné). Guinea-Bissau, with a population of about 650,000 is one of the smallest and poorest of African countries, forming a little triangular wedge of territory between Guinea and Senegal. It is low-lying; the coastal areas are full of deep inlets, rivers and mangrove swamps. The chief food crop is rice, the chief export crop, groundnuts. There are, at the moment, no known resources outside agriculture. The population consists of many different ethnic groups, most of which have the small-scale political institutions we discussed earlier in this book (see page 99). Like the small-scale societies of eastern Nigeria and southern Ivory Coast, they put up a long and fierce resistance to the imposition of colonial rule. The Portuguese fought almost constant campaigns between 1878 and 1936, and for a long time, there were only outposts of Portuguese authority in a sea of undefeated peoples.

It was the double misfortune of Guinea-Bissau that it was both lacking in natural resources, and that it was ruled by a colonial power which has shown singularly little concern for the welfare of the colonised. In 1926 the Republican government of Portugal was overthrown and a military government established. By 1932 Salazar had established a personal dictatorship which was to last, incredibly, until his death in 1970. (When he died his policies were continued by Marcello Caetano.) Under his regime, there was no real economic or social development in the colonies, and no prospect, even remotely, of political independence. No political parties, demonstrations, debates or assemblies were allowed. There were no rights for trade unions. There was no thought of voluntarily abandoning the colonies. Because Portugal was small, weak, impoverished and underdeveloped, she clung to the last relics of her past greatness the more obstinately. And since the Portuguese themselves lacked rights and liberties, they were not likely to be unduly troubled by the lack of the same rights and liberties among Africans. In one respect, Guinea-Bissau was better off than Portugal's other colonies – there was no substantial white population, so the people were spared much, though not all, of the burden of forced labour, which reduced the peoples of Angola and Mozambique to a state worse than slavery.

In theory, Portugal practised the assimilation policy. In practice, just eleven of the inhabitants of Guinea-Bissau had won the rights of citizenship by 1960.

Guinea-Bissau was a classic instance of a colonial economy dominated by a vast monolithic foreign combine. The Uniao Fabril (CUF) monopolised Guinea-Bissau's import and export trade, so that even the Portuguese sometimes referred to the struggle which developed as the Company's war. CUF was closely linked with British, French and West German firms.

In a regime so resistant to change, and so insensitive to the welfare of the governed, change could only be effected by violence. It is a paradox which is true of all revolutionary movements that those who suffer most from a regime's injustices – in the case of Guinea-Bissau, the peasants – cannot themselves provide the leadership to overthrow it. This leadership must be provided by those who could benefit from the existing regime. A revolution depends on some of the relatively privileged being willing to sacrifice their privileges for the general good. It was fortunate that Guinea-Bissau produced such a man, in Amilcar Cabral, who qualified in Portugal as a hydraulic engineer. A métis from Cape Verde, he was so completely assimilated to Portuguese culture that the only language he spoke fluently was Portuguese. Like Eduardo Mondhlane of Mozambique, he was a brilliant and successful man, who instead of plucking the fruits of prosperity and professional advancement, chose to live, and ultimately die, for the liberation of his people.

The revolutionary movement in Guinea-Bissau traces its ultimate origins to a small group of African students in Portugal – Cabral, and the future Angolan revolutionaries Agostinho Neto and Mario de Andrade. They studied Marxist classics, and embarked on their own re-Africanisation. Later, Cabral conducted an agricultural census for the Portuguese in Guinea-Bissau, building up detailed knowledge of the land and its people. Then he spent a period in Angola, where he played an active role in the foundation of the MPLA.

The Guinea-Bissau revolutionary party, the PAIGC,* was founded at a secret meeting at Bissau in 1956. There were just six people present, and Cabral himself was the leading spirit. In August 1959, the dockworkers of Bissau went on strike. They were suppressed with great brutality by the Portuguese (both the military and civilians, for the African troops refused to fire). Fifty of the dockers were shot dead, and some of the survivors imprisoned. The Portuguese could scarcely have given a clearer demonstration of the futility of peaceful techniques. Immediately, Cabral returned from Angola and the PAIGC entered a new, more militant, phase, resolved to seek liberation 'by all possible means, including war'.

The next phase, 1959–63, was when the groundwork was laid. Cabral, now based in Guinea-Conakry, devoted himself to recruiting and training devoted revolutionaries who would later work among the peasants and win them over to their cause. These revolutionaries were recruited largely from among the poorer section of the urban population.

To win the support of the peasants, it was essential to show them that liberation would bring them real concrete benefits in their daily lives. In countries which proceeded constitutionally to independence, the masses played a basically passive role. On occasion, a minority erupted on to the scene of action, as in the Gold Coast ex-servicemen's disturbances in 1948, but the rural masses were essentially spectators. If Guinea-Bissau was to win a liberation war, the peasants had to do much more. They must fight in the guerilla army, grow food for it, and endure Portuguese reprisals. As it proved, they had to endure the bombing of their fields and villages with napalm and high explosives. They could not do all this just to see a white privileged elite replaced by a black privileged elite. In the words of the revolutionaries themselves:

> To be masters of our destiny, that's not simply a question of having African ministers. What we need is that our work, our riches, should belong to all of us, to the people who labour to create this wealth . . . If we make this war only to chase out the Portuguese, then it's not worth the trouble. Yes, we make it to chase out the Portuguese, but also so that nobody shall exploit us, neither white men nor black men.

Like most revolutionary movements in the modern world, they adopted a Marxist ideology, and worked towards the formation of a socialist state. They emphasised

* Usually referred to by its initials, which stand for African Party for the Independence of Guiné and Cape Verde.

Amilcar Cabral during the struggle in Guinea-Bissau

A napalm bomb

that they had no intention of being controlled by any particular communist state. Socialism in Guinea-Bissau would take the particular form dictated by local conditions. In fact, Cabral and his followers embarked on a very detailed sociological analysis of Guinea-Bissau society. He always emphasised that each nation must follow its own path: 'National liberation and social revolution are not for export'. Internationally, apart from the other liberation movements – MPLA and Frelimo – in Portuguese Africa, the movement with which they seemed to have felt the most affinity was the Liberation Front in Vietnam.

To convince the peasants that a new order was really going to come, it was not sufficient to paint rosy pictures of a fine new world 'after the war'. This has happened so often in world history. People suffer and die in the name of an ideal, but the survivors have often felt bitterly disillusioned with the world they actually found. The PAIGC determined to start building the new society *during the war*. As time went on, they liberated even more of the country from Portuguese control, and in these areas they began the construction of the kind of society they envisaged.

Schools were built on a massive scale in liberated areas – 164 in all during the war. This was a difficult task because of the great shortage of literates who could act as teachers. Health services expanded with a similar heartening rapidity. By 1967 there were, in the liberated zones, 6 field hospitals, 120 clinics and 23 mobile medical units. Large numbers of personnel were sent to the USSR and Eastern Europe for training, including doctors, nurses and technical trainees (motor mechanics, electricians and so on). Appeals to Britain were less successful. When a PAIGC delegate asked the British Red Cross for medical supplies, she was told to ask Portugal! By the end of the war, they had 10 fully trained doctors, 11 assistant doctors, 45 nurses and 237 auxiliary nurses.

It was not simply a matter of improvements imposed from above. In each village, a committee (three men and two women) was elected by the villagers.

> You have to show our people that the world doesn't begin and end at the village boundary . . . that it's a struggle for the whole of Guiné, an international struggle, that they must run their own lives, resolve their own village problems, develop production, send their children to school, and have frequent meetings.

Foreign observers had long predicted that the burdens and strains of her unsuccessful colonial wars would ultimately topple the dictatorship in Portugal. In a sense, this is what happened. Her futile colonial wars exacted an ever increasing price in Portugal. In the one year of 1967, in the three African colonies, 10,000 Portuguese conscripts were killed or wounded, 7,000 deserted or mutinied, and 15,000 dodged conscription. In 1971 her 'defence' expenditure was estimated at 398 million American dollars. It was Portugal's poverty and weakness that led her to try and keep her colonies by force in the first place. Paradoxically, it was these very wars which wrecked her economy.

In late April 1974 a coup overthrew Portugal's dictatorship, amid scenes of delirious rejoicing. Africa had changed a European government. More precisely, little Guinea-Bissau had, for Spinola, the Portuguese general who headed the new government, had been convinced of the hopelessness of Portugal's wars by his own unsuccessful attempts to subdue the revolutionaries of Guinea-Bissau between 1968 and 1973.

But it is essential to realise, that although Guinea-Bissau contributed to the liberation of Portugal, her own liberation *preceded* the coup in Portugal. In September 1973 Guinea-Bissau was proclaimed an independent sovereign state. International recognition followed rapidly. She entered the United Nations Organisation as the 138th member nation. When Portugal finally recognised her independence too, in the month in which she completed the withdrawal of her troops, in September 1974, she was rather late in the day.

Tragically, the great Amilcar Cabral did not live to see the hour of victory. He had been brutally assassinated eight months earlier, in January 1974. Like Moses, he led his people from bondage, and through unspeakable perils, but did not live to enter the promised land.

In one sense, his admirers all over the world may feel a certain grim satisfaction. Unlike so many nationalists, he did not live too long for his glory.

The present leaders of Guinea-Bissau, such as Aristide Pereira, the Secretary-General of the PAIGC, and Luis Cabral, the country's President (Amilcar's brother), continue, with the same 'rocklike devotion'. One notable aspect of the war's end was their remarkably forgiving spirit to the Portuguese. Even during the war, under Amilcar Cabral's leadership, they had shown the same compassion to their prisoners of war. He, indeed, lost his life because of his compassion, which made him surround himself with malcontents and those in disgrace, in the hope of their rehabilitation.

In a sense, the Portuguese, strangely enough, benefited their colonies by their very failure to develop them, their very refusal to grant them freedom. The years of colonialism have left hardly any impression on the country at all. Its people have a much wider range of options open to them, to shape the kind of society they really want.

The very patriotism, idealism, and close attachment to the rural base which make Guinea-Bissau so promising, were forged in war. In poverty, hardship and danger, there was no plunder or privileges for the elite to divide. The foundation of their success was the growth of political awareness in the countryside, the formation of policies which the peasantry found acceptable.

But other states have attained independence with high hopes, and found them disappointed. Much will depend on the determination of the leadership to resist the charms of affluence, which have wrecked so many young nations in the past. If they do, it may well be that Guinea-Bissau, small and impoverished, will light a beacon of hope for the whole of West Africa and, indeed, the world.

11

Independence Regained

Themes

If we analyse the post-independence experience of West Africa's states, we discover a great number of common themes and problems, and it is these which form the subject of this chapter. Generalisations are necessary for the purpose of analysis, but we should never forget the tremendous differences between West Africa's nations, in size, population and most important, economic resources. Nigeria in population, size and wealth is West Africa's giant. The 1973 census (now officially discarded) revealed a population of almost 80,000,000. She is one of the world's seven leading producers of petroleum, and this is one of the very few raw materials in the world where the producer dictates terms to the buyer, and is now doing so with disastrous consequences to western capitalism. The outlook is very different in a country like Niger, which is landlocked, largely desert, and has a population of perhaps four million. It has no railways or even good roads and between 1972 and 1974 its natural difficulties were cruelly intensified by a prolonged and terrible drought. It had depended on the export of groundnuts but the drought left it with too few groundnuts even for seed. An expatriate expert estimated at the beginning of 1974 that a million Nigeriens were dying of starvation and another million were badly affected. Upper Volta is another Sahelian state where much of the land is desert and the problems of life are multiplied by the prevalence of river blindness in river valleys. Its main source of income is thought to be the earnings of migrant workers. De Gaulle called it 'the land of men' because they needed such courage to live there. Mauritania was desperately poor in the colonial era. The discovery of extremely rich iron ore deposits has transformed her export earnings but as yet provides little wage employment and seventy per cent of her population remain nomads.

Poverty is not confined to the Sahelian zone. The boundaries of modern African states were determined not by their economic viability nor by their cultural unity but by a 'scramble' by European states. It was a question of whose representative reached which point first, and of which territories were exchanged for which at a remote conference table in distant Europe where the minds and policies of statesmen were

Drought in the Sahel

filled with a dozen considerations, but concern for the welfare of African peoples was not among them. This has left West Africa with tiny countries like Gambia and Guinea-Bissau. Gambia is on average only twenty-four kilometres wide. These face a future of extreme difficulty and uncertainty in a modern world.* The same applies to Dahomey (now Benin).†

The form of government

When the former colonies became independent, the departing rulers took it for granted that they would and should follow the English or French form of democracy, which they assumed was the best form of government any state could possibly have.

Democratic government in France and Britain differs, in fact, in several important respects. Britain has elections where the man who has the highest number of votes in a constituency wins it. This means that a party which won a third of the votes in every constituency would have, not a third of the seats, but no seats at all. The electoral system encourages the domination of political processes by two major parties. A voter who likes the policies of neither can do little about it and even if the party he votes for wins, it may well follow policies on specific issues of which he disapproves bitterly.

The French follow a system of proportional representation. A party which polls a tenth of the votes in the whole country gets a tenth of the seats, a system which has encouraged the development of a large number of political parties. These differences are reflected in seating arrangements. In England the two major parties sit on two opposite sides of the House. In France they sit in a semi-circle, one party merging into the next. The French system has meant that France has normally been governed by coalitions and has a history of very frequent changes of government.

In West Africa, the democratic system broke down with amazing rapidity and completeness. With the exception of little Gambia, and even there the opposition is very weak, West African states are either ruled by one-party, or military, governments. In this, as in so much else, Liberia anticipated the experience of independent West Africa. The True Whig party has ruled constantly since 1877 and office, power and privilege have been monopolised by a group of highly inter-related Americo-Liberian families. Nigeria, until 1966, has sometimes been cited as an exception to the pattern of one-party government, but the difference is illusory for what one had in practice was

* Gambia became independent in 1965 amid prophecies of doom. Since then she has achieved a modest prosperity based on expanded groundnut production, the growth of a tourist trade, and smuggling across the Senegalese frontier, so that her economic condition is now generally accepted as better than that of Senegal. But these are fragile bases for prosperity. The Gambia depends heavily on British aid and imported food. Less than five per cent of her population is in wage employment and graduate unemployment is increasing.

† Both old and new names are given in this book to avoid confusion with Benin, Nigeria.

one-party domination of each of the three (later four) Regions. Dahomey (Benin), in its fleeting and troubled days of civilian rule, followed the same basic pattern of three regional groupings; one, led by Migan Apithy was predominantly Yoruba and Catholic and based on Porto Novo in the south-east; one, led by Justin Ahomadegbe was predominantly Fon, with its chief centre in Cotonou; the third, led by Hubert Maga, had its power base in the north.

One-party rule

It is not difficult to see why multi-party rule collapsed so rapidly. The financial attractions of office were overwhelming, especially to members of parliament for whom political success had meant an almost magical transition from poverty to affluence. Too often they were prepared to use any means, legitimate or illegitimate, to keep it. It became normal for party funds to be fed from government sources. It became normal for a man in office to flood his constituency with economic benefits, so that a man out of power could scarcely hope to challenge him. Those in power were united, if in nothing else, in their grim resolution to retain it. Politicians out of power very often joined the government. On this, as on so much else, President Nyerere of Tanzania makes the best possible comment:

> Which is the politician who went to the people at election time and asked them to elect him so that he could provide for his future? . . . Whenever a person seeks political work, whether it is through election or by appointment, he says he wants the opportunity to serve the people, to guard their interests and to further their aspirations. What right has such a person, once he has the appointment he sought on this basis, to use his responsibility for his own betterment?

One-party government has received a great deal of theoretical justification by African scholars and intellectuals and, perhaps surprisingly, by western liberals. It has been justified in terms of African tradition which emphasises government by agreement. It has been pointed out that countries which lack highly skilled manpower should not squander their scarce human resources in unnecessary conflict. It has been justified in Marxist terms by those who claim that in Europe parties represent different classes, the property owners and the workers, and that such a class structure does not exist in Africa. They claim that in Africa the conflict was between colonisers and colonised and that now that the colonisers have gone, the unity of the colonised should not be lost.

More convincingly, it has been claimed that in practice in West Africa different political parties have tended to have, not an ideological but a tribal or regional base; we have noted this in Nigeria and Dahomey (Benin). A one-party structure makes it possible for these potentially conflicting elements to be united in a common organisation, and in practice the heads of one-party governments have usually taken care to achieve this. This is true of Sekou Touré in Guinea, and Siaka Stevens in Sierra Leone.

One-party government is not necessarily undemocratic. This can be seen from the experience of Tanzania, where members of the same party contest seats, and ministers have not infrequently lost them. But it very easily becomes so, and most one-party states have tended to be caught in a vicious circle. As constitutional opposition becomes impossible or hopeless, opposition is forced into non-constitutional channels, such as conspiracy or assassination. The threat that these pose makes the government ever more authoritarian and repressive. Political prisoners have become commonplace in many West African states, and so have treason trials. The political opposition of Mali is sent to the salt mines of the Sahara. Nkrumah's Ghana, Acheampong's Ghana, Touré's Guinea, Stevens' Sierra Leone and Houphouet-Boigny's Ivory Coast, have all had their history of conspiracies and treason trials.

There has been no obvious link between the policies followed by governments and their stability. At almost the same time, coups overthrew a socialist government in Ghana and a far from socialist government in Nigeria. Nor is there any obvious link between stability and prosperity. One finds coups equally in the relative prosperity of Nigeria and Ghana and the absolute poverty of Upper Volta and Niger. Some governments which have survived coups successfully derive from this a false image of popularity and stability. There have been several unsuccessful coups in Ivory Coast. In 1962 in Senegal, personal rivalries between President Senghor and his Prime Minister, Mamadou Dia, led to an attempted coup by the latter which failed only because the army was divided and the paratroop leader, Jean Diallo, backed Senghor. Dia went to prison and has remained there, Diallo became head of the Armed Forces, and Senghor, after a referendum, merged the powers of Prime Minister with those of President.

It is noteworthy that West African intellectuals who are on the whole very much the products of the western liberal tradition, have accepted one-party rule with such few apparent misgivings. Several explanations have been suggested. One is that it is arrogant of Europeans to think that all countries of the world must follow in the particular path that they have followed, a path moreover which has often led to crises and difficulties. This view says that African intellectuals are and ought to be looking for new political forms more compatible with African tradition. A more cynical view says that African intellectuals, with a handful of brave exceptions, tend not to be critics of government or society. The government employs most of them, whether as civil servants or university teachers. More basically it is said, it is feared that if they are too outspoken in their criticisms of society, they might cause a major revolutionary upheaval which would destroy them and their privileges and much else as well.

But why are western liberals favourable, on the whole, to one-party rule? The concept has a perennial attraction for socialists, who see their own party as the party of the common man. Many western commentators are afraid of being arrogant, of having the same heartless and incomprehending attitude to modern Africa that their ancestors had to pre-colonial societies. Because one-party government is practically universal in the whole African continent, except for South Africa, they feel it must have real justification.

The present writer, however, believes that the multi-party system of government, whatever its shortcomings in practice in the western world, has real and indeed essential advantages. The party in opposition keeps a constant watch on the actions of those in power. Much of its criticism may be petty and dictated by party interests. But those in power act in the constant knowledge that their every action will be discussed and criticised. In a one-party state, the role of criticism is left essentially to the press. This places too heavy a burden on too few shoulders and some brave spirits have suffered bitterly for bearing it. The prospect of a coming election, when the loss of power is a real danger, is the best possible antidote to the corruption, extravagance and indifference to the public good for which West Africa's rulers are so often criticised. In historical reality, opposing parties rest less on differing class interests than on opposing *policies*. In West Africa, at the present time, there is a very real set of alternative policies – socialism and free enterprise – each of which has ardent and numerous African adherents. At the moment, a socialist in Ivory Coast or a supporter of capitalism in Guinea must choose between silence, conspiracy or exile. Only a multi-party system can re-establish *the right to choose* on which the first generation of nationalists laid such emphasis.

A minor but not unimportant consequence of one-party government is ageing leadership. At the time of writing three West African heads of state, Senghor in Senegal, Houphouet-Boigny in Ivory Coast and Siaka Stevens in Sierra Leone, are on the verge of seventy.

It is essential to realise that none of the political difficulties we have discussed are peculiar to Africa. England has experienced both civil war and military rule; the U.S.A. went through a disastrous civil war, and, at the time these words were written had a non-elected President, since both the elected President and the elected Vice-President had proved unworthy of the office they held. France has experienced not one, but several, revolutions.

Military rule

In many West African countries, civilian regimes have been overthrown by a military coup. Some of these have given way fairly rapidly to another civilian government, whereas in others the soldiers have retained power in their own hands. Some countries, such as Dahomey (Benin) and Ghana, been through coups of both kinds. All military regimes are in theory commited to the ultimate restoration of civilian rule but in some the prospect appears fairly remote.

The motivation for these military interventions has varied considerably. Sometimes, army career grievances appear to be prominent. This was the case in the first West African coup in Togo, in 1963, which killed the highly gifted Sylvanus Olympio. The background to this was a reorganisation of the French army which meant that large numbers of French West African soldiers needed to be incorporated into the armies of the new states. Olympio felt that to build up a large army was a waste of the resources of his small and poor country. Career grievances ap¡ ear to have been important also in both the Ghana coups, in 1966 and 1972.

Many military coups have been essentially a protest against government extravagance and corruption. This was very much the case in the coup of January 1966 which overthrew Nigeria's First Republic. In the words of one of the ringleaders, Chukwuma Nzeogwu, who was destined to die fighting in the Nigerian civil war:

> Our enemies are the political profiteers, swindlers, the men in high and low places that seek bribes and demand ten per cent, those that seek to keep the country permanently divided so that they can remain in office as Ministers and VIPs of waste, the tribalists, the nepotists, those that make the country look big for nothing before international circles.

One cannot always say that the motives of the soldiers and the movement of popular discontent coincided, but there can be no doubt that many coups have given expression to a very widespread discontent with corruption and extravagance in high places. Successive coups in Dahomey (Benin) have sprung largely from the contrast between the country's disastrously unsatisfactory balance of trade, leading to government demands for austerity, and the contrast this provided with 'the glittering Presidential palace in Cotonou . . . and an enormous (and as yet unfinished) independence monument'. The coup which overthrew President Maurice Yameogo in Upper Volta in 1966 sprang very much again from the contrast between an 'austerity' budget and the spectacle of a regime which was at once extravagant and authoritarian.* Very often, however, military governments have quickly lost their original reforming impetus and have fallen victim to the corruption and extravagance of their civilian predecessors. The extensive enquiries and dismissals which occurred in Nigeria's then twelve states after the fall of General Yakubu Gowon's government in July 1975 made this very clear.

Some commentators see military governments as the true successors of colonialism, which was imposed by military violence, was maintained by its capacity for military violence, and was extremely authoritarian.

Military governments are frequently characterised by their rejection of 'politics' and of political discussion and debate in general. A commissioner in Colonel Acheampong's government is said to have warned against 'bogus ideologies and theories', and criticised a university teacher who advocated 'Marxism, Leninism or democracy, or whatever he calls it'. Lieutenant Colonel Kerekou's government, which seized power in Dahomey (Benin) in 1972, has a reputation for Marxist sympathies but has also gone on record as saying, 'We do not want communism or capitalism or socialism. We have our own Dahomean social and cultural system'. This rejection of ideology is not peculiar to the military. A leading political figure in Ivory Coast, Philippe Yace (generally regarded as Houphouet-Boigny's likely successor) said, 'We have no time to spend on ideologies'.

Experience, however, tends to show that reaction against the abuses committed by one's predecessor is not an adequate political programme. 'Ideology' is simply a description of the kind of society one hopes to achieve, and a possible plan of how to

---

* It is believed that Voltaic Catholics were also alienated when Yameogo married a second wife.

achieve it. The present writer believes that real change in the African situation demands above all else an ideology which can win men's hearts. A famous military ruler in seventeenth-century England defined a patriot as one who knows what he fights for and loves what he knows.

One evil of authoritarian regimes, whether civilian or military, and the restraints they impose on candid public debate, can be seen in the extraordinarily unbalanced assessments often made of contemporary events in the West African press. Many commentators have remarked on this in the Ghanaian context. When Nkrumah was in power he received nothing but adulation. When he fell from power he was utterly condemned. The same was true later of Busia, and of General Gowon's regime in Nigeria.

Ethnic nationalism

Ethnic nationalism, called tribalism by its critics, has been to a very large extent the product of urban life and of the colonial experience. Many tribal groups which developed a lively common consciousness, such as the Ewe or the Igbo, had no sense of common identity in pre-colonial times and saw themselves as citizens of small local communities. An Igbo from Owerri saw himself as an Owerri man. An Igbo from Ohafia was a stranger, and perhaps an enemy. Yorubaland consisted of a large number of states which were often at war with each other, not infrequently in alliance with non-Yoruba communities. The very word 'Yoruba' originally referred to the Oyo dialect.

Ethnic consciousness became stronger in the conditions of urban life, where men from many different tribal backgrounds competed for jobs, contracts and accommodation. When men meet strangers, they tend to see them first and foremost in terms of the tribe they belong to. Deeper and longer acquaintance may show them the inadequacy of this impression, but its very existence acts as a barrier between individuals and hinders their mutual understanding. 'Tribalism' becomes a blanket explanation for imperfectly understood events. If a man of another tribe, or clan, succeeds, his competitors attribute it to his successful manipulation of tribal and kinship ties. To attribute it to his superior abilities or qualifications would be more damaging to their self-esteem.

Some ethnic and regional consciousness was the direct result of the policies and attitudes of colonial officials. This is especially true of the extremely artifical division between northern and southern Nigeria, where it was said that if the Nigerians left, the white officials could go to war!

A great deal of tribal consciousness and hostility was created by competing politicians exploiting their own tribal background in order to build up a following. Tribalism was useful to the elite politician because it cuts across class and economic boundaries. It would have been, to say the least of it, inconvenient for them, if parties had formed on class lines instead. Nigeria and Dahomey (Benin) are the classic examples of ethnic politics but the phenomenon was much more widespread. Dr Kofi Busia, a scholar who has spent much time at Oxford and was highly esteemed among the English intelligentsia, deliberately exploited Asante tribalism in his efforts to find a base for opposition to Nkrumah.

Tribalism rests to some extent on a contradiction, which is almost impossible to avoid. All educated Africans are deeply aware of the need to identify and understand their roots in their own culture. 'African personality', 'negritude', are much too general and universal ideas to shed a real light on the individual's experience. Ever since the nineteenth century, West African intellectuals have been trying to explore their own history, language, culture and religion more profoundly. But by doing this, they concentrate on the factors which divide them. A man from Ekiti may explore Ekiti culture and, to a lesser extent, Yoruba culture, but by definition, the factors which shape his past and define his own Ekiti identity are those which distinguish him from the cultural heritage of others.

It is conventional to criticise tribalism as an evil and it has undoubtedly produced infinite evils. For example, there was an attack on educated Dahomeans in Ivory Coast in 1958, and massacres of Igbos took place in northern Nigeria in 1966. Yet basic to the discussion is a real problem: to what should a man be most loyal? In the modern world, including the OAU, the conventional answer is, the nation state. But it is an answer which is not universally accepted, and Basque separatists in Spain and German-speaking separatists in north Italy have a different answer. A great eighteenth-century English political philosopher said with truth, 'No cold relation makes a zealous citizen', meaning that those who are most intensely attached to the local or tribal loyalty are, at least potentially, the most fervent patriots. He would have sympathised with the twentieth-century Efik and Nigerian patriot who said, 'The love of Calabar must consume us . . . We are either Calabarians or nothing'.

A nineteenth-century Nigerian church leader had a different formula but it is one which few men have ever been able to put into practice – mankind before Nigeria, Nigeria before Yorubaland, Yorubaland before Ekiti, Ekiti before the Agbebe family, and the Agbebe family before himself.

The anatomy of under-development

The absolute poverty of the workers and peasants of West Africa is not a matter of controversy. Some West African countries, Dahomey (Benin), Guinea, Niger and Upper Volta among them, are among the twenty-five most under-developed countries in the world. If one divides the gross domestic product by the number of people in the country, one is left with a per capita income of $286 a year for Ghana, $345 for Ivory Coast, $176 for Sierra Leone, $167 for Mauritania, $94 for Dahomey, $84 for Niger, $71 for Guinea, $57 for Upper Volta, and $54 for Mali. Because in fact a small section of the population earns vastly more than this, the labouring masses actually earn much less.

Under-development, however, must be defined not only in terms of national incomes but in terms of a characteristic kind of social structure, which can be found in under-developed societies all over the world. An under-developed economy commonly has a very small sector of modern development, which is largely in foreign hands. Only a small proportion of the population work for wages. The economy is heavily dependent on primary exports, either minerals, which are frequently unprocessed, or agricultural products. These societies are the victims of long term changes in the terms of world trade which mean, with several exceptions which we shall discuss later, that prices of primary products are steadily declining on the world market, and that those of industrial manufactures are rising. Because the modern sector is largely in foreign hands, there is a steady flow of capital from the under-developed to the metropolitan country. The more she expands her exports, the greater this outflow becomes. No under-developed country has ever broken out of the vicious circle of under-development simply by expanding her exports. After bitter experience, the Ghanaians defined their own situation in the following sentence: they were running very fast in order to stay still.

The under-developed nation contains a miniature version within its boundaries of the unequal distribution of world resources. It has a wealthy elite, often working closely with expatriate business interests. This retains its members' loyalties with shares in businesses or directorships, a process sometimes misleadingly called indigenisation. Most of the elite, however, are in government employ, where their salaries consume a vastly excessive' proportion of the national income. In Dahomey (Benin), government salaries consume 65 per cent of her budget; in Senegal in the mid 1960s 47 per cent of government revenue went on administrative salaries. In Ivory Coast civil servants form 0.5 per cent of the population and consume 58 per cent of the budget.

This misuse of scarce resources is a direct result of colonial rule. White officials were paid high salaries, related to the salary structure in Europe, plus inducements to compensate for the supposed hardships of life in West Africa. One of the points which nationalists agitated for most strongly was equal pay for Africans. It seemed a matter of elementary justice that Africans in their own country should receive the same pay for the same work as Europeans. But it has meant that the salaries of the highly paid are vastly excessive in terms of average incomes. The gulf between rich and poor is made worse by corruption. It is also made worse by the tendency to what is called 'conspicuous consumption' – luxury cars, expensive clothes and sumptuous wedding or burial ceremonies. One European critic* puts it this way:

> Africa is a continent of mass poverty, but the obsession of the ruling groups is with luxuries. The same could be said in indictment of countless societies. But those who came to power mouthing the rhetoric of change faced the critical poverty of their countries with frivolity and fecklessness . . . The newly rich . . . are obsessed with property and personal performance in countries where all but a tiny fringe own hardly more than a hoe, a plastic bucket, an ironware cooking pot or two, and perhaps a bicycle.

* Ruth First.

Frantz Fanon was a doctor from Martinique, who took part in the Algerian independence struggle, and died in 1961, of leukemia, at the age of thirty-six. In the year of his death, he published a searing, impassioned and controversial book called *The Wretched of the Earth*. This is what he said then about the bourgeoisie. The words are especially notable, because they *predict* so much of the social history of the next fifteen years:

> There exists inside the new regime . . . an inequality in the acquisition of wealth and in monopolisation. Some have a double source of income and demonstrate that they are specialised in opportunism. Privileges multiply and corruption triumphs, while morality declines. Today the vultures are too numerous and too voracious in proportion to the lean spoils of the national wealth.

Even in a supposedly prosperous state, such as Nigeria with its petroleum boom, the workers and peasants live in poverty and deprivation. The workers in the slums of Nigeria's cities have neither adequate living space nor a balanced diet, nor a good water supply, nor an adequate sewage disposal system. Many children in hospital have no disease but malnutrition. Every year both primary and secondary school leavers engage in an exhausting, dispiriting and often unsuccessful search for employment. An official document of 1963 said that 100,000 children left primary school each year in western Nigeria, of whom only half gained admission to more advanced schools or found 'useful employment'. Since then, the numbers have vastly increased. The fact that so many West Africans still prefer the life of the urban slum dweller or 'applicant' to that of the village is the best possible commentary on the hardship of rural life. All West African countries face a crisis in food production. They depend increasingly on imported foods because farming is left in the hands of the elderly and unsuccessful, and of women, as labour migration removes ever more able-bodied men from rural life.

Scholars disagree as to whether the rural areas are better or worse off than they were in pre-colonial times. The optimists point to the earnings of cocoa farmers, for instance, which are spent on better houses or schooling for their children. The pessimists point out that much of West Africa is not really involved in the production of cash crops and that even where it is, it often leads, as in Senegal, to a serious under-production of food for home consumption. This under-production of food becomes more serious as the population increases. A nutritionist,[*] summarising research done in Nigeria in the early 1960s, states that some areas have a fifty per cent child mortality rate, and that this is largely caused by malnutrition. He writes, 'Most of our adults are so grossly underfed that they are poorly motivated for increased productivity and hope for a better world. This was clearly seen in the Ekiti farming community . . . where the people do not have food enough to eat, and are therefore not willing to work for more than three or four days in the week on farms which they fatalistically believe cannot be improved'.

[*] I. S. Dema.

Supply of capital

For development to take place it is necessary to have money, or capital, to invest. This capital can be obtained in one of two ways. It can be borrowed from abroad, or built up within the society. The latter involves policies of severe austerity. Russia is the classic case of a society which generated the capital for her own industrialisation but she did so at the cost of much suffering and compulsion, which no-one would wish for West Africa. For most West African states, in any case, this is not a suitable choice – probably only Nigeria has the resources to go it alone in this way. West Africa as a whole, however, has both a large population and excellent natural resources, the two things which made Russia's industrialisation possible. There is the iron ore of Mauritania and Mount Nimba, the bauxite of Guinea, the electricity generated by the Volta dam, Nigeria's petroleum. Nkrumah dreamed of, but was unable to attain, this kind of international co-operation by which West African countries would help each other to develop. West Africa has now moved much closer towards it with the formation of the Economic Community of West African States (ECOWAS) in 1975.

At the present time, most of West Africa's industries are either engaged in processing her natural products or in manufacturing goods which would otherwise have to be imported. Most economists agree that to create a truly industrialised economy, one must first create a basis of heavy industry. This is really only viable at the West African, not the national, level. It seems clear, in any case, that West Africa will not become truly industrialised while development takes the form of import substituting factories, set up within the artificial boundaries of fifteen different countries.

Even if a totally self-financed development strategy is impossible, most West African countries could go much further in the direction of self-reliance, which means austerity. This would probably mean both higher rates of taxation and cutting down sharply on imports of non-essentials. Countries can succeed in carrying out such policies either by extreme coercion, or by generating a tide of enthusiasm and patriotism. The essential requirements for such enthusiasm are that the political leadership should set an example of austerity in its own life style and that government spending should be channelled in directions which can be seen to be helpful to the average man – not in empty prestige projects, or a massive standing army. If such an army exists, and cannot be disbanded without creating a massive unemployment problem, it could be used in development projects.

The other way of financing development is with money from abroad. Nothing has confused the popular understanding of the real situation in Africa today more than by calling all forms of capital from outside sources 'aid'. In the words of a European commentator:*

> Two-thirds of all aid consists of private investment and loans on commercial terms, and is in fact a normal operation of finance capital undertaken in the

* L. Barnes.

interests of the creditor. Long-term advantage for the 'aidee' is here neither sought nor found. After a few years, debt servicing charges involve a net transfer of resources from Africa abroad, instead of vice versa. The drain begins to flow towards Europe.

As Liberia discovered in the nineteenth century, borrowing money from abroad can soon lead to a situation where much of a nation's income goes on paying interest on her debts. In the 1960s, many West African countries contracted loans on very disadvantageous terms, such as the now notorious system of suppliers credits (see page 332).

Much aid is 'tied', which means goods must be purchased in the lending country, even if they can be obtained more cheaply elsewhere. Private firms invest in West Africa for one reason only – to make money – and their primary loyalty is to their overseas shareholders. Various factors attract them – mineral resources, such as petroleum or bauxite, the nearness of raw materials, such as palm oil for soap factories, or energy sources, such as hydro-electricity, or the buying power of the large Nigerian market. They placate local opinion by Africanising senior staff, but usually not their key policy-making posts. But the test as to whether a firm is truly indigenised is surely its policy. If a foreign firm is expatriating large profits every year, it is not really indigenised whether its staff are African or not. A classic example was the Nigerian Indigenisation Decree of 1972 which was implemented by 1974. It benefited only those with spare money to invest; that is, it enabled the prosperous to become still more prosperous. To the average Nigerian wage earner, concerned with how to feed his family in the last days of the month before he gets his pay, the sale of shares might as well have been on the moon.

We have noted the long-term trend in world trade which has tended to mean that the prices of primary exports decline in relationship to the prices of manufactured goods. In several areas, this trend has been reversed, with a new militancy among primary producers following the extremely successful example of the Organisation of Petroleum Exporting Countries, OPEC. There are limits to what can be attained in this way. If prices are forced too high, the purchasing countries will simply cut down on non-essentials, such as cocoa and coffee, or will look for artificial substitutes. Thus a ceiling is placed on rubber prices by the existence of artificial rubber. Nevertheless, this type of militancy seems more promising than dependence on 'aid'. One European expert on aid writes, 'The real motives for providing aid are fear and greed', and yet another European authority urges the use of 'the power to withhold the supply of minerals . . . the power to withdraw money balances or default on debt, and the power to tax private foreign investment'.

Middle level technology

One partial answer to this problem of capital shortage may lie in middle level technology. In countries where there is little capital but plenty of labour, it may not be wise to copy the factory system of the west which is designed for conditions where labour is scarce and very expensive. The first Industrial Revolution in England began in small workshops, where simple mechanical processes were used which needed little capital. In a developing country this may make more sense than setting up very complex machinery, dependent on spare parts from abroad and foreign experts to maintain it. A French agriculturalist has made this point with regard to the grinding of millet. To grind millet by hand with a pestle and mortar is obviously a waste of time and energy. Motorised mills have proved too expensive. His solution is middle level technology – a mill driven by wind or water power, or by oxen walking in a circle.

Middle level technology has been widely supported as the best form of development in agriculture. Experiments with highly mechanised agriculture and expensive farm settlements have usually been disastrous failures. In an earlier section of this book, we noted the vast sums consumed by the Niger Office irrigation scheme in Mali. In Mokwa in northern Nigeria, where mechanised groundnut production was undertaken, at one time the cost of destroying termite mounds for a single season was equivalent to the cost of the whole crop.

Obvious improvements could be made by rationalising land holdings, since many farmers waste hours walking between their widely scattered plots, in irrigation where possible and appropriate, in organising peasant consumer and producer co-operatives, and improving seed varieties and fertilisers. Much may be gained through the cultivation of new crops, such as varieties of tropical vegetables from South China. The soya bean is an excellent source of protein. Many other suggestions have been made, such as the cultivation of edible cactuses and trees with edible leaves, to feed stock in the Sahel, and the rearing of goats for their milk as well as their meat.

Education

One of the most popular forms of investment in West Africa, both among governments and among individuals, is in education. Undoubtedly at independence, the new states needed skilled manpower badly and since the expansion of educational opportunities is one of the things the average man wants most, there is tremendous pressure on governments to provide them. But in many cases the expansion of education has been ill-planned and ill-considered. It is much easier to build a school or university than to create employment opportunities for its products.

Estimates made some years ago showed that it then took ₦2,000 of investment to employ one man in a textile mill, ₦20,000 in an oil refinery. Nigeria has a steadily rising threshold of educated unemployment. The openings for graduates and the production of graduates can be compared with water being poured into a jug – the jug is not yet full but it soon will be, and the universities will still pour out graduates at the same rate as before.

It is almost impossible to find solutions to the problem. At the moment we have an educational system which makes its products reluctant to work on the land. We have an economy which means that most people must live on the land. For many reasons, the prospect of a prosperous mechanised system of agriculture, which makes rural life really attractive in a country like America, is very remote indeed. Farm schools have been suggested, to train rural children for farm life. This will only work if the whole salary structure is radically revised. As long as clerks or civil servants earn much more money for much less work, rural schools of this type will be second class schools for second class citizens.

What kind of a society?

Industrialisation and improved agricultural productivity do not necessarily lead to a better standard of living for the masses. Italy is an example of an industrialised country where there is still a great deal of poverty. The prosperity of the masses will depend partly on the natural resources of the country, and partly on the way in which wealth is distributed within the society. Here there are the two possible models of socialism (not necessarily the same thing as communism), and capitalism.

Capitalism

This type of society is called free enterprise by its admirers, and capitalism by its critics. Supporters believe that the workings of the economy should be left to the private individual, with a minimum of government interference. They say that this type of economy is more productive because the individual businessman is basically concerned with making a profit for himself and so makes every effort to improve productivity.

There is also an economic situation which is termed state capitalism. This is quite a different thing from socialism, though people sometimes confuse the two. One has state capitalism when the state owns and controls certain spheres of activity, such as cement manufacturing, which private capitalists lack the resources or expertise to run effectively. This can be a half-way house towards a socialist or a capitalist society. Ivory Coast is officially committed to capitalism but in the absence of a suitable class of local businessmen, has an economy dominated by state capitalism.

In a capitalist society, such state-owned enterprises tend to run at a loss. For example, in West Africa, they have often been run by civil servants with little aptitude for business. Since their salaries are paid whether the corporation makes a profit or not, they have little interest in efficiency. It has too many salaried employees. They are often negligent, or corrupt, or both, in their work. Advocates of capitalism say that if these corporations were owned privately, the owner would do everything possible to make them run at a profit.

Karl Marx, analysing industrial societies in the mid-nineteenth century, thought that capitalism had played a useful role in human development. He admired its energy and its capacity for work and investment, but thought its ruthless selfishness would lead to its overthrow. West Africa has never seen the kind of capitalism to which Marx was referring. The West African middle class consists of civil servants, not industrialists as was the case in nineteenth-century Europe. Their wealth, instead of being productively invested, is often wasted on luxuries and prestige symbols.

Relatively few West African leaders say that they believe in capitalism. They tend to follow capitalist principles in practice and to avoid ideologies altogether. Yet an ideology is nothing but a clear concept of where the state should be going and how to get there. In a sense, the statesmen of the independence era did not take up their intellectual responsibilities. Nkrumah, Azikiwe and Awolowo, all wrote books about politics before independence. After independence they turned to autobiography.

The critics of capitalism say that if some are allowed to accumulate wealth without restraint, others will not be free from poverty, hunger and disease. It is important to realise that neither capitalism nor socialism are found in their pure form anywhere. The Russians and the Chinese would be the first to admit that they have not achieved pure socialism. England is not generally regarded as a socialist state but it has carried the redistribution of wealth to great lengths, with extremely heavy taxes for the rich and many benefits, such as old age pensions and widows' pensions, for the less privileged.

The present energy shortage has created a crisis for international capitalism, which has led to a renewed questioning of its basic values.

Socialism

Socialism means different things to different people. Some people are put off socialism altogether by Russian and Chinese communism which was accompanied by a hostility to religion and a high degree of compulsion or coercion (but it also made a tremendous improvement in the standard of living of ordinary people). Basically, socialists believe that the wealth created by the peasants and workers should be used for their benefit and not for the benefit of a class of industrialists. It is normally suggested that this can be achieved by the public ownership of the means of production, distribution and exchange. But all socialist countries have in practice a sphere for private ownership, particularly of peasant land holdings. Many who call themselves socialists in Africa are thinking less of the public ownership of large sections of the economy than of the same kind of redistribution of wealth which exists now in England. They want higher taxes, and lower elite salaries but minimum wages for all the workers. They want the introduction of social security benefits, in as much as the economy permits it. They want strict import restrictions so that the country's valuable foreign exchange is spent on machinery or fertilisers instead of luxury cars or alcohol.

Measures of this kind would mean hardship and sacrifice for the elite, but it is only the elite who can provide people sufficiently well educated to understand the problems of a society and ways in which they might be tackled. All over the world, fortunately, countries have produced elite leaders who are willing to make this kind of renunciation.

Many people are discouraged from following this path by the fact that African elites are so small that even if they renounced their privileges this would not produce an improved standard of living for the masses. This overlooks the point that poverty is relative. A yam farmer in an Igbo village a hundred years ago could be content with few possessions. If he was an expert farmer, his neighbours hailed him as Yam King. He owned little, but so did most other people. A modern yam farmer walks to his farm while cars roar past him, covering him with mud or dust, depending on the season. When he sees houses with cement walls and 'zinc' roofs, the traditional thatch roofs and adobe walls cannot satisfy him. His bitterness increases, when he sees that his lack of money condemns his children, regardless of their abilities, to live in the same way.

Our understanding of socialism in West Africa is made more difficult by the fact that many statesmen have paid lip service to socialism but made no real effort to transform its ideals into practice. Nigeria has produced politicians who have called themselves socialists but socialist policies have never been followed in Nigeria. Senghor is a celebrated theorist of African socialism, but Senegal is not a socialist state. The only real attempts made in West Africa to build socialism have been made in Ghana under Nkrumah, in Mali until the overthrow of Modibo Keita, in Guinea, and in Guinea-Bissau. We shall look at the experience of these states in the case studies which follow on page 323. (Ruben Um Nyobe of Cameroon was killed before he had a chance to follow the same road.)

The outstanding theorist and practitioner of African socialism comes not from West but from East Africa. After Julius Nyerere had led Tanzania to independence he became concerned at the increasing gap between rich and poor, and at the lack of real benefits independence had brought to the peasants and workers.

The fact that he sought a solution to this problem in socialism can be connected with his strong Christian beliefs. But he knew that this was not an ideology that would appeal to Tanzanians as a whole, who include many Muslims and traditionalists, and a few free thinkers. Therefore he rooted his theory in a description of traditional African society.

> In an acquisitive society, wealth tends to corrupt those who possess it. It tends to breed in them a desire to live more comfortably than their fellows, to dress better, and in every way to outdo them . . .
>
> When a society is so organised that it cares about its individuals, then, provided he is willing to work, no individual within that society should worry about what will happen to him tomorrow if he does not hoard wealth today. Society itself should look after him, or his widow or his orphans.

In 1967 Nyerere issued the Arusha Declaration which translated his aims into cold hard practice. According to this every party and government leader must be a peasant or worker; none could earn two or more salaries, hold shares in any company or a directorship in any private firm or rent out houses to others. At a blow, all the avenues of private enrichment were closed. Some grumbled, but they followed him. There have been some inefficiencies and injustices, as was probably inevitable. But it may be said that Tanzania is moving towards the creation of a just society.

No set of political arrangements has ever produced a perfectly just society. It was inevitable that the prospect of political independence in Africa should arouse boundless hopes and expectations. In West Africa, the promise that when independence was achieved, everything else would follow, was one that could not have been kept. Too much hope was bound to lead to cynicism and despair – and despair and corruption are very closely allied. It is essential that West Africans should realise that on the one hand the ideal society cannot be attained, and that on the other hand the attempt to realise it must be made continuously, and the strategy for doing so rethought by every generation.

The Islamic tradition and social reform
In some West African states, socialist ideas of social change have been joined with the Islamic tradition we discussed in an earlier section of this book. This has been particularly the case in Guinea and Mali. A Malian statesman can look for inspiration, not to remote figures in distant continents, but to the example of the Massina Caliphate, and Sheikh Ahmadu's austerity, self-denial, and concern for the common man. The same connection can be seen in Sekou Touré's Guinea. Sekou Touré is himself a descendant of Samori – and there were other living links with the past. Fanta Mady, a supporter of Touré who died in 1955, was a great Muslim teacher and mystic, and was the son of Samori's spiritual guide. When he died, Sekou Touré praised him 'as the living example of a being who believes in God'. Many PDG meetings begin with the first sura of the Quran:

> In the Name of God, the Merciful, the Compassionate,
> Praise belongs to God, the Lord of all Being . . .

The same linking of the Islamic tradition and western socialist ideas can be seen in Alhaji Aminu Kano, of northern Nigeria, who was the leader of NEPU. His mother was literate in Hausa and Arabic, his father an Islamic judge, and he himself is a Tafsir Mallam.*

Christianity and Islam share many of the same ideals of social justice. Both lay great stress on concern for the poor and believe that a man's salvation depends largely on what he does for them. Both belong basically to the same great religious tradition, and are far closer to each other than either is, for instance, to Buddhism, Hinduism, or traditional African religions. The tradition of nineteenth-century western Sudan government, piety and learning, joined with western and secular ideas about social justice, can be an inspiration to West African Christians, as well as West African Muslims.

Trade unions
In democratic countries, trade unions have been the main means of improving the conditions of the workers. In a country like England, the history of working class betterment is very largely a history of union organisation, and the unions' fight for legal recognition and protection. Historically, unions have fought for better wages, shorter working hours, safer working conditions, protection against arbitrary dismissal and victimisation, and so on. In the western world, today, unions are extremely powerful; so much so that it lies in their power to disrupt the economy. Sometimes

* Authorised interpreter of the Quran.

they have used this power unwisely, and thus have had the opposite effect from what they sought. By disrupting the economy, they have caused unemployment.

In West Africa, with the exception of Guinea, unions have tended to be weak and disunited, with little say in political processes. During the period of the nationalist struggle, they sometimes provided support which helped to bring elite politicians to power. To take Nigeria as an example, the General Strike of 1945 gave force to the demands of the nationalist movement. But when independence was achieved, the workers were disillusioned to see that the politicians grew richer, while they themselves obtained no tangible benefits. As a trade union pamphlet of 1962 put it,

> The edifice of privilege remains; only its proprietors are different . . . This situation, in which a senior official may receive fifty times the salary of a junior official, or a daily labourer, is politically explosive and economically intolerable

In 1964 Michael Imodou led a group of unions in a General Strike, which was successful in a sense but which did not, in the long run, yield the hoped for benefits. The fate of the General Strike has parallels elsewhere in West Africa. Occasionally – in Dahomey (Benin), or in Upper Volta – union action has threatened, or even toppled, a government. But it has not been successful in realising unionism's main aim – the long term progressive improvement of workers' conditions.

West African unions have been weak for three reasons; disunity, leadership rivalries and ambitions, and the high rate of unemployment. The Nigerian trade union movement has a history of chronic division. There are about three hundred unions in the country. Many of these are 'house unions' which means they are unions of the employees of a particular firm. At the moment (late 1975), attempts are being made to rationalise the union structure, and unite them in a single body.

Successful unionism demands dedicated leadership – men for whom the improvement of the condition of the workers is the major commitment of their lives. Partly because of the ideology of free enterprise which is popular in their country, Nigerians have tended to lack this kind of commitment. Union leaders sent abroad for further studies have often used the opportunity as a springboard to a better job. When every cleaner hopes to be a typist, when every typist hopes to enter university, the gifted cleaner will devote himself to evening classes in typing, not to the long term improvement of conditions for cleaners.

But the greatest weakness of organised labour is the high rate of unemployment. In a country like Nigeria, even people with skills, such as drivers, mechanics, carpenters, cooks, find that the supply outstrips the demand. When a Lagos department store sacked a thousand workers in 1964, the streets were crammed with crowds of applicants for the vacancies. In this situation the strike, which is the classic weapon of the worker, loses its effectiveness, and union leaders have often found their own jobs in danger. Paradoxically, the groups who are least in need of union protection, such as doctors and university teachers, are able to form unions more effectively than other groups, because the high level of their skills makes the threat to withhold their labour effective, and because their ranks can easily supply dynamic and gifted leadership.

Relations with Africa and the rest of the world

Neutralism

Whatever their domestic policies, most West African leaders have chosen neutralism at least in theory. That is, they have refused to make a definite commitment to either West or East, retaining what has been called a freedom to choose. In this they were very much influenced by the example of India. While willing to stay within a loose grouping such as the British Commonwealth, or the French Community, they were, on the whole, unwilling to bind themselves by specific defence agreements. Despite the close links between France and the Francophone states, when France carried out atom bomb tests in the Sahara she met a unanimous outcry of protest. The Sardauna of Sokoto defined neutralism well:

> We must not find ourselves in such a position in international affairs that we should feel morally bound to support some policy which does not win our whole-hearted or intellectual backing, or attract us by its obvious rightness.

In practice, West African states have tended to retain close links, especially economic links, with the former colonial masters. Even Nkrumah, who made deliberate attempts to develop trade links with the East, in fact borrowed most of his capital from the West.

Probably the country which has come closest to real neutralism is Guinea. France's abrupt withdrawal in 1958 left a vacuum which was partly filled with trade, and technicians, from the communist countries, and later from the USA. Mali, under Keita, made a similar deliberate attempt to extract the utmost possible benefit and help from both East and West. Nigeria, during the civil war, obtained arms impartially from Britain and Russia.

Panafricanism

In its origins, Panafricanism was an expression of black rather than African identity, formulated especially by black men in the New World. Panafricanism came, in a sense, more readily to them, because enslavement, and long residence in the Americas, had robbed them of their tribal identities, languages and cultures.

From the 1945 Manchester Conference onwards, Panafricanism ideals, at least in theory, became widely accepted among nationalists. But most, in practice, were mainly concerned with their own countries.

Nkrumah was the one nationalist for whom African unity was a consuming passion. He was utterly convinced that only through unity could Africa overcome her own poverty, and the grip of foreign exploitation and control. He lent £100 million to Guinea at her independence, and gave much financial help to movements struggling against white domination.

Various attempts were made to start a union on a small scale. We have already seen the short-lived federation of Senegal and Mali (see page 293). In 1960 Ghana, Mali and Guinea formed a 'union'; in 1961 they met with North African leaders at Casablanca.

This Casablanca bloc immediately provoked the formation of rival groupings. Nigeria led the formation of the Monrovia bloc. There was yet another organisation of former French colonies, led by Houphouet-Boigny, called the Brazzaville bloc.

It was a great triumph for African unity, when, in 1963, despite these divisions, a meeting of thirty-two African independent states was held at Addis Ababa, which led to the formation of the Organisation of African Unity – a step forward which was largely the work of Nkrumah.

Hardly any African leaders shared Nkrumah's desire for unified political institutions. Having just won their independence from Europe, they did not want to surrender it to the United States of Africa. (The three East African states came close to union, a move which was strongly backed by Nyerere, and mistakenly opposed by Nkrumah.) The emphasis on the territorial integrity of member nations was strongly stressed, from the OAU's beginnings, not least because most of its member statesmen were uneasily aware of potential divisions within their own boundaries. This fundamental emphasis of the OAU was to be of great importance during the Nigerian civil war.

As the sixties progressed the prospects for African unity, if anything, receded. Leaders of liberation movements complained bitterly that the amount of financial backing they were given was inadequate (although the confrontation with a common, white, enemy in southern Africa was a powerful stimulus to unity). And if individual countries such as Nigeria had such difficulty in remaining one, what were the chances for a United States of Africa?

Probably the most promising form of unity lies in regional groupings for economic ends, such as the West African Economic Community, ECOWAS, first projected at a meeting at Lomé in 1973, and finalised in 1975.

The artist as critic of society

It is very striking that in independent West Africa the most courageous and outspoken critics of society have been the creative writers, and especially the novelists, rather than those whose professional concern is with the analysis of society, and changes in it over time – historians, political scientists, or sociologists.

There are several reasons for this. The mask of fiction enables a man to be more outspoken, in societies where to be outspoken is sometimes dangerous. Professional scholars usually have only one period in their lives for full-time research and writing, which is when they do their doctorates. These have to be acceptable to the norms of a western – some would say bourgeois – university. Professional scholars have to be able to show evidence for what they say. A creative writer distills the essence of his own experience – what he sees around him, hears, feels . . .

Many creative writers, both in French and English, have shown a radically critical vision. Here we shall look at a few outstanding examples.

Chinua Achebe, an Igbo novelist, began with a novel on the transition from traditional to modern life. In 1966, the year of the Nigerian coups, he published his fourth novel, *A Man of the People*, an unsparing indictment of the First Republic:

A regime which inspired the common saying that a man could only be sure of what he had put away safely in his gut, or, in language ever more suited to the times: 'you chop, me self I chop, palaver finish'.

Elsewhere in the same book, he isolated, with unfailing insight, the sickness of his time:

> A man who has just come in from the rain and dried his body and put on dry clothes is more reluctant to go out again than another who has been indoors all the time. The trouble with our new nation . . . was that none of us had been indoors long enough to be able to say, 'To hell with it'. We had all been in the rain together until yesterday. Then a handful of us – the smart and the lucky and hardly ever the best – had scrambled for the one shelter our former rulers left, and had taken it over and barricaded themselves in.

Wole Soyinka, a Yoruba poet and playwright from western Nigeria, is an outstanding example of a writer who assumes a prophetic role, and not only denounces the ills of his society, but attempts to change them. In 1966 he greeted the news of the Igbo massacres in the north with grief and outrage:

> oh God
> They are not strangers all
> Whose desecration mocks the word
> Of peace – *salaam aleikun* . . .
> I borrow seasons of an alien land
> In brotherhood of ill, pride of race around me
> Strewn in sunlit shards.

When the Nigerian civil war broke out, he denounced a conflict which he thought no-one could win, and appealed for a cease fire. He got two grim years in detention for his pains, which form the theme of his book, *The Man Died*.

Another indomitable Yoruba intellectual, the radical school master Tai Solarin, has earned the admiration of his compatriots for his fearless, forthright honesty.

The same prophetic voice was heard in Ghana. Ayi Kwei Armah's *The Beautyful Ones are not yet Born*, was published in 1968 when he was twenty-nine. It is a searing indictment of corruption in the last years of Nkrumah's regime, the story of the sufferings of a poor upright man who refuses to play the game that everyone else is playing. It is ablaze with a powerful vision – constant images of filth reinforce the theme of corruption and, towards the end, the riches of the corrupt Party man lead only to terror and flight. The book ends with a series of unforgettable contrasting images. A mad woman walks down the beach, her words echoing the perplexities of the sane:

> They have mixed it all together! Everything! They have mixed everything. And how can I find it when they have mixed it all with so many things?

The day after the Revolution, a policeman stops a vehicle and demands a bribe . . .
A vehicle carries a painted motto, 'The beautyful ones are not yet born . . .'

Among Francophone West Africans, David Diop emerges as perhaps the most clearly prophetic figure. He was born in 1927, and died in 1960 and throughout his short life, he was plagued with ill health, which cut short his medical studies. The air crash which killed him, and his entire family, meant also the loss of many of his manuscripts. But despite all this, he managed to produce a small body of white hot poems, lashing out at those he called 'the vultures' and 'the renegades', yet frantic with hope for the dawning of a new age.

> Despite your songs of pride amid the slaughter houses
> The desolate villages, Africa torn apart
> Hope lived within us like a citadel
> And from the mines of Swaziland to the heavy sweat of
> > Europe's factories
> Spring will come to life under our steps of light.

I2

Case Studies

We have analysed a number of themes which are common to the post-independence history of all or many of West Africa's states. But each, of course, has its own unique history. To discuss them all in turn would make this book too long. Therefore five states have been selected as case studies. They have a special interest because their history illustrates a number of possible approaches to the problems of national unity and development.

Nigeria

The post-independence history of Nigeria falls into four sharply contrasting phases:
1 The years of civilian rule, which lasted from independence to the coup of January 1966.
2 The years of crisis, 1966–70, which saw several coups and a civil war.
3 The post-war years under General Gowon's government, 1970–5.
4 A new military government which came to power in 1975 and was headed by Brigadier (later, General) Murtala Ramat Muhammed until his assassination.

The years of civilian rule

We have seen (page 287) that parliamentary representation was based on population and that the north received an absolute majority, so that if it had been unanimous, it could have ruled Nigeria indefinitely. In fact, at independence a sixth of the northern seats was held by NEPU and the Action Group so that a coalition was necessary. Despite all the differences that had divided northern and southern politicians in recent years, the NCNC, the predominantly eastern party, and the Northern Peoples Congress united to form a government. This has been interpreted by commentators in different ways. Some believe that the jealousies and ambitions of the Igbo and Yoruba elites prevented them from uniting, and that the NCNC believed (wrongly) that they could dominate their northern partner. Others see the NCNC's decision as a praiseworthy attempt to reduce the potentially dangerous divisions between north and south.

Two themes were important in the political history of the First Republic. The first was the political breakdown at the centre, and the second was the rise of protest first among the peasants, then among the urban workers, and finally and most effectively among the military. Both in the regional governments and at the centre politicians became notorious for their extravagance and corruption, arousing the hostility of the more politically conscious of the masses who came to wonder what independence was all about. 'The edifice of privilege remains; only its proprietors are different'.

The forms of parliamentary democracy collapsed with amazing rapidity. Awolowo, the leader of the Action Group, embarked on a nationwide campaign against the coalition in power. As the only possible way of uniting different ethnic groups, he supported 'democratic socialism'. A section of his party opposed him for two reasons. As wealthy businessmen, they had no sympathy for socialism, and as politicians hungry for office, they wanted to try and enter the coalition rather than challenging it from the outside, and antagonising its members. By what amounted to a regional coup in the west, the leader of this faction, Akintola, replaced Awolowo as Western Region Premier. Despairing of democracy, Awolowo turned to conspiracy. After a celebrated trial, he was imprisoned.

Meanwhile, the NPC–NCNC alliance was crumbling. In 1962 a census was held. Since political representation depended on population, the census was of crucial political importance, for it would determine whether or not the north would keep its dominant role. The 1962 census, which confirmed northern dominance, was bitterly attacked by southern politicians. A second census was held, giving much the same picture. It seems that all parts of Nigeria deliberately inflated their population figures, sometimes beyond the bounds of possibility. This meant that Nigeria was deprived of the basic requirement for economic planning – accurate statistics of population. Since the 1973 census was suppressed, like its predecessor, this is still true twelve years later.

By the time of the General Election of 1964, the pattern of alliances had changed. The NPC allied with Akintola's wing of the Action Group, which was now christened the Nigerian National Democratic Party, but which was like its predecessor of the same name, neither Nigerian, nor national nor democratic. This new coalition was called the Nigerian National Alliance. The NCNC allied with what was left of the Action Group and the northern opposition parties to form the United Progressive Grand Alliance. The election campaign was marked by a sinister crescendo of Igbo criticisms of northerners and vice versa. There was a massive incidence of pre-election irregularities, an increasing amount of thuggery and intimidation, and the nominations of opposition candidates were suppressed. At the last minute the Progressive Alliance leaders lost their nerve and boycotted the election, giving their opponents a landslide victory.

The 1965 regional election in the west was destined to be literally the election to end all elections. This is how a European political scientist, then living in the west, described it:

Electoral officers hid to avoid receiving opposition nomination forms; ballot papers were distributed to government supporters; local government policemen and thugs were used to drive opposition supporters from the polls; counting of votes was falsified . . .

By such means, Akintola and his party won a victory. As events were soon to show, the victory was a hollow one.

It would be wrong to see the First Republic as a total failure. In education, in the expansion of the infrastructure, and in industrial growth, Nigerians made far more progress than under any colonial government. But in the country generally, the incidence of corruption and political intimidation caused a great sense of disappointment.

The breakdown of government

The peasants' protest broke out first in Tivland which broke into open revolt in 1960 and again in 1964, in passionate protest against 'an imposed, inefficient and corrupt local government authority'. When Gowon came to power, he released over a thousand of these Tiv resisters from prison. Akintola's corrupt victory in 1965 led to another peasant revolt, this time in the West. The majority of the Yoruba, whether intellectuals, workers or peasants, disliked his regime and came increasingly to see the imprisoned Awolowo as a symbol of Yoruba identity. But where the intellectuals grumbled, the peasants exploded in rage. They drove the representatives of the party in power from the villages. They burnt some of them alive. They set up road blocks and destroyed cars and property, sometimes together with their inhabitants. From a protest against a party, it turned into something very like class warfare, an attack by the poor on the prosperous in general.

The peasants of the west set up road blocks; the urban workers turned to a General Strike. In 1964 under the leadership of a brave, flamboyant mid-Westerner, Michael Imoudou, a railwayman, there was a General Strike which temporarily paralysed the economy and won substantial wage increases. These gains, however, like later wage increases, had little effect because of inflation and dismissals.

The final blow which toppled the First Republic came not from the peasants, nor from the workers, but from a group of young army officers who could no longer endure the plight of their unhappy country. Some, but not all, were Igbo. Some high-ranking northern army officers were killed and a number of eminent politicians, among them Akintola and the two northern leaders, Tafawa Balewa and the Sardauna of Sokoto. The fact that no Igbo politician was killed gave the coup of 15 January 1966 the unintended appearance of an Igbo takeover, and when one of the ringleaders learnt this, he said immediately that the coup had failed. Balewa himself was an extremely popular figure overseas, where his death attracted immense sympathy. Nigerians, however, tend to point out that he was Prime Minister in an era of corruption and political violence, for which he could not escape some responsibility. An eighteenth century radical said of one who mourned the victims of the French Revolution: 'He pities the plumage and forgets the dying bird.'

Like many revolutionaries, the coup makers knew more clearly what they wanted to destroy than what they wanted to build. In the event, they did not even have the chance to try. Major-General Johnson Aguiyi Ironsi, the head of the Nigerian army, who was an Igbo who had risen from the ranks and had once been a storeman, intervened. With the help of Ojukwu, stationed in Kano, the coup was put down and its leaders imprisoned. The discredited and terrified politicians eagerly handed over to army rule, not to the coup makers, but to Ironsi.

The years of crisis

Ironsi realised clearly that it was essential that his regime should not appear to be Igbo-dominated. With great courage, he surrounded himself with northern soldiers (Gowon did the same thing later, when he entrusted his life to an Igbo pilot). But he was advised by a group of largely Igbo senior civil servants who, like many other people, thought that the regions were the source of Nigeria's ills, and who supported the idea of a unitary government. In May decrees abolished the political parties and the regions, and unified the civil service. (The last decree affected only a very few individuals, but still, to northerners, seemed a first instalment of Igbo domination.)

In May peaceful demonstrations by students and civil servants in the north escalated into mob violence, in which some hundreds of Igbos were killed. In July, there was a counter-coup when Ironsi and a number of senior Igbo officers were killed – also Lieutenant Colonel Fajuyi, a Yoruba with whom Ironsi had been staying at the crucial time. With extraordinary gallantry, he insisted that he must share the fate of his guest. Major-General Yakubu Gowon, a Christian from a northern minority group who had apparently not taken part in the coup, emerged as the new Head of State.

It seems that the July coup was first thought out by northerners determined to break away from the rest of Nigeria, but that they were dissuaded at the last moment by other northerners, on economic grounds. At this point, many of the Igbo elite, including university teachers, civil servants and so on, went back to the east.

In September–October, thousands of Igbos living in the north were massacred. These events, it has been said, added the word 'pogrom' to Nigerians' vocabulary. The massacres showed signs of being organised which made them the more appalling. But as with all pogroms, the killings were the expression of a host of social and economic grievances, many of which had little real connection with the Igbos.

After October the east was in a state of undeclared secession. The Igbos poured back to their overcrowded homeland, which, miraculously, was able to absorb them. Ojukwu and Gowon met at Aburi but little was achieved.

In May 1967 Gowon's government issued a decree dividing Nigeria into twelve states. The aim was to prevent the confrontation of the three major ethnic groups and to win the support of the minorities, by giving them their place in the sun. But to the Igbo, cut off by the new boundaries from the predominantly Igbo city of Port Harcourt, and from most of the petroleum-producing areas, the states were the last straw. Three days later, Ojukwu proclaimed 'The Republic of Biafra'.

Few phases of African history have aroused so much excited attention in the world at large. To the Igbo, the justification of their action was simple. 'They were leaving a state in which they had not been permitted to live.' Many people throughout the world thought that they were fighting for the principle of self-determination, and this won them many sympathisers even in countries whose governments supported Nigeria. The outcome of the war was decided by the question of international recognition. Four African states – Tanzania, Zambia, Gabon and Ivory Coast – recognised the new regime. France gave some help, but never recognition. For the rest, the great powers supported Nigeria. Disagreeing on most other issues, they agreed on this. Their policy was probably decided by their view of their own economic interests and a realistic assessment of who would win, but there were many more arguments than this on the Nigerian side. The most important was, that it would be a tragedy to destroy her potential prosperity and greatness, and replace it with a chain of small and weak states.

The absence of external recognition meant that the Biafran secessionists lacked arms and food. The soldiers fought with hardly any ammunition. The children starved to death. But the length of the struggle, which lasted over two and a half years, astonished the world. At last, when courage, tenacity and despair could fight no longer, the Biafrans made an unconditional surrender in January 1970.

But there was a real sense in which the secessionists defeated themselves. The old extravagance and corruption, which had wrecked the First Republic, had reappeared, made infinitely more shocking by the suffering of the masses – the blinded or crippled peasant soldiers, the fleeing and starving villagers, the dying babies. The Ahiara Declaration of June 1969 was meant to signal a fresh start.

> Our revolution is a historical opportunity given to us to establish a just society; to revive the dignity of our people at home and the dignity of the black man in the world.

But by then, there was no time left for fresh starts and had time been given, one must doubt whether a fresh start would have been made.

The Yoruba poet, Wole Soyinka, has said that one must envy the oppressed black masses of South Africa, for the hope of the fresh start has not yet been taken away from them.

The years of reconstruction

Just as the Biafrans won the admiration of Nigeria and the world for their courage in war, Nigeria won the admiration of the rebels and the world for her generosity in victory. It is impossible to better the verdict of an English commentator:

> When one considers the brutality, the proscription, the carefully maintained, immensely durable hatred that have so often followed wars in the 'civilised West' ... it may be that when history takes a longer view of Nigeria's war it will be

shown that while the black man has little to teach us about making war he has a real contribution to offer in making peace.

As far as ethnic relations go, on the whole the early seventies were a period of reconciliation. The war taught the former enemies a new respect for each other, and a new awareness of the dangers of ethnic nationalism. Strangely enough, ethnic divisions proved the easiest to remove. They require, essentially, a change of heart, which has often, in human affairs, proved surprisingly easy to effect. A problem which proved far more difficult to solve concerned the redistribution of wealth in society – a problem which was the more insoluble precisely because it required a lead from those who were benefiting from the existing situation.

The gulf between rich and poor was made intolerable by two things – the corruption of the prosperous, and the nation's vastly increased revenues, thanks to petroleum. In 1965, the last year of civilian rule, the state's total revenue was £200 million. By 1973 the total revenue was £1,100 million, £600 million of it from oil. The following year, oil revenues trebled. With far more money than any civilian regime, or the colonial government, had ever enjoyed, Nigeria's people might hope at last to find their own place in the sun.

But like many West African states in the 'seventies, Nigeria was gripped with a complexity of problems. One of the nine points of the army's self-imposed programme was to combat corruption, but it became obvious that many of those in power looked on their office mainly as an avenue to self-enrichment. When the regime fell in 1975, many investigations, startling disclosures and dismissals, followed. This example at the top led to a general cynicism and disillusionment in public life. Urban unemployment and rural poverty continued, and beggars, who had given up the unequal struggle, filled the city streets. The armed forces, estimated at 157,000 in 1973, consumed a large part of the national income.

As the 'seventies progressed, inflation and shortages became more pronounced. The Udoji award, intended to make salaries in the public sector keep pace with prices, released ₦370 million into circulation, by backdating the awards nine months. It helped to deal with the very real hardship of the lower income bracket of the public sector, but it also gave large cash bonuses to those who by the standard of the average man were overpaid already. It led to galloping inflation, which weighed equally heavily on those who had not benefited from Udoji at all, including employees in the private sector,* and the long-suffering peasants.

The frequency of armed robbery, which is a common sequel to war, especially civil war, diminished as the 'seventies progressed, apparently because of the extremely severe punishments. Armed robbers faced a firing squad, whether they injured anybody or not, which to some observers meant that life is less esteemed than property. The existence of armed robbery was fairly obviously a consequence of serious unemployment.

---

* Some private employers, not all, matched the awards.

Shortages became common – power cuts, water shortages, a chronic scarcity of petrol, and a lack of imported goods worsened by disastrous port congestion. These affected both industry and the elite. Most of the peasants were not so affected as they had no piped water or electricity anyway, and were more concerned with scarcity of food than scarcity of petrol.

The 'seventies had their brighter side. The National Youth Service Corps was introduced in 1973. It compels graduates to work for a time, often in rural areas, outside their own home area for relatively little pay. It seems to have worked well, though its introduction was very understandably resented by the students, who felt that they were being called on to display a patriotism and self-sacrifice which was not shown in the lives of their elders.

A scheme for universal compulsory free primary education is promised for 1976. One commentator has called it 'one of the greatest social endeavours the world has seen'. It is immensely popular and is intended to equalise the educational resources of Nigeria's states and classes. But educationalists warn of the likelihood of a fall in academic standards and in the absence of a major rethinking of the *content* of education, it seems likely to increase still further the problem of unemployment, since even a low standard of education is seen as an escape route from rural life. Agricultural under-production, and consequent high food prices, remain among Nigeria's enduring problems.

Nigeria's inability to solve her domestic problems contrasted sharply with the increasingly important role she played on the world stage. Her Head of State played an ever more prominent part in international affairs. Nigeria played the key role in the formation of ECOWAS – the Economic Union of West African States. Some of the small poor Francophone nations began to develop closer links with Nigeria as a counter-weight to French domination. Nigeria's international standing reached its height in 1973 when Gowon was elected chairman of the OAU.

But in 1974 and 1975 domestic criticism sharpened. Gowon went back on his promise to bring back civilian rule in 1976. The post-Udoji inflation, the much criticised census exercise, the growing shortages, seemed to indicate a fundamental sickness in the national life. Gowon himself diagnosed the illness accurately enough: 'want in the midst of plenty'. Like Balewa, he was extremely popular in the western world but lacked the essential strength of character necessary to cut through a jungle of corruption and injustice. In late July 1975, when Gowon was attending an OAU meeting at Kampala, his government was overthrown in a bloodless coup.

The new military government

The new Head of State was Brigadier (later General) Murtala Ramat Muhammed, from Kano. He had been a prominent northern spokesman in 1966, and played a distinguished role in the early stages of the war. It is a sign of the way in which social problems had replaced ethnic divisions that the change was welcomed by southerners, and Igbos. He at once replaced the twelve state governors, some of whom had become notorious for corruption and profoundly unpopular, and began an energetic inquiry into corruption, followed by widespread dismissals. Such measures are not without their dangers, since they mean dismissing many men of experience and there is a risk that careers may be wrecked by secret accusations and private feuds. The perennial demand for new states intensified, a demand created largely by the elite's restless hunger for new career opportunities. But on the whole the fresh start was popular, a popularity increased by a new promise of civilian rule in 1979.

On 3 February 1976 seven more states were created, making a total of nineteen. This move enables the resources of the nation to be spread more evenly, but means also that much of the national income must be consumed in salaries and in the building of new state capitals. This is also true of the plan to build a national capital at Abuja.

On Friday, 13 February 1976, General Murtala Ramat Mohammed was cut down by an assassin's bullet. He was thirty-eight years old. He had ruled Nigeria for two hundred and one days. His government had been notable especially for its fearless attack on corruption and its energetic and principled foreign policy. He was buried with the simplicity his religion enjoins, without so much as a coffin, and was mourned as no Nigerian leader has as yet been mourned.

Reaction against the errors of a past regime can carry a government just so far. At the moment there is a spirited debate in the mass media on the shape of the new

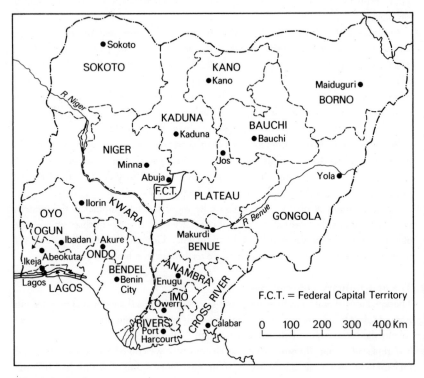

Nigeria in 1976

Nigeria. Some intellectuals advocate socialism; a military leader probably speaks for many Nigerians when he says he fears this will lead to 'indolence and chaos'. The return to civilian politics will provide a forum for the debate on the shape Nigeria is to take, and the use she will make of her freedom and opportunities.

Ghana

Nkrumah

Nkrumah's career as ruler of independent Ghana falls into two sharply contrasted phases: the 'liberal' or 'moderate' phase to 1961, and the socialist phase, 1962–6. The liberal policies of the first phase developed during the years of joint control, when power was still shared with the British. Even in those years he called himself a socialist but his policies often appeared to be right wing, as when he expelled a group of radical trade unionists from the party in 1952. If Nkrumah himself became less socialist during his period in office, this was much more true of the party he led. Many individuals in it had begun in a spirit of idealist enthusiasm, but it was an enthusiasm for independence rather than for a restructuring of society. In power they became increasingly interested in their own gain, whether in salaries or in contracts. Corruption became increasingly widespread and separated the party even more from the masses. It was this tendency in the CPP that was ultimately to hinder Nkrumah's movement towards socialism, for as Fidel Castro says, 'You can't build socialism without socialists.'

In 1961–2 Nkrumah became increasingly dissatisfied with the condition of Ghana. He felt that Ghana's political independence was not matched by any real economic independence. Her economy appeared a classic case of what has been called growth without development. She was overwhelmingly dependent on the export of natural products – cocoa, wood, gold and diamonds. The quantity of her exports increased to the point where her forest reserves were threatened and the efforts of her cocoa farmers could be called heroic. But this did not prevent her continued dependence on foreign capital and foreign markets, a rising level of imports and an increasing amount of debt. A distinguished Ghanaian civil servant said that his country was running fast in order to stay still.

At this point Nkrumah decided on a radical change of policy. (Some commentators believe that his change of policy was due to the experiences of the Congo and the murdered Lumumba.) In 1961 he made a famous dawn broadcast attacking corruption. Some high party officials were dismissed from office but they were soon back again because of the difficulty he found in finding other satisfactory co-workers. Corruption continued and Nkrumah himself permitted what some observers regarded as a very high level of prosperity. Party members were allowed to own two houses, jointly worth £20,000, which is a very great deal for men who were previously on three-figure incomes.

Nkrumah could not hope to find enthusiastic and convinced support from a CPP corrupted by prosperity and power. Yet his policies continued to arouse the hostility of the urban workers and the rural masses whose support he should surely have sought.

In July 1961 he introduced a savage budget which deducted compulsory savings from the earnings of peasants and workers. This seemed intolerable when contrasted with the extravagant life-styles of the governing class. Although strikes were illegal, there was a major strike in Takoradi which ended, incredibly for a so-called socialist left-wing government, with nineteen unionists in detention. The cocoa farmers continued to be upset by the fact that the government was still keeping the difference between the price they were paid for their cocoa and the much higher price it fetched on the world market.

The socialist phase
Between 1962 and 1966, Nkrumah made a tremendous attempt to transform the Ghanaian economy. Despite his attacks on neo-colonialism and international capitalism his plans for development laid down that this was to be done in collaboration with foreign private business interests.

Like many other African states in the 'sixties, Ghana obtained much finance under an extremely disadvantageous system called contractor finance, or suppliers' credits. One observer comments

> The repayment period is cruelly short, varying in the case of western countries between two and a half years and six years. The commercial interest rate is stingingly high. Repayment is generally required entirely in foreign currency, no matter what proportion that contractor's local costs bear to his total costs. Prices are always suspect . . .

The Volta dam, which produces a vast amount of electricity and has been of the greatest use to Ghana in the recent energy crisis, was finished a year before schedule. In Nkrumah's original plan this was to be part of an aluminium processing complex, but he was deposed before it was completed. Ghana has vast quantities of bauxite. One plant was needed to turn bauxite into alumina and a second to turn alumina into aluminium – a process which requires vast quantities of electricity. Only the second was built, so for years an American consortium has used Ghana's electricity to process alumina from Australia, while Ghana's bauxite remains undisturbed. In those years, too, he did much to develop the country's infrastructure, particularly by building a deep water port at Tema. But his enterprises ended in disaster for two reasons: falling cocoa prices and a lack of genuine popular participation.

Towards the end of his regime cocoa prices fell disastrously. This fact and their subsequent rise has led some to think that they were deliberately manipulated by western powers, hostile to his socialism and his growing links with Russia, and hoping for his downfall. In 1954, cocoa sold at £350 per ton. Nkrumah's Seven Year Plan for Work and Happiness assumed a price of £180 a ton. By August 1965, prices were down to £90 a ton. If his regime could have survived into the era of rising cocoa prices, its long term success might have appeared very differently.

His other great weakness was lack of mass support. He never succeeded in stirring up revolutionary or socialist zeal in the party he led and the people generally. Some other African leaders have done it with great success – Julius Nyerere in TANU, Amilcar Cabral in the PAIGC – and it is an interesting question for reflection and discussion why some have succeeded while others have failed, and the different strategies they have used. He cut himself off from the party he led by his socialism, from the urban workers by his repression and from the cocoa farmers by his economic policies. Thus Nkrumah became increasingly isolated and authoritarian. An extravagant cult of personality grew up around him which even his admirers found repellent. Like Sekou Touré, he was often called a dictator. In 1958, as a response to several seditious movements against him, he passed a Preventative Detention Act. Estimates of the numbers of political prisoners detained under it range from 400 to 1,100, but only one terrorist was put to death. These figures, which were shocking at the time, appear less shocking today in a West Africa where political detention and treason trials have become almost commonplace. What one had, basically, was a vicious circle. The opposition, with little hope of gaining power by constitutional means, resorted to conspiracy. Attempts were made on his life in 1962 and 1964. In a natural reaction to these conspiracies, Nkrumah became more repressive and more intolerant of criticism. In 1964 one-party rule was established after a fraudulent referendum.

The difficulty remained – 'one cannot build socialism without socialists'. He attempted to fill the gap partly by bringing in foreign socialists, such as the distinguished Nigerian intellectual Samuel Ikoku, and partly by setting up the Winneba Ideological Institute, but Winneba's products were inexperienced and lacked the 'pull' of the more experienced politicians.

One of the aspects of his policy for which Nkrumah has been most consistently criticised is the fact that when he came to power, Ghana had very large foreign reserves and when he fell he was heavily in debt. Years of rising cocoa prices and the profit taken by the marketing boards, had indeed built up large reserves in England which had significantly assisted that country's post-war recovery. He was quite right to use this money for developing Ghana, since it would have been absurd to allow it to slumber on in English banks. What is open to criticism is the actual use that was made of it. Many loans were negotiated on very unfavourable terms. A contract was awarded, for instance, to Stahlunion of West Germany, for £9.5 million, to set up a water and sewage system in Accra. A plan for the same work drawn up by the UN was independently professionally estimated at a maximum of £6.5 million. There was much corruption and waste, and, as in other African countries, much expenditure on empty prestige products.

As we have seen, however, the money was not entirely wasted – there were real steps forward as well. The Volta dam, the port of Tema and many less conspicuous aspects of a developing infrastructure were built at this time. Nkrumah greatly expanded education and social services. His plan for universal free education failed, like comparable projects in southern Nigeria – fees reappeared thinly disguised as text book fees – and forty per cent of Ghana's children are still not in school. Nevertheless, he made much progress. In 1964 there were seven times as many children in primary schools and ten times as many in secondary schools as there had been in 1950, and three flourishing universities were either established or on the way.

Pan-Africanist as ever, he was deeply convinced of the need for a real African political union. Because it was not shared by the elites of other newly independent countries, it was not realistic, but the OAU Charter of 1963 was deeply influenced by his ideas. President Nyerere of Tanzania worked for East African union as a step towards African union but, surprisingly and mistakenly, Nkrumah opposed it. But whatever the rights and wrongs of his individual policies in foreign affairs, Nkrumah was a commanding figure on the international stage. His work did much to restore the dignity of the African in the world. After he fell a Ghanaian said, 'Ghana succeeded in making Africans everywhere feel proud of their Africanness.'

But in 1965 the crisis deepened. Heavily burdened with debts, Nkrumah sought aid in vain from various financial institutions in the western world. There were serious food shortages. The mismanagement of import controls meant that there were all sorts of shortages in imported goods such as razor blades and matches which have been used from that day to this to make his regime look ridiculous. Seeking an exit from these difficulties, a Ghanaian mission began to negotiate a trade agreement with Russia. If this had been brought to a successful conclusion and implemented, the Russian market might have done for Ghana's cocoa what it did for Cuba's sugar. But there was no more time. In February 1966 Nkrumah went abroad, on a mission concerned with peace in Vietnam. Army officers, partly motivated by army career grievances, staged a successful coup. Like many other coups, it was the work of a tiny group of actors, watched by an apparently indifferent public.

Assessment

No figure in independent Africa has been as sharply controversial as Nkrumah. Most commentators would agree in criticising some aspects of his regime, such as the cult of personality, and the repression of political opponents. Where they differ most profoundly is in their assessment of the basic value of the socialist policies he followed in his last years of power.

The first interpretation which is basically the one put forward in this book, is that he followed the right policy, but failed in practice because of a number of internal and external factors, such as falling cocoa prices, the failure to generate real popular support, and a whole series of errors in detailed implementation. Among these were the disastrous farming projects, embarked on without adequate pilot studies, the unfavourable method of financing, through suppliers' credits, and the prevalence of corruption.

It is important to realise that there is another pattern of interpretation, which holds that Nkrumah's economic policies were catastrophically badly chosen, that he turned a prosperous country with healthy foreign reserves into a chronic debtor, and that the lack of positive achievements among his successors has been due to his economic legacy.

Nkrumah had often been accused of accumulating wealth but the pattern of his remaining years seems to show otherwise. He went to live in Guinea where Sekou

Touré, whose unfaltering loyalty to his old friend brightens the sombre history of his last years, not only welcomed him but made him co-President. He lived in a house by the sea and devoted himself to writing. Gradually his health declined and he went abroad in search of medical treatment. At the age of sixty-three he died in a Rumanian hospital, apparently of cancer, and Guinea and Ghana competed as to who could pay him the most honour in death. In the end Ghana gave him a state funeral. His mother said at his graveside, 'He was the salt that seasoned Ghana and Africa.'

Military rule, 1966–9

After Nkrumah's fall, a National Liberation Council was set up under General G. A. Ankrah. In 1969 General Ankrah resigned because of charges of accepting money from business interests, and was replaced for a short time by Major A. A. Afrifa. This army government saw itself essentially as a temporary regime, pledged to the early return of civilian rule. It began with lengthy investigations into corruption, but there were soon rumours that corruption was continuing, and the same kind of conspicuous extravagance in the governing class which had been criticised in the days of Nkrumah. A record issued in Ghana in 1968 and later banned was called, 'The Cars are the same, only the Drivers are Different'. If Nkrumah had made mistakes in his attempt to put an ideology into practice, his successors appeared to have no ideology at all. Ghana's financial crisis continued and expenditure on agriculture, communications and industry were cut. Yet various elite groups received salary rises and defence expenditure increased by forty-one per cent in three years, consuming more foreign exchange than any other state department.

The new regime relied heavily on foreign business enterprise. Lonhro was given a fifty-year lease in the gold fields and to the indignation of many Ghanaians (two newspaper editors were dismissed for criticising it), the state pharmaceutical corporation was handed over to an American firm.

But in western eyes, all these shortcomings were outweighed by the return to civilian rule in 1969.

Dr Kofi Busia's government, 1969–72

Busia's government came to power with several advantages. It had an unmistakable electoral victory and a high degree of acceptability in the western world. From his self-chosen exile, Busia had long been a bitter and unsparing critic of Nkrumah, yet in his own period of office he did not do as well.* He had criticised Nkrumah for the debts he had incurred but incredibly Busia's government, in little over two years, incurred an even greater burden of debt, so that by the time he fell from power, most of the state's revenue was going to pay the interest on debts. Unlike Nkrumah, he had very little to show for it. He had been an outspoken critic of corruption, but he did not force his ministers to declare their assets, as the constitution required, and after he fell the investigations of the Taylor Assets Committee revealed the corruption of his

---

* It is only fair to record that he faced the same problem in falling cocoa prices.

own regime. He blamed Nkrumah for autocracy, yet in 1969 he expelled 'foreign' Africans, in an unsuccessful attempt to lessen unemployment. He upset the trade unions by abolishing the TUC and by his severity to strikers. He even aroused the hostility of the cocoa farmers of his own area. Most dangerously of all, from his own point of view, he won the enmity of the army, when he cut defence expenditure by ten per cent in 1971. In February 1972 a second coup ushered in Ghana's second phase of military government.

Colonel Acheampong's government, 1972–

Colonel Acheampong's government has tried to steer a middle course between Busia type elitism and Nkrumah type socialism. His government has been greatly helped by the rise in cocoa prices which reached a world record level of £583 a ton in 1973. He energetically tackled the enormous problem of Ghana's debts. Some debts were repudiated, others re-negotiated on much more favourable terms. The state acquired an interest in major foreign mining enterprises. One particularly popular and successful aspect of his policy has been his attempt to reduce Ghana's dependence on imported food in Operation Feed Yourself. There has been a boom in rice-growing reminiscent of the cocoa boom of earlier years, which has actually led to a shift of population towards the north. His government has followed a strategy of selective indigenisation, very much like that of Nigeria. The government has 55 per cent holdings in mining and banking, and a number of large industries, and foreigners are restricted from re-tailing, and limited to 50 per cent ownership in many other enterprises. But the vast aluminium plant remains in foreign hands.

But Ghana's fundamental position remains unchanged. She is still heavily dependent on primary exports, especially cocoa, which in 1975 formed 70 per cent of all her exports. The high degree of foreign investment means that much capital is expatriated – an economist has estimated this at 6 per cent of her gross domestic product. Although the regime began with a vigorous attack on corruption, cries of corruption have again been heard, the Logistics Committee for the allocation and distribution of essential goods was so discredited that all its members were suspended. Like other military regimes, the government, if anything, prides itself on its absence of ideology. One highly placed officer warned the 'politically ambitious' not to confuse government with 'bogus ideologies and theories'.

As yet, no promise has been made about a return to civilian rule.

Ivory Coast

The economy

In 1957 Nkrumah gave President Houphouet-Boigny of Ivory Coast a famous chal-lenge. He said that in ten years' time, the world would be able to assess the success of their respective policies. In a sense, Nkrumah was a bad prophet. In ten years time he was an exile, whereas some eighteen years later Houphouet-Boigny is not only still in power, but enjoys the good opinion of a large sector of the western world. An

American economist* writes 'By all the obvious measures . . . the Ivory Coast has been one of the truly star performers in the less-developed world . . . a world of dazzling economic expansion.'

But there is a sense in which Nkrumah's challenge still echoes. Just as scholars differ about the value of Nkrumah's socialist years, so they differ about the real achievements of Ivory Coast. Like the Nkrumah experiment, the recent history of Ivory Coast has a significance which extends far beyond its own boundaries, for it has opted decisively for a free enterprise economy, and for the closest possible links with the western world. If this policy has really produced 'dazzling economic expansion' it would suggest that the solutions of socialism and self-reliance are mistaken, and that other developing countries could scarcely do better than do likewise. This is why the supporters of socialism and free enterprise have embarked on as much impassioned debate about the Ivorian, as about the Nkrumah experience.

Basically, instead of rejecting its dependence on the western world Ivory Coast has embraced it, attempting to gain all the profit possible from the relationship. She extends a welcome to foreign capital and expatriate personnel which makes a country like Nigeria look radical in comparison – 'No nationalisation, no indigenisation, no Africanisation'. Insistent in his hostility to socialism, Houphouet-Boigny was one of the last African statesmen to break with Taiwan and recognise Communist China, in company with Liberia, and Malawi. He has shocked much African opinion by his advocacy of 'dialogue' with South Africa.

Ivory Coast has embarked on a very successful policy of agricultural expansion and diversification. She is among the world's leading exporters of coffee, cocoa, palm oil, bananas and pineapples, and has made good use of scientific research in establishing, for instance, well planned, high-yielding plantations of oil palms. She has embarked upon an energetic programme of diversification, which means that she exports, among other things, avocados and cut flowers. (Both, however, like pineapples, are luxuries, and so extremely dependent on favourable economic conditions abroad.) In the early 'fifties, she exported an average of sixty thousand tonnes of cocoa and of coffee annually. By the early and mid-'sixties, this had risen to an average of 212,000 tonnes of coffee and 122,000 tonnes of cocoa. She lacks mineral resources, and her industries are mainly import substituting.

So far, the facts are not in dispute. It is agreed that although lacking in mineral resources, Ivory Coast has expanded her agricultural exports to a point where she has the highest growth rate in French-speaking West Africa. Where they disagree is in their reasons for this growth, and of the real value of what has been achieved.

Socialist commentators tend to look for other reasons to explain Ivory Coast's growth rate. One scholar claims that it is because Ivory Coast got off to a late start. In the early 1940s, her agricultural potential was very under-developed. What really happened was that she went through, in the 'fifties, the kind of agricultural expansion which the Gold Coast went through earlier, at the time of the first cocoa boom. This

* Elliot Berg.

argument is not very satisfactory since it ought to apply to a country like Guinea as well, which has not gone through the same kind of agricultural growth. A more persuasive argument is that Ivory Coast was luckier in the prices for her export crops. But this again was not really luck, but the reward for her programme of diversification, whereas Ghana was too closely tied to one crop and suffered accordingly.

A much more convincing criticism of Ivory Coast is that she has achieved growth without development. Her dependence on foreign capital and personnel has created not only a very large expatriate community in Abidjan, but, more important, a constant flow of capital abroad. In 1965 Ivory Coast had a capital inflow of 15,400 million francs, and an outflow of 23,300 million francs. In other words, the outflow – payment of interest on debts, profits repatriation and so on – had become greater than the inflow, and although exports boomed, much of the proceeds from the export sales were being creamed off overseas.

Ivory Coast is committed to capitalism, but lacks a class of substantial indigenous businessmen. Whereas some states adopt state capitalism as a half-way house to socialism, Ivory Coast has adopted it as a half-way house to capitalism. In practice this has tended to produce, not businessmen, but salaried bureaucrats, who consume much of the national income, like their counterparts in other West African states.

There are obvious examples of inequality in Ivory Coast. The classic symbol of privilege is the Presidential palace in Abidjan, which cost over six million pounds, in French aid funds. Incredibly, malachite for it was imported by air from Russia. A visitor some years ago wrote that 'Nothing is missing: from chandeliers and antique-style furniture in subtly contrasted colours to embossed chinaware and cutlery for over 1,000 guests, and a single table that seats hundreds . . .'

One cannot know exactly what kind of society the Ivorian strikers and rioters of the late 'forties thought they were struggling for. But one may guess that those who lost their jobs and risked prison in the fight for freedom, would have grieved to know that it meant this.

The counterpart to the chandeliers in the Presidential palace is the labour of an under-privileged group of Mossi labourers from Upper Volta, who form between half and two-thirds of the plantation labour force, and whose exertions create so much of the country's 'growth'.

The government
Since independence, Ivory Coast has been ruled by Houphouet-Boigny's Parti Démocratique de la Côte d'Ivoire. Some western commentators, who condemned one-party government and personality cults in Ghana, look at them more kindly in Ivory Coast. In the purely political sphere, the differences between Houphouet-Boigny and Nkrumah appear much less:

> . . . both gave short shrift to the opposition, handled coups or putative coups in a similar repressive fashion and held tight rein on non-party intermediary structures such as trade unions, youth groups, and so on.

Each faced crises and opposition, but Houphouet-Boigny, now seventy, has trium-
phantly surmounted it (some observers believe that he still owes much popularity to
his opposition to forced labour, nearly thirty years ago). In 1962–6 there was a whole
series of inter-connected crises in Ivory Coast. In 1963 perhaps two hundred people
were arrested, and eighty-six secretly tried – sixty-four were found guilty, and thirteen
sentenced to death (their sentences were later commuted). More arrests followed.
Some saw the opposition as socialist inspired, others as a protest against the dominance
of the Baoulé tribal group. In 1964 a former student leader, Ernest Boka, died in
mysterious circumstances. The government claimed that it was suicide, preceded by
confessions of anti-government conspiracies, especially in the sphere of witchcraft!
More trials followed, but the atmosphere relaxed after the fall of Nkrumah, whom
Houphouet-Boigny saw as the external focus of opposition to his regime.

Much potential opposition has been stilled by the practice of offering office to the
regime's opponents. But in 1973 there were again allegations of a planned coup, this
time in the army. In the official version, this was strange indeed, beginning with the
sacrifice of five foreign fishermen to win the favour of traditional gods! An unofficial
version says that these details were invented to discredit what was simply a socialist
discussion group.

Whatever the truth about this conspiracy may be, it is unquestionably true that there
has been at the time, and since, a strong undercurrent of discontent. There have been
many accusations of corruption, for example, in 1973 seven men were tried for
embezzling 432 *million* CFA francs. Observers pointed to the damaging effects of
personal rivalries within the one-party structure. An astute commentator summarised
the weaknesses – which are not peculiar to Ivory Coast:

> An inactive single party; the scourges of regionalism, nepotism, the growth of
> an economically privileged political class and endemic corruption; they lack any
> clear-cut direction or ideology and tolerate the coercion of the rural population
> by party bureaucrats and administrators . . .

Guinea

If we except recently independent Guinea-Bissau, only two other West African
countries have followed the programme of socialism and self-reliance on which
Nkrumah embarked in his last years of power.

Guinea came to independence in circumstances which were unique, and which
provided a peculiar blend of advantages and disadvantages. On the credit side, she had
a high level of political consciousness, forged originally in the General Strike of 1953.
The radical commitment of the PDG was not lost, as so often happened elsewhere.
This is perhaps because of its trade union origins, its long years as an opposition party,
and the effects of its alliance with the peasants for the abolition of chieftaincy in 1957,
and the more democratic system of village councils which accompanied it. The sudden withdrawal of the French, after Guinea voted 'Non', created tremendous problems.

The many skilled expatriates working in Guinea were suddenly almost completely evacuated* taking with them files and other records. The rapid expatriation of capital by private firms and banks created an immense crisis. For better or for worse, it meant that Guinea could no longer look to the western world for support. Guinea had, at the time, exactly twelve graduates.

In his desperate need for finance and skilled personnel, Sekou Touré turned to the communist countries. This in its turn made the West even more hostile as they believed, incorrectly, that Guinea had chosen communism.

The search for independence led Touré to be concerned with economic freedom, and the dependence of the Third World on the metropolitan countries. He said,

> We seek the independence of our society; the prisoner does not consider the liberty he enjoys inside the walls of his jail but only his liberty in relation to the outside world. Socially we consider ourselves prisoners in relation to the developed nations, and it is this liberation we seek.

The logic of this chain of thought led him, indeed, to socialism, but he sought trade relations with communist countries primarily because of his desperate need to fill the vacuum which France's sudden departure created. Later, Guinea's relations with Russia worsened, and trade links with West Germany and the United States became important – but this did not imply, though it was sometimes called, a swing to capitalism. When independence was first attained, the overwhelming concern was less for the restructuring of society than with *nationalism* – independence. As far as socialism is concerned, the attitude which the Guinea leadership has adopted for many years is that socialism is the ultimate goal, but that it has not yet been attained. They call their policies the 'non-capitalist alternative' – not wishing to discredit the socialist ideal by what they recognise as the imperfection of their present practice.

Interestingly enough, in view of Touré's left-wing reputation in the west, his leadership has twice been attacked by left-wing groups within Guinea itself. The first was in 1957, after the landslide electoral victory which returned fifty-six PDG Deputies out of sixty, and before the vote 'non' in 1958, which set Guinea on an irrevocably radical road. A small group of radical intellectuals, based at, of all places, Mamou, the stronghold of one of the two Almamis of Futa Jallon – attacked the tendency of the elected Deputies to become 'an elected bourgeoisie', with their relatively high salaries (£250 a month) and their large chauffeur-driven cars. One of the radicals was a woman, married to a serf:

> The Party came and I realised I was the slave of a slave. We struggled among the women to awaken their consciousness too. I was often in trouble with the police

---

* Although they were told their careers would not be guaranteed, a tiny devoted handful stayed on anyway. One of them was Jean Suret-Canale, who later wrote a classic work on French colonialism in West and Equatorial Africa, and the standard study of Guinea's post-independence economic history.

. . . We went into the slave villages, and also attacked the chiefs through their wives . . .

The radicals, out-manouevred by the party leadership, failed, but their indignant questioning still echoes. When raising questions on ministers' transport they asked 'Why can't they use bicycles?'

A similar, unsuccessful, left-wing protest, the 'teachers plot' of 1961 was an even less effective movement among intellectuals.

In 1960 Guinea left the franc zone, replacing the CFA franc★ with a Guinea franc which could not be converted into any other currency. This was intended to stop the flow of capital abroad, and to end the external commercial domination of the economy which membership of the franc zone implied. But the French reaction was extremely damaging. She cut off nearly all financial ties with Guinea, and stopped paying both civil and military pensions. (This meant that Guinea had to waste part of her pitifully scarce resources in paying pensions to, for instance, French army veterans.) It also meant that many of those who had previously sent capital overseas turned to smuggling, expatriating it in the form of goods instead.

The obstacles to development, especially, perhaps, in a socialist direction, were formidable. Guinea was surrounded on all sides by neighbours who did not share her economic views. Her small population of under four million was an inadequate industrial market, and this was made much worse by its poverty. The very shape of the country, with its vast curving frontiers, which make smuggling easy, and the provision of transport difficult, was an economically troublesome legacy from colonialism. It had potential riches in its iron ore and bauxite, but lacked the finance, the skilled manpower and the infrastructure to develop them.

The first development plan, introduced in 1960, planned that development should be mainly by borrowing, especially from communist countries. As elsewhere in West Africa, and as in Nkrumah's Ghana, much went wrong in the execution. Less than was planned was actually spent on industry and agriculture; more was spent in administration. Like other West African states, Guinea invested in a number of prestige projects, money which could have been put to more productive use (a 26,000-seat sports stadium, an international airport, a national airline). One of the difficulties in drafting and implementing any plan lay in the extreme shortage of skilled and trained personnel. There was practically no high-level Guinea manpower, and foreigners, especially from communist countries, tended to be unfamiliar with local conditions. (A famous story is told of how the Russians imported snow ploughs!)

★ The former colonies of French West Africa, except Guinea (and, for a time, Mali) have a currency called CFA francs (pronounced 'sayfah' the initials stand for African Financial Community). The CFA franc is linked to the French franc, and was devalued with it. It is controlled by BCEAO (The Central Bank of the States of West Africa), which has its headquarters in Paris, and its reserves, including the foreign exchange earnings of its members, in French francs. To buy foreign exchange, BCEAO needs the permission of the Bank of France.

The state took over a number of concerns at the centre including banking, importing and exporting, and experimented with the control of retail trade. It attempted to introduce peasant co-operatives and mechanised farming in the countryside, but failed, as so many other such endeavours have failed. The peasants had no real desire for co-operatives, or understanding of them. For such a scheme to succeed it must be preceded, not followed, by the same kind of long education and persuasion which the PAIGC embarked on in Guinea-Bissau. Guinea still depends on food imports (though this is partly because of increased standards of consumption, which are, of course, a good thing). But her agriculture remains obstinately unchanged, and her productivity low.

Guinea exports bananas, coffee and pineapples, but all agricultural products together form only a third of her exports. The other two-thirds are mineral exports, mainly aluminium.

Her mineral resources posed newly-independent Guinea with a problem. They contained, potentially, the solution to many of her economic problems, but she lacked the finance and personnel to exploit them effectively. Her freedom of action was further limited by the fact that several agreements with foreign firms had been negotiated before independence. One of these, La Minière de Conakry, exported iron; unable to compete with new sources of iron ore, such as Mauritania, and disliking the political climate, it did as so many white plantation owners did in the same circumstances. As they 'mined' their soil, extracting the last ounce of profit before leaving, the mining company failed to maintain its equipment, leaving Guinea, when it was liquidated in 1966, with totally unworkable equipment, and a mass of debts. Guinea has another immensely rich source of iron, at Mount Nimba, on the Liberian frontier. This has not yet been exploited because of transport problems, which make it hard to compete with Liberia itself, or Sierra Leone and Mauritania.

Before independence, an agreement for exploiting Guinea's bauxite had been negotiated with a vast international consortium, comprising American, French, British, Swiss and West German interests, called Fria. Fria mined bauxite and turned it into alumina, starting production in 1960. The alumina was exported to Cameroun where it was turned into aluminium, its value trebling in the meantime.

There is a further centre of bauxite mining at Boke. This was negotiated later than the Fria agreement, and on much more advantageous terms. Guinea owns 49 per cent, and an American consortium, Halco, owns the rest.

These bauxite mines add greatly to Guinea's foreign exchange earnings. They are highly mechanised, and the firms concerned have built model towns for their workers. But the numbers they employ are fairly low; they are, in effect, islands of prosperity in a sea of underdevelopment, a frustrating example of a way of life it is impossible to make available for everybody.

In a sense it seems to be a contradiction that in Guinea, which tends towards socialism, the key economic resources should be in the hands of big foreign firms. Is this neo-colonialism? Basil Davidson replies that it is not, if the sense of national purpose remains intact, if the country retains real control over her own destinies.

Neo-colonialism . . . consists not in small and impoverished ex-colonial countries having to remain in a posture of economic dependence on powerful outside buyers: nothing else is remotely possible in the world of the 1970s. Neo-colonialism consists in allowing these buyers to secure control over domestic policy: even more, it consists in handing power to domestic cliques or elites who became, willingly or not, the local representatives of foreign interests. Neo-colonialism, in short, is the situation which reproduces in an ex-colony a necessarily weak and corrupt copy of a 'middle class' society.

One of the areas where clearest progress has been made is in the sphere of education and health services. In 1958 there were 40,000 pupils in school; by 1973, there were 300,000. In 1958 there were no institutions of higher education at all. By 1973 universities and polytechnics were producing a thousand graduates a year. In 1958 there was one first-class hospital, and one second-class hospital. By 1966 there were five of the first category, and twenty-nine of the second.

How successful has Guinea really been in preventing the formation of a prosperous elite, and in fighting social inequality. Like Nkrumah, Touré has attacked this kind of tendency ceaselessly. The Deputies, whose salaries offended the Mamou radicals in 1957, now get paid when the House of Assembly is actually in session, which is seldom. Many foreign observers, who have criticised the gulf between rich and poor elsewhere, speak with approval of the relatively low level of conspicuous consumption in Guinea, and the relative austerity and dedication of its leadership. But the evidence is conflicting. Sekou Touré would not need to encourage austerity so insistently if he was preaching to the converted. And an English observer comments grimly, 'One cannot observe the contemporary Guinean situation – the Ministers with their large cars and several houses and the widespread diversion of public resources into private pockets – without reconsidering Mamou's 1957 manifesto'.

In any country which attempts to lessen the gap between rich and poor, the elite suffer a strong inner conflict, between their patriotism and sense of justice on the one hand, and their very natural desire for self-enrichment on the other. A Frenchman who lived for a long time in Guinea described this conflict between devotion to the public good, on the one hand, and ethnic consciousness, and 'the frantic will to succeed and to enrich onself' produced by the colonial period.

In Guinea, this conflict has not always been confined to the individual consciousness. If the regime has faced, from time to time, attacks from the left, who wish the regime to be more socialist, it has also met, not once but repeatedly, attempts at overthrow from the right. In 1966, and again in 1969, an anti-socialist group plotted against the regime, with help from outside forces. In November 1970 there was a much more dramatic external threat, when the Portuguese organised an unsuccessful invasion of Conakry, which was apparently intended to destroy the PAIGC headquarters.

Like Nkrumah, and Houphouet-Boigny, Touré reacted against these threats to his position by intensifying his personal authority, and clamping down on his opponents.

The sympathy the attempted invasion might have won him internationally was lost by the extensive trials which followed, when ninety-one death sentences were passed. (It should be noted, however, that thirty-three were not present and so could not be executed, and only eight are known to have actually been executed.) He is not willing to accept open opposition within his own country – 'They are free to be against the Revolution, but not in Guinea'. This has meant that a very large number of his political opponents live in exile, in France, Senegal, or Ivory Coast. Like political exiles everywhere, they become even more out of touch with the complicated realities of their homeland, and engage in a continual chorus of attack which does much to intensify Touré's authoritarian tendencies, and intolerance of opposition. It is the same vicious circle – conspiracy, dictatorship, conspiracy . . .

By 1971 Touré's standing in the west was lower than it had ever been. There were constant rumours of intended coups and conspiracies, constant arrests, and denunciations of Senegal and Ivory Coast. Much attention focused on a group of Frenchmen, imprisoned in Guinea for alleged involvement in plots against the regime; since these numbered about twenty, concern in the West seemed exaggerated, when compared with the hundreds, if not thousands, of black political prisoners in both black-dominated and white-dominated Africa.

Since then, Touré seems to have followed a deliberate policy of improved relations both with other African states, sometimes acting as a mediator in their disputes, and with the West. The culminating point came in 1975, when France and Guinea resumed diplomatic relations, ending the long estrangement which had lasted, with one short break,★ since 1958.

Mali

In 1960, Modibo Keita led his country to independence as the leader of the Union Soudanaise, the local sector of the RDA. Until his overthrow in 1968 he made great efforts to achieve the economic development of his country and break the bonds of poverty which constricted so many of her people. He faced, however, tremendous difficulties. Mali is entirely landlocked and stretches far into the Sahara. Most of her population live in the area of the Niger bend. The only large town was Bamako. What little foreign exchange she managed to earn came from groundnuts, cattle and fishing, but her lack of export earnings posed a tremendous obstacle to any development plans. Despite its lack of material resources, the area had a very ancient political tradition which still lives in Malian awareness as a consciously treasured heritage. It is the memory of the ancient empire of Mali and the nineteenth-century empire of Al Hajj Umar, but most of all, of the small and short-lived caliphate of Hamdallahi and Sheikh Ahmadu's tradition of austerity and devotion to the common good.

It will be remembered that Soudan came to independence as part of the Federation of Mali (see page 293). Keita and his supporters had planned this with passionate pan-

★ The two countries were briefly reconciled between 1962 and 1965.

African zeal. In 1959 Keita had called on his fellow delegates to swear the following oath: 'If I am called on to make the ultimate sacrifice for the Federation of Mali, political unity and African unity, I swear that I shall neither hesitate nor retreat'. In the event the Federation of Mali lasted exactly two months, largely because of his own strong support for socialism, though Soudan retained the name Mali. Keita applied the same idealism to economic life, and was determined to make war on exploitation, poverty and injustice. He wrote, 'We are convinced that victory belongs to the majority, that victory belongs to the exploited, that victory belongs to the under-paid, and that wars will never succeed in extinguishing this determination to liberate mankind exploited by mankind'.

In his attempt to put these ideals into practice, Keita tried to go too far too fast. He drew up a very ambitious development plan, which involved a high degree of state investment and a programme of austerity to halt current expenditure. Government corporations were set up to control groundnut exports and key imports; a transport department was set up which created a lorry pool of three hundred lorries; attempts were made to form the peasants into rural co-operatives; Mali left the franc zone and established her own currency and her own bank.

Many of these ventures were unsuccessful. The big irrigation scheme run by the Niger Office continued to swallow vast sums to no good purpose, as in the colonial era (the only success was sugar-cane grown with the aid of communist Chinese technicians). In general, agriculture stagnated and groundnut exports fell. With insufficient food being produced, Mali came to rely increasingly on food imports. Great efforts were made to build up the infrastructure, especially in the sphere of transport. Industries were set up, some of which ran at a loss, and again, those which were most successful, such as the matches factory and the Segu textile factory, were run with Chinese help.

But the country was in the grip of an apparently insoluble financial dilemma. As in other West African countries, the bureaucracy expanded and became more expensive. Not only were exports inadequate but much of what revenue might have been gained from exports and imports was lost by smuggling. As with Nkrumah, it was an attempt to impose socialism from above. The masses for whom this transformation was intended remained almost totally outside it. Most remained outside the cash sector so there was little revenue from taxation. The lack of internal revenue drove Mali to depend more and more on foreign aid. By 1967 the country was bankrupt. Mali was forced to return to the franc zone and the Malian franc was devalued by half. She was deeply in debt, her three main creditors being, in this order, the Soviet Union, France and China. The coup which overthrew Keita in November 1968 was essentially a consequence of this disaster.

Since then Keita has lived in detention. Whatever his failings may have been, and they were essentially errors of judgement and understanding, he lacked neither courage, idealism, nor self-sacrifice. It is not impossible that one day he will return to political life. At the moment much opinion, both within Mali and in the world at large, hopes fervently for his release.

The coup which overthrew Keita was led by Lieutenant, now President, Moussa Traore. For a short time the new government was headed by Captain Diakite who later fell from power, apparently as a result of personal differences. He was sentenced to forced labour for life in the salt mines of Thiasselet and later died there. Since then the government has been headed by President Traore.

Predictably the new government reversed Keita's policies. French experts were called in, the state corporations were either handed over to private enterprise or abandoned, and expenditure both on the infrastructure and social services, especially education, was cut down. The regime adopted the close links with France which were common in the other states of the Sahelian zone. None of this has solved the basic problem of Malian government which is also the problem of Niger and Dahomey (Benin), the great imbalance between exports and imports, the great dependence on external finance, and the apparent, near-impossibility of generating economic development in a country so lacking in natural resources. Since 1972 these difficulties have beeen cruelly intensified by the Great Drought.

At the moment the regime seems to be contemplating a return to civilian rule and in 1974 there was a referendum on a new constitution. Whatever the form civilian rule might take, Keita himself will be remembered as one of the great figures of African independence, a leader who used his position not to accumulate advantages for himself but to fight for the welfare of the common man.

Epilogue: Looking Forward

The last words in this book are those of Africans – the anonymous Africans, some now dead, who drafted the party directives of the PAIGC. They were written in the late 'sixties when the PAIGC was still fighting for survival. They could stand as an inspiration to other West Africans who are technically at peace, but really at war with poverty, ignorance, disease, and the unjust economic structures of their societies, and the whole world.

Educated ourselves, educate other people, the population in general, to fight fear and ignorance, to eliminate little by little the subjection to nature and natural forces which our economy has not yet mastered. Fight without useless violence against all the negative aspects, prejudicial to mankind, which are still part of our beliefs and traditions . . .

Demand from responsible citizens* that they dedicate themselves seriously to study, that they interest themselves in the things and problems of our daily life and struggle in their fundamental and essential aspect, and not simply in their appearance . . . Learn from life, learn from our people, learn from books, learn from the experience of others. Never stop learning.

Responsible citizens must . . . take life seriously, conscious of their responsibilities, thoughtful about carrying them out, and with a comradeship based on work and duty done . . . Nothing of this is incompatible with the joy of life, or with love for life and its amusements, or with confidence in the future and in our work . . .

Every responsible citizen must have the courage of his responsibilities, exacting from others a proper respect for his work and properly respecting the work of others. Hide nothing from the masses of our people. Tell no lies. Mask no difficulties, mistakes, failures. Claim no easy victories . . .

---

* The original, which was addressed to PAIGC members, says 'Party members'.

Independent West Africa

	Benin	Guinea	Ivory Coast	Mali	Mauritania
1957					
1958		Independence under Sekou Touré's Parti Démocratique de Guinée			
1959				Federation with Senegal	
1960	Independence under President Hubert Maga		Independence under President Félix Houphouet-Boigny's Parti Démocratique de la Côte d'Ivoire	Independence under Modibo Keita's Union Soudanaise	Independence under President Muhktar Ould Daddah's Parti du Regroupement Mauritanien
1961					
1962					
1963	Coup. Christopher Sogbo in power				
1964	President Sourou Migan Apithy and Prime Minister J. Ahomadegbe in power				
1965	Sogbo returns to power				
1966					
1967	Coup. Major M. Kouandete in power				
1968	Return to civilian rule under President E. Zinsou			Coup. Lt. Moussa Traore becomes Head of State	
1969					
1970	Government of National Union. Three leaders in turn (Maga,				
1971	Ahomadegebe, Apithy)				
1972	Coup. Lt. Col. M. Kerekou takes power. National Council of				
1973	the Revolution				
1974					
1975		**Formation of Economic Community of West African States**			
1976					

Niger	Senegal	Togo	Upper Volta	Guinea-Bissau	
					1957
					1958
	Federation with Mali				1959
Independence under President Hamani Diori's Parti Progressiste Nigérien	Independence under President Leopold Senghor (Bloc Démocratique Sénégalais)	Independence under President S. Olympio (Comité de l'Unité Togolaise)	Independence under President Maurice Yameogo (Union Démocratique Voltaique)		1960
					1961
					1962
		Olympio assassinated. Army instals Nicholas Grunitzky as President			1963
					1964
		Military rule under Major-General Etienne Eyadema	Yameogo resigns. Army rule under Lt. Col. S. Lamizana		1965
					1966
					1967
					1968
					1969
			Return to civilian rule under Prime Minister Gerard Ouedraogo.		1970
			Military and civilians share power		1971
					1972
				Independence under PAIGC	1973
Coup. Lt. Col. Seyni Kountche takes power			Coup. Lamizana becomes Head of State		1974
	Formation of Economic Community of West African States				1975
					1976

Independent West Africa

	Gambia	Ghana	Nigeria	Sierra Leone	Liberia
1957		Independence under Kwame Nkrumah's Convention Peoples Party			Ruled by True Whig party since 1877 and by President William V. S. Tubman since 1944
1958					
1959					
1960			Independence under N.P.C.-N.C.N.C. alliance (Nnamdi Azikiwe President and Sir Abubakar Tafawa Balewa Prime Minister)		
1961				Independence under Sir Milton Margai, leader of Sierra Leone Peoples' Party.	
1962					
1963					
1964			N.P.C.-N.N.D.P. alliance in power	Death of Sir Milton Margai. Succeeded by Sir Albert Margai	
1965	Independence under Sir Dauda Jawara's Peoples Progressive Party				
1966		Nkrumah deposed in coup. Replaced by National Liberation Council led by Maj. Gen. J. A. Ankrah	Coup. Maj. Gen. Aguiyi-Ironsi takes power. 2nd coup – General Yakubu Gowon becomes Head of State		
1967				Two coups. National Reformation Council under Lt. Col. Juxon-Smith	
1968				New coup instals civilian rule under Siaka Stevens leader of All Peoples Congress	
1969		Ankrah replaced by General Afrifa. Return to civilian rule under Dr Kofi Busia's Progress Party	Civil War		
1970					
1971					Death of Tubman. Succeeded by Vice-President William R. Tolbert
1972		Coup. National Redemption Council under Col. I. K. Acheampong			
1973					
1974					
1975	**Formation of Economic Community**		Coup. Brig. Murtala Muhammed comes to power	**of West African States**	
1976			Murtala Muhammed assassinated. General Obasanjo takes over		

Questions

Chapter 1

1 How strongly established was Islam in West Africa in 1800?
2 How do you account for the lack of impact which Christianity had in West Africa during the first centuries of contact with Europe?
3 Assess the relative importance of sea-borne trade, trans-Saharan trade and internal trade in West Africa in 1800.
4 Examine critically the consequences of the Atlantic slave trade for nineteenth-century West Africa.

Chapter 2

1 Compare the roles of Usuman dan Fodio and Ahmadu of Massina as statesmen and religious reformers.
2 Can one describe the Sokoto jihad as the expression of Fulani ethnic nationalism?
3 Write a short account of two of the following:
   a) the city of Hamdallahi;
   b) the Bambara kingdoms in the nineteenth century;
   c) Al Hajj Umar.
4 Give an account of the various jihadist movements in the western Sudan, and how they were related to each other.
5 Should Al Hajj Umar be considered mainly as a religious leader, or an expansion-minded empire builder?
6 Give an account of the spread of Islam in nineteenth-century Senegal.
7 Compare the differences and similarities between Usuman dan Fodio and Al Kanemi as religious leaders and statesmen.
8 What were the problems facing the Borno state after the death of Al Kanemi?
9 What was the importance of the Tijaniyya in the western Sudan in the nineteenth century?
10 Describe the political organisation of either the Sokoto Caliphate or the Caliphate of Massina.

11 To what extent was the conflict between the French and Al Hajj Umar a conflict between two expanding imperialisms?

Chapter 3

1 Why did the Fante and the British often find themselves in alliance in the nineteenth century?

2 Why did the power of Asante decline in the fifty years after 1824?

3 What were the factors which caused Asante-British hostility in the nineteenth century?

4 Account for the decline and collapse of the Oyo empire.

5 What were the most important causes of the Yoruba wars of the nineteenth century?

6 Give an account of the growth and policies of either Abeokuta or Ibadan in the nineteenth century.

7 Give an account of two of the following:

(a) Afonja; (b) Gezo of Dahomey; (c) the Ekitiparapo.

8 Describe the political and economic organisation of Dahomey in the nineteenth century.

9 Evaluate the role of women in the Dahomey state.

10 When and how did King Gezo of Dahomey and his son Glele attempt to expand their kingdom eastwards?

11 Describe the difficulties which confronted the Benin kingdom in the nineteenth century, and her response to them.

12 Write an essay on the nineteenth-century history of one of the following:

(a) Nri; (b) Awka; (c) the Ezza; or (d) Ohafia.

13 Compare the career and achievements of Nana and Ja Ja.

14 Give an account of the main civil wars and revolts in the Niger Delta city states in the nineteenth century.

15 How did the transition from the slave trade to the palm oil trade affect the Niger Delta?

Chapter 4

1 Analyse the impact of the Creoles of Freetown on the rest of West Africa.

2 Describe the reasons for the decline of the Creole community in commerce and the professions.

3 Assess the career and achievements of any outstanding Freetown Creole in the nineteenth century.

4 What was the 'Sierra Leonian' impact on Nigeria in the nineteenth century?

5 Compare the difficulties faced by successive settlers at Freetown, and the settlers in Liberia.

6 Assess the historical significance of either the Egba United Board of Management or the Fante Confederation.

7 'The policies of the settlers in Liberia towards the local people were essentially the same as those of white settler communities in different parts of Africa.' Discuss.

8 Give a short assessment of two of the following:

(a) Joseph Roberts; (b) Edward Wilmot Blyden; (c) E. J. Roye.

Chapter 5

1 Give an account of the Atlantic slave trade in West Africa in the nineteenth century.

2 Analyse the difficulties faced by any one West African state as a result of the decline of the external slave trade. What efforts did it make to surmount them?

3 Give an account of either the palm oil trade or the groundnut trade in nineteenth-century West Africa.

4 Why did trans-Saharan trade decline in the nineteenth century?

5 Analyse the motives behind French and British imperialism in nineteenth-century West Africa.

6 Give an account of nineteenth-century mission activity, and its impact in one of the following:

(a) Nigeria; (b) Ghana; (c) Sierra Leone; (d) the Gambia.

7 How important a part did Africans play in Christian mission work in West Africa in the nineteenth century?

8 Give a short account of any two of the following:

(a) Faidherbe; (b) the Royal Niger Company; (c) George Maclean.

9 Assess the career and achievements of one of the following:

(a) Bishop Samuel Ajayi Crowther; (b) Bishop James Johnson; (c) William Wade Harris;* (d) Garrick Sokari Braide.*

Chapter 6

1 Why were West African states unsuccessful in their attempts to prevent conquest by European colonial powers?

2 'Divide and Rule'. Is this an accurate summary of British and French policies in West Africa?

3 Can Samori be described as a modernising ruler?

4 Account for Samori's initial successes, and ultimate overthrow.

5 Do you agree with the view that Samori's government imposed heavier burdens on conquered peoples than French rule?

6 Analyse the opposition to colonial conquest among the small-scale societies of either southern Ivory Coast, or south-eastern Nigeria.

7 Describe the career and achievements of Bai Bureh.

Chapter 7

1 What do you understand by the French policies of Assimilation and Association, and what was their importance in West African history?

* Discussed in Chapter Seven.

2 Compare the methods and aims of French and British colonial governments in West Africa.

3 Assess the merits and defects of Indirect Rule in Nigeria.

4 Do you agree with the view that colonial economic policies in West Africa were basically concerned with 'standing still'?

5 Why, in the colonial era, were African merchants unable to compete successfully with expatriate firms?

6 Analyse the growth of communications in West Africa in the colonial period.

7 With reference to the colonial period, write a short essay on one of the following: (a) cocoa cultivation; (b) groundnut cultivation.

Chapter 8

1 Analyse the spread of either Islam or Christianity in twentieth-century West Africa.

2 With reference to any two West African countries assess the success of the education policies of the colonial powers.

3 Assess the West African contribution to the First and Second World Wars.

4 Do you agree that the policies of colonial governments in West Africa were primarily intended to benefit the metropolitan countries?

Chapter 9

1 Do you agree that nationalist movements in British West Africa before 1939 sought mainly to further the interests of the western-educated elite?

2 Critically assess the career and achievements of either Blaise Diagne or Herbert Macaulay.

3 What were the aims, strengths and weaknesses of the National Congress of British West Africa?

Chapter 10

1 Discuss the development and significance of the R.D.A. (*Rassemblement Démocratique Africain*) to 1958.

2 What was the impact of the Second World War on West African nationalist movements?

3 How do you account for the differences in the aims of the post-war nationalist movements of French and British West Africa?

4 Assess the contribution of Azikiwe to the Nigerian nationalist movement.

5 'The greatest West African nationalist.' Do you agree with this verdict on Amilcar Cabral?

6 Why were the nationalists of Guinea-Bissau unable to win independence by peaceful means? How did this need for an armed struggle affect their general aims and policies?

7 Write an essay on the nationalist movement in Sierra Leone.

Chapter 11

1 Why have military governments become so widespread in independent West Africa?

2 Outline the arguments for and against one-party states, and assess the success of the system in any one West African country since independence.

3 Describe the formation and significance of ECOWAS (the Economic Community of West African States).

Chapter 12

1 Evaluate the strengths and shortcomings of Nkrumah, as the ruler of independent Ghana. Why did he fall from power?

2 Write an essay on ethnic nationalism, with special reference to either Ghana or Nigeria.

3 Compare the policies followed by Sekou Touré in Guinea and Houphouet-Boigny in Ivory Coast.

4 How successful was Modibo Keita in his attempts to overcome the social and economic problems in Mali?

Reading Guide

P = available in paperback
$\star$ = recommended
$\star\star$ = strongly recommended

Books are referred to in full, once, and subsequently by the name of the author (plus a short title if more than one book by the author is included).

Making material available

Especially in rural areas, teachers need a lot of energy and persistence to make sure that the books they need are available for their own use, and for students. Books need to be ordered by post from a good bookshop. It may be quicker for schools, once a year, to draw up a list of books recommended by teachers in various subjects, and send someone to the nearest large town, where there are good bookshops, to bring them all back. Even university teachers experience much delay and frustration in getting access to the books they need!

In my own experience as a university teacher, I have found it very useful to prepare stencils for students. This is an excellent solution to the shortage of books, and students' low buying power. There is no point in preparing stencils of what is readily available; but summaries of, or extracts from, important articles and books can be of great value – also stencils of contemporary documents. I make a point of preparing a certain number of new stencils each year. These must be carefully kept (e.g. in a labelled carton) with each stencil labelled, so that the collection builds up each year and can be used by new staff members. In tropical conditions, stencils will not last indefinitely. When they start to deteriorate, you can get enough run off for three years or so ahead.

Examples of material it could be profitable to stencil: Flint's and Hargreaves' contributions to L. H. GANN and PETER DUIGNAN (Eds.) *The History and Politics of Colonialism 1870–1914*, Cambridge University Press, 1969, vol. I. This is an expensive book, much of which is not really useful for schools, for this course.

What books to buy

There are two main types of book in West African studies. The first are specialised texts, usually in hard cover and fairly expensive (e.g. S. A. AKINTOYE, *Revolution and Power Politics in Yorubaland 1840–1893*, Longman, 1971, or L. BRENNER, *The Shehus of Kukawa*, O.U.P., 1973). The typical school library, or individual, can only acquire a few of these, concentrating on books relevant to its area or his interests.

It is possible for teachers to stay fairly up-to-date, and to build up a good working library for themselves and their schools, by making good use of the steady stream of paperbacks which appear year by year. These include those intended specifically as textbooks or general surveys, like this one, and collections of essays by different experts in particular fields. Penguin Books issue many important topical paperbacks which are quite cheap. Because African studies is a rapidly changing discipline, one never reaches a point where one can sit back and say, 'Thank goodness, I've mastered that at last'. All textbooks, including this one, get out of date quickly.

Schools are advised to subscribe to *West Africa*, which will keep them up to date with current events and reviews many important books. If possible, schools should also subscribe to their own country's historical journal (e.g. in Nigeria, *The Journal of the Historical Society of Nigeria*). A careful study of both these will make a teacher aware of most important new books.

★★ *Tarikh*, Longman. This journal is intended specifically for schools. Buy all back numbers if necessary and bind it volume by volume. Encourage students to read each new number as it appears, like a magazine.

★★ O. IKIME, (Ed.) *Leadership in Nineteenth-Century Africa*, Longman, 1975, **P.** Contains reprints of some *Tarikh* articles.

★★ J. F. ADE AJAYI and MICHAEL CROWDER, (Eds.) *History of West Africa*, Longman, 1972 and 1974, **P.** 2 vols., I to 1800, and II after 1800. As with all symposia, some articles are better than others, and some are less up to date than the publication date would suggest. But they are still the standard big books, essential for both schools and teachers.

★★ J. D. FAGE, *A History of West Africa, An Introductory Survey*, Cambridge University Press, 1969, **P.** This is a standard short history, though the later sections were written long ago, and were written from a European viewpoint which historians may now find less acceptable.

★★ MICHAEL CROWDER, *West Africa under Colonial Rule*, Hutchinson, 1968, **P.** This is a substantial general survey which teachers will find invaluable.

★★ MICHAEL CROWDER, (Ed.) *West African Resistance*, Hutchinson, 1971, **P.** This is valuable, not only for resistance, but for its treatment of West African states in the nineteenth century.

** J. B. WEBSTER and A. A. BOAHEN, *The Growth of African Civilisation: The Revolutionary Years, West Africa since 1800*, Longman, 1967, **P**. A very good survey, now getting out of date (this is especially evident in the bibliographies, and in parts of the contents, e.g. the chapter on the Igbo).

** A. G. HOPKINS, *An Economic History of West Africa*, Longman, 1973, **P**. Too difficult for students but essential for teachers.

For the stimulus of a contrasting, controversial view:
* W. RODNEY, *How Europe Underdeveloped Africa*, Bogle Louverture, 1972, **P**.

National histories
There is a lack of really satisfactory national histories.
** JOHN E. FLINT, *Nigeria and Ghana*, Prentice-Hall, 1966, **P**., and
** J. D. HARGREAVES, *West Africa: The Former French States*, Prentice-Hall, 1967, Spectrum Books, **P**. These are useful general surveys dealing fairly briefly with the period covered by this book.

On Nigeria, there is an important book in preparation, by many contributors,
** *Groundwork of Nigerian History*. Watch out for it.

* MICHAEL CROWDER, *The Story of Nigeria*, Faber, third edition 1973, **P**. This is still the standard study, but getting out of date.

Two brilliant shorter accounts are:
** THOMAS HODGKIN's introduction to his new edition of *Nigerian Perspectives*, Oxford University Press, 1975, **P**., and JOHN FLINT, 'Nigeria, the Colonial Experience', in L. H. GANN and PETER DUIGNAN, (Eds.) *The History and Politics of Colonialism*, Cambridge University Press, vol. I, 1969.

A brilliant short economic history can be found in ROBERT GAVIN's contribution to the *Groundwork of Nigerian History*.

For a completely different perspective, see ELIZABETH ISICHEI, 'Images of a Wider World in Nineteenth Century Nigeria', *Journal of the Historical Society of Nigeria*, December 1973, VII, 1, pp. 111–119.

There is no satisfactory general history of Ghana. Both
* W. E. F. WARD, *A History of Ghana*, Allen & Unwin, revised edition, 1966, and the brief account by J. D. FAGE, *Ghana, A Historical Interpretation*, University of Wisconsin Press, 1966, **P**., are out of date, the former especially.

★ KWAMINA DICKSON, *A Historical Geography of Ghana*, Cambridge University Press, 1969, **P.**, pp. 143 ff. Useful for social and economic history.

On Sierra Leone, CHRISTOPHER FYFE, *A Short History of Sierra Leone*, Longman, 1962, **P.**, was written specifically for schools, and is fine for the purpose.

HARRY A. GAILEY, *A History of the Gambia*, Routledge & Kegan Paul, 1964, is the standard study.

★★ MICHAEL CROWDER, *Senegal – A Study of French Assimilation Policy*, Methuen, 1967, several reprints, **P.** Useful.

Historical anthologies
These can be an invaluable teaching aid. For example, when the class is studying Samori, the teacher can find the appropriate contemporary account (cf. p. 368 below) and use it to make the subject come alive.

★★ T. HODGKIN, *Nigerian Perspectives*, **P.**,
★★ C. FYFE, *Sierra Leone Inheritance*, Oxford University Press, 1964,
★★ F. WOLFSON, *Pageant of Ghana*, Oxford University Press, 1958
are three companion volumes, published by Oxford University Press. Get them all, or at least the one on your own country.

For Francophone Africa see:
★★ J. D. HARGREAVES, *France and West Africa, An Anthology of Historical Documents*, Macmillan, 1969, **P.**

On recent African history, politics, etc.
There are many paperbacks – I recommend the following:
★★ BASIL DAVIDSON, *Which Way Africa?*, Penguin, 1967, **P.**
★★ RUTH FIRST, *The Barrel of a Gun*, Penguin, 1972, **P.**
★ W. F. GUTTERIDGE, *Military Regimes in Africa*, Methuen, 1969, **P.**
★★ P. C. LLOYD, *Africa in Social Change*, Penguin, 1967, **P.**
★ BASIL DAVIDSON, *The Liberation of Guiné*, Penguin, 1969, **P.**

Lighter reading
Some of the books in this reading guide need a high degree of concentration. One of the beauties of historical studies is that much can be learnt from books such as novels and biographies and autobiographies – which can be profitably read when one is tired, or not in the mood for serious studies. For example:

Autobiographies of politicians
OBAFEMI AWOLOWO, *Awo*, Cambridge University Press, 1960, **P.**
★ K. NKRUMAH, *Ghana, An Autobiography*, Nelson, 1959, often reprinted, **P.**
N. AZIKIWE, *My Odyssey*, Hurst, 1971, **P.** So far only volume one, to about 1938.
AHMADU BELLO, *My Life*, Cambridge University Press, 1962, **P.**

Novels etc.
A. K. ARMAH, *The Beautyful Ones are Not Yet Born*, Heinemann African Writers' Series, 1968, **P.** The end of Nkrumah's Ghana.
C. ACHEBE, *Things Fall Apart*, 1958, **P.**, and *Arrow of God*, 1966, **P.**, both Heinemann African Writers' Series. These deal with traditional Igbo society.
C. ACHEBE, *No Longer at Ease*, 1963, **P.**, and *A Man of the People*, 1966, **P.**, both Heinemann African Writers' Series. These cover the period of Independence and the First Republic in Nigeria.
FERDINAND OYONO, *Houseboy*, Heinemann, 1966, **P.**, and *The Old Man and the Medal*, Heinemann, **P.** Acid comment on colonialism and white society in Cameroon.
SEMBENE OUSMANE, *God's Bits of Wood*, Heinemann, 1970, **P.** 1947 railway strike in Senegal.
CAMARA LAYE, *African Child*, Fontana, 1959, **P.**, and *The Radiance of the King*, Fontana, new impression 1970, **P.** Sensitive and profound.

Autobiographies of colonial officials
These give a different viewpoint—for example,
B. SHARWOOD-SMITH, *But Always as Friends*, Duke, 1969.
J. SMITH, *Colonial Cadet*, Duke, 1968.
STANHOPE WHITE, *Dan Bana*, Cassell, 1966.

There are a large number of biographies of West Africans, of varying interest and value. Try:
C. FYFE, *Africanus Horton*, Oxford University Press, 1972. Short.
E. A. AYANDELE, *'Holy' Johnson, Pioneer of African Nationalism, 1836–1917*, Cass, 1970. Longer, more difficult.
ELIZABETH ISICHEI, *Entirely for God: A Life of Michael Iwene Tansi*, in the press. About an obscure Nigerian priest who became a monk.

Chapter 1

On the geographical environment, R. J. HARRISON CHURCH, *West Africa*, second edition, Longman, 1960. and especially, W. B. Morgan and J. C. Pugh, *West Africa*, Methuen, 1969.

The standard economic history of West Africa is A. G. HOPKINS, *An Economic History of West Africa*, Longmans, 1973, **P.** This provides extremely full reading guides on all aspects of the subject, including the slave trade.

The standard account of slavery in the Western Sudan is A. G. B. FISHER and H. J. FISHER, *Slavery and Muslim Society in Africa*, Hurst, 1970. (Teachers.)

There are some useful articles in I. M. LEWIS, (Ed.) *Islam in Tropical Africa*, Oxford University Press, 1966 and J. R. WILLIS (Ed.) *Studies in the History of Islam in West Africa*, Cass, 1972.

On traditional religion see:

The traditions collected by M. ONWUE JEOGWU and R. ARAZU in ELIZABETH ISICHEI, (Ed.) *Igbo Worlds*, Macmillan, **P.**, forthcoming and M. GRIAULE, *Conversations with Ogotemmeli* (Dogon religion), Oxford University Press, 1965, **P.**

There is no really satisfactory general book on this subject, but note E. G. PARINDER, *African Traditional Religion*, S.P.C.K., 1962, **P.** and *West African Religion*, Epworth Press, 1961.

On pioneer Christians see: F. L. BARTELS, 'Philip Quaque', *Transactions of the Gold Coast & Togoland Historical Society*, 1955, and 'J.E.J. Capitain', *Transactions of the Historical Society of Ghana*, 1959.

Chapter 2

The jihad in Gobir and the Sokoto Caliphate

For the jihad in Gobir, both teachers and students should try MERVYN HISKETT, *The Sword of Truth: The Life and Times of the Shehu Usuman dan Fodio*, Oxford University Press, New York, 1973, **P.** Beautifully written, the most recent study, and fairly short – 169 smallish pages of text.

There are three big books on the Sokoto Caliphate – teachers should try to compare their approaches:

H. A. S. JOHNSTON, *The Fulani Empire of Sokoto*, Oxford University Press, 1967.

MURRAY LAST, *The Sokoto Caliphate*, Longman, Ibadan History Series, 1968. Read up to page 141 only; the second half is a detailed study of the office of Vizier.

R. A. ADELEYE, *Power and Diplomacy in Northern Nigeria 1804–06*, Longman, Ibadan History Series, 1971. More emphasis on external relations and British encroachment.

There are many relevant articles which teachers will find listed in the above, especially Hiskett.

For a shorter account, see:

MURRAY LAST, 'Reform in West Africa: The Jihad movements of the nineteenth century', pp. 1–13 only, in AJAYI and CROWDER, *History of West Africa*, vol. II, and R. A. ADELEYE, 'The Sokoto Caliphate in the nineteenth century' in the same book.

The jihad in Massina

There is no full acount of this in English; all but the last of the short studies listed below (and my own) are based on the same book – a French compilation of oral traditions. There are valuable extracts from this in English in J. D. HARGREAVES, *France and West Africa*, Macmillan, 1969, **P.**, pp. 122–127. All the following are suitable for students.

MURRAY LAST, 'Reform in West Africa', (see above), pp. 14–17.

JOHN D. HARGREAVES, *West Africa: The Former French States*, pp. 53–55.

J. SPENCER TRIMINGHAM, *A History of Islam in West Africa*, Oxford University Press, 1970, pp. 177–181.

For the background to the jihad, teachers should consult:

J. R. WILLIS' chapter in AJAYI and CROWDER, vol. I, 'The Western Sudan from the Moroccan Invasion'.

Borno

For a short account, see:

RONALD COHEN and LOUIS BRENNER, 'Bornu in the Nineteenth Century', in AJAYI & CROWDER, vol. II, Ch. 4.

The standard book is:

LOUIS BRENNER, *The Shehus of Kukawa*, Oxford University Press, 1973. This is relatively short: 130 pages of text.

Some of the correspondence between Muhammad Bello and Al Kanemi is given in THOMAS HODGKIN, *Nigerian Perspectives*, Oxford University Press, 1960, pp. 198–205.

Al Hajj Umar and his empire

Shorter accounts suitable for students are:

MURRAY LAST, 'Reform in West Africa', pp. 18–23.

MICHAEL CROWDER, *West Africa under Colonial Rule*, pp. 38–42 and pp. 80–86.

A. S. KANYA-FORSTNER's account in MICHAEL CROWDER, (Ed.) *West African Resistance*.

For the religious background, see:

J. M. ABUN NASR, *The Tijaniyya*, Oxford University Press, 1965, especially Chapters III (on Tijani teachings), and V, which is mainly concerned with Al Hajj Umar.

For a more detailed study suitable for teachers, see:

B. O. OLURUNTIMEHIN, *The Segu Tukulor Empire*, Longman, Ibadan History Series, 1972.

The Senegambia

On Lat-Dior, see VINCENT MONTEIL, 'The Wolof Kingdom of Kayor' in DARYLL FORDE and P. M. KABERRY, (Eds.) *West African Kingdoms in the Nineteenth Century*, Oxford University Press, 1971.

CHARLOTTE A. QUINN, 'Maba Diakhou Ba: Scholar-Warrior of the Senegambia, *Tarikh*, 1968, vol. 2, no. 3.

B. O. OLURUNTIMEHIN's chapter on Mahmadou Lamine, in MICHAEL CROWDER, (Ed.) *West African Resistance*.

DONAL CRUISE O'BRIEN, 'The saint and the squire' (an essay on Ahmadu Bamba and his followers) in CHRISTOPHER ALLEN and R. W. JOHNSON, (Eds.) *African Perspectives*, Cambridge University Press, 1970. (He has also written a longer study, published by Oxford University Press, *The Mourides of Senegal*.)

Chapter 3

Fante and Asante

There is a good general account, to 1874, by A. BOAHEN, 'Politics in Ghana, 1800–1874' in AJAYI and CROWDER, II, pp. 167–261.

A shorter account by the same author is in WEBSTER and BOAHEN, pp. 121–136 and 210–227.

IVOR WILKS, 'Ashanti Government' in FORDE and KABERRY, pp. 206–238. He has also written a vast book on Asante history.

J. K. FYNN, 'Ghana – Asante (Ashanti)' in M. CROWDER (Ed.) *West African Resistance*.

F. AGBODEKA, 'The Fanti Confederacy 1865–1869', *Transactions of the Historical Society of Ghana*, VII, 1964, pp. 82–123.

DAVID KIMBLE. *A Political History of Ghana, 1850–1928*, Oxford University Press. Teachers should read this selectively. Don't be put off by the size – it is full of interest. See for instance:

pp. 135ff. on Southern Ghana elite,

pp. 192ff. on King Aggrey,

pp. 222ff. on Fante Confederation,

pp. 264ff. on late nineteenth century Asante.

F. WOLFSON, *Pageant of Ghana*. A historical anthology – teachers can select extracts for class use.

Yorubaland

The best starting points are:

J. F. ADE AJAYI, 'The aftermath of the fall of old Oyo', in AJAYI & CROWDER, II; and

★ ROBERT S. SMITH, *Kingdoms of the Yoruba*, Methuen, 1969, **P.**, pp. 133ff.

Yoruba students, especially, will like to own and browse in SAMUEL JOHNSON's superb work of pioneering scholarship, *The History of the Yorubas*, C.S.S. Bookshops, **P.**, first completed in 1897. Note that this should be read as well as, not instead of, modern accounts.

Those who wish to go into the subject more deeply will find a very large number of specialised books and articles, many of which are the work of Yoruba historians. They include:

BOLANLE AWE, 'Militarism and Economic Development in Nineteenth Century Yoruba Country: The Ibadan Example', *Journal of African History*, 1973, XIV, 1, pp. 65ff.

P. MORTON-WILLIAMS, 'The Yoruba Kingdom of Oyo', in FORDE and KABERRY.

J. A. ATANDA, 'The Fall of the Old Oyo Empire, a Reconsideration of its Cause', *Journal of the Historical Society of Nigeria*, 1971, V, 4, pp. 477ff.

S. A. AKINTOYE, *Revolution and Power Politics in Yorubaland*, Longman, Ibadan History Series, 1971. A detailed study of the Ekitiparapo.

J. F. ADE AJAYI and R. S. SMITH, *Yoruba Warfare in the Nineteenth Century*, Cambridge University Press, 1964.

Dahomey

The main references are:

W. J. ARGYLE, *The Fon of Dahomey. A History and Ethnography of the Old Kingdom*, Oxford University Press, 1966, Ch. III, pp. 34–54.

J. LOMBARD, 'The Kingdom of Dahomey', in FORDE and KABERRY.

DAVID ROSS, 'Dahomey' in *West African Resistance*.

J. C. YODER, 'Fly and Elephant Parties: Political Polarisation in Dahomey, 1840–1870', *Journal of African History*, 1974, XV, 3, pp. 417ff.

Additional references are:

DAVID ROSS, 'The first Chacha of Whydah, Francisco Felix De Souza', in *Odu*, October 1969, NS no. 2, pp. 19ff.

DAVID ROSS, 'The Career of Domingo Martinez in the Bight of Benin, 1833–1864', *Journal of African History*, 1965, VI, 1, pp. 79ff.

I. A. AKINJOGBIN, *Dahomey and Its Neighbours 1708–1818*, Cambridge University Press, 1967. A full and interesting, though controversial study, but it deals with an earlier period.

Benin

Students should read:

PHILIP IGBAFE, 'Oba Ovonramwen and the Fall of Benin', *Tarikh*, 1968, vol. II, no. 2.

An interesting account based on oral tradition by an outstanding local historian is:
★ JACOB EGHAREVBA, *A Short History of Benin*, Ibadan University Press, 1968 reprint, P., pp. 42–51.

For teachers:

ALAN RYDER, *Benin and the Europeans*, Longman, 1969, pp. 227–294.

R. E. BRADBURY, 'The Kingdom of Benin', in FORDE & KABERRY, pp. 1ff.

The Igbo
For students:

A. E. AFIGBO, 'The Indigenous Political Systems of the Igbo', *Tarikh*, 1973, IV, 2, pp. 13ff.

A. E. AFIGBO, 'Patterns of Igbo Resistance to British Conquest', *Tarikh*, 1973, IV, 2, pp. 14ff.

The standard account of Igbo history is:
ELIZABETH ISICHEI, *A History of the Igbo People*, Macmillan, 1976, **P**.

An earlier work by the same author concentrates on the first phase of contact with Europeans:
The Ibo People and the Europeans: The Genesis of a Relationship to 1906, Faber, 1973.

Anybody interested in Igbo history should consult:
The Interesting Narrative of Olaudah Equiano, **P**., the autobiography of an Igbo who lived from 1745 to 1797, was a victim of the trans-Atlantic slave trade, but managed to win his freedom. Chapter One consists of his memories of mid-eighteenth century Igboland. It is readily available in an inexpensive abridgement and is suitable for both teachers and students, PAUL EDWARDS, (Ed.), *Equiano's Travels*, Heinemann, 1970.

Teachers who wish to go into the subject more deeply could tackle the following:
ELIZABETH ISICHEI, (Ed.) *Igbo Worlds* (a historical anthology), Macmillan, forthcoming.
F. I. EKEJIUBA, 'The Aro Trade System in the 19th century', *Ikenga*, I, I, January 1972, pp. 11–26.
A. E. AFIGBO, 'Trade and Trade Routes in nineteenth century Nsukka', *Journal of the Historical Society of Nigeria*, December 1973.
P. A. IGBAFE, 'Western Igbo Society and its Resistance to British rule', *Journal of African History*, XII, 1971 (about the Ekwumekwu).
G. I. JONES, 'Ecology and Social Structure among the North Eastern Ibo', *Africa*, XXXI, 1961 (about the Ezza, etc.).

The Niger Delta
For students:

WEBSTER & BOAHEN, pp. 193–208.
O. IKIME, 'Colonial Conquest and African Resistance in the Niger Delta States', *Tarikh*, 1973, IV, 3, and the same author's studies of Nana in CROWDER, (Ed.) *West African Resistance*, and *Tarikh*, I, 2, pp. 39–50.
E. J. ALAGOA, 'Nineteenth Century Revolutions in the Eastern States and Calabar', *Journal of the Historical Society of Nigeria*, June 1971, V, 4, pp. 565–574.

Teachers should try to become familiar with the large body of historical writing on the Delta, such as:

S. J. S. COOKEY, *King Ja Ja of the Niger Delta*, Nok, 1974. The standard life, by an Opobo historian.

G. I. JONES, *The Trading States of the Oil Rivers*, Oxford University Press, 1963. An important general book by an anthropologist, covering a time span of about four hundred years.

K. O. DIKE, *Trade and Politics in the Niger Delta*, Oxford University Press, 1956. A pioneering classic, partly outdated by later research.

O. IKIME, *Niger Delta Rivalry*, Longman, Ibadan History Series, 1969. Urhobo-Itsekiri relations; and note the same author's full-length biography of Nana.

On Calabar, see contrasting studies:
A. J. H. LATHAM, *Old Calabar, 1600–1891*, Oxford University Press, 1973; and
K. K. NAIR, *Politics and Society in South Eastern Nigeria*, Cass, 1972.

Chapter 4

The leading authority on the history of Sierra Leone is CHRISTOPHER FYFE, who has done more than anyone else to make people appreciate the achievements of the Creoles, and their culture. His *A Short History of Sierra Leone*, Longman, 1962, **P.** has already been mentioned. Another suitable account by the same author is his chapter in AJAYI and CROWDER, Vol. II.

For other scholars' interpretations, see:
H. R. LYNCH, 'Sierra Leone and Liberia in the 19th century', in AJAYI & ESPIE, *A Thousand Years of West African History*, Nelson, 1965. A shorter account.
JOHN PETERSON, *Province of Freedom: A History of Sierra Leone, 1787–1870*, Faber & Faber, 1969.

For a complete contrast, see:
E. A. AYANDELE, *The Educated Elite in the Nigerian Society*, Ibadan University Press, 1974, Ch. I 'Deluded Hybrids'.

CHRISTOPHER FYFE, *Sierra Leone Inheritance*, Oxford University Press, 1964, is an anthology of extracts from contemporary sources; teachers can use it selectively to make aspects of the subject more real and interesting.

For the indigenous people of Sierra Leone, see two articles by A. IJAGBEMI, 'The Mende of Sierra Leone', *Tarikh*, 5, 1, pp. 46–56, and 'A Note on Temne Kingship in the early nineteenth century', *Tarikh*, 4, 2, pp. 24–29.

Liberia
There is a great lack of good recent books on Liberian history, a sharp contrast with the

scholarly attention devoted to Sierra Leone. There is a good short account in WEBSTER and BOAHEN, pp. 155–173.

This may be compared with an account by a Liberian scholar:
ABEODU B. JONES, 'The Republic of Liberia' in AJAYI & CROWDER, Vol. II, Ch. 8.

Two standard older works are:
R. L. BUELL, *Liberia: A Century of Survival,* reprinted 1969 by Kraus Reprints, and
C. H. HUBERICH, *The Political and Legislative History of Liberia,* published in America in 1947.

For a comparison of Liberia and Sierra Leone, see:
J. D. HARGREAVES, 'African Colonisation in the Nineteenth Century: Liberia and Sierra Leone', *Sierra Leone Studies,* 1962, pp. 189–203.
HOLLIS LYNCH, *Edward W. Blyden, Pan-Negro Patriot,* Oxford University Press, 1967, is a useful biography.

Abeokuta
J. HERSKOVITS KOPYTOFF, *A Preface to Modern Nigeria, The 'Sierra Leonians' in Yoruba 1830–1890,* University of Wisconsin Press, 1965, pp. 178ff.
S. O. BIOBAKU, *The Egba and their Neighbours,* Oxford University Press, 1957.

Chapter 5

On economic life
A. G. HOPKINS, *An Economic History of West Africa,* pp. 112–166. This includes many suggestions for further reading.
RALPH A. AUSTEN, 'The Abolition of the Overseas Slave Trade, A Distorted Theme in West African History', *Journal of the Historical Society of Nigeria,* 1970, pp. 257–274. p. 274 summarises the uses of palm oil.
COLIN W. NEWBURY, 'Trade and Authority in West Africa' in L. H. GANN and PETER DUIGNAN, (Eds.) *Colonialism in Africa 1870–1960,* Cambridge University Press, 1969.

Missions
The standard general study, now really out of date, is:
C. P. GROVES, *The Planting of Christianity in Africa,* Lutterworth, 1958, vols. II and III.

There are a number of detailed studies, of which note especially:
J. F. ADE AJAYI, *Christian Missions in Nigeria, 1841–1891,* Longman, 1965.

The spread of European rule
The chief authority on the scramble is JOHN D. HARGREAVES. As well as a series of detailed books he has also written a number of short accounts, such as:

'The Chronology of Imperialism: The Loaded Pause', *Journal of Historical Society of Nigeria*, June 1974.

'West African States and the European Conquest' in GANN & DUIGNAN, I, pp. 199ff. Note the account in his *West Africa, The Former French States*, Ch. 7 and Chapter 11 in AJAYI and CROWDER, II.

Note also OLURUNTIMEHIN's chapter in AJAYI and CROWDER, II.

Students will find the account in FAGE, *A History of West Africa*, Ch. 11, most useful.

Chapter 6

Resistance to colonial rule

The key sources here are:

JOHN D. HARGREAVES, 'West African states and the European conquest', in L. H. GANN and PETER DUIGNAN, *Colonialism in Africa*, I, pp. 199–219.

** MICHAEL CROWDER, *West African Resistance*, Hutchinson, **P**. A volume of nine case studies. The earlier sections of the present study contain short accounts of other examples of resistance to the imposition of colonial rule. Teachers should draw on the material included in these sectors as well.

Samori

Students will benefit from R. GRIFFETH, 'Samori Toure', *Tarikh*, I, 4, pp. 26–42.

But *the* authority is:

YVES PERSON, whose studies make earlier works out of date. 'Guinea-Samori' in *African Resistance*, pp. 111ff., and a further essay in R. I. ROTBERG and A. A. MAZRUI, (Eds.) *Protest and Power in Black Africa*, Oxford University Press, 1970, pp. 37ff.

See also:

MARTIN LEGASSICK, 'Firearms, horses and Samorian army organisation', *Journal of African History*, 1966, VII.

For a contemporary account of Samori's empire, see:

'Samori's Revolution in Government', pp. 134–140 in J. D. HARGREAVES, *France and West Africa*.

Rabih

R. A. ADELEYE, 'Rabih b. Fadlallah and the Diplomacy of European Imperial invasion in the Central Sudan, 1893–1902', *Journal of the Historical Society of Nigeria*, V, 3, December 1970, pp. 399ff.

For his earlier career, see the same author's:

'Rabih b. Fadlallah, 1879–1893: Exploits and Impact on Political Relations in Central

Sudan', *Journal of the Historical Society of Nigeria*, V, 2, June 1970, pp. 223ff. (especially pp. 236–242, specifically on Bornu).
See also 'Rabih ibn Fadlullah' by JOHN E. LAVERS in J. R. WILLIS, (Ed.) *Studies in the History of Islam in West Africa*, Cass, 1972.

A short but useful survey:
LOUIS BREHNER, *The Shehus of Kukawa*, pp. 123–128.
HODGKIN, *Nigerian Perspectives*, pp. 60–61.

For a valuable account of the eastern Sudan Mahdist movement (necessary background for teachers), see:
L. CARL BRAUN, 'The Sudanese Mahdiya', in ROTBERG & MAZRUI, pp. 145–168.

Ivory Coast
** JEAN SURET-CANALE, *French Colonialism in Tropical Africa*, Hurst, 1971, pp. 95–103.

Bai Bureh
Students should start with:
C. FYFE, *A Short History of Sierra Leone*, pp. 130–131, 141–148.

The standard accounts are those in:
ROTBERG and MAZRUI, pp. 169ff. (by LA RAY DENZER and M. CROWDER)and
M. CROWDER, *West African Resistance*, by LA RAY DENZER.

Chapter 7

Colonial Government
There is a very large literature on this but much of it is concerned with the question of whether colonial government in particular areas should be called Direct or Indirect Rule.

For a short introductory survey, students should see:
J. D. FAGE, *A History of West Africa, An Introductory Survey*, pp. 175–188.
The account by A. E. AFIGBO in E. A. AYANDELE, A. E. AFIGBO, R. J. GAVIN and J. D. OMER-COOPER, *The Growth of African Civilisation, The Making of Modern Africa, vol. II, The Late Nineteenth Century to the Present Day*, Longman, 1971, **P.**, pp. 147–159.

For a description of Indirect Rule in four different areas of Nigeria, see:
The articles by O. IKIME (on northern Nigeria), J. A. ATANDA (Yorubaland), P. A. IGBAFE (Benin), in *Tarikh*, III, 3, 1970, and by A. E. AFIGBO (south-eastern Nigeria) in *Tarikh*, IV, 4.

The account in MICHAEL CROWDER, *West Africa under Colonial Rule*, Hutchinson, 1968, **P.**, pp. 165–248. (pp. 241–248 are an account of German rule in Togo, omitted in this book for reasons of space).

★ The introduction to MICHAEL CROWDER and OBARO IKIME, *West African Chiefs*, University of Ife Press, 1970, **P**. The rest of this book is full of lively and interesting material about chiefs, which teachers will like to browse in rather than read from cover to cover.

For a very critical viewpoint, see:

★★ JEAN SURET-CANALE, *French Colonialism in Tropical Africa*, pp. 71–90 and 307–349.

Teachers could also try:

I. F. NICOLSON, *The Administration of Nigeria, 1900–1960*, Oxford University Press, 1970. Very critical of Lugard – otherwise sympathetic to white officialdom in Nigeria, by a former colonial official.

D. A. LOW, *Lion Rampant: Essays on the study of British Imperialism*, Cass, 1973. An interesting theoretical discussion of Africa and Asia.

The Colonial Economy

Students can start with:

WEBSTER and BOAHEN, pp. 278–292.

M. CROWDER, *West Africa under Colonial Rule*, pp. 271–353.

CROWDER and AJAYI's chapter (15) in AJAYI and CROWDER, II.

For teachers, the most generally acceptable account is probably:

★★ A. G. HOPKINS, *An Economic History of West Africa*, Chs. 5–7. This provides much detailed reading guidance as well.

For a contrasting view, see:

★★ JEAN SURET-CANALE, *French Colonialism*, pp. 3–69 and 155–304.

For a simpler version of the same basic approach, see:

★ WALTER RODNEY, *How Europe Underdeveloped Africa*, Bogle Louverture, 1972, **P.**, Chs. 5 and 6.

Chapter 8

Attitudes and Elites

A controversial rethinking of this subject is:

★ E. A. AYANDELE, *The Educated Elite in the Nigerian Society*, Ibadan, P. Teachers would find extracts from this an excellent starting point for class discussions.

Christianity and Islam

In each case, there are excellent studies of particular aspects, such as the Mourides, the Ahmadiyya, or the Aladura churches, but a great lack of good general surveys, for which there is a great need.

At the moment, the only general studies are:

J. SPENCER TRIMINGHAM, *Islam in West Africa*, Clarendon Press, 1959, and
C. P. GROVES, *The Planting of Christianity in Africa*, Lutterworth, 1958, IV.

There is a useful brief survey in CROWDER, *West Africa under Colonial Rule*, pp. 356–369.

Both teachers and students will profit from:

J. D. Y. PEEL, 'The Aladura Movement in Western Nigeria', *Tarikh*, III, 1, pp. 48–55, and
J. B. WEBSTER, 'Independent Christians in Africa', *ibid.*, pp. 56–81.
Something can be gleaned from JAMES KRITZECK and WILLIAM H. LEWIS, (Eds), *Islam in Africa*, Van Nostrand Reinhold, 1969, but on the whole it contains disappointingly little detail about the present century. But note VINCENT MONTEUIL's chapter on Marabouts, pp. 88ff., H. J. FISHER, 'Separatism in West Africa', pp. 127ff., and N. LEVTZION, 'Coastal West Africa', pp. 301ff.
I. M. LEWIS, (Ed.) *Islam in Tropical Africa*, Oxford University Press, 1966, is much more substantial but contains relatively little on twentieth century West Africa, and many of the articles deal with other areas.

Western Education

Again, there are some useful detailed case studies, but a lack of good general syntheses. But see the following:

CROWDER, *West Africa under Colonial Rule*, pp. 372–389.
S. O. OSOBA and A. FAJANA's article in *Groundwork of Nigerian History* (forthcoming).
JOHN WILSON, *Education and Changing West African Culture*, Oxford University Press, 1966, **P.**
L. G. COWAN, J. O'CONNELL and D. G. SCANLON, *Education and Nation-Building in Africa*, Praeger, Pall Mall, 1965, **P.**
N. H. HILLIARD, *A Short History of Education in British West Africa*, Nelson, 1957.

Alien Wars

MICHAEL CROWDER, Chs. 13 and 17 in AJAYI and CROWDER, II.
Also pp. 252–266 and 482ff. of his *West Africa Under Colonial Rule*.
J. SURET-CANALE, pp. 118–146 and 462–488.
EDWARD MORTIMER, *France and the Africans*, Faber, 1969, pp. 45–49.

Chapters 9 and 10

Nationalism

Students should begin with the following articles in *Tarikh*:

G. I. C. ELUWA, 'The National Congress of British West Africa: A Pioneer Nationalist movement', *Tarikh*, 1971, III, 4, pp. 12ff.

F. AGBODEKA, 'Nationalism in the Gold Coast, 1900–1945', *ibid.*, pp. 22ff.

B. O. OLURUNTIMEHIN, 'Constitutional Development and the Achievement of Independence in French West Africa, 1914–1960', *ibid.*, pp. 33ff.

T. N. TAMUNO, 'The Independence Movement in Nigeria', 1971, IV, 1, pp. 1ff.

P. O. ESEDEBE, 'The Independence Movement in Sierra Leone', *ibid.*, pp. 15ff.

And then read:

CROWDER, *West Africa Under Colonial Rule*, Chs. 15, 16, 18 and 19.

G. O. OLUSANYA, *The Second World War and Politics in Nigeria, 1939–1953*, Evans, 1973, **P**. This has a wider scope than its title implies and is fairly brief.

A number of important paperbacks were written in the 'fifties and early 'sixties. Though out of date in some ways, they still merit attention:

★ THOMAS HODGKIN, *Nationalism in Colonial Africa*, New York University Press, 1955, **P**.

★ THOMAS HOGKIN, *African Political Parties*, Peter Smith, **P**.

★ RONALD SEGAL, *African Profiles*, Penguin, 1962, **P**. Portraits of nationalist leaders.

★ KEN POST, *The New States of West Africa*, Penguin, 1964, **P**.

Teachers should try to read among the 'big books' on the subject, concentrating especially on the country where they live.

R. W. JULY, *The Origins of Modern African Thought*, Faber, 1968. 19th and early 20th century nationalists.

On Panafricanism see IMANUEL GEISS, *The Pan-African Movement*, Methuen, 1974 reprint, **P**.

Nigeria

★ J. S. COLEMAN, *Nigeria – Background to Nationalism*, University of California Press, 1960, and reprints. Written before Nigeria became independent, but still essential reading. Richly deserves re-issuing in paperback.

Ghana

DAVID KIMBLE, *A Political History of Ghana*, Clarendon Press, 1963. A very long book which is a mine of information, but unfortunately the promised sequel has never appeared and it ends in 1928.

D. APTER, *Ghana in Transition*, Atheneum, 1962. A sociologist's analysis.

F. M. BOURRET, *Ghana, the Road to Independence*, Oxford University Press, 1960.

D. AUSTIN, *Politics in Ghana*, Oxford University Press, 1970, **P**.

★ BASIL DAVIDSON, *Black Star*, Allen Lane, 1973, **P**. Teachers and students. Some people consider it too favourable to Nkrumah. Very readable.

Sierra Leone

M. KILSON, *Political Change in a West African State*, Harvard University Press, 1966, Oxford University Press, 1967.

Francophone West Africa

G. W. JOHNSON, 'Blaise Diagne, Master Politician of Senegal', *Tarikh*, I, 2, pp. 51–57 (students).

EDWARD MORTIMER, *France and the Africans, A Political History*, Faber, 1969. A useful, straight-forward, political history of French West and Equatorial Africa. (Teachers.)

RUTH SCHACHTER MORGENTHAU, *Political Parties in French-speaking West Africa*, Oxford University Press, 1964. Very detailed: a book to read selectively rather than straight through. (Teachers.)

V. THOMPSON and R. ADLOFF, *French West Africa*, Stanford University Press, 1957. Older; a wider range of subject matter.

Teachers should try to master the broad outlines of world twentieth century history, at least to the point that expressions such as 'the campaign in Burma', 'the Cold War', have a real meaning to them.

Two good books to start with, both thematic in approach, are:

★★ G. BARRACLOUGH, *An Introduction to Contemporary History*, Penguin, 1969, many reprints, **P**.

J. MAJOR, *The Contemporary World*, Methuen, 1970.

Two first class books, written for secondary schools, but limited to Europe:

★★ MARTIN ROBERTS, *Machines and Liberty*, Oxford University Press, 1973, and *The New Barbarism*, Oxford University Press, **P**.

Guinea Bissau

★★ BASIL DAVIDSON, *The Liberation of Guiné*, Penguin, 1969, **P**. Though written when the war was still on, this is *the* study. Watch out for the flood of new studies the independence of Portugal's African colonies is bound to produce.

There are a number of general books getting out of date, on Portugal in Africa, such as:

R. H. CHILCOTE, *Portuguese Africa*, Prentice-Hall, 1967, **P**.

J. DUFFY, *Portuguese Africa*, Harvard University Press, 1959.

373

Chapter 11

General books

There are a large number of stimulating paperbacks on recent West African – or African – history. One to two years always elapse between the finishing of a book and its publication, so it is impossible for any book to be completely up to date. Schools should subscribe to *West Africa*, and keep and bind the copies. Students can take it in turns to summarise the main events, week by week, for the class.

COLIN LEGUM (Ed.) *Africa Contemporary Record*, Rex Collings, six volumes so far, starting in 1968, gives a very useful commentary year by year, but its size and expense make it difficult for individuals, or schools, to buy it. If the individual parts of the second section – 'West Africa', etc., were printed as separate paperbacks, it would add greatly to its usefulness.

Important paperbacks worth buying for teachers and students include:
** BASIL DAVIDSON, *Which Way Africa?* Penguin, 1967, most recent reprint, **P.**, Chs. 7, 8, 9, 10, 12. Lively and controversial, as is:

* RUTH FIRST, *The Barrel of a Gun*, Penguin, 1972, **P**. The first three chapters are a general analysis of the state of society in independent Africa; Chs. 4 and 5 give full accounts of coups in Nigeria and Ghana, and pp. 205ff. a useful summary of African coups in general.

** W. F. GUTTERIDGE, *Military Regimes in Africa*, Methuen, 1975, **P.**, is more recent, but less interesting.

** P. C. LLOYD, *Africa in Social Change, Changing Traditional Societies in the Modern World*, Penguin, 1969, **P**. A fascinating book by a sociologist – about *West* Africa, despite its title.

* SAMIR AMIN, *Neo-Colonialism in West Africa*, Penguin, 1973, **P**. An important Marxist analysis, worth study by teachers. Note especially his analysis of Ivory Coast. If you find it difficult, try a bit at a time.

RENE DUMONT, *False Start in Africa*, Deutsch, 1962. This is more readable than many novels. Note that it is by an expert in agricultural economics, and covers all Francophone Africa and Madagascar.

Chapter 12

Nigeria

WALTER SCHWARZ, *Nigeria*, Pall Mall, 1968. A lively well informed journalist's account, to the end of 1966. Would be enjoyed by students, especially in Nigeria.

JOHN DE ST JORRE, *The Nigerian Civil War*, Hodder & Stoughton, 1972, **P.**, is the standard account of the war.

JAMES O'CONNELL has written a number of important articles in various symposia, such as 'The Fragility of Stability: the Fall of the Nigerian Federal Government, 1966', in ROTBERG and MAZRUI, and 'Political Integration, the Nigerian Case', in HAZELWOOD, (Ed.) *African Integration and Disintegration*, Oxford University Press, 1967.

Ghana

Note the books listed under nationalism. Davidson is very suitable for student use, but it is essential to compare his interpretation with other different ones, e.g.:

H. L. BRETTON, *The Rise and Fall of Kwame Nkrumah*, Pall Mall, 1967.

I. L. MARKOVITZ, 'Ghana without Nkrumah, the Winter of Discontent', pp. 252ff. in MARKOVITZ, (Ed.) *African Politics and Society*, Free Press, 1970.

JONES, *Ghana's First Republic*, Methuen, 1976, **P.**

Ivory Coast

P. FOSTER and A. R. ZOLBERG, (Eds.) *Ghana and the Ivory Coast, Perspectives on Modernisation*, University of Chicago, 1971. Note especially the chapter on Berg, (pp. 187ff.) and compare it with the book by Amin (pp. 48ff.).

I. WALLERSTEIN, *The Road to Independence, Ghana and the Ivory Coast*, Mouton, 1964.

VICTOR DUBOIS, *Ivory Coast*, Cornell University Press, forthcoming.

A. ZOLBERG, *One-Party Government in the Ivory Coast*, Princeton University Press, 1969 edition.

M. MIRACLE, 'The Economy of the Ivory Coast', in P. ROBSON and D. A. LURY, (Eds.) *The Economies of Africa*, Northwestern University Press, 1969.

Guinea

Note the chapters by L. G. COWAN in CARTER, (Ed.) *African One-Party States*, and by DUBOIS in COLEMAN and ROSBERG (Eds.).

L. G. COWAN and V. DUBOIS, *Guinea*, Cornell University Press, forthcoming.

LADIPO ADAMOLEKUN, *Sekou Touré's Guinea*, Methuen, 1976, **P.** A useful and recent study.

Mali

Note the chapter by HODGKIN and MORGENTHAU in COLEMAN and ROSBERG, and the brief discussion in Amin.

Index

Muridiyya, *see under* Mourides
Musa, Mallam (Emir of Zaria), 25

Nana, 122ff.
National Congress of British West
  Africa, 268
National Council of Nigeria and the
  Cameroons, 283ff.
Nationalism, 215-6, Chapters 9 and 10
  passim
Nembe, *see under* Brass
NEPU (Northern Elements Progressive
  Union), 286, 323
Niger, 300
Niger Delta, 2, 9, 104, 110-11, 114ff.,
  152, 168: *see also* names of individual
  states
Niger expeditions (British, in 19th
  century), 160-1
Niger office, 220, 345
Nigerian Youth Movement, 272
Nkrumah, Kwame, 281-3, 293, 319,
  331ff.
Northern Peoples Congress, 286ff.,
  323ff.
Nri, 57, 100ff.
Nupe, 26, 71

Opobo, 57, 116ff., 120ff.
Oseo Bonsu, 61ff.
Oyo (Oyo-Ile), 69ff., 81, 84, 92
Oyo (new Oyo), 73ff.

Palm oil trade, 84-5, 97, 116ff., 151ff.,
  233
Panafricanism, 270-1
Park, Mungo, 158
Pepple, King George, 119
Pepple, King William Dappa, 119
Portugal, in West Africa, 294ff.
Prempeh, 66ff.

Qadiriyya, 21, 31, 41, 248

Quaque, Philip, 16

Rabih Zubair, 40, 165, 191
Railways, 144, 163, 231
RDA (Rassemblement Démocratique
  Africain), 289ff.
Richards Constitution, 283-6
Roberts, Joseph Jenkins, 140, 143
Royal Niger Company, 169, 240
Roye, Edward James, 142-3
Rubber, 97, 146, 153, 234

Sahara, 1-5
Salaga, 60
Samori Touré, 48, 163-4, 181ff.
Sarbah, J. Mensah, 67
Second World War, 260-3, 278-9
Segu, 31, 34, 41, 42ff.
Sekou Touré, 291, 293, 317, 335, 339ff.
Senegal, French in, 42, 47ff., 51
Senghor, Leopold, 275-6, 289, 291-2,
  304, 305, 316
Serer, 48ff.
Shuwa, 36
Sierra Leone, 11, 125ff., 165, 194ff.,
  237, 287ff.
Slave revolt, 11, 85, 117ff., 138
Slave trade (trans-Atlantic), 5ff., 58-9,
  72, 82ff., 88, 91, 96, 101, 103-4,
  115ff., 127ff., 149ff.
Slaves, in Africa, 10-11, 27-8, 33, 39,
  62, 72, 85, 94, 104, 110, 115ff., 152ff.,
  228ff.
Society of African Missions, 155ff.
Sodeke, 78
Sokoto, 23, 29, 39, 41, 171
Solanke, Ladipo, 270
Songhai, 31
Soninke, 50ff.
Stevens, Siaka, 288, 305
Strikes, 267, 269, 274, 285, 332
Sufism, 18-19, 21, 39-40, 247-8: *see
  also* Qadiriyya, etc.

379